Carlism and crisis in Spain

FOR MY PARENTS

Carlism and crisis in Spain
1931–1939

MARTIN BLINKHORN
Lecturer in History, University of Lancaster

CAMBRIDGE UNIVERSITY PRESS

CAMBRIDGE

LONDON · NEW YORK · MELBOURNE

Published by the Syndics of the Cambridge University Press
The Pitt Building, Trumpington Street, Cambridge CB2 1RP
Bentley House, 200 Euston Road, London NW1 2DB
32 East 57th Street, New York, NY 10022, USA
296 Beaconsfield Parade, Middle Park, Melbourne 3206, Australia

Library of Congress Catalogue Card Number: 75–2727

ISBN: 0 521 20729 0

First published 1975

Photoset and printed in
Malta by St Paul's Press Ltd

Contents

Preface

The book which follows is a study of political extremism in the Spain of the Second Republic and the Civil War: to be precise, of that traditionalist subspecies of right-wing extremism which in Spain was – and is – represented by one of the curiosities of contemporary European history, namely Carlism. In the narrow context of the 1930s, Carlism's most obvious importance resides in its role as a vital element within Nationalist Spain, one without which, indeed, the rebels of 1936 might never have established the military position from which they were able to win the Civil War. Even before the outbreak of hostilities, however, Carlism had played a significant part as one of the political forces most antagonistic towards the Second Republic. As such, it not only contributed its own share in the undermining of that regime, but also by virtue of its existence helped to tug other, less automatically reactionary forces away from the path of constitutionalism.

Yet there is more to Carlism than this. The 1930s marked the centenary of a movement which had throughout that time exercised a powerful influence upon Spanish history, either directly or as a point of reference for other parties, interests and ideologies. In a broader, European setting, Carlism represents the outstanding example of a popular movement of the ultra-conservative, as distinct from the fascist right. Fascism has been intensively studied in recent years, ultra-conservatism or traditionalism less so; study of a traditionalist movement of so classic a type as Carlism may therefore enhance appreciably our understanding of the extreme right in all its forms. The Carlist movement thus merits scholarly attention not only on account of its role in the affairs of Spain, but also by virtue of its place in the wider spectrum of European right-wing politics and ideas.

I should like to thank all those persons and institutions who have contributed in their various ways towards the accomplishment of this study. The staffs of the following archives and libraries deserve special gratitude for their competence and tolerance: in Madrid, the Hemeroteca Municipal, the Biblioteca Nacional, the Archivo Histórico Nacional and the Hemeroteca Nacional; in Barcelona, the Archivo de la Ciudad; in Pamplona, the Archivo de la Diputación de Navarra; in London, the British Museum Reading Room, the British Museum Newspaper Library at Colindale, and the London Library; and in Oxford, the Bodleian Library.

Particular appreciation is due to two distinguished scholars whose inspiration underlies this book. Raymond Carr, Warden of St Antony's College, Oxford, first awoke my interest in the history of Spain through his undergraduate lectures, and subsequently supervised the doctoral thesis of which this study is a development; Professor Gordon Wright, of Stanford University, aroused a parallel interest in the history and politics of the European right through his wise teaching of French history during my year as an M.A. student. Several friends and colleagues in the field of Spanish history have read all or part, either of the original doctoral thesis or of the present manuscript, and my thanks are offered to them for their helpful and critical comments: Dr Richard Robinson of the University of Birmingham; Professor Stanley Payne of the University of Wisconsin; Professor Alistair Hennessy of the University of Warwick; Professor Robert Whealey of Ohio University; Mr Paul Preston of the University of Reading; Don Joaquín Romero Maura; and my own research students, Raymond Steele and Stephen Lynam. Valuable help and encouragement has also come from Professor Gabriel Jackson of the University of California, San Diego; Professor Hugh Thomas of the University of Reading; Mr Herbert Southworth; Don Julio Caro Baroja; and Don Jaime del Burgo. The responsibility for all the interpretations, judgements and errors contained in the book is, of course, entirely my own.

Finally, I wish to thank the William Waldorf Astor Foundation for granting me the financial assistance which made it possible to visit Spain in 1971 in order to supplement the original research carried out between 1965 and 1968; the University of Lancaster for allowing me periods of sabbatical leave in 1971 and 1973–4, during the latter of which the greater part of this book was written; and my wife, Irene, for her constant encouragement and her tolerance towards my many absences in Spain.

Lancaster　　　　　　　　　　　　　　　　　　　　M. B.
March 1975

Glossary

Acción Popular: Originally founded in April–May 1931 as *Acción Nacional*. A Catholic political organization initially embracing several strands of conservative opinion, but eventually crystallizing around an 'accidentalist' programme. After March 1933 it formed a part of the CEDA (q.v.).

AET: *Agrupación Escolar Tradicionalista* or *Agrupación Estudiantil Tradicionalista*. Carlist student organization.

a.e.t.: Weekly newspaper of the AET (see above), published in Pamplona during 1934.

afrancesados: 'frenchifiers' – those Spaniards who, during the Napoleonic occupation of 1808–14, collaborated with the French in the cause of modernizing Spain.

aplec, aplech (Cat.): Mass rally, specifically those held by the Carlists during 1935 at Catalonian monasteries.

apostólicos: Members of the ultra-clerical faction at the court of Ferdinand VII and in Spain at large, and hence the direct precursors of Carlism.

arrendamiento: The practice of leasing large estates to a single tenant or *arrendador*, who either cultivated the land directly or divided and sub-let it to a number of lesser tenants or *arrendatarios*. Direct cultivation was commoner in southern Spain, sub-letting in Old Castile and León.

cacique: Local 'boss' (see *caciquismo*).

caciquismo: Local bossism, involving extensive patronage and the managing of elections, as practised throughout the greater part of rural Spain during the Liberal Monarchy and surviving in some areas into the Republic.

Casa del Pueblo: Left-wing, usually Socialist local headquarters and meeting-place.

caudillo: A leader. A term used to describe (i) a military commander; (ii) a Carlist pretender; and (iii) after 1936, Franco as Leader of Nationalist Spain (i.e. '*El Caudillo*').

CEDA: *Confederación Española de Derechas Autónomas* (Spanish Confederation of Autonomous Right-Wing Groups). A conservative, Catholic political organization formed in March 1933 through the confederation of *Acción Popular* (q.v.) with numerous regional and provincial Catholic and landholders' groups. Under the leadership of Gil Robles it accepted social-Catholic doctrines but was also influenced by contemporary European authoritarianism and fascism.

ix

CNCA: *Confederación Nacional Católico-Agraria*. A Church-sponsored farmers' organization, particularly important in the sphere of credit extension, and powerful in León and the Castiles.

CNT: *Confederación Nacional del Trabajo* (National Confederation of Labour). Anarcho-Syndicalist labour organization, founded in 1911 and particularly strong in Catalonia and Andalusia.

decuria: In the Requeté (q.v.) a detachment of ten men.

dictablanda: 'soft dictatorship' – a play on words derived from *dictadura* (dictatorship) and *blanda* (soft) and referring to the interim regimes of General Berenguer and Admiral Aznar which followed Primo de Rivera's fall and preceded the coming of the Second Republic.

Diputación: Provincial representative body.

DRV: *Derecha Regional Valenciana*. Regional Catholic right-wing party formed in March 1930 in Valencia by Luis Lucía, a former Carlist, and subsequently one of the most important component elements of the CEDA.

empleomanía: Frenzied quest for posts in the bureaucracy, often dependent upon changes of government. A distinctive characteristic of nineteenth- and twentieth-century Spanish life, graphically depicted in the novels of Benito Pérez Galdós.

enchufe: Literally a 'plug', used colloquially to denote a 'contact'.

enchufista: A 'fixer'.

españolismo: Spanish super-patriotism.

Esquerra (Catalana): Catalan Left: a fusion of left-of-centre Catalanist groups effected during the 1920s under the leadership of Francesc Macià.

ETA: (*Euzkadi Ta Askatasuna*, loosely translatable as 'Freedom for the Basques'). Clandestine revolutionary organization founded in 1967, aiming at the creation of a Basque Socialist Republic straddling the Pyrenees.

FET: Shortened form of *FET y de las JONS*, itself an abbreviation of *Falange Española Tradicionalista y de las JONS* (see JONS), the unified party formed by Franco in April 1937, principally out of the Falange and the Traditionalist Communion.

FUE: *Federación Universitaria Escolar*. Republican students' organization.

fuero: Local or regional rights, laws and freedoms; of medieval origin and gradually eroded by the central government during the eighteenth and nineteenth centuries. Those of Navarre and the Basque region survived longest and were thus the crux of autonomist politics.

grupo: In the Requeté (q.v.) a platoon of around twenty men.

hispanidad: 'Spanishness' i.e. an inherent or intrinsic quality of being or feeling Spanish (cf. the Italian word *italianità*).

huerta: Fertile irrigated plain, specifically in the Valencian region and in the province of Granada.

JAP: *Juventud de Acción Popular.* Youth movement of the CEDA (q.v.). Literally a 'chief'; a leader, either regional, provincial or local, in the Carlist organization. (N.B. *jefatura*: the position or rank of leader).

JONS: *Juntas de Ofensiva Nacional Sindicalista.* Fascist organization founded in October 1931 by Ramiro Ledesma and Onésimo Redondo; in February 1934 it fused with José Antonio Primo de Rivera's Falange.

junta: Committee – specifically the governing committee of the Carlist organization at national, regional, provincial or local level. Also, ruling committee of insurgent Spain: *Junta de Defensa Nacional.*

Levant (Sp. *Levante*): The coastal provinces of eastern Spain: Castellón, Valencia, Alicante and sometimes Murcia.

Lliga: Strictly *Lliga Regionalista* (Regionalist League): conservative Catalan regionalist party, founded at the beginning of the twentieth century and closely associated with business interests.

Maestrazgo: Range of mountains situated in Castellón and Teruel provinces which was one of the principal fastnesses of nineteenth-century Carlism.

mendigoixales (Basque): Paramilitary wing of the Basque Nationalist Party.

patrulla: In the Requeté (q.v.) a unit of from four to six men.

pidalismo, -ista: Tendency associated with Alejandro Pidal, one-time Carlist who in 1883 led his ultra-clerical organization, Unión Católica, into Cánovas' Conservative Party: hence an inclination on the part of some Carlists towards 'collaboration' with liberal regimes.

piquete: In the Requeté (q.v.) a section of around seventy men.

pistolerismo: The phenomenon of political gunfighting between rival Spanish political groups or, more commonly, trade unions.

PNE: *Partido Nacionalista Español.* Spanish Nationalist Party of Dr Albiñana, founded in 1930 and fused with Carlism after the death of its leader early in the Civil War.

PNV: *Partido Nacionalista Vasco*: Basque Nationalist Party.

pronunciamiento: A peaceful military *coup d'état*, involving the 'pronouncement' of rebellion by one garrison or group of officers and the acquiescence of the rest of the army.

PSP: *Partido Social Popular.* A social-Catholic political party founded in 1922 and attracting support from a number of prominent Catholics, among them some Carlists. Although its existence was cut short by Primo de Rivera's *coup d'état* in September 1923, several of its leading figures later became prominent in the CEDA (q.v.).

rabassaires: Catalonian tenant farmers occupied in the cultivation of vines, whose leases were traditionally tied to the life of a vine. After the *phylloxera* epidemic hit Catalonia in the 1880s, and new American vines were planted, the effective duration of a lease was cut drastically owing to the shorter life of the new vines: hence the social radicalism of the *rabassaires*.

requeté: A term used loosely by Carlists to apply to (i) the Carlist paramilitary arm as a whole; (ii) a company of 250 men within this body; and (iii) a single militiaman. In this book, the word Requeté is used to denote (i), requeté for (ii), and the alternative term 'Red Beret' (*boina roja*) for (iii).

ribera: The low-lying district of Navarre which lies along the northern bank of the river Ebro and belongs geographically to Rioja (Logroño) and Aragon rather than to the Basque–Navarrese region proper.

Sanjurjada: Sanjurjo's revolt of 10 August 1932.

señorío: Seigneurial estate. Before 1811 nobles had held only jurisdictional rights over these estates, but thereafter usurped them as private property. They formed a special category for confiscation under the 1932 Agrarian Reform.

tercio: In the Requeté (q.v.) a battalion of 700–800 men.

UGT: *Unión General de Trabajadores* (General Union of Workers). Socialist trade union organization, founded in 1883, four years after the Socialist Party itself, and strongest in Madrid, Asturias, the Basque region and, during the Second Republic, rural Extremadura and Andalusia.

TYRE: *Tradicionalistas y Renovación Española*: joint electoral office of the Carlist and Alfonsist political organizations.

UME: *Unión Militar Española*: clandestine officers' lodge, closely involved in preparations for the 1936 rising.

yunteros: An impoverished class of sub-tenants in the two Extremaduran provinces of Badajoz and Cáceres.

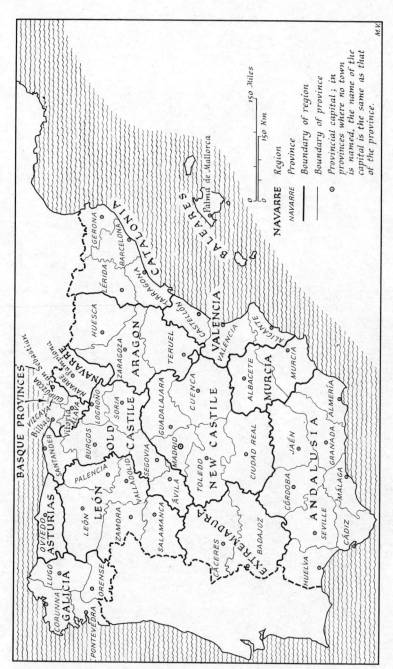

Spain: regions and provinces

I

A classic form of counter-revolution

On 12 April 1931, the men of Spain enjoyed the unusual experience of going to the polls. The elections were only local, but the politically informed were well aware that their importance extended far beyond the municipality, that on their outcome might rest the very survival of the king, Alfonso XIII, and the 'Liberal Monarchy' of which he was the incarnation. Little more than a year previously, Spain had emerged from the disappointing experiment of the dictatorship of General Miguel Primo de Rivera; this six-year regime, far from saving the monarchy as had been intended, had actually lowered its credit and at the same time injected a new vigour into Spanish Republicanism, a cause which had been in the political shadows since the short-lived and chaotic Republic of 1873. The 'Dictablanda' of General Berenguer and Admiral Aznar which followed Primo de Rivera's fall merely postponed the reckoning, warning of which came in the shape of a pact between Republican, Socialist and Catalan autonomist politicians, signed in San Sebastian in August 1930, and an unsuccessful Republican rising at the end of the year. The present electoral contest supposedly represented the opening stage in a gradual return to the full-scale parliamentary government which had operated before Primo de Rivera's *coup d'état* in September 1923; in reality, however, with monarchist candidates throughout the country opposed by a coalition of Socialists and middle-class Republicans, it had been raised into what amounted to a plebiscite on the monarchy's future.

The local elections dealt a largely unexpected death-blow to the Liberal Monarchy which, in the persons of Alfonso XII, the regent María Cristina and Alfonso XIII, had ruled Spain since 1875. Over the country as a whole a large majority of monarchist councillors was returned, but the Republican–Socialist alliance swept urban Spain, winning control in all but nine of the fifty provincial capitals. The effect upon the king, his ministers and his personal circle was shattering. Later monarchist – and, after 1936, Nationalist – propaganda was to make much of the monarchist victory in the country-side. Yet monarchists and Republicans alike knew how little this might actually reflect the true state of rural opinion, given the traditional and continuing management of Spanish rural politics by local bosses (*caciques*) and bigwigs still attached to the monarchy. Since the turn of the century it had been generally recognized that public opinion was most accurately expressed via the more or less open and honest elections in the cities. Hence those close to the king concluded that the wisest course in the present crisis was one of strategic withdrawal. During 13 April, as it was realized that neither the army nor the paramilitary rural police force, the Civil Guard, was inclined to rally to the king's side, pressure on Alfonso to leave Spain mounted. On the fourteenth, as he prepared to quit Madrid for the coast, the Republican leaders, astonished at their sudden apotheosis, assumed political power and launched the Second Republic on its course. Early the next morning Alfonso sailed from the Mediterranean port of Cartagena into what he hoped and believed would be a brief exile, having first issued a statement declaring that he was leaving in order to prevent civil war and that he had neither abdicated nor renounced any of his rights. [1]

While the streets of Spanish towns and cities overflowed with celebrating Republicans and leftists, the king's supporters sulked in their tents, scarcely able to take in what had happened. Not all monarchists mourned for Alfonso, however. One monarchist daily newspaper, with more than a hint of approval, described the election result as a 'popular explosion'; [2] another remarked that the monarchy's collapse was the inevitable consequence of attempting to combine the irreconcilable principles of monarchism and liberalism; [3] and a third positively gloated at Alfonso's humiliation, a fall 'without grandeur, with no gesture of gallantry, amid the ovations of a people amazed by its victory, as desired as it was unexpected'. [4] Any Spaniards capable of deriving this kind of satisfaction from Alfonso's overthrow obviously could be no lovers of the Liberal Monarchy. And indeed they were not; they were in fact Carlists, supporters of a rival monarchist cause born early in the nineteenth century, battered by repeated defeat, yet surviving almost miraculously into the 1930s.

Carlism in 1931 was indisputably the oldest continuously existing popular movement of the extreme right in Europe. Since the 1830s, and even earlier in the form of its immediate precursors, it had embodied the Spanish brand of that Catholic traditionalism most fluently articulated by Frenchmen such as the Vicomte de Bonald, and the best-known organized manifestation of which was probably French legitimism. Carlism, however, also possessed that mass element which had been present during the 1790s in the Vendée and the Chouannerie, but which was already effectively lost to French legitimism by the time its Spanish counterpart came into being. Around the often undeserving persons of the Carlist pretenders to the Spanish throne, there grew up a cause which attracted a substantial minority of mostly rural Spaniards to a crusade against the dominant developments of the age: urbanism and industrialism in the socio-economic sphere; tolerance, scepticism and atheism in that of religion; centralization of administration; and in the world of politics, liberalism and socialism. To counter these horrors, Carlism slowly formulated a programme calling for the 'installation' of a 'traditional' but not absolute monarchy; administrative devolution in the name of the historic *fueros* (rights, laws and privileges) of the Spanish regions; a corporative social and political system guaranteeing universal well-being and harmony; and, infusing everything, 'Catholic Unity' involving uniformity of belief, expression and behaviour.

Three times during the nineteenth century – between 1833 and 1840, in the late 1840s, and again between 1870 and 1876 – the Carlists took up arms and went to war against Spanish liberalism, and three times they were defeated. Between risings, and down to the turn of the century, sporadic outbursts of Carlist violence were an accepted part of the Spanish political scene, and at no time in the nineteenth century could a government afford to ignore Carlism completely. Until 1876 the Carlist threat to an often vulnerable liberal system was constant and at times acute; thereafter the danger subsided, yet Carlism refused to die. For more than fifty years, as their cause gradually declined, Carlists consoled themselves by predicting the eventual collapse of the hated Liberal Monarchy. Hence their elation in April 1931: at a time when Carlism was at its weakest ever, their seemingly tired and absurd prophecy had been suddenly and surprisingly fulfilled. Having thus received an eleventh-hour kiss of life, the moribund Carlist cause now embarked upon a new phase of counter-revolutionary activism which was to culminate in its playing a crucial role in the destruction of the Second Republic and the creation of the regime which succeeded it. This revival of an apparently doomed and anachronistic movement is the subject of this study.

Perhaps the best point at which to begin an introductory discussion of Carlism is not 1833, when it was officially born, nor even 1808, the year from which the history of modern Spain is conventionally dated, but 1700. It was in that year that the grandson of Louis XIV ascended the Spanish throne as Philip V, first Bourbon king of Spain – though of course it took the long war of the Spanish Succession to render his position secure. The Bourbons brought innovation and eventually 'enlightenment' to a Spain whose institutions and economy had been stagnating for several decades; Philip V set in motion a process of governmental rationalization and centralization which, when combined by his successors Ferdinand VI and Carlos III with the social reformism and religious erastianism of the Spanish Enlightenment, seemed to the traditionalists of the nineteenth century to have gone a long way towards destroying the central strengths and virtues of Spain's Golden Age. This hostile view of the eighteenth century, widespread among the European conservatives of later generations, constituted one of the life-giving myths of Carlism, a Bourbon cause paradoxically wedded to Spain's pre-Bourbon past.

Within this paradox there lay another, for there was one Bourbon innovation which Carlism embraced gladly – without which, indeed, it could not have existed at all. In 1713 Philip V, anxious to prevent a possible future union of the French and Spanish crowns, introduced into Spain the Salic Law limiting the royal succession to males. The law, of Frankish origin and applied in France for several hundred years, was quite unknown in Spain, in all of whose constituent kingdoms custom had preferred the succession of a monarch's female children to that of, for instance, younger brothers. Since a Pragmatic Sanction of Carlos IV in 1789, seeking to reverse the law, was never promulgated, this eighteenth-century novelty survived to give the Carlist pretenders of the nineteenth and twentieth centuries their claim to legitimate kingship.

Enlightened ideas and various aspects of their practical application naturally provoked indignant opposition among certain sectors of the Spanish population: defenders of lost or threatened corporate privileges, displaced nobles and, above all, conservative ecclesiastics. From the 1760s onwards, the Spanish political and religious elite was riven between the friends and enemies of 'enlightened' government, especially where it seemed likely to impinge upon the Church's monopoly of ideas – and, by no means unrelated, its economic wealth. It was this mainly clerical current of hostility towards rationalism, enlightenment and like 'foreign' notions, and their employment by the crown and its ministers in order to transform a traditional society and polity, which provided Carlism with its first recognizable ideological precursors.[5]

Conservative resistance to new ideas, and especially those deemed foreign, rose to an unprecedented pitch during the period of the French Revolution and the Revolutionary Wars. Thus far, however, its actual expression was still effectively confined to the clergy and aristocracy. Popular conservatism, while it certainly existed, remained silent until 1808, when Napoleon I's forcible placing of his brother Joseph on the Spanish throne ushered in a whole new era in the country's history. For six years, while a small minority of self-consciously 'modernizing' Spaniards, the *afrancesados* ('frenchifiers'), collaborated with the French, the great majority resisted the occupation in what Spain now knows as the War of Independence. The struggle was a complex one, not least in the ideological sphere, for those who fought to rid Spain of the French included both reformers and traditionalists. It was also crucial in the development of Carlism, for while the armed struggle made conservatism a mass cause and thereby gave birth to the popular element in what later became Carlism, the debate between patriot factions provoked traditionalists into the first systematic formulation of what was subsequently adopted as the Carlist programme.

The most distinctive form taken by the Spanish struggle against the French, and the one which caused most annoyance to the occupying forces, was the rural guerrilla band. As the imperial army advanced southwards, its control of most towns and cities was made more or less secure, albeit sometimes after long sieges like those of Zaragoza in 1808 and 1809; but in the surrounding countryside it remained eternally vulnerable to the harrying of the guerrillas. Although in the nature of things they inflicted few major defeats on the French, their achievement over a period of years, in cutting lines of supply and communication and in tying down a disproportionate number of French troops, was enormous. The guerrilla bands recruited overwhelmingly from among humble Spaniards, which in the early nineteenth century meant that *guerrilleros* were mostly country people. Their view of the conflict was the simple and conservative one of their kind: defence of the Spanish crown in the person of the exiled Ferdinand VII and devotion to the traditional Spanish Catholicism epitomized by the Inquisition. Although their role has been greatly exaggerated, parish priests and members of religious Orders were active in the fight and sometimes led the guerrillas in action; Wellington himself wrote that 'the real power in Spain is the clergy. They kept the people right against France'. From the point of view of our understanding of Carlism, the importance of the 'Throne and Altar' element in the guerrilla was lies in its inauguration, throughout much of central, northern and eastern Spain, of what soon became a tradition, almost an instinct of popular militancy on behalf of monarchy, religion and other, less fundamental causes associated with them.[6]

Popular conservatism, concentrated coincidentally in those regions where the occupation was most thorough, was nevertheless only one part of the picture. Elsewhere, and especially along the southern periphery where the French conquest advanced slowly and was never completed, the formation of mainly urban *juntas* (committees) of resistance announced the beginnings of Spanish liberalism. When Cortes were convened in 1810 in the unoccupied city of Cádiz, the occupation of the more conservative regions meant that a considerable majority of the deputies were liberals. In 1812 the Cortes of Cádiz enacted a Constitution which was to serve as a model for southern European liberals for the next forty years. It involved the introduction of a single-chamber legislature elected on the basis of universal but indirect male suffrage and limited only by a suspensive royal veto; the centralization of the administrative system to a point undreamed of by the 'enlightened' rulers of the previous century; the final dismantling of an already dying guild system; the abolition of all aristocratic legal privileges, seigneurial jurisdiction and right of entail; and the destruction of the chief symbol of the old Spain, the Inquisition. The voice of conservative opposition to this radical document was not heard until the first regular Cortes met in 1813; it then became clear just how powerful an opposition did exist among the threatened aristocracy, the military hierarchy and the clergy. As the war drew to a victorious close and the last French troops left Spain, and as the country prepared to welcome back Ferdinand VII, Spaniards were already polarizing according to their opinion of the Constitution.[7]

Many conservatives would have been happy to return to the *status quo ante* 1808, but not all. In 1814 a group of conservative deputies drew up a document, the Persian Manifesto, for submission to Ferdinand. In it they argued that Spain had been travelling the wrong road since the first stirrings of personalist rule under the Habsburgs, and more particularly since the coming of the Bourbons; the interruption of normal politics between 1808 and 1814 had presented Spain with a golden opportunity for making a fresh start, one which must be seized in order to replace liberalism, not with the royal and ministerial despotism of the eighteenth century but with the 'tempered' monarchy of the medieval kingdoms and the early sixteenth century, wherein the king's power was limited by Cortes, Royal Council, *fueros* – and the Church. This, the first coherent utterance of a 'traditional monarchist' alternative to both liberalism and Bourbon absolutism, constituted the essence of what was to become the Carlist programme. This is not, of course, to suggest that it actually inspired the actions of all Carlists or even all the Carlist pretenders.[8]

Ferdinand paid little heed to the 'Persians', but his cancellation of the Constitution and the generally conservative tone of his first five years as king were enough to keep traditionalists relatively quiet. In 1820, however, a military rising forced on him a new liberal regime, bringing with it the return of the Constitution and a degree of anticlericalism which had been largely absent at Cádiz. This liberal phase lasted three years before the regime's collapse in the face of another French invasion, that of the '100,000 sons of St Louis' sent at the behest of the Quadruple Alliance. For us, the chief importance of the liberal triennium lies in the fact that the liberals' policies of political centralization, legal anti-clericalism and renewed assault on noble privilege provoked the reappearance of 'royalist' bands in parts of northern and north-eastern Spain, and especially where economic hardship forged an alliance between the politically threatened and the materially abject. The royalist bands were simply one expression of the emergence of a more or less clearly defined 'apostolic' interest dedicated to restraining the Spanish crown from the least inclination towards liberalism, and whose figurehead if not leader was Ferdinand's brother and heir presumptive, Don Carlos. It is probable, though not certain, that Don Carlos personally encouraged some of the royalist guerrillas of 1820–3; certainly by 1824 the government was informed of the continuing existence of armed bands determined to replace Ferdinand by his brother.[9] The king was trusted by no one, so that although for the moment he was content to let himself be protected from the clutches of the liberals, the *apostólicos* could never feel confident that he might not at some future date sell out to liberalism again.

From 1824 onwards, the Carlist cause existed in all but name.

Don Carlos openly became the focus for *apostólico* hopes; Ferdinand might shrink from crushing liberalism once and for all, they told themselves, but his devout, intolerant brother could be relied upon to carry out the holy task when, as it seemed must happen, he became king. The *apostólico* cause was strengthened by the possession of a potential army in the 120,000 Royal Volunteers formed in 1823 as a substitute for the 'liberal' army, while even in the latter a rash of badly planned and unsuccessful 'royalist' military risings between 1824 and 1826 hinted at what might come. Continued popular support for Don Carlos' cause was revealed during the Catalonian 'War of the Malcontents' in 1827–8, when armed bands issued the first formal demands for his installation as king. The Malcontents' aims stood in direct line of descent from those of the 'Church and King' guerrillas of the War of Independence through the royalist bands of 1820–3: a wholesale return to the past, the Inquisition included.[10] Malcontents and *apostólicos*, it must be noted, displayed little of the relative sophistication of the Persian Manifesto, reverting instead to a much cruder 'Throne and Altar' programme. The Malcontents' action was contained and failed to ignite the nationwide rural rising that its *apostólico* backers apparently had in mind. As for Ferdinand, while no liberal, neither was he disposed to become the *apostólicos'* prisoner; in choosing therefore to maintain an opening to the more moderate liberals, he merely confirmed the worst fears of the *apostólicos* and caused them still greater agitation.

One thing only held back Don Carlos' supporters from really desperate measures in the late 1820s – the general expectation of his succession to the throne and the automatic triumph of their cause. The king was childless after three marriages, and a sick man, so that there was good reason for their optimism. Hence the universal astonishment and, among the devotees of Don Carlos, dismay, when Ferdinand's fourth marriage to María Cristina of Naples produced two daughters in as many years. For over two years, with the king's death clearly looming, the Spanish court seethed with bitter factionalism and labyrinthine machinations, as Don Carlos sought to assure his succession and the queen, supported by all anti-*apostólicos*, that of her eldest daughter Isabella.[11] Don Carlos' advocates invoked Philip V's Salic Law, and the queen pointed to the Pragmatic Sanction of 1789, hastily promulgated by Ferdinand in 1830. When the latter finally died in 1833 the initiative rested with María Cristina. Don Carlos had been forced into exile in Portugal; the Royal Volunteers were being gradually disbanded, with the encouragement of the army, in which elements sympathetic to Don Carlos were also being weeded out; and *apostólico* influence both at court and in provincial and local government was on the wane. Don Carlos' protagonists had thus lost the peaceful battle for place and influence, and rebellion was the only alternative left to them. The announcement of Ferdinand's death and the proclamation of Isabella II at the end of September 1833 was soon followed by the formation of rebel juntas and armed bands, first in Extremadura and Castile and then in the real Church and King strongholds of Navarre, the Basque country, Catalonia and Aragon. The Carlist cause was born.[12]

It is the unhappy fate of legitimist causes that their leaders are preordained, that while dynasticism provides a focus of activity and, with luck, both cohesiveness and continuity, the pretenders themselves are often less than ideally suited to their calling. So it was with Carlism, one of whose wonders is that such extremes of self-sacrificial loyalty could be commanded by so mediocre a line of 'kings'.[13] The first Don Carlos, Carlos V, was a dull, pious bigot, ungrateful towards those who fought and died for him, deaf to good advice, and utterly incapable of the flexibility and breadth of vision necessary to bring him victory. His power over his followers rested almost exclusively upon the genuine if somewhat ostentatious devotion to the Church which made him a religious as much as a political leader. Carlism's later history was touched at every turn by the legends and symbols of Carlos V and his war. On the credit side, this fostered a powerful element of myth which unquestionably helped to perpetuate popular identification with the dynastic cause, but on the other hand it ensured that Carlos V's personal legacy of religious fanaticism and political myopia remained far more potent than was good for his descendants' chances of success.

Carlos V was nevertheless obsessively attached to his own destiny, surely the least to be expected of any pretender. His two successors lacked this kind of single-mindedness without supplying much by way of compensation. His son Carlos VI, Conde de Montemolín, assumed the leadership of Carlism on his 'abdication' in 1845, and spasmodically pursued the throne for the next fifteen years. By any reckoning Montemolín was a second-rate character, whose warlike posturings smacked more of the musical comedy stage than the battlefield – and even his calculatedly 'heroic' exterior was marred by the squint which deterred Isabella II from taking him as a husband and ending the dynastic quarrel then and there. In the late 1840s, even as Carlism revived in Catalonia, he came close to abandoning his claim in order to wed an English commoner, and in 1860 actually did so in payment for his freedom at the hands of the queen, following a farcical landing and attempted *pronunciamiento* at San Carlos de la Rápita (Tarragona). Once safely in exile, Montemolín tried to retract his renunciation, and for a year the Carlist claim was disputed by him and his brother Don Juan. In 1861 he died of cholera, leaving Don Juan as sole Carlist claimant.

Juan III (Juan I and Juan II had been Kings of Castile during the later Middle Ages) was the most bizarre of all the Carlist pretenders. On occasions Montemolín had raised Carlist temperatures by flirting with liberals in the pursuit of support, but Don Juan went much further in his willingness to separate the dynastic issue from the ideological apparatus surrounding it. He was in fact not only a convinced liberal but an advanced one, and eventually pursued his position to its logical conclusion by recognizing Isabella II as queen.

This development served to prove that Carlism, while needing a royal figurehead, had already become more than a mere dynastic movement, for at this low ebb in its fortunes Carlists showed themselves ready to cast aside a heterodox claimant and rally to another. In doing so, they gave the first practical expression to what subsequently became known as the 'dual legitimacy' principle, whereby a Carlist pretender must not only possess 'legitimacy of blood' but also exhibit 'legitimacy of conduct' by conforming closely to the central principles of Carlist Traditionalism. On this occasion, the new Pretender was Don Juan's own son, another Carlos. Raised by a mother, María of Modena, who was anxious to keep him out of Spain's endless dynastic dispute, Carlos and his younger brother Alfonso were virtually taken over and groomed for the Carlist leadership by Carlos V's formidable widow, the Princess of Beira. When his father cleared the air by recognizing Isabella, the young Carlos assumed the claim as Carlos VII – just in time to witness the queen's overthrow in 1868. Tall, magnificently bearded and with a commanding presence, the young Carlos VII actually looked like the popular idea of a king – unlike the dwarfish Carlos V and the cross-eyed Montemolín. And for thirty years of his forty-two year 'reign' he did indeed prove to be by far the worthiest member of his line, leading the Carlist forces bravely during the war of 1870–6 and presiding over the movement's difficult post-war phase successfully enough to guide it into the new century, alive if hardly flourishing. Only in his last years, under the influence of his second wife, Princess Berta of Rohan, did his commitment to Carlism weaken and his popularity among Carlists decline.

Carlos VII's son, Don Jaime, took up the Carlist claim on his father's death in 1909. The new Pretender was a warm, attractive character with an enquiring mind and a taste for travel. As a young man he had dabbled in liberalism, but by now he was already settling into a fairly conventional, if refreshingly unbigoted form of Carlism (or, more strictly, Jaimism). To a great many Carlists, Don Jaime remained disturbingly cosmopolitan and even 'liberal', and the bond between him and his followers was never as strong as Carlism's effectiveness demanded. More ominous still, after an early romantic tragedy he had chosen to stay unmarried; since his heir presumptive was his equally childless uncle, Don Alfonso, Carlism by the 1920s confronted an alarming problem of succession.

An unfortunate but probably inevitable side-effect of fusing a dynastic claim with a much broader ideological and political programme was a tendency towards schism on the part of elements considering themselves more Carlist than the Pretender. Don Juan's timely withdrawal prevented one serious crisis, but splits occurred in 1888 and 1919. On the former occasion it was the Integrists, critics of Carlos VII's refusal to shut his mind to modernity, who broke away under the leadership of Ramón Nocedal. Few but vociferous, the Integrists maintained an independent existence until 1931–2; officially unconcerned with the dynastic quarrel, and indeed with all forms of government, they preached 'the Social Reign of Jesus Christ', a theocratic notion which eschewed consideration of practical details. Through their Madrid daily *El Siglo Futuro* they sniped at the 'liberal' leadership of Carlos VII and Don Jaime, while exercising an austerely conservative influence out of all proportion to their numbers, both within the Spanish Church and among the more reactionary supporters of the Alfonsine Monarchy itself.[14] In 1919 the Carlists' most prominent ideologue and politician, Juan Vázquez de Mella, led a number of important figures in revolt against Don Jaime's leadership. This schism also deprived Carlism of outstanding personalities and, like that of the Integrists, spread disillusionment even among those who stayed loyal to the Pretender; in this instance, however, personalities were more involved than fundamental ideological differences, and Mella's death in 1928 made reconciliation likely.[15] Where the Integrists were concerned, only a jolt in Spain's historical development could bring to an end a schism which continued through sheer inertia.

Despite these crises, which over so long a period were bound to occur, and the uneven stature of the pretenders themselves, the Carlist dynasty, with the help of the myth of the wars, on balance fulfilled its essential role of contributing cohesion and continuity to the wider cause of which it was the central core. The mere existence of a dynastic claim was not enough, however, to guarantee its own survival and vitality – as the fate of other legitimisms bears witness. In order to comprehend both Carlism's persistence and its failures, we must look elsewhere.

Carlism would have little claim on the historian's attention had it simply been one more of the many legitimist causes which decorated the politics of nineteenth-century Europe. Where Jacobitism, its closest British equivalent, quickly passed from the defeat of 1745 to become a hobby for eccentrics, and French legitimism was reduced after 1880 to being the obsession of a diminishing number of dreamy aristocrats, Carlism continued as an important minority force in Spanish politics down to the twentieth century, thanks to its consistent ability to mobilize a mass following which, if never sufficient to bring victory, nevertheless prevented it from dying. This remarkable achievement was assisted by the peculiarities of Spain's economic and social development: in particular its slowness compared with Britain, Germany, Italy and France, and its extreme regional variations. These had the effect of preventing the ultraconservative hostility to change which Carlism represented from being ruthlessly swept aside by irresistible social and economic forces, and permitting its entrenchment in one or two well-defined regions.

The Carlist masses were mostly though not exclusively rural; widespread throughout Spain at the start of the First Carlist War in 1833, after the defeat of 1839–40 they were to be found concentrated within a large, mainly mountainous triangle of territory embracing the Basque provinces, Navarre, Aragon, and the inland districts of Catalonia and the Levant.[16] These were regions characterized by moderate-sized land holdings, owned or leased by peasant farmers; yet to classify Carlism crudely as a movement of conservative peasants is to tell only part of the story. For one thing, the Carlist ranks always contained a sizable minority of artisans;[17] for another, the so-called peasantry itself was a far from homogeneous class. Within the peasant society and economy of northern and north-eastern Spain there existed at the time of Carlism's birth and for much of the nineteenth century a crucial division between the secure and relatively prosperous Basques and Navarrese and the depressed peasantry of Aragon, Catalonia and the Levant. Popular Carlism thus presented two faces to the world: the face of conservatism and the face of protest.

In his classic study of modern Spain *The Spanish Labyrinth*, Gerald Brenan wrote that Carlism was 'nothing else than the hostility of a sturdy race of mountaineers and farmers to industrial life'.[18] It was rather more than that, yet Brenan's words accurately conjure up an image of that element of primitive, predominantly rural hostility to contemporary 'progress' which undoubtedly drove thousands of individuals to enlist in the Carlist armies. The early nineteenth century in Spain was a time not only of political upheaval but also of recurrent economic difficulties wrought by general European conditions and more specifically by the gradual loss of the country's American empire between 1806 and 1826.[19] In Spain, where regionalism was perhaps more extreme – and certainly was more complex – than anywhere else in western Europe, economic developments and crises tended to be highly selective in their impact, so that some regions prospered while others, sometimes adjacent, stagnated or declined. Naturally enough, many of those rural and small-town Spaniards who found themselves the victims of progress reacted to economic difficulty and the pressures of infant industrialism by looking back nostalgically to the days before the turn of the century when – or so it seemed – life had been ordered and secure; and since the hand-maid of change was liberalism, they responded readily to the appeal of liberalism's most resolute enemies – royalists, *apostólicos* and finally Carlists. Until the second half of the century, the greater part of rural Spain knew no other vehicle of social protest.

Although over the course of a century the staunchest bastion of Carlism was to be Navarre, during much of the nineteenth century it was Catalonia, Aragon and the Levant which were most militant in their defence of the cause. In all three regions, a depressed and declining upland area looked down on a prosperous plain, and in each it was the sierra which poured forth Carlists. By the early nineteenth century, coastal and lowland Catalonia had already developed a thriving, progressive agrarian economy based on secure tenure and the cultivation of vines, olives, vegetables and fruit. Upon the foundations of this rural prosperity, Barcelona and the neighbouring towns had become the stage for Spain's first experience of modern industrialism. The Catalonian textile industry was already second only to that of Lancashire by 1800, though other foreign rivals were later to overtake it; at this stage, with the partial exception of Valencia, industrialization had not even begun to affect the rest of the country. The contrast between Catalonia's cities and plain on the one hand, and the mountainous interior on the other, was brutal. In the latter a miserable peasantry scraped a meagre and deteriorating existence, raising poor subsistence crops on insecure leases, the normal tedium of its life interrupted only by a vigorous tradition of feuding and banditry which now proved susceptible to politicization. The factories of the Barcelona district drew off some surplus manpower from these Pyrenean valleys and their stagnating townships, leaving many of the farmers, artisans and marginal groups remaining to commit their frustrations to the cause of Church and King as embodied in the Royalists of 1820–3, the Malcontents, and the Carlist guerrillas of the next forty years.

Conditions in Aragon and the Levant were broadly similar. The Valencian *huerta*, a fertile irrigated plain which was – and is – one of Spain's richest agricultural districts, scattered in the early part of the nineteenth century with several prosperous towns in the first phase of industrialization, was juxtaposed with a parched and half-starved mountain hinterland. The uplands of Aragon produced sparse crops and fed vast migrant flocks of sheep, owned by the richer villages and by magnate families. These too were regions in decline; the once vibrant pastoral economy and related local industries of upland Huesca, Teruel and, above all, the mountainous area of Castellón known as the Maestrazgo, were contracting in a manner ill understood by the peasant and artisan population, conscious both of a relatively recent prosperity and the more fortunate circumstances of the coast and the Ebro basin. Regretting a lost arcadia, they too were to seek its recovery through Carlism.

Somewhat resembling eastern Carlism, though with shallower roots, were its more sporadic manifestations in Castile, Extremadura, Galicia and Andalusia. Here, and especially in parts of Old Castile, Carlism lingered on through the middle years of the nineteenth century chiefly in the form of ephemeral bands of marginal peasants, artisans and land-workers turned bandits. Their appearance closely coincided with periods of short-term economic hardship; assembling in villages or small towns, they would call for the reduction or removal of the *consumos* (excise taxes), proclaim their devotion to the current Carlist pretender, ravage the surrounding district and, if not apprehended, return to their normal lives as quickly as they had left. The Carlism of Catalonia, Aragon and the Levant may often have seemed to differ little in practice from brigandage, but that of Castile and of the west and south was in truth scarcely more than a façade behind which brigandage operated.[20]

Eastern Carlism possessed certain characteristics in common with the Carlism of Navarre and the Basque country which will be discussed shortly. In both, popular enthusiasm for Church and King was perfectly genuine even if it also served – or was believed to serve – other, more material ends. At the same time, however, it was patently harnessed by Carlism's local leadership: the Carlist elite, as it were, of clerics, lesser aristocrats, and a middle-class element made up of anti-liberal professional men, wealthier landowners and retired army officers. In the case of struggling communities, this alliance of the comfortable and the desperate might seem a curious one. It was nevertheless quite natural; deference on the part of the poor towards their social superiors and religious mentors was still the normal thing in these traditional societies, where economic hardship had not yet generated local class antagonisms. Any feeling of economic grievance nursed by the indigent peasants and insecure artisans of Pyrenean Catalonia, upland Aragon or the Maestrazgo was aimed not against their more fortunate neighbours, often mortgaged or indebted to urban interests themselves, or against an equally poor local clergy, but at what they reasonably regarded as their real exploiters – the *rentiers*, bailiffs, usurers and factories of the large towns and cities.

This brand of Carlism, which enjoyed its heyday from 1830 to 1876, was in its popular dimension a genuine movement of social protest expressed in reactionary terms, and as such a doomed one. Doomed, because like the Luddism which was one of its chief ingredients, it existed to combat changes in the pattern of rural and small-town life, and in the relationship between countryside and city, which had already irreversibly taken place or else were irresistible. In this situation, Carlism provided a convenient political refuge for something which transcended banditry but stopped well short of social revolution. Social protest in this context was heartfelt but completely negative; however zealous their Catholicism and monarchism, the Carlist guerrilla bands of eastern – and central – Spain depended for their manpower upon economic casualties whose zest for violence very often exceeded that of their far from squeamish commanders. The priest Merino, whose bands roamed Castile during the First Carlist War, confessed his inability to control the passions of his men; Ramón Cabrera, guerrilla commander in Aragon, saw his followers smash machinery and destroy factories when they fell upon the Valencian plain; and in Catalonia Carlist guerrillas, like the royalist and Malcontent bands before them, sacked entire towns and levied 'taxes' upon the livers of the soft life along the coast. Such activities, which appalled not only non-Carlists but also many of the Carlists themselves, had little to do with the Carlist cause proper, and everything to do with a disintegrating traditional society's outcry against the visible evidence of change and modernity.

Carlism as social protest displayed remarkable persistence, but carried the seeds of its own decline. Rural-based guerrilla bands were difficult for government forces to defeat and eradicate, but incapable in the form in which they existed of the co-ordinated campaigning indispensable for overall victory. Since superbrigandage was also unable to alter underlying economic conditions, repeated failure was sooner or later bound to bring disillusionment and a search for alternative courses of action. The mere passage of time worked against ultimate success. Social change may have been slow, or Carlism would not have functioned for so long as a virile if inchoate form of protest, but take place it did. Spanish cities, especially in the last third of the century, increasingly absorbed surplus, discontented rural populations, in Catalonia to such a degree that stability and peace finally came to the hills and valleys which had once been the home territory of Carlist guerrillas. Having taken a firm hold in Catalonia, industrialism began to affect other regions, advancing too rapidly to allow effective conservative resistance. And perhaps most important of all, Spain's traditionally atrocious communications at last began to improve, making sustained bandit or guerrilla activity far less easy to conduct. This was crucial, for in order to live, the Carlism of declining areas *needed* violent expression. Rather than a constant, rooted popular conviction, it was simply the customary form assumed by endemic discontent in a period when no alternative was available. Between risings it effectively ceased to function as a political force, and after the defeat of 1876 it vanished completely from many districts. Carlism did not die out altogether in eastern Spain, but contracted to become a residual movement of those peasants, secure or struggling, who remained firm in their Catholicism. But in Aragon especially, generations of rural hardship finally bred loss of religious faith, so that in many areas peasant dissent passed from right to left, from Carlism to anarchism.

Unlike the Carlism of Catalonia, Aragon and the Levant — not to mention that of central, southern and western Spain — Navarrese and Basque Carlism remained a mass phenomenon down into the twentieth century, and therefore needs to be considered separately. Carlism in Navarre and the three Basque provinces of Álava, Guipúzcoa and Vizcaya was above all a movement of the economically satisfied.[21] The countryside of most of the region was divided into moderate-sized family farms, either privately owned or rented on long and secure leases from generally conscientious and benevolent landlords. Whether owned or leased, farms were customarily passed on by inheritance, not always to the eldest son but usually by prior family agreement and without rancour. Since Basque and Navarrese farms were sufficiently large and productive to support entire families from generation to generation, the families themselves remained tightly integrated and their loyalties and traditions extremely strong. Village communities were in turn bound together by the shared interest in this equitable distribution of property. In a region where acute poverty and social conflict were less apparent than anywhere else in Spain, all forms of conservatism flourished, under the protective mantle of a homely, unquestioning Catholicism whose parish priests came from the communities over whose souls they had care. Here more than in any other region, the local clergy provided Carlism with leadership and inspiration; here as a result, fervent Catholicism, symbolizing social harmony and distrust of outsiders, was the chief driving force of a Carlism whose worst wartime excesses were committed in the Church's name.

In a society of this kind, the simple prospect of change constitutes a threat to all. The Basque country and Navarre had traditionally enjoyed a large measure of self-administration on the basis of their ancient *fueros*; liberalism threatened their elimination in the cause of uniformity and centralization, thereby driving members of the local ruling class into the arms of the Carlists, who somewhat calculatedly grafted the cry of 'fueros' on to that of 'Dios, Patria, Rey!' Liberalism also meant secularization and in particular the alienation of ecclesiastical property – an abomination to the people of a region where the Church was genuinely and deservedly popular. And, of course, it promised 'progress', the infliction of urbanism and industrialism upon members of a society which, while not exploited by urban interests like the rural communities of other Spanish regions, was no less suspicious of cities for that. All in all, liberalism and 'progress' offered an uncertain and disturbing future to almost all sectors of a society which found little to complain about in its present lot. 'Liberal' cities such as Bilbao, San Sebastian and Pamplona were near enough to permit the countryman to taste the meaning of progress and to convince him that he disliked it. The rural populace of the Basque–Navarrese region thus flocked to the standard of Carlism: not so much as a protest against its present condition as an insurance against the future.

Where Carlism in most parts of Spain resembled, when mobilized for battle, a higher form of banditry, in Navarre and the Basque country it came closer to being a *levée en masse* of an entire population. This wholeheartedness and near unanimity, animated by religious and regional conviction, made it possible during the wars of 1833–40 and 1870–6 to erect in the region something approximating to a Carlist state and to construct at least a passable imitation of a full-scale army. From 1840 onwards, even if eastern Carlism was more militant and quicker to take up arms, it was Navarre and the Basque provinces which stood out as the Carlist country *par excellence*, an extensive region in which Carlism was a living cause during peace as well as war. Where family and local tradition was powerful and respected, there was more to inheritance than mere property. Devotion to the Carlist cause, with its colourful history, its 'heroes and martyrs', its songs and symbols, was handed down from one generation to the next as smoothly and automatically as the family farm and livestock. In a stable, well-fed, little-changing community, the extended family circle kept alive an oral tradition of exceptional vigour, in which the feats of war-heroes like Zumalacárregui and Cabrera, the strange exploits of fighting priests such as Merino and Santa Cruz, and the shame of General Maroto's betrayal of Carlos V at Vergara, were as real to the Carlists of the 1900s as to their grandparents and great-grandparents who had lived through them. In the twentieth century, the most potent Carlist symbolism was that which recalled the Basque–Navarrese region's identification with the cause: 'Oriamendi', the rousing Carlist anthem, tells of the greatest victory of the First Carlist War near the Guipúzcoan town of Hernani; Montejurra, the sacred mountain upon whose summit Carlists still assemble on the first Sunday in May, was the scene of the relief of Carlos VII's Navarrese capital of Estella in 1873.

Basque and Navarrese Carlism thus possessed stronger and deeper roots than that of any other Spanish region and continued to prosper even after the cause had withered almost everywhere else. The very conservatism of the rural population which had originally underlain its support of Carlos V also made it slow to abandon Carlism despite repeated defeat and the advance of the changes to which it had been opposed. Thus the sale of ecclesiastical property during the 1830s and 1850s, which in most of Spain enriched liberals and strengthened liberalism, in Navarre benefited the same farmers and professional men who, as Carlists, had opposed its introduction; instead of transforming them into grateful liberals, however, it actually reinforced the material basis of their conservatism. The industrialization which from the last quarter of the nineteenth century occurred in the coastal Basque provinces of Vizcaya and Guipúzcoa caused relatively few harmful convulsions in the rural hinterland, yet agrarian aversion towards urban Babylons was undiminished. Only one political development, it transpired, had the power to threaten Carlism's grip on rural Guipúzcoa and Vizcaya, and less seriously its monopoly in Navarre and Álava. This was the emergence of Basque Nationalism, which will be examined later.

The nature of Carlism's popular base in the early and mid-nineteenth century was thus such as to ensure the movement's longevity — though not necessarily its immortality — while at the same time rendering its triumph unlikely. It was also a contracting base, thanks to the very social and economic developments against which early Carlism militated. By the later nineteenth century, urbanism and industrialism were becoming irreversible, while social protest, urban and rural, was assuming the very different forms of socialism and anarchism.

These developments did not necessarily add up to a death sentence on Carlism. The last quarter of the nineteenth century saw the birth in many parts of Europe of organized expressions of right-wing hostility to liberalism; the twentieth century was to demonstrate their power. Assuming that some such phenomenon was probably bound to emerge in Spain, Carlism had a head start over any potential challenger. But the very depth of its historical roots was also a hindrance, in making it difficult for Carlists to accept changes in their movement's outlook and policies. This was a serious problem, since in order to flourish in twentieth-century conditions as an effective opponent of Spanish liberalism, to retain existing support and win new adherents, Carlism would have to move with the times. In particular, it would have to develop its ideology and programme and formulate a credible and efficacious political strategy.

Before the middle of the nineteenth century, Carlism could lay little claim to ideological distinction. One school of modern Spanish historians holds that Carlism represented a 'middle way' of reform between the extremes of liberalism and ministerial despotism, yet while some Carlists doubtless did subscribe to the kind of traditionalist reformism enshrined in the Persian Manifesto, it is even more certain that Carlos V spoke for the mass of his followers in preferring a more basic 'Throne and Altar' conservatism.[22] Where the cannon fodder of the Carlist armies was concerned, ideas mattered far less than simple loyalties and instinctive antagonisms. After 1840 a degree of intellectual respectability was lent by two non-Carlist admirers, the Catalan theologian Jaime Balmes and the less impressive Donoso Cortés; these were the first important contributors to Spanish Traditionalist thought, yet their ideas were for the most part imported directly from French Catholic propagandists.[23]

Serious formulation of Carlist theory had to wait until the 1860s and 1870s, with the entry into the movement of converts from the 'Neo-Catholic' religious and intellectual revival. Two of these converts, Cándido Nocedal and Antonio Aparisi y Guijarro, were responsible for providing the reviving Carlist movement of the late 1860s with a more or less systematic corpus of anti-liberal thought, the constructive side of which involved a politico-religious programme essentially similar to that of the 'Persians'.[24] The propagandistic achievements of Nocedal and Aparisi did much to make Carlist ideas respectable among conservative Spanish Catholics, but made scant impact on the Carlist rank and file, most of whom responded more readily to the unsophisticated urgings of the war party which, in 1872, succeeded in pushing Carlos VII into another rising. When the war ended in 1876, Carlism was left once again saddled with the image of obscurantism, bigotry and fanaticism, and identified in the popular mind with a naïve attachment to absolute monarchy, clericalism and rural localism.

Fortunately, Carlos VII was disinclined to tolerate such a situation. Even before the end of the war, he had caused some consternation in the Carlist ranks by proclaiming his belief in the need to adapt political programmes to changing circumstances,[25] a view which he continued to hold during the decades which followed, despite the criticism and eventual schism of Nocedal's son, Ramón, and the Integrists. The ideologue equipped to 'modernize' Carlist thought proved to be on hand in the person of yet another convert, an Asturian, Juan Vázquez de Mella. Between the late 1880s and his death in 1928, Mella made a deliberate and in many respects successful attempt at creating a complete and coherent system of modern Traditionalist theory, in the hope of clarifying Carlism's ideas and policies both for the education of committed adherents and the attraction of converts. The end product of his efforts was a species of Catholic corporativism related to contemporary movements in other parts of Europe, influenced by the Encyclicals of Leo XIII and claiming to offer a modern, 'authentically Spanish' solution to the problems of the day.

As a convert rather than the product of a Carlist background, Mella was free from the obsessive harping on the dynastic quarrel and the exaggerated glorification of the movement's violent past which were so typical of Carlists and their propaganda. Spain, he wrote in 1889, must be shown that a Carlist was not, as generally caricatured:

a kind of crow lurking in the crevices of feudal keeps, disposed to damn every scientific discovery and condemn all the marvels of industry . . . a kind of romantic poet who, bowed down with present-day reality and a nostalgia for the past, turns tearful eyes towards bygone centuries.[26]

On the contrary, he argued, Carlism was 'modern' in as much as it possessed the answer to contemporary social and political problems. To strengthen his case, Mella chose to employ the fashionable vocabulary of liberalism as a weapon against the liberals themselves. True 'progress' thus became impossible unless tied to tradition, while genuine 'freedom' and even 'democracy' lay not in liberalism but within an organically based 'federative' or 'representative' monarchy.[27] As this implies, Mella made no attempt to tamper with the fundamentals of Carlist Traditionalism as expounded by Cándido

Nocedal and Aparisi: the dynastic claim, the 'inviolability of the Holy Faith', the *fueros* and the limited — but not constitutional — monarchy, all governed by the all-embracing sovereignty of God. Unlike the Integrists, however, he displayed positive enthusiasm in tackling the problematical implementation of God's sovereignty through secular institutions, advancing beyond the ideas of his precursors by acknowledging the need to adapt those institutions hallowed by tradition rather than restoring them *in toto*.

The central theme and ultimate goal of Mella's thought, as of that of all those who in nineteenth-century Europe countered liberalism with one or other form of corporativism, was 'unity' — the creation of a system of government and social relationships free from the divisive ideological, class and regional conflicts rampant in late nineteenth-century Spain. The guarantee of unity was a Catholic, monarchic and traditionally based system; national consciousness would be ensured by the unequalled social bond of religious uniformity or 'Catholic Unity', rigidly enforced; the nation itself was not produced by race or language but was a 'psychological principle' derived from a vast fund of ideas, feelings, aspirations, and above all traditions.[28]

Temporal institutions, Mella believed, existed to embody and protect the spiritual unity bequeathed a people by its traditions. Since the Church's role was that of maintaining 'unity of doctrine' and of providing 'sap' for every organic unit within society, it must enjoy total freedom over its internal affairs and exercise a monopoly over education. This was what Carlists called 'religious freedom'. It had no room either for religious toleration or for laic education, since tolerance of heresy, even of heterodoxy, was believed to destroy 'doctrinal unity' and thereby erode the very foundations of society.[29]

Thus far, Mella's ideas were hardly original. His personal contribution to Spanish Traditionalist ideas lay in his detailed discussion of a 'representative monarchy', based upon the proposals of the Persians, and of Aparisi, yet updated in such a way as to assume — in Mella's own eyes at least — a relevance to contemporary problems: the practical as distinct from the theoretical shortcomings of liberalism, the intensifying regionalism of Catalonia and the Basque region, and the increasingly bitter social unrest now finding its expression in socialism and anarchism. Mella was thus particularly eager to kill off the Carlist incubus of 'absolutism', a label he claimed was more suited to Spanish liberalism, in which a much-vaunted freedom and democracy barely concealed a governmental despotism based on oligarchy, self-interest and dishonesty. To Mella these tendencies were the inevitable by-product of liberalism. The liberal Cortes, he charged, were founded upon the erroneous principle of individualism; 'numerical' suffrage produced results which at best were unrepresentative and in the Spanish context were further distorted by all manner of corruption and coercion. The Cortes therefore contained nothing but a collection of abstract opinions and competing greeds, and served as the arena for institutionalized conflicts. In fact if not in theory, liberal government was a tyranny against which the people were defenceless, headed by a monarchy as expensive as it was useless and which was committing a slow suicide through its dependence on its foes.[30]

The role of the monarchy, according to Mella, was to complement that of the Church by providing 'external' or political unity.[31] The Traditional Monarch whom he wished to see supersede the Liberal would rule actively but not absolutely, assisted by an appointed Council of Notables and 'truly representative' Cortes. The Cortes, their sessions private, would exist to bring the people's needs and feelings before the king; they would not actually legislate, but their approval would be required for the imposition of new taxation or any alteration in the 'fundamental laws of the kingdom'.[32] In order to be 'truly representative' the Cortes would be organized not on the basis of divisive political parties, but of the 'natural' constituent elements of society. Six 'orders' would accordingly elect members: agriculture, industry and commerce, the clergy, the armed forces, the aristocracy and the intelligentsia.[33]

Anxious to reverse the prevailing trend towards the centralization of authority, Mella urged that the central government's powers be strictly limited. Apart from the areas of foreign relations, international trade, the armed forces and judiciary, and arbitration in interregional and interclass disputes, all administration ought to revert to regional, provincial and local bodies.[34] This demonstrated Mella's desire to elevate the characteristic localism of the regions where Carlism was strongest into a fundamental constitutional principle, capable of being exploited against both centralizers and separatists; by devolving power instead of concentrating it in Madrid, the appeal of separatism might, it was hoped, be destroyed. Mella recognized that the various regions of Spain possessed distinct personalities, institutions, traditions and problems which were the fruit of historical development and of variations in race, language, terrain and climate; since regional and local issues were best understood at their own level, that was where they were also best tackled – as long as wider, perhaps national implications were not involved. Carlist 'regionalism', Mella insisted, was not divisive but 'integrative' in its perception of the vital and inextinguishable relationship between the Spanish nation and its constituent parts.[35]

Here Mella came into direct conflict with the Catalanist and Basque Nationalist movements which emerged in the latter part of the nineteenth century. Both owed much to the intellectual contributions of writers who, if not Carlists, were ex-Carlists or the product of Carlist backgrounds. In Catalonia these included the poet Verdaguer, the politicians Cambó and Estelrich, and the Bishop of Vich, José Torras y Bages, whose work *La Tradició Catalana*, published in 1893, became the bible of the Catalanist right and remains a classic of Traditionalist theory. Yet Catalanism, the result of a century's development, was always an alliance of left and right; Carlism contributed to it a strong sense of the region's history and popular culture, of the underlying stability of its rural society, and of the distinctiveness of its legal system. In no real sense can it be said that Carlism was the chief foundation for the evolution of Catalanism as it undoubtedly was for that of Basque Nationalism. Most of the latter's early leaders were originally Carlists, and the programme of the *Partido Nacionalista Vasco* (PNV) as elaborated in the 1890s showed a clear debt to Carlism, placing a similar emphasis upon Catholic Unity, opposition to liberalism, and the pre-eminence of clerical interests.[36] Intolerant in religious matters and indifferent on the question of republic versus monarchy, early Basque Nationalism could be regarded as upholding the wish to implement the Integrists' 'Social Reign of Jesus Christ' within an area defined by the limits of the Basque race and tongue.

It was this preoccupation with race which, more than anything else, created an ideologically unbridgeable gulf between Basque Nationalism and Carlism. Basque Nationalist propagandists claimed the Basque race to be not only unique but superior to the Spanish;[37] their frank hostility to Spain was symbolized by the burning of the national flag at meetings to cries of 'Death to Spain!' The confessed goal of Basque Nationalism was the exclusion from the entire Basque country – on both sides of the Pyrenees – of non-Basque language, culture and authority.[38] No genuine Carlist could stomach such 'excesses', and Mella attacked Basque Nationalism bitterly. Race and language were not in themselves, he insisted, the lifeblood of nationality; neither Basques nor Catalans enjoyed that 'spiritual unity' which alone created a nation. Spain on the other hand did, and was consequently the *patria* of Basques and Catalans just as much as of Castilians. This being so, to question national unity was *lèse patrie* — treason.[39] The way to satisfy the yearnings of Spain's regions was not separatism but regionalism as the Carlists defined it: the devolution of administrative power within a framework of inviolable national unity.[40]

In spite of his protestations that Carlism was a modern movement qualified to tackle the accentuating social problems of the late nineteenth and early twentieth centuries, it was in confronting what Spanish conservatives were wont to call the 'social question' that Mella was at his least confident. Influenced by the example of Leo XIII and by European corporativist and social-Catholic contemporaries, with several of whom he corresponded,[41] Mella found it easy enough to bemoan prevailing conditions in agriculture and industry and to belittle the remedies suggested by others — especially on the left. His own proposals, however, reflected the limited horizons of a northern Spaniard ignorant or careless of the problems of the latifundist regions of the south and west, with their vast areas of unused land and armies of unemployed or underemployed rural labourers. Irresponsible landowners he condemned, it is true; yet he also rejected all question of confiscation, voicing instead the ingenuous wish to extend to these regions the totally inappropriate systems of land tenure and exploitation indigenous to the north.[42] The result of this failure, the outward evidence of Carlism's decline as an outlet for social protest and withdrawal into regions of rural self-sufficiency, was an inescapable, if unstated alliance with agrarian conservatism.

With industrial problems Mella was even more uncomfortable. Carlism, born of rural aversion to all that liberalism represented, admitted to no love for large-scale capitalism, which Mella declared unacceptable and doomed.[43] At the same time, Carlism's roots — and those of Mella himself — in a deeply religious, rural society wherein social injustice and inequality were not extreme, and where charity remained the normal and honoured remedy for such hardship as did exist, prevented them from grasping the complexities of modern industrialism and the real causes of social misery and unrest. The blame, not unfairly, was placed at the door of liberalism, which it was claimed had destroyed charity and replaced it with pauperism; work, instead of a rewarding Christian duty, had become a mere business, and man himself a machine. In undermining religious faith, liberalism had also weakened the principal restraint upon social unrest.

Mella was clear and explicit as to the system with which liberal economics and industrial relations must be replaced: within the total system of Catholic Unity and representative monarchy, industry would be reorganized along corporative lines and the old guilds restored.[44] Neither Mella nor any other Carlist could offer a convincing suggestion as to how this desired state of affairs could be brought about; solutions were presented as ends, without the slightest indication of the means, peaceful, violent or downright miraculous, necessary to achieve them. How such pious hopes as the unity of master and man, an end to the tyranny of capital and the law of supply and demand, and the emancipation of the worker through Christianity were to be realized in the face of cynical liberal employers and an overwhelmingly socialist or anarcho-syndicalist labour force, was a question which Mella evaded. Now and then, however, he would toy with a theory of catastrophe: capitalism, like the Liberal Monarchy which encouraged it, was destined to collapse through its own internal contradictions; its probable successor would be socialism, which system would in turn disintegrate, thus opening the way for a restoration of traditional values as a repentant proletariat once again embraced the Church and accepted the Carlist monarchy. Thus Mella moved a step beyond Marx and dreamed of a New Carlist Man.

This utopian vision illustrates the serious limitations of Mella's ideological accomplishment. The Carlist state which he sketched was vivid enough and by no means unattractive to Spanish Catholics of a conservative temper. What remained painfully unclear was whether it could be achieved against the apparent current of history, and if so, how. The central dilemma facing thoughtful Traditionalists after 1876 was that their maximum goals, a state free from unnecessary bureaucratic and coercive powers and a society free from economic exploitation and class conflict, with a universal, voluntary religious faith acting as a kind of social cement, were logically unattainable through the use of coercion and control, and realistically unattainable through peaceful persuasion. For while it was unlikely that the vague and charitable piety of Mella's social policies would ever succeed in re-Christianizing the Spanish working class and converting it to Traditionalism, the Carlists' deliberate rejection of the coercive apparatus of the detested modern state prevented them from making the vital ideological leap necessary to transform their movement into a party of the modern, authoritarian right. As long as an acute social and political crisis lay in the future, this problem was only latent; sooner or later, however, the Carlists would be forced to resolve their dilemma or else be swept aside by more 'modern' competitors.

In spite of these contradictions, Traditionalist ideology gained a new prestige as the result of Mella's work. In bringing Carlist ideas as up to date as it was possible to do, relating them – however questionably – to contemporary issues, and generally adding a measure of sophistication to what had previously been a limited and simplistic collection of ideas and prejudices, he won the esteem of a significant sector of conservative opinion. The respect openly paid him by eminent non-Carlist intellectuals such as Marcelino Menéndez Pelayo, statesmen like the Conservative leader Antonio Maura, and not least the Dictator, Primo de Rivera, transcended the merely personal and rubbed off on the Carlist cause itself. They and other conservative Spaniards used Carlist Traditionalism as an important element within their own ideas and programmes, however much they may have adapted, distorted or added to it – especially in the direction of the modern authoritarianism which Carlism avoided. Indeed, it would not be going too far to suggest that by the early twentieth century, Carlist principles as developed by Aparisi, Cándido Nocedal and Mella had come to form the main ideological source for the Spanish anti-liberal right.

Mella's tendency to divorce his vision of an idyllic traditional Spain from the problems, theoretical and practical, associated with its achievement was typical of Carlist intellectuals and surpassed by most of the rank and file, few of whom ever considered such abstract matters. The same went for the more mundane realms of strategy. Carlism was never satisfactorily to resolve the crucial question which confronted it at the end of the First Carlist War in 1840: not so much whether the Traditionalist arcadia was capable of re-creation as how liberalism was to be defeated in the first place. It would only be when this stage was reached, or at least was at hand, that the ideological dilemma discussed above was likely to be clearly perceived. In the meantime, Carlists hovered between two alternative but frequently converging paths: war and persuasion.

The experience of the First Carlist War had starkly illuminated Carlism's military limitations, which were closely related to the sociological limitations discussed earlier. Notwithstanding the widespread popular feeling behind Carlos V when fighting began, it soon became evident that his cause was truly strong only in northern and eastern Spain. In its home territory, from its north-western limit of Vizcaya to Alicante in the south-east, Carlism often appeared militarily impressive, whether in the form of the Catalonian or Maestrazgo guerrillas or the more regularized armies of Navarre. Here victories could be won, foreigners bewitched, and dreams of future triumph nursed. This was simply not enough, however. As the war dragged on and the liberals gained in strength, Carlist support in other regions fell away. Time and resources were squandered in besieging liberal strongholds within Carlist country, especially Bilbao; without large-scale support on the far side of Madrid, there was no chance of a pincer attack which might capture the capital and smash the liberal system at a stroke; and when the Carlist armies did try to break out of their provincial confinement, in the peripatetic Gómez expedition and Carlos V's own march on Madrid, lack of resolution produced by an uneasy sense of remoteness from a reliable base stood in the way of decisive success. In the end, collapse came not through dramatic defeat so much as sheer absence of progress.[45]

One military failure ought perhaps to have been enough. But already by 1840 violence had assumed for Carlists a mythical role which had little or nothing to do with rational assessment of the chances of victory. One former guerrilla, Cabrera, was sufficiently shrewd to realize eventually that a cause which relied on insurrection in strictly confined regions was doomed to defeat, but others refused to accept the inevitable. In Catalonia and Aragon, where rural unrest was endemic, intermittent Carlist violence spluttered for a quarter of a century after 1840. In the late 1840s it rose to such a level as to merit, at least from the Carlists themselves, the label of Second Carlist War, though the commoner title is the War of the Early Risers (*Matiners*). With little echo in other regions, even Navarre, these troubles annoyed but did not threaten Isabella's crown. If Carlism's geographic constriction was not enough to ensure defeat, what did guarantee it, now and for several decades more, was the hostility of the Spanish army. This was now a solidly 'liberal' institution, immune to Carlist subversion and always capable, sooner or later, of overcoming Carlist violence.[46] When one military convert to Carlism, General Ortega, joined Montemolín in issuing the *pronunciamiento* of 1860, his pathetic failure proved precisely what a freak he was. Even so, military failure did little to inspire the majority of Carlists to think any further than violence. The fact that the harmonious Spain of which Carlists spoke was hardly likely to be built on the ashes of civil war was not, of course, considered; not surprising, perhaps, when one remembers that Carlists continued to thrill to Carlos V's singularly unharmonious bigotry rather than to the benevolent 'reformism' of the Persian tradition.

If Carlism had any hope of success between 1840 and 1868, it lay not in rebellion but in an undermining of the Isabelline system. The queen herself, and still more her husband, Francisco de Asís, were nagged by the feeling that the Carlist claim to the throne was indeed legitimate. Carlist influence was still powerful at Court, in the aristocracy and, for the moment, in the episcopate and the Church at large; with the line separating Carlism from conservative 'moderate' liberalism often a blurred one, and with a revival of religious piety seizing the privileged classes, the crown found itself threatened with a possible takeover from within. Attempts, urged by the Catholic intellectual Balmes, at resolving the dynastic issue through a marriage between Montemolín and either the queen, her sister or daughter, came to nothing. In the 1860s, the plummeting prestige of the Isabelline monarchy gave a new opportunity to Carlism, which with the 'accession' of Carlos VII in 1867 at last seemed in a position to grasp it. The influx of 'neo-Catholics' before and after Isabella's fall in 1868, and the vigorous leadership of Cándido Nocedal, meant that by the early 1870s Carlism had become a powerful parliamentary party which, in a highly fluid political situation, could anticipate an important role, with the eventual succession of Carlos VII not utterly out of the question. Grass-roots violence, however, resumed in 1870; and two years later, following a decline in the party's electoral fortunes, the Pretender succumbed to the pressure of the Carlist war party and the Third Carlist War began in earnest. As Spain experienced first the brief monarchy of Amadeo I of the House of Savoy, and then the one-year Republic, the Carlists fought a repeat performance of their first war. At the end of 1874, a military *coup d'état* brought about the restoration of the old monarchy in the person of Isabella's son, Alfonso XII. By 1876 the Carlist cause was defeated again, gloriously but, it seemed, finally; the factors which had bred failure between 1833 and 1840 had been at work again.

Until now, the possibility of a Carlist victory over Spanish liberalism, while unlikely, had never been totally absent – and certainly had not appeared so. After 1876, although Carlism survived just as it had done in 1840, its prospects of success were reduced almost to nil. In terms of everyday Spanish politics, it became a mere minority movement of the far right, albeit one with influence beyond its own membership and possessing considerable nuisance value from time to time. Quite apart from the devastating effects of another defeat, the new political climate was ominous for a cause of Carlism's character. Alfonso XII and his 'Liberal Monarchy', thanks to the traumatic experiences of the years since his mother's fall, enjoyed from the outset a degree of acceptance and even popularity which Isabella had never known. Its constitution indicated the intention that it should stand as the very embodiment not only of the monarchic principle itself but also of religion and order; this role, which Carlism had always sought to fill, was swiftly recognized by the Papacy, almost all the Spanish episcopate, the armed forces, the entire liberal oligarchy – and not a few former Carlists. Being more Catholic than the Pope was no novelty for members of a movement which had always received less enthusiastic support from Rome than it felt it deserved, but when the Spanish hierarchy, which in the past had contained many active or passive Carlists, turned its collective back on them, they had every reason to feel alarmed.[47] As the years passed, this alarm was amply justified. Although a number of bishops retained sympathy for Carlism, and even more for Traditionalist attitudes towards religion, active support was rarely forthcoming as the Alfonsine regime continued to command the loyalty of the Spanish Church and the approval of the Vatican.

Carlos VII consoled himself with the classic placebo of the exiled pretender: the belief that the 'usurper' would enjoy but a brief honeymoon with the Spanish people, that the Liberal Monarchy was doomed by its very nature, and that its imminent death-throes would bring Spanish conservatives rushing shamefacedly back into the Carlist fold.[48] His hopes were not rewarded. Far from it – as it became increasingly plain that the Liberal Monarchy, whatever its long-term prospects, was unlikely to oblige the Pretender by an early collapse, still more Carlists began to defect, mostly into an independent neo-Catholic party, *Unión Católica*, whose leader Alejandro Pidal was himself a lapsed Carlist seduced — as the faithful saw it — by the doctrine of 'lesser evil' into accepting the constituted power. Experience had already proved that Carlism prospered amid conservative insecurity, and when conservative Spaniards found reassurance in the ruling regime, Carlism was condemned to struggle.

The political mechanics of the new system only made Carlism's problems worse. In place of the fluid liberalism of the pre-1868 days, constantly interrupted by military *pronunciamientos* and encouraging Carlism by virtue of its very instability, a system was now artificially introduced by the regime's architect and colossus, Antonio Cánovas del Castillo, which offered few openings to extremists of either wing. In a political game shared between oligarchic Conservative and Liberal parties, led respectively by Cánovas and his opposite number Práxedes Sagasta, power passed peacefully from one to the other via elections carefully controlled by the Minister of the Interior and, at constituency level, by the *caciques*. With working-class unrest localized and small-scale until the end of the century, and with conservatives, army and Church squarely behind the system, a generation passed without the kind of instability and uncertainty upon which Carlism depended for life.

Amid this depressingly hostile atmosphere, the Carlists could do little but concentrate upon keeping their movement ticking over while hoping against hope for better times. Carlos VII, displaying qualities of patience and common sense for which his line had not previously been distinguished, made the best of a difficult situation by presiding not only over Mella's intellectual overhaul but also the creation for the first time of a recognizable party organization. This was constructed first of all by Cándido Nocedal, who after the war became Carlos VII's 'Delegate' in Spain, and after his death by another outstanding royal servant, the Marqués de Cerralbo. It was Cerralbo who as Carlos VII's Delegate-General after 1888 set up a formal hierarchy of regional, provincial and local juntas or committees, together with 'circles' — centres for social and political activity — in districts where Carlism was still relatively thriving. Cerralbo's goal was a nationwide Carlist organization, backed up by a healthy press and capable of carrying Carlism into regions other than the north and east. Officially the purpose of the party organization was peaceful: discussion, social intercourse, charity and the dissemination of information and propaganda; just the same, there was no question that should the need arise, local organizations might be transformed overnight into foci of violence — nor that this facility was uppermost in Cerralbo's mind.[49] His achievement, like Mella's, was a considerable one; although after the turn of the century much of the national organization was to run down, it nonetheless helped to keep the Carlist cause alive during a difficult period and survived with only minor modifications until the livelier days of the Second Republic.

Carlist strategy in the wake of the 1876 defeat was inevitably governed by circumstances. Confidence that nemesis would eventually overtake the Liberal Monarchy and permit its replacement by that of Carlism lived on, as it had to do, yet few could seriously doubt that the great day lay far distant. For twenty years, violence was officially played down as Carlos VII and his chief advisers forbade a renewal of rebellion — not as in any sense immoral but simply as untimely. At first they pursued a policy of almost complete voluntary isolation from political affairs; then in 1890, as Cerralbo's efforts began to bear fruit, the Pretender announced a return, not to violence but to the electoral and parliamentary politics last practised before 1872. Carlism, the Spanish people were now assured, wished to be 'a hope, not a fear'; to most it was by this time neither.

The road of peaceful politics was a risky one to take, since the results of elections only advertised the depths of Carlism's decline since 1876.[50] For most of the period between 1890 and Primo de Rivera's *coup* in 1923, the number of Carlist deputies wavered between seven and thirteen, rising to the dizzy height of seventeen in 1907 only by virtue of the Catalonian Carlists' participation in *Solidaridad Catalana*, a broad, shaky and short-lived alliance of parties from all parts of the Catalonian political spectrum. When the parliamentary regime met its end in 1923 the Carlists had only six deputies.[51] Peaceful politics, besides being intrinsically uncongenial to the great majority of Carlists, thus appeared to do nothing to hasten the day of reckoning. Nevertheless at a time when rebellion was out of the question they were valuable in keeping Carlists active, the organization functioning, and Traditionalist ideas circulating for anyone willing to listen to them. Pending the millennium, survival was of the essence, and to this end any kind of action was better than none.

The political experience of Carlism between 1876 and 1931 illustrates perfectly the difficult task faced by a Traditionalist movement within a modernizing society and a political system dominated by conservative interests. The world to which the Carlists of the 1833 generation had tried to cling was receding even further, giving way to one in which it was becoming harder for the Carlists to gain acceptance for their message, however relevant they might consider it. Mella's achievement in giving Carlism a more or less coherent programme was in its way a remarkable one, but while it may have helped to prevent Carlism from dying it did little actually to attract new blood into a movement which desperately needed it. If anything, the elaborating and publicizing of Carlist ideas probably put off as many Spaniards as it attracted, by presenting them with a highly demanding, integralist system of ideas not one of which was regarded as dispensable or even capable of compromise. In consequence Carlism failed not only to win converts from the working class but also from among conservatives. Members of the expanding working class were alienated by Carlism's religiosity, its attachment to an archaic guild system which meant nothing to them and, in Catalonia, its growing deference towards capitalism and involvement in 'yellow' unionism. By 1923 the dream of winning over the hapless victims of liberalism was further away than ever, with the Spanish labour force overwhelmingly organized in the Socialist UGT (General Union of Workers) and the Anarcho-Syndicalist CNT (National Confederation of Labour). As for the more fortunate, they continued to see little point in encouraging a movement which called for total – and retrogressive – change when their own special concerns could be more realistically and effectively looked after either by the Liberal Monarchy itself or by particular parties within it. Thus those satisfied by a generally conservative, but completely non-ideological brand of monarchy settled happily for the Alfonsine regime, while the more piously inclined embraced *pidalismo* or even Integrism rather than soldier on in an apparently lost cause. And as time passed, there arose new forces to challenge Carlism by stressing only a part of its integral programme: political regionalism, social-Catholicism and conservative authoritarianism.

Catalonian Carlism never fully recovered from the defeat of 1876. During the last quarter of the nineteenth century it beat a retreat before a conservative regionalism which initially differed little from it save in its abandonment of dynasticism. Eventually this

strand compromised with the conservative wing of Catalonian liberalism and was absorbed within the Lliga Catalana, a moderate party
chiefly representing the region's industrial elite and standing for
regional devolution within the Alfonsine monarchy. The details of
Carlism's decay in the valleys of inland Catalonia remain mysterious,
but so far as can be discerned Catalanism was its beneficiary rather
than its cause.[52] In the Basque–Navarrese region, the emergence of
Basque Nationalism late in the nineteenth century confronted Carlism
with a direct competitor for essentially the same predominantly rural
constituency, and that in the one part of Spain where its mass support
had so far remained loyal. Devotion to the *fueros* had always been
an important element in Basque–Navarrese Carlism, even if it had
originally been distinctly pragmatic. After 1876 the liberal regime
reduced the scope of the *fueros* to a nugatory level; Carlist failure to
resist this encroachment led to discontent, mainly in the more solidly
Basque coastal provinces of Guipúzcoa and Vizcaya. During the
1880s dissatisfied race-conscious Basques expressed their feelings via
foralism, a loosely organized movement with autonomist leanings
founded and for the most part supported by Carlists.[53] The Basque
Nationalist Party (PNV) was eventually founded in 1894, again
mainly by Carlists or by ex-Carlist foralists, but once the amorphous
sentiments of foralism were crystallized by Sabino de Arana y Goiri
into the more modern, strident, outright separatist demands of
Basque Nationalism, continued overlapping between the two movements became impossible. By the early years of the twentieth century,
rural Vizcaya and Guipúzcoa were at last being drawn into the
modern world of Bilbao, San Sebastian and the smaller Basque industrial towns, a world to which Basque Nationalism, while by no
means a progressive force, appeared more attuned than Carlism.
Here the drift of the rural population from Carlism to Basque
Nationalism went on, led throughout whole districts by the politically
vital parish clergy, until by 1914 the PNV was the larger party in
both provinces. In Navarre and Álava, where the proportion of
Basque speakers in the population was much lower, and interest in
Basque Nationalism commensurately weaker, Carlism continued to
dominate the Catholic right and the rural areas down to the coming
of the Second Republic.[54]

This widening gap brought into the open certain differences of
emphasis which had always existed between Basque and Navarrese
Carlism but which for most of the nineteenth century had lain beneath

the surface. In the coastal Basque provinces of Guipúzcoa and Vizcaya, cut off from the Castilian plateau by a range of mountains and looking outwards, as it were, from Spain, nineteenth-century Carlism was an expression of a deep-rooted regionalism of which the Basque language was an important but by no means the only element, especially in view of the Basques' distinctive economic interests in relation to any Madrid government. Basque Carlism began to flourish when it took up the cause of the Basque *fueros* – a conservative rather than a strictly Carlist concern, as Raymond Carr has pointed out[55] – and, when its defence of the *fueros* failed, lost ground before a modern nationalism which more accurately articulated the true nature of Basque aspirations. In contrast, Carlism in Navarre – and to a great extent in Álava – was above all an expression of *Spanish* patriotism. The declining force of Basque language in the two inland provinces only partly explains this phenomenon, which in Navarre at least would probably have been scarcely less apparent even had Basque been more widely spoken. Navarre and Álava, situated on the landward side of the Basque mountains, were drawn economically and, perhaps more important, psychologically towards Spain rather than to the Atlantic or into a mythical Basque nation. Navarrese Carlist regionalism, while genuine enough, drew its inspiration from the traditions of the old Kingdom of Navarre, one of the constituent parts of that Spanish state on whose strength and spiritual unity the Carlists of Navarre continued to insist; the intensity of this regionalism was always related to the general degree of acceptability of the regime in Madrid, and over the years it became clear that clericalism, monarchism and a broad social conservatism were the principal ingredients of what was actually a particular form of Spanish nationalism.

The overall effect of the emergence of Catalan and Basque regionalism was thus seriously damaging to Carlism in two of its key areas. It drew off Carlists whose chief motive in supporting the cause had been to defend regional interests, as well as attracting new adherents who might have found Carlist regionalism appealing but were repelled by other aspects of its integral programme.

Carlism's failure to project itself as a social-Catholic movement provided further evidence of the dangers inherent in integralism. After the turn of the century, with the Alfonsine party system disintegrating and social unrest on the increase, social-Catholicism began to make serious headway within both clergy and laity, yet despite Mella's efforts there were few outside the Carlist ranks who even briefly considered Carlism a possible vehicle for the application of social-Catholic ideas in Spain. Eventually in 1922 an assortment of Spanish Catholics who drew their inspiration from Leo XIII came together to form the *Partido Social Popular* (PSP). They took as their models the German Catholic Centre Party and the Italian *Popolari* of Don Luigi Sturzo, and were encouraged by the new Papal Nuncio, Tedeschini. The followers of Don Jaime would have little truck with the new party, but some of the dissident Mellists took their interest to the point of participating in its formation and activities. Mella himself refused to get involved, but his chief *protégé* Víctor Pradera played a leading role in the PSP's foundation along with other prominent Carlist dissidents such as the sincere social-Catholic Salvador Minguijón. Primo de Rivera's *coup* in 1923 effectively strangled the PSP in its infancy, but its short life indicated that if allowed to do so it would have emerged as a significant political force and one capable of wooing the less die-hard, more 'socially' minded Carlists away from the fold.[56] Firm evidence of this was forthcoming from the Levant, where a former Carlist PSP activist, Luis Lucía, during the 1920s gradually put together his own social-Catholic organization and in doing so attracted a sizable following among former Carlists in the region. In March 1930 the organization was formally constituted as a political party, the *Derecha Regional Valenciana* (DRV). Between them the PSP and the DRV suggested that a future national party fighting on a social-Catholic platform but rejecting other, less comfortable aspects of Carlism's ideology would present Carlism with a serious problem.

The first glimmerings of modern right-wing authoritarianism provided additional evidence that Carlism's anti-liberal past and continued invocation of patriotism and order were not enough to win over Spanish conservatives, even when liberalism was on the defensive. It has been rightly suggested that the Carlists of the 1890s were the first of the 'regenerationists', those Spaniards who reacted to the gradual disintegration of the Canovite party system and to Spain's humiliation at the hands of the United States in 1898 by urging a drastic transformation of the country's institutions. Nevertheless, it was not to Carlos VII but to generals like Polavieja and Weyler that disgruntled *fin de siècle* conservatives looked – in vain – for a miracle. Later, during the crisis-torn years between 1909 and 1923 it was not Carlism but Maurism which blossomed as the result of an appeal to public order, national unity and that superpatriotism which Spaniards call *españolismo*. The call of the Conservative statesman Antonio Maura to the 'essential Spain' and his desire to resist an apparently impending social revolution echoed at least parts of Carlism's programme while ignoring its less practicable aspects. It was therefore not surprising if Maurism won support which the Carlists might otherwise have hoped to attract — and, indeed, that of a considerable number of the Carlists themselves.[57] The respect which Mella and Pradera felt towards Maura was mutual; however, Maura remained a constitutionalist to the end in spite of the decidedly authoritarian—nationalist bent of his 'street' following. Had this not been the case, and had he not finally committed himself to parliamentarism in 1918, there can be little doubt that Mella's schism in the following year would have boosted the Maurist forces and been far more serious than it was for Carlism. As things stood, Víctor Pradera's sympathy towards a movement of 'unity' embracing all lovers of order was symptomatic of the temptation for Carlists of compromise and *rapprochement* with other groups on the right when a national emergency threatened.[58]

The frustrations of what Carlists were inclined disparagingly to dismiss as 'politics' served chiefly to convince the devotees of violence that theirs was the right, indeed the only course for true Carlists to follow. By its very nature as a Traditionalist movement, Carlism was emotionally rooted not simply in the past as a whole but also in its own early history. And when Carlists glorified their cause's past, it was on the wars that they focused their nostalgia, with their glorious victories and no less glorious defeats. Young Carlists drew their inspiration not from the remote and frequently unexciting pretenders, much less from 'politicians' such as Cándido Nocedal or Cerralbo, but from warriors like Zumalacárregui or the fearsome young Cabrera, 'tiger of the Maestrazgo'.[59] The fact that Carlism, while repeatedly defeated in war, had never been totally crushed or humiliated, allowed Carlists to attribute failure to betrayal and keep alive a military legend which for the unsophisticated rural mass of the movement remained the core of their creed, something infinitely more immediate than the carefully worked out corporativism of a Mella. Veterans of the 1870–6 war occupied a special place among Carlists down to the 1930s, when this military legend assumed a new significance.

The strength of what amounted to the myth of civil war was such that even when violence was officially discouraged between 1876 and 1900, a renewal of rebellion never ceased to be the goal of many, perhaps most, of the Carlist rank and file. During the late 1870s and 1880s, veterans and young Carlists in particular continued to dream of a final, victorious Carlist War and to hatch bootless conspiracies. There was no appreciable threat to the Alfonsine monarchy, yet the mere consciousness of the Carlists' persistent strength in one or two regions still worried liberal politicians, while at the same time providing them with a bogey invaluable in staving off 'advanced' legislation.

Sooner or later, as long as a Carlist movement still existed, its violent strain was sure to resurface. It did so at the turn of the century, after a decade of declining fortunes for the Liberal Monarchy had been climaxed by the assassination of Cánovas and the disaster of 1898. With the regime in a state of crisis for the first time, the possibility of a Carlist rising began to be taken seriously both by the Carlists themselves, not least Mella and Cerralbo, and by their enemies. The gradual formation of a nationwide conspiratorial network was followed in 1900 by the outbreak of unco-ordinated and unsuccessful insurrections in Catalonia and the Levant. Carlos VII, exiled and softened by his new, anti-Carlist wife, withheld his blessing from a rising which he correctly believed hopeless, and thereby lost the affection of hosts of disgusted Carlists.[60]

The importance of this fiasco, apart from the weakness which it laid bare, lay in a novel development: a direct, albeit abortive approach by the Carlists to elements in the army. The 'liberal' army's evident immunity to Carlist blandishments had seen sealed by its restoration of the 'usurping' branch of the Bourbons in 1874–5. This event coloured the Carlist attitude towards the army for several years afterwards, and it was usual for Carlists to call for economics in military expenditure.[61] Early in the 1890s, however, as the liberal system began to show cracks and attract criticism, Carlos VII and Mella could be heard expressing a new sympathy towards the army. 'Tomorrow,' Mella predicted in 1892, 'it will be our ally.'[62] Five years later the Pretender executed a neat about-turn in calling for an increased military budget and an 'honoured place' for the army in Spanish society.[63] As Carlists planned a rising, he made tentative approaches to the right's hero of the moment, General Weyler, but here again it was the Pretender's own lack of resolution which prevented an alliance from being forged.[64] It is unlikely that an agreement would have led to a significant part of the officer corps' siding with a Carlist rebellion, but the mere attempt was noteworthy.

Carlist sympathy for the army, once taken up, was maintained. Mella led the way in upholding the army's right and duty to act in defence of public order, and in doing so defined the common ground which Carlists and army officers shared.[65] The once-liberal army which Carlists had considered the 'praetorian' tool of freemasonry was thus granted an honorary place in the Carlist system. As long as it remained in broad sympathy with the incumbent regime, the officer corps would have no need for the Carlists as allies; but once the Liberal Monarchy, having lost the army's confidence, gave way to a regime which quickly became as uncongenial to many officers as it was to all Carlists, the way was clear for a *rapprochement*.

The abortive resumption of violence at the turn of the century had one other consequence of importance for the period after 1931. In Catalonia, the armed squads of Carlists suppressed by the authorities between 1900 and 1902 revived, if on a small scale, the regional tradition of direct action. During the Catalonian crises of 1908–12, the squads were reconstituted in the form of the Requeté, a paramilitary force made up of young men clad in the traditional red beret of the Carlist guerrilla. The Requeté, although not reluctant to engage in trials of strength with left-wing militants, was hardly a terrifying expression of Carlist aggressiveness; it nonetheless did represent the birth of a modern paramilitarism which the Carlists of the 1930s were to raise to maturity.[66]

The combined effect of the aforementioned difficulties was to render Carlism incapable of reaping benefit from the accentuated social and political crisis of 1917–23, which was finally ended by Primo de Rivera's *coup*. Carlism's weakness was not in itself a barrier to revival, as 1931 was to show; the real barrier was the survival power of the Alfonsine – though now no longer strictly 'Liberal' – Monarchy, and its ability, temporary as events were to prove, to rally Spanish conservatives behind a monarchist–military alliance. Given the Dictator's restoration of 'order' and his stress upon traditional values, it was to be expected that many Carlists would receive his regime warmly as a relief from the troubles which had preceded it.[67] The Dictatorship, if far from exemplifying every virtue of the Traditional Monarchy, did share many Traditionalist assumptions and could therefore be considered a step in the right direction. Pradera, who had long envisaged a 'regenerative dictatorship' as the only solution to the problem of how the Carlist monarchy could be installed, co-operated wholeheartedly with the regime.[68] Others, including Mella, who shared the hope that the Dictatorship, after destroying liberalism, would remove Alfonso XIII and instal the Traditional Monarchy, were soon disillusioned by Primo de Rivera's continued loyalty to the reigning monarch and the 'principles of 1876', as well as by the artificiality and opportunism of his political organization, the *Unión Patriótica*. Most of Don Jaime's supporters moved into a position of ineffectual opposition under the flaccid leadership of their elderly Delegate, the Marqués de Villores, and were joined there by the schismatic Mella, alienated by the Dictatorship's centralizing policies and lack of fundamental purpose.[69] By now, however, Carlist strength had sunk so low that neither support nor opposition could have much effect upon the regime or its eventual fall.

When Primo de Rivera surrendered power in January 1930, Carlism was at its lowest ebb since the 1870s. Each of its principal appeals had been taken up more successfully by political rivals, thus preventing expansion and, indeed, causing actual loss of support; internal quarrels had split the movement into three factions; worst of all, perhaps, the movement appeared to be stranded in a society increasingly indifferent to its myths and ideas. Had the monarchy of Alfonso XIII been able to escape convincingly from the shadows of the Dictatorship, either by recourse to another, more successful authoritarian regime or by returning decisively to a parliamentarism more genuine than that which died in 1923, it is not unreasonable to suppose that Carlism's decline, which all the efforts of Carlos VII, Mella, Cerralbo and the rest had merely slowed down, would soon have become irreversible. Alfonso's fall thus came in the nick of time for the demoralized Carlist cause. The Carlists' jubilation at the sudden arrival of a regime which was almost certain to launch an attack on the Church and, in all probability, would also wage war on private property, the sanctity of marriage and who knew what other bastions of the traditional Spanish way of life, may seem strange. It was, however, perfectly natural. Carlists had come to realize that their cause would never flourish amid the conservative atmosphere of the so-called 'Liberal' Monarchy. Its collapse not only vindicated their prophecies, but also, in ushering in a Republic, ensured the general upheaval and conservative insecurity on which a renascent Carlism could hope to feed.

2

The Vaticanist Gibraltar

Even as the Carlists danced on the political grave of Alfonsism, they were full of apprehensiveness at the arrival of a Republic. The exiled Don Jaime for once spoke not only for his own followers but also for the Integrist and Mellist schismatics when he warned that the most conservative of republics represented the first step in an accelerating lurch into what was indiscriminately labelled 'bolshevism' or 'anarchy'; the new Republic in Spain, he was sure, was likely to be crushed beneath 'the avalanche of international communism', however patriotic and well-meaning the Republican leaders might be.[1] The Integrist daily *El Siglo Futuro* discovered evidence of this in the nationwide disturbances with which it chose to fill its columns. Blaming them on 'communists', it urged its readers to stand firm against the social hurricane now sweeping Spain.[2] A rather more sophisticated and, from the Carlists' own point of view, prophetic analysis was offered by the daily of the Navarrese establishment, *El Pensamiento Navarro*. Recent events, it suggested, were a triumph for the Socialists and their trade union organization, the UGT; having exploited the favourable treatment which they had received from Primo de Rivera, they were now collaborating with Republican moderates and intellectuals in creating a system which they were certain to find incompatible with their long-term social goals. When they came to realize this, the UGT's masses would bring disorder and revolution to Spain.[3]

Carlism's historic role, its ideological anti-Republicanism and the probable reforming and anti-clerical orientation of the new regime made it inevitable that the Carlists would from the outset oppose not only Republican policies and legislation but also the Republic itself. For the moment, however, weakness dictated prudence. From Paris, Don Jaime urged his followers to assist the Provisional Government of the Republic in maintaining public order;[4] in Catalonia, where the proclamation on 14 April of a Catalonian Republic within an 'Iberian Federation' was rescinded only in return for

Madrid's concession of a Generalitat, or regional administration, the Carlist[5] leaders actually offered their patriotic co-operation to Francesc Macià, head of the left-wing autonomist Esquerra party and, *de facto*, the dominant political figure in the region. Predictably, their offer was spurned.[6] Elsewhere most Carlists followed the Pretender's promptings and upheld public order simply by refraining from disrupting it themselves.

Looking further ahead, Don Jaime and many of his supporters saw in the new situation an opportunity for Carlism to take over the entire Spanish monarchist cause and eventually challenge the Republic for the allegiance of Spain. On 23 April the Pretender issued an official call for all monarchists to join a Carlist-led 'monarchist, federative, anti-communist party' in time for the expected election of Constituent Cortes. Don Jaime naïvely hoped that the election would offer voters a clear choice between the infant Republic and his 'renewed, progressive, amply decentralized monarchy'.[7] A strategy based upon monarchist unity under Carlist leadership was in the circumstances logical and not necessarily unrealistic, but any talk of achieving it in a matter of weeks was quite absurd. In order to succeed, it would require the great mass of Spaniards who had accepted Alfonso XIII to abandon him and his family; at present, however, they were too numbed by the king's sudden fall to be capable of admitting the validity of the Carlist position, much less of actually crossing the dynastic divide and forming up behind the little known Don Jaime. Besides, it was not as if Carlism itself looked like a serious opposition force in the spring of 1931. Even if Don Jaime was correct in claiming that the 'immense majority' of those who had voted against the monarchy on 12 April were not convinced Republicans, this did not alter the fact that the overthrow of one monarchic system implied no more than a moral victory for the advocates of another.

The elections which had precipitated Alfonso's fall had also, as was only to be expected, revealed the chronic limitations of Carlism's popular appeal.[8] Real success was confined to Navarre, Álava and parts of rural Guipúzcoa; although some Carlists and Integrists were elected in Catalonia and in an isolated Integrist outpost bound by the Andalusian towns of Cádiz and Jerez, in both cases it was glaringly obvious that the successful candidates owed more to their alliance with Alfonsists against the 'revolutionary' coalition than the Alfonsists owed to them.[9] In other words, outside Navarre and the Basque provinces, Carlism and its schismatic offshoots together added up to a mere splinter group of the Catholic right, able to achieve electoral success only within a broad alliance. The very existence of three rival Traditionalist factions did nothing to enhance Carlism's claims as the vanguard of the anti-Republican opposition, especially since all three were poorly organized and incompetently led. If Don Jaime seriously hoped to see his monarchy peacefully installed as the result of an imminent and democratic election, then he was living in a private dream-world. Many of his followers in Spain recognized the potential value of seeking monarchist unity, while also appreciating that its fulfilment would be a long-drawn-out business; others, especially the younger generation, had different ideas. Like the Pamplona student Jaime del Burgo, they started to carry guns and scheme rebellion on the day of the Republic's foundation. As they realized, a final, victorious Carlist War could also only be a distant vision while Carlism itself was so weak. Even if, with the Liberal Monarchy dead and discredited, Mella's distinctive dialectic seemed to be working itself out, the day of triumph still lay a long way off.

The realities of Spain's new situation quickly confirmed Carlist prejudices. The Provisional Government itself, although headed as had been anticipated by Niceto Alcalá Zamora, a moderate, Catholic former minister of the monarchy, and having another Catholic, Miguel Maura (son of Antonio Maura), at the Ministry of the Interior, was otherwise solidly anti-clerical. Dogmatic anti-clericalism was represented by the Minister of War, Manuel Azaña; the Minister of the Navy, Casares Quiroga; the Minister of Public Instruction, Marcelino Domingo; and the Minister of Public Works, Álvaro Albornoz. Somewhat more restrained opponents of the Church were the Communications Minister, the Radical Republican and prominent freemason Martínez Barrio, and at the Foreign Ministry his party leader Alejandro Lerroux, an ambitious and cunning opportunist whose active radicalism had long ago deserted him. As if this were not enough to worry Carlists, the inclusion of three Socialists – Indalecio Prieto at Finance, Fernando de los Ríos at Justice, and Franciso Largo Caballero at Labour – and a Catalanist, d'Olwer, at the Ministry of Industry, superimposed the spectre of social upheaval and national dismemberment upon that of religious 'persecution'.

The Carlists' most immediate – and justified – fears, which they shared with most Spanish Catholics, were for the future of the

Church. These took two forms: fears, inspired by memories of church-burnings and violence against clerics in the early years of the century, of actual physical attacks which might be launched under the Republic's protective wing; and fears of the legislative action expected from Spain's new rulers against the Church's property, its relationship with the state, and above all its vital role in education. From the beginning of the Republic Carlists warned that, while they would submit to any regime which guaranteed 'order, peace and natural progress', legislation harmful to the Church would drive them into opposition.[10] The statement was disingenuous; since, as they well knew, such legislation was a certainty, so was Carlist opposition to the regime which sponsored it.

Official anti-clericalism got under way, modestly but decisively, as early as 15 April, when the Provisional Government promised freedom of religious practice within a 'Juridical Statute' designed as a statement of the Republican–Socialist alliance's minimum programme. Tolerance of all or no beliefs was not 'religious freedom' as Carlists understood it, and they wasted no time in saying so. According to the regional junta of Aragon, the government's announcement was an act of 'dictatorial despotism' which, in conjunction with the antici-pated separation of Church and state, constituted 'a challenge hurled at the Catholic conscience of the Spanish people'.[11] The Carlists also accused the government of inspiring in sympathetic newspapers a defamatory campaign against the Primate, the Integrist-inclined Cardinal-Archbishop Segura of Toledo. The Integrist *El Siglo Futuro* vehemently denied that Segura had said or done anything hostile to the Republic; early in May, however, it published his Pastoral letter, the tone of which did nothing to allay Republican criticism.[12]

Segura's intransigence was an embarrassment to the Vatican, which despite its generally good relations with the Alfonsine Mon-archy, had no taste for a confrontation with the new Republic. The same pragmatism which in 1929 had inspired Pius XI to make the Lateran Treaty with the Italian state also, in 1930, persuaded him that a change of regime in Spain was at the very least a con-tingency for which the Church must be prepared. The Nuncio, Tedeschini, was accordingly instructed to establish working relations with the leaders of the moderate Republican opposition; when the Opposition became the Provisional Government, those relations were maintained.[13] The hope of the Vatican was that if the Spanish episcopate and laity could be restrained from antagonizing the new government, and indeed persuaded to abandon their misgivings, nourished by tales of the First Republic, and embrace the Second, then official anti-clericalism might be kept within acceptable bounds and the Republic evolve in a moderate, that is conservative, direction. Fulfilment of this wish was hardly likely to be facilitated by Segura's truculence or, for that matter, by the very existence in the Carlist and Alfonsist camps of devout and vociferous Catholics who had no intention of meeting the Republic half way.

The task of the Catholic Republicans like Alcalá Zamora and Maura who earnestly sought a *ralliement*, and of Tedeschini, was thus not an easy one. It became all but impossible after the events of 11–14 May, when urban crowds of somewhat mysterious origin burned churches and convents in several cities including Madrid. The incidents, and the government's hesitancy in quelling them—hesitancy which in its critics' eyes indicated unwillingness — confirmed Catholic suspicions of the Republic and provided fuel for the Carlists' two overriding fears — for the safety of the Church and the maintenance of public order. The Carlist press reported little else for days, although discretion or, in *El Pensamiento Navarro*'s case, orders from the Republican authorities themselves, prevented it from blaming the government outright as it was later to do.[14]

The government charged that ultimate responsibility for the troubles rested with the provocative Primate, who was ordered to leave Spain. Segura's departure and that of the monarchist Bishop Múgica of Vitoria heralded a new governmental assault on the Church's privileged position, including the promised decree of religious freedom and another ordering the removal of religious images from schools. The 'expulsion of the crucifix' was seen by outraged Carlists as a symbolic act of enormous significance;[15] protests against the anti-clerical climate came from local Carlist juntas and from the rank and file as well as from the press. Carlist and Integrist organizations in Navarre, the Basque provinces, Huesca and elsewhere complained officially to Alcalá Zamora and Maura, flooded the Catholic press with indignant letters, and issued public declarations in support of the exiled prelates and the religious *status quo*.[16] Alcalá Zamora and Maura were patently embarrassed by the position in which they found themselves, and impressed by a Catholic reaction which threatened their political ambitions, but as a minority of two they were also powerless to change the direction of the government's religious policies.

During the first few weeks of the new regime the religious issue occupied the Carlists' attention to the virtual exclusion of all else. Despite *El Pensamiento Navarro*'s predictions concerning the future role of the Socialists, little heed was paid to Largo Caballero's purposeful beginnings at the Ministry of Labour. The only working-class member of the Provisional Government, Largo Caballero lost little time in issuing a series of decrees, which became full laws later in the year, aimed at improving the position of Spain's urban and rural workers. Besides measures introducing rent relief for the rural poor and an unprecedented provision for accident insurance, these included a decree covering the settlement of labour disputes by means of mixed juries of workers and employers and another, that on municipal boundaries, which sought to end the widespread practice of undercutting rural wages through importing cheap labour from outside the locality. These were important measures, which apart from promising to alter the balance of economic power in favour of the employee, were also to strengthen the position of the UGT and the Socialist Party. Here, surely, was something to disturb the Carlists; yet little heed was paid to Largo Caballero's activities – perhaps because they were unaccompanied by disorder.

While thus ignoring the real fruits of Socialist participation in the government – a state of affairs that could only be temporary – the Carlists allowed their imaginations to run riot. Beneath their dislike of the Republic, dark suspicions were at work in the shape of those fears of foreign agencies and international conspiracies which characterize the extreme right everywhere. The Soviet Union, it was confidently claimed, was watching events in Spain with great interest, and even now was preparing to use her resources to release another bolshevist revolution there.[17] Communism, *El Siglo Futuro* warned at the beginning of May, was already a serious danger to Spain.[18] Inevitably, international Jewry was thought to be pulling the strings which worked the men of Republican Spain, among them three allegedly Jewish members of the cabinet – Alcalá Zamora, Maura and Fernando de los Ríos.[19] Carlist anti-semitism was as yet little more than a mild reflex action, but it was to intensify in the fertile soil of the Republic.

The immediate pressure on Carlism during the spring of 1931 was to assert itself as a credible movement of protest against Republican legislation, if not as yet the Republic itself. To do this on a national level, however, was out of the question at this stage; there was no real sign yet of the revival which was to come, and the movement's concentration in the Basque–Navarrese region ensured that it would be here that its first serious, organized response to the coming of the Republic would be based. The nature of that response was nevertheless dictated less by the Carlists themselves than by the Basque Nationalists, who immediately following the change of regime and the news that Catalonia was to have the right of enacting an autonomy statute, launched an autonomy campaign of their own.

Once the autonomy campaign got under way, officially sponsored by the PNV, conducted for the most part by Basque Nationalist-dominated local councils, and led by the dashing and ambitious mayor of Guecho, José Antonio Aguirre, the Carlists had little choice but to join it. However uneasy they might be at the Basque Nationalists' talk of 'nationhood' and a 'Basque Republic', regional autonomy and the restoration of the historic *fueros* were, after all, cornerstones of the modern Traditionalist programme accepted, in essence, by all three factions. Co-operation with the Basque Nationalists was not a matter of principle, however, but of hard political necessity. For one thing, the Basque–Navarrese Carlists were anxious not to concede further ground to the PNV by allowing it the political limelight; more important still, there existed the possibility, though a slender one, that autonomy might prove the means whereby Spain's most Catholic region would be able to isolate itself from the anti-clerical plague emanating from Madrid, to become what the Finance Minister and Bilbao Socialist, Prieto, was soon to dub a 'Vaticanist Gibraltar'.[20] This was undoubtedly the major attraction of Basque–Navarrese autonomy for the region's Carlists, especially in Navarre and Álava where Basque consciousness among leadership and rank and file alike was appreciably lower than in the two coastal provinces.

Although most Carlists' conception of autonomy differed significantly from that of the Basque Nationalists, being far less ambitious juridically while more demanding in the religious sphere, some degree of unofficial co-operation was thus inevitable from the moment the campaign began. Neither party was sufficiently powerful throughout the four provinces of the region to enable it to act unilaterally, the PNV's dominance in Vizcaya and Guipúzcoa being balanced by that of the Carlists in Álava and Navarre. The Basque Nationalists regarded the inclusion of all four provinces as central to the very notion of a 'Basque State' and therefore could not dispense with

Carlist help; the Carlists were in turn obliged to involve themselves rather than allow the PNV the political initiative in the region and conceivably be confronted at the end of the day by an uncongenial Statute of Autonomy. Collaboration was made easier by the fact that the campaign was officially conducted by the region's mayors and local councils and not by the political parties directly.

The autonomy campaign had the Provisional Government profoundly worried. The PNV's willingness to recognize the Republic failed to dispel Republican mistrust of a party well-known for its religiosity, whilst concerning the Carlists' attitude towards the regime no doubts could be entertained. On 22 April Maura, eager to circumscribe Carlist and Basque Nationalist influence in the region, authorized the replacement of the four Basque–Navarrese *Diputaciones* (Provincial Councils) by appointed Temporary Committees. The same policy was adopted towards numerous local councils where monarchist majorities were deemed to have been dubiously won on 12 April; among them were a large number of councils in Navarre and the Basque provinces. The Temporary Committees, at both provincial and local level, invariably had pro-Republican majorities.[21]

The Carlists and Basque Nationalists protested angrily at this cynical attempt to loosen their grip on local and provincial government – protest largely justified in so far as the *caciquismo* which produced unrepresentative results elsewhere in Spain barely existed in their region.[22] They were given further cause for complaint when the Temporary Committees, with governmental connivance, decided to challenge the autonomy campaign by producing a rival, safely 'Republican' autonomy statute of their own. The committee of mayors which was spearheading the original campaign tried vainly to persuade the Temporary Committees of what was certainly the truth – that it was they, the mayors and councils, who commanded the popular support of the Basque and Navarrese people.[23] The Temporary Committees' spokesmen forbore to reply that popular support would not be enough to prevent or overcome the governmental veto which the Basques would in all likelihood have to face.

The Temporary Committees were slow off the mark, however, and it was the mayors' campaign which won a non-existent race to produce the first draft statute. On 31 May the Society for Basque Studies, the 'Academy' of Basque culture, to which the mayors had entrusted the task of drawing up a statute, published its proposals.[24] The majority of Basque and Navarrese Carlists found them very disappointing. True, much of what was on the whole a moderate document was reasonably in tune with Carlist sentiment. Navarrese fears of a centralized state dominated by Bilbao and the PNV were at least partly allayed by the provision of extensive provincial autonomy within the region as a whole, and the knowledge that any of the constituent provinces might pull out of the autonomous region if it so wished; Carlist *españolismo* was also satisfied by the assurance that Madrid would continue to control the important areas of foreign relations, the armed forces, communications, mercantile and penal law, and suffrage in national elections. Two points, however, more than outweighed these positive elements in the eyes of most Carlists. Reference was made to a 'Basque State ... autonomous within the totality of the Spanish State' – an ambiguous expression to say the least, but one which ran counter to Traditionalist regionalism; and far worse, the draft surrendered to Madrid the one power which the Carlists were desperate to keep within the region – power over Church–state relations and religious matters generally.[25] The frail bond between the Carlists and the PNV might have snapped there and then, had not the predominantly Basque Nationalist local councils of Guipúzcoa, scarcely less concerned than the Carlists about the religious issue, met and produced an amendment designed to bring Church–state relations within the competence of the autonomous region and empower it to make its own Concordat with Rome.[26] For the dissident Traditionalists of the region this was still not enough. The Basque Integrists, led by the national *jefe* of Integrism, Juan Olazábal, let loose a torrent of anti-PNV criticism, whilst the *de facto* spokesman for the shrinking Mellist faction, Pradera, repudiated the Statute flatly. The probable inclusion of the religious amendment nevertheless proved sufficient to win the support of Don Jaime's followers for the draft Statute.[27] Amid all the excitement, few stopped to consider that the amendment would also ensure the Statute's unacceptability to those who ruled in Madrid.

As the Statute's supporters prepared for an assembly of local councils in Pamplona which would discuss and, it now seemed certain, approve the amended draft, opposition within the region was revealed as ill organized and for the moment impotent.[28] The Integrists sniped from the right; the Basque left, led by Prieto, offered a foretaste of what was to come by attacking the Statute as 'clerical and reactionary', while discreetly refraining from systematic resistance; the Temporary Committees dabbled unproductively with an assortment of alternative schemes but the autonomist impetus appeared irresistible. Relations between the Carlists and the Basque Nationalists remained difficult, especially in Navarre where Carlist enthusiasm for the Statute was visibly lower than in the other provinces. The Navarrese PNV openly complained of the Carlists' less than wholehearted commitment to the autonomy campaign,[29] while the latter riposted with jibes at the PNV's republicanism and failure to appreciate the 'true *fueros*'.[30] Quite apart from their genuine misgivings regarding the Statute, the Carlists were cut off from the PNV through belonging to a 'Spanish', indeed *españolista* party, at a time when the pull of national politics was making itself felt. The Navarrese Carlists, led by an urbane, gregarious aristocrat, the Conde de Rodezno, and by the brothers Joaquín and Ignacio Baleztena, were now preoccupied with attempting to forge a strong 'anti-revolutionary' alliance for the forthcoming general election, and were irritated when the Basque Nationalists hesitated about joining. The Carlists' order of priorities was graphically demonstrated when they arranged for a 'Catholic–Foralist' rally to take place in Pamplona on the same day as the councils' assembly.[31] When the local authorities refused to permit the holding of two potentially troublesome meetings on the same day, Rodezno led the Navarrese Carlists in insisting that the Catholic–Foralist rally must go ahead. At the last minute, the councils' assembly was transferred thirty miles to Carlos VII's old capital of Estella.[32]

On 14 June Navarre was thus the scene of two mass meetings, symbolizing the division within Basque–Navarrese Catholicism. In Pamplona the Carlist-run rally drew several thousand Catholics from throughout northern Spain; those present affirmed their defence of the Church against Republican laicization and of the *fueros* against the Scylla of Madrid and Charybdis of Bilbao.[33] A message of support was, however, sent to Estella, where in an atmosphere of febrile nationalism the councils' assembly approved almost unanimously the amended form of the proposed Statute.[34] That evening the cause of Carlist–Basque Nationalist collaboration received an unexpected boost, when participants of both meetings, returning home to Bilbao and Zaragoza, were physically attacked by supporters of the Republic.[35] The left-wing press reported the incidents with every evidence of relish and approval.[36]

The election for Constituent Cortes was eventually called for 28 June. The Carlists, in spite of their abhorrence of the theory and practice of parliamentarism, threw themselves into the fray with enthusiasm. Perhaps the keenest of all was Don Jaime who, out of touch with the true state of affairs in Spain, approached heterodoxy in his pleasurable anticipation of an electoral confrontation between Republicanism and his brand of 'renewed and progressive monarchy', which he apparently believed would dispel the ambiguities of the April results and lead to his cause's triumph.[37] Most of his followers inside Spain, conscious of the prevailing climate of sympathy towards the young regime, as well as of the weak and disorganized state of all the monarchist forces, kept a firmer grip on reality. The issue of a monarchic restoration or 'installation' was, they realized, a non-starter in the election. The desire of leading Carlists to take part in the election stemmed, in fact, not from optimism but from an exceedingly gloomy defensiveness. Knowing that the Constituent Cortes, however much they might dislike the fact, would provide Spain with a body of fundamental legislation which, for the foreseeable future, would have to be obeyed, and which was certain to include measures affecting the Church, the Carlists concluded that they and all Catholics must use all available means to defend their faith, elections included. Otherwise, they were wont to argue, the Spanish Church might go the way of the Mexican.[38] After these apprehensions had been strengthened by the church-burnings of May, *El Pensamiento Navarro* exhibited the Gibraltar mentality once again by exhorting the electorate in Catholicism's northern strongholds to use its votes wisely in order to prevent such horrors from recurring.[39]

Realism and defensiveness also counselled electoral collaboration with other elements on the right. It quickly became evident that the almost total disintegration of the political forces of Alfonsism did not automatically present Carlism with the leadership of the Spanish right, not least since a considerable proportion of Alfonso's supporters was showing a tendency to sit on the fence where the question of the regime was concerned. Late in April, while Don Jaime dreamed of monarchist unity behind his standard and Alfonsist diehards tried without much success to regroup their forces in an Independent Monarchist Circle, a new right-wing organization was founded in Madrid. This was Acción Nacional, the brainchild of Ángel Herrera, a leading figure in Spanish Catholic Action and the editor of the influential daily *El Debate*. It was claimed that Acción Nacional was 'an electoral organization . . . of social defence' rather than a political party; it invoked a string of unimpeachably conservative principles and took what was described as an 'accidentalist' position on the question of the regime.[40] Accidentalism involved regarding neither republic nor monarchy as intrinsically more desirable, since a regime's form was held to be less important than its content. The Republic was therefore considered a *de facto* regime, a legally constituted power deserving of dutiful obedience but whose machinery might be employed to transform or even destroy it. The intention was obviously to appeal to all conservatives, principally those who had formerly been devoted to the fallen monarchy, but also Carlists and right-wing Republicans.

Acción Nacional reflected a very different attitude towards the Republic from that of Alcalá Zamora and Maura, one at best ambivalent and at worst hostile. Since it enjoyed the sympathy of Tedeschini and, it was to be assumed, the Vatican, it gained a head start over outright Catholic Republicanism, which was thus effectively cancelled out as a serious political force. For some Catholics, it was true, accidentalism might conceivably serve as a half-way stage in the transition from monarchism to eventual acceptance of the Republic; for others, the Nuncio and a large part of the Spanish hierarchy among them, it was a useful formula through which to respond not to the existence of a Republic so much as to its actions; but for a great many more it was merely a convenient façade behind which to conceal a variety of self-interests and a common hostility towards the Republic and everything that it represented.

Armed as it was with the papal blessing and the support of much of the episcopate, Acción Nacional's foundation provided little encouragement for a Carlist cause so long starved of official Church sponsorship. Even so, many prominent Carlists, aware of the need for a short-term pooling of resources in order to achieve even a respectable Catholic representation in the Constituent Cortes, responded favourably to Herrera's approaches. Rodezno, a Navarrese senator under the monarchy and a man sensitive to the demands of politics, joined Acción Nacional's directive committee, as did *El Siglo Futuro*'s editor, Manuel Senante.[41] The Acción Nacional committee in Seville, though composed mostly of ex-Alfonsists, also contained a dour Integrist, Domingo Tejera, who shortly afterwards became owner and editor of the city's independent Catholic daily, *La Unión*.[42] In Jerez, Acción Nacional was dominated by an energetic group of middle-class

Integrists and financed by wealthy local wine-producers such as the Domecqs and Palominos. [43] The Integrists were also active in Salamanca, under the leadership of a wealthy, locally powerful stockbreeder and landlord of French legitimist antecedents, José María Lamamié de Clairac. In 1930 Lamamié had been one of the founders of Acción Castellana, a Catholic landowners' pressure group which now attached itself to Acción Nacional. [44]

During the month of June, Acción Nacional and its various provincial satellites drew up lists of candidates for the election. Although monopolized by ex-Alfonsists and accidentalists, some of these lists also included Carlists and Integrists. That of Acción Castellana contained the name of Lamamié, another candidate being a young, little-known lawyer of Carlist parentage, Herrera's *protégé* and a onetime PSP activist, José María Gil Robles. [45] Two more Integrists appeared in the list for Burgos, while in Madrid the presence of a single Carlist among the Acción Nacional candidates indicated the extreme weakness of Carlism in the Spanish capital. [46]

Acción Nacional was essentially a Madrid-based expression of conservative resistance to anti-clericalism and impending social reform, which inspired emulation and attracted Carlist support in areas where the eclipse of Alfonsism had left a vacuum on the right. In Navarre and the Basque country the strength of Carlism and Basque Nationalism made any such organization superfluous. The success there in the April elections of 'anti-revolutionary' alliances dictated their reconstitution for the national campaign, broadened if possible to include the PNV. In Vizcaya and Guipúzcoa, where Carlist enthusiasm for autonomy was greatest, the consequent good relations with the Basque Nationalists made it possible to do this with relative ease, and in each province one Carlist appeared in the right's list. [47] In Álava most of the province's Basque Nationalists gave their support to a Carlist, José Luis Oriol, in return for his above-average dedication to the Basque cause. [48] The formation of a right-wing candidature in Navarre was a more difficult and protracted affair, owing to the mutual dislike of the Navarrese PNV and an Alfonsist-inclined group of independents led by Rafael Aizpún. Their relations, and those between the Basque Nationalists and the Carlists, deteriorated still further towards the end of May, when the PNV abstained from contesting the repeated election for the Pamplona city council made necessary by Maura's decree. Throwing their support behind the Republican candidates, the Basque Nationalists helped to reverse the right's victory of 12 April and give the left control of Navarre's capital.[49] The Carlists were disgusted; however, the relaxing of tensions after the Pamplona and Estella assemblies, together with the harmonious example set by the other provinces, finally produced the desired result: a 'Catholic–Foralist' candidature consisting of two Carlists, Rodezno and Joaquín Beunza; two Catholic independents, Aizpún and Miguel Gortari; and Aguirre for the Basque Nationalists.[50]

The remaining Carlist candidacies pinpointed three areas of residual support and possible expansion: Catalonia, the Levant and western Andalusia. The Catalonian Carlists joined a Conservative 'regionalist coalition' led and dominated by the Lliga; they were allotted a mere three candidates throughout the entire region – one each in the city and province of Barcelona and one in Tarragona.[51] In the Levant the level of Carlism's vitality was cruelly exposed by the advanced age of its three candidates and the refusal of the region's other right-wing parties to ally with them.[52] Another doomed candidacy, but one, as things turned out, not without significance, was the Integrist 'Independent Right' of Cádiz, one member of which was an obscure Sevillian lawyer unknown outside the region, Manuel Fal Conde.[53]

The electoral propaganda of the Carlist candidates and press was as carefully moderate as the watchfulness of Republican censorship and the pugnacity of left-wing crowds dictated.[54] Tacitly accepting that the Republic, at least for the time being, was a fact of life, candidates went out of their way to insist that they were not attacking the Republic as such but merely the 'tyrannical oligarchy' of politicians at its head.[55] Defensiveness was still the main motif; the purpose of seeking parliamentary representation, it was announced, was to register a protest against the enormities already committed in the Republic's name, and to insure against worse to come.[56] Only the more fervent advocates of the *fueros* saw a constructive side to the forthcoming Cortes. Their spokesman, Oriol, saw them as offering 'a providential opportunity for the reintegration of the racial personality of the Basque country and the complete restoration of its racial traditions'.[57] But this view, both of the Cortes and of the Statute to be submitted to them, was untypical; most Basque and Navarrese Carlists, especially the latter, regarded the foral issue as inextricably bound up with an overall defensive reaction to the godless and centralizing Republic, and displayed no such enthusiasm or optimism. For them, as for Acción Nacional's rich Castilian and Andalusian backers, the future was dark with the shadow of communism and, in *El Pensamiento Navarro*'s colourful words, 'anarchy, violence, hunger and ruin'.[58] Against a prospect as bleak as this, what good was a parliament? None at all in the view of most Carlists, whose opinion of elections was well conveyed in the manifesto of their lone candidate, the veteran Hernando Larramendi, to the voters of Madrid:

If not honestly conducted, they produce the victory of fraud; if they *are* honestly conducted, they normally bring about the triumph of cultural inferiority − that is, of the majority.[59]

The outcome of the election confirmed the Carlists' worst fears. A crushing victory for the continued alliance of Republicans and Socialists meant that out of a chamber of 478 members only between forty and fifty seemed likely to defend the Church's interests. The scale of the Republican triumph may have been exaggerated by the right's disorientation, the restriction of the franchise to men, and the eccentricities of a voting system which favoured alliances,[60] but there was little doubt that a clear majority of Spaniards − culturally inferior or not − were willing to give the Republic an extended trial. Yet although the overall result was distressing to the Carlists and the right generally, the position in the north provided consolation. Of the twenty-four seats contested in the Basque−Navarrese region, sixteen were won by the alliance of Carlists, independent Catholics and Basque Nationalists. Five of these were Carlists, eight were Basque Nationalists and three independents. In the light of the Republican and Socialist successes across the rest of Spain, these results offered evidence of the emergence of the very Vaticanist Gibraltar of which Prieto had warned.[61]

The right also achieved some success in the regions of Old Castile and León, where the fears of small farmers for the Church's position had been exploited to bring mass support behind the social intransigence of the privileged. Among the deputies elected in this way were the three Integrists in Burgos and Salamanca. They owed their election to their religion rather than their politics, and their presence in the Cortes could not be interpreted as reflecting popular support for Integrism or Carlism in the provinces they represented. All the other Carlist and Integrist candidates were defeated. Those standing in Madrid and Barcelona each came a poor last of the right's candidates, a harsh reminder of Carlism's lack of urban appeal. Some grains of comfort could none the less be gleaned from the respectable performances of the independent candidatures presented in Valencia, Castellón and Cádiz, which if nothing else indicated nuclei of enthusiasm which might serve as the basis for future expansion.[62]

The first general election of the Second Republic had thus brought defeat to the right in general and the Carlists in particular, but a defeat which only the most short-sighted of Republicans believed was final. The Carlists, heartened by their successes in the north and the first signs of a revival, gave themselves over to an optimism which few outside the movement would have thought justified. The excited language of *El Cruzado Español*, organ of the cause's veterans, was typical:

We are in possession of the truth. We are in possession of the religious and patriotic truth. We are the salvation of Spain! Why not surrender to optimism and be ready to achieve a triumph? We are on the side of Christ…Who can stand against us?[63]

If the election results demonstrated Carlism's geographical limitations in mid-1931, the newly elected deputies exemplified perfectly the advanced years and narrow class background of the movement's upper echelons. In a party which clung stubbornly to the myth of virile combat, gerontocracy was the order of the day. Of the Basque–Navarrese Carlist deputies only Marcelino Oreja (Vizcaya-Province) was under fifty; Julio Urquijo (Guipúzcoa) was sixty, and Oriol (Álava), Beunza and Rodezno (Navarre) all in their mid- or late fifties. This contrasted vividly and, Basque Nationalists believed, significantly, with the youth of the eight PNV deputies, only one of whom was over fifty and whose leader, Aguirre, was a mere twenty-eight. Of the Integrist trio, only the dapper Lamamié could be said to present a youthful image.

Apart from the grandee Rodezno, who owned extensive estates in the province of Logroño and a *señorío* (seigneurial estate) in Extremadura, the Basque–Navarrese Carlists were as middle-class as they were middle-aged. Beunza and Urquijo were successful lawyers, the former with a practice in Madrid as well as in Pamplona. Urquijo, who belonged to the same Basque financial dynasty as the owner of the influential conservative Bilbao daily *La Gaceta del Norte*, also held considerable interests in Basque industry, as did the engineer Oreja and the architect Oriol.[64] The rural preoccupations

more traditionally associated with Carlism found their main representation via the three Integrist deputies. Lamamié was one of the
largest landowners in the Salamanca district, while Estévanez
(Burgos) owned lucrative estates principally devoted to the cultivation of wheat. He was also a practising lawyer, owned two small
local newspapers, and was well known in and around Burgos for
his charitable works and his efforts in organizing Catholic farmers'
associations.[65] Carlist concern for the Church, and the latter's now
lukewarm interest in Carlism, was incarnate in the substantial form of
Estévanez's fellow-deputy from Burgos, the Cathedral canon Gómez
Rojí.

These eight individuals, if hardly a cross-section of Carlism and
Integrism, were not unrepresentative of a movement whose numbers
had steadily contracted, whose leadership had ossified, and which
was run at provincial and local level by middle-aged and elderly
members of the professional bourgeoisie and minor aristocracy. A
national organization barely existed during the Republic's early
months, and in the Marqués de Villores Carlism was saddled with
a political chief who lacked the powers of leadership – the right
man, perhaps, for the quiet years of the Dictatorship, but not for the
more challenging times of the Republic. If Carlism was to offer any
sort of threat to the system, let alone attempt to install its variety
of monarchy, changes were going to be necessary. One hopeful
portent was the closing of the much-divided Traditionalist ranks in
the face of real or imagined threats posed by Spain's new condition.
If Don Jaime's calls for 'monarchist unity' were aimed primarily at
repentant Alfonsists, they were certainly not intended to by-pass
the Carlist schismatics who, in the event, paid them far more heed.
Mellism, which lost its principal justification for existence with the
death of its leader in 1928, by now maintained its independence
more through inertia than will, while Integrism's semi-accidentalism,
tenable under the Alfonsine monarchy, came under severe strain once
the reality of a Republic struck home. From late April onwards,
de facto unity at local level was increasingly common in many areas,
as the three factions moved gradually but inexorably towards a grand
reconciliation.

On 12 July the five Carlists elected in the Basque–Navarrese
region joined their Catholic–Foralist colleagues in Guernica, the
Basques' spiritual capital, for an official send-off. A euphoric audience

received an impression of unity among the deputies in favour of the 'Statute of Estella' and in opposition to the continued existence of the Temporary Committees. Shrewd observers, however, might have detected cracks in the façade. The Basque Nationalists waxed aggressive in their obsession with the autonomy issue. Aguirre, apotheosized by one of the Guipúzcoan deputies, Canon Pildáin of Vitoria, as the Basques' O'Connell, threatened that his people would seize their autonomy if it were not conceded them. Except for the slightly eccentric Oriol, who hailed Aguirre as a 'man of providence', the Carlists were noticeably cooler towards the Statute. Intimations of future discord came when Rodezno, the least Basque-minded of the Carlist deputies, concentrated in his speech on the religious issue, invoked the *fueros*, implied a fundamental and permanent division between 'these [Basque] provinces and the Kingdom of Navarre' and praised the latter's contribution to 'Spanish greatness' – a sequence of ideas scarcely calculated to delight the Basque Nationalists.[66]

Continued unity was necessary, however, so that the Carlists, Basque Nationalists and independent Catholics elected in the Basque–Navarrese constituencies might form a parliamentary party large enough to qualify for representation on Cortes committees. When the deputies arrived in Madrid they accordingly formed themselves in a Basque–Navarrese Bloc, with the Carlist Beunza as parliamentary leader and Aguirre as secretary. It was announced that close association would be sought with autonomists from other regions and with other right-wing deputies.[67] Most of the latter, including the three Integrists, were organized in the Agrarian group, a broad alliance of fifteen deputies mainly from Castile and León, led by a former Liberal Monarchist, José Martínez de Velasco, and sharing a common Catholicism, conservatism, and concern for landowners' interests. Within this loosest of associations the Integrists constituted the ultra-conservative wing, the other extreme being liberal in politics and economics alike. The Agrarians reciprocated the Basque–Navarrese wish for close relations and declared that they too would limit their parliamentary interventions to the 'basic questions' of the Constitution, the statutes of autonomy, and the defence of public order.[68]

The most urgent and important issue facing the Cortes was, of course, the creation of a Constitution for the new Republic. The first attempt to produce an acceptable scheme collapsed when the

Socialists, the largest group in the Cortes, condemned as 'reactionary' the preliminary draft of an Advisory Juridical Committee headed by the moderate Catholic legalist Ossorio y Gallardo.[69] The draft reflected the outlook of conservative Republicans like Alcalá Zamora and Maura, and upset the Carlists for very different reasons; they saw in the Ossorio committee's attempt to republicanize the 1876 Constitution and separate Church and state 'a bad copy of some modern constitutions' unsuited to Spain and tainted by the pernicious influence of Versailles and the League of Nations.[70]

Ossorio's committee was replaced by a committee of the whole Cortes, constituted in rough proportion to the various parties' parliamentary strength. This meant that only three of its twenty-one members were Catholics, a fact which convinced Carlists that the end-product would be a revolutionary 'diktat'. The Constitution, *El Siglo Futuro* warned, would be born with 'irreconcilable enemies'.[71] Although the point was not made explicit, there could be no question that the Carlists would be foremost among them.

The early sessions of the Constituent Cortes took place against a backcloth of the kind of violent unrest that the right had been expecting since April. A national telephone strike, inspired by the Anarcho-Syndicalist CNT, began on 4 July and reached a bloody climax later in the month in Seville, where martial law was declared and order restored at the cost of thirty dead and two hundred wounded.[72] *El Siglo Futuro*, never too fastidious with regard to the finer distinctions of left-wing ideology, renewed the cry of 'communism' and agreed with Largo Caballero – if for different reasons – that CNT extremism as displayed in Seville would be the ruination of Spain.[73] In the Cortes, Beunza demanded a public enquiry into the Seville troubles, while the irascible Estévanez openly accused the government and the Republic itself of responsibility. Against a bedlam of angry interruptions he declared that the Republic was already reaping a revolutionary harvest from seeds it had sown itself.[74]

The Basque–Navarrese and Agrarian deputies found life in the Cortes harassing. Whether like Beunza they behaved with what the Speaker, the moderate Socialist Besteiro, praised as 'exquisite parliamentary correctness',[75] or else like Estévanez and Gómez Rojí repeatedly vented their irritation at parliamentary procedure and, indeed, all things Republican,[76] they were subjected to ceaseless interruptions and insults from left-wing deputies who regarded them as 'troglodytes' and 'cave-dwellers'. Such conduct, which Besteiro found difficulty in restraining, was certainly reprehensible; and yet the Republic's supporters, accustomed to regarding Carlism as the quintessence of all that they most deplored in Spain, could perhaps be forgiven for reacting cynically when Carlists like Beunza and Lamamié spoke of their movement's willingness to 'collaborate' with the Republican authorities.[77] For in practice Carlist 'collaboration' was and continued to be confined to supporting the maintenance of order against the militant left. Beyond that it was entirely conditional upon the Republic's operating in a totally improbable manner – especially on the religious question.

Relations between the Republic and the Church were still deteriorating in spite of all the Vatican's efforts. From his exile, Segura advised Spanish Catholics that their due obedience to the constituted power ceased to apply when the laws of God and the Church were infringed. Understandably, the Primate's requests to be allowed re-entry into Spain were turned down. Then on 14 August frontier guards claimed to have found on the person of the Vicar-General of Vitoria documents in which Segura instructed Spanish bishops to forestall Republican confiscation of ecclesiastical property by selling off as much as possible and exporting the proceeds. Segura denied the charge, but the damage was done. Church–state relations suffered yet another blow when the government issued a decree secularizing cemeteries; this new symbolic attack on their sensibilities convinced Catholics that there was to be no let-up in the 'persecution' of the Church and that anti-clericalism was likely to be enshrined in the Constitution itself.[78]

While the Cortes prepared to discuss the draft Constitution, in Catalonia and the Basque–Navarrese region interest in the autonomy issue burned as fiercely as ever. The situation of the Catalonian Carlists differed drastically from that of the Basque–Navarrese, in as much as their ideas made them unwelcome as allies to the Esquerra-dominated Generalitat, while their lack of political weight made them unnecessary. Their offer to co-operate in drafting a Catalan Statute was therefore brushed aside and the Statute was eventually drawn up by a committee controlled by the Esquerra. Published on 12 July, it provided for an autonomous Catalonia within the Spanish Republic, possessing moderate powers over internal affairs, including education and public order. Foreign affairs, customs and tariffs, and relations between Church and state were left in Madrid's hands.[79] In other words, the draft broadly resembled the unamended draft of the Society for Basque Studies, and in this instance an Estella-style amendment was out of the question.

Catalonia's Carlists reacted confusedly. In principle any autonomy, short of separation, conformed with their ideas. Yet in the absence of the clear-cut contrast which existed between the political climates of Madrid and the Basque–Navarrese region, it was doubtful whether rule from Barcelona was in any way preferable to rule from Madrid. *Reacción*, a new Carlist weekly reflecting a 'young' outlook, initially urged rejection of the draft on account of its laicism, but fell obediently into line once the regional leadership of Miguel Junyent decided that Carlists might support the Statute in the forthcoming referendum. Notwithstanding its shortcomings, especially in the religious sphere, it was conceded to be a genuine if limited affirmation of Catalonia's personality.[80]

The referendum on 2 August produced an overwhelming majority in favour of the draft statute. Interestingly, in view of the many doubts cast upon the genuineness of the figures, Junyent accepted the 'almost unanimous' verdict of the Catalonian electorate. But although he acknowledged that the Statute offered the best way out of a tricky situation, he also remained depressed about Catalonia's future. The bourgeois Esquerra, he predicted, would henceforward be the captive of the Anarcho-Syndicalists whose votes it had solicited four times in as many months.[81] Confirmation came swiftly, when late in August violent strikes organized by the CNT occurred in and around Barcelona. The handful of Catalonian Carlists was impotent in the face of this unrest, however loudly the movement's press cried 'anarchy' and called on the 'elements of order' to take firm action. The prevailing feeling among the Carlists of Catalonia was one of imprisonment in an utterly hostile environment. According to their own lights they had, in accepting a potentially autonomous Catalonia, surrendered themselves to what their leader, Junyent, described as a 'corpse'.[82]

The Basque autonomy issue was becoming increasingly complicated by the challenge of the Temporary Committees' rival campaign, which gathered momentum during the summer as its leaders turned for their model to the original, unamended draft of the Society for Basque Studies.[83] The religious amendment continued to drive a wedge between the Temporary Committees and the devotees of the Statute of Estella, but it was already apparent that the Basque

Nationalists were less fanatically attached to the religious clauses than were the Carlists. In Navarre and Álava, indeed, it was the Carlist opposition which in August led assemblies of local councils to reject the Temporary Committees' proposals and reassert their support for the Statute of Estella.[84] The Temporary Committees' campaign was stopped dead in its tracks, and nothing could now prevent the Statute of Estella from going before the Constituent Cortes.

The passions surrounding the autonomy campaign and the open antagonism of many of its protagonists towards the Republic's religious policies gave rise during the summer of 1931 to rumours of conspiratorial activities in the north. The role in the campaign of the Carlists, with their tradition of anti-liberalism, conspiracy and violence, would on its own have been enough to encourage such notions; the presence of influential supporters of Alfonso XIII in coastal resorts on both sides of the French frontier only reinforced them. Certainty of anti-Republican plots was voiced by Prieto and the leading Navarrese Socialist Ansó, who was convinced that the Carlists of his own province were deeply involved. Prieto for his part believed that the whole autonomy campaign was a mere front for sedition on the part of 'Alfonsists, Jaimists, Nationalists and Jesuits' who were actually training armed groups to strike at the Republic.[85] The rest of the government were sufficiently infected by this alarmism to cancel a planned visit of ministers to the Basque–Navarrese region on 4 August for fear of hostile demonstrations. On 20 August the government went further and suspended almost the entire Catholic press of northern Spain, as well as selected right-wing newspapers in other regions.[86] The leading Integrist Juan Olazábal was detained in prison for three days for printing in his newspaper *La Constancia* an editorial entitled 'The New Diocletians', and other Catholic editors were released only on bail.[87] Maura, who not long before had listened not unsympathetically to the Basque–Navarrese deputies' request for the dissolution of the Temporary Committees, was now as convinced as anyone of the seriousness of the situation; feeling over the religious issue, he announced, made resolute action necessary against those periodicals 'which dedicate themselves to a hostile and subversive campaign against the Republic'.[88]

The northern Catholic press had undeniably been intemperate; moreover, Maura's claim that the Carlists and Basque Nationalists had been inciting their younger brethren to 'get out and form armed groups' was by no means unfounded. The PNV's paramilitary youth organization, the *mendigoixales*, was growing fast, whilst by now the Carlist Requeté was also slowly reforming in Navarre. Immediately after the church-burnings of May, during which young Carlists had stood guard outside churches and convents in Navarre (where all was quiet), the first detachments of illegally armed 'Red Berets' were reorganized in the Pamplona district in a system of ten-man squads or *decurias*. The official seal of approval was applied to this new stirring of Carlist militancy in the middle of June, when delegates from Navarre, the Basque provinces and Logroño met in the Navarrese village of Leiza and decided to embark on a new course towards rebellion. Don Jaime's agreement to what was bound to be the most long-term of strategies was obtained forthwith,[89] and the work of improving the Navarrese Requeté went ahead. A retired army officer, Eugenio Sanz de Lerín, was appointed its instructor, subject to the overall control of the Regional Junta. Five parish priests were given the task of winning the local clergy's sympathy for the activities of Sanz de Lerín's two main field commanders, Generoso Huarte and Jaime del Burgo, who were soon busy conducting a propaganda and recruiting campaign among the Navarrese youth.[90] Their job was not a difficult one; where Navarrese Carlism was not already active, it was simply dormant and easily reawakened through the use, zealously encouraged by the local clergy, of the religious issue. By late summer, clandestine drilling was commonplace, and the Requeté's reservoir of support could be numbered in thousands; talk of '10,000 youths ready to march' well before the end of the year may not have been too wildly exaggerated.[91]

Nevertheless the government's alarm, which finally drove it to send troops to the north on spurious 'exercises', was excessive. For while a rudimentary conspiracy did exist, its threat to the Republic's security was paltry. Its principal movers were retired Alfonsist army officers such as General Orgaz; individual Basque Nationalists like those who helped to arrange a meeting between Orgaz and Aguirre late in August, and odd Carlists such as Urquijo, were not uninterested in the idea of a general Catholic rising based in the north, but wider enthusiasm and response from the leadership of the two movements was largely absent. The Orgaz–Aguirre meeting proved fruitless, with Orgaz unimpressed by the PNV's paramilitary potential and Aguirre alienated by the conspirators' monarchism and evident lack of real sympathy towards Basque autonomy.[92] Orgaz's approaches to the Navarrese Carlists were equally abortive.[93] The Carlists had no wish to commit the reviving Requeté to a rising which, in the highly unlikely event of success, was plainly designed to benefit the Alfonsist cause which they believed dead. In any case, they had enough common sense to appreciate that they as yet commanded insufficient military strength to risk insurrection when, as far as could be ascertained, the army was unlikely to move against the Republic. The Navarrese Requeté, if beginning to possess numbers, possessed little else. Had the '10,000' been called upon to march it would have been as a fervent but untrained and poorly armed rabble, doomed to certain defeat. A century of struggle and disappointment had taught the Navarrese Carlists patience.

Although the government soon realized that the atmosphere in the north was one of protest rather than rebellion, the press ban stayed in force until 15 September. Public meetings on behalf of the Statute of Estella continued, with Carlist speakers concentrating more than ever upon the religious clauses. As the plans for submitting the Statute to the Constituent Cortes neared completion, and the mood of its supporters grew increasingly excited, the Basque–Navarrese deputies were brought face to face with harsh reality. Leizaola, the Basque Nationalist representative on the Cortes Constitutional Committee, reported back that the 'events' of late August had strengthened feeling within the Committee against Basque autonomy;[94] in the chamber, the deputies could tell for themselves how little chance there was of the Statute's being accepted. By the time a special train from the north arrived in Madrid on 22 September, bearing the Statute and a mass deputation of four hundred Basque–Navarrese mayors, those prepared to accept the truth knew that the submission of the Statute of Estella to the Cortes would amount to nothing more than an empty propaganda gesture.

Discussion of the draft Constitution opened early in September and lasted three months. From the outset a flood of minority reports from the two Catholics on the Constitutional Committee, Leizaola and Gil Robles, indicated that religion was going to be the principal focus of dispute. In addition to the draft's strictly religious clauses and others, such as those dealing with education and the family, which affected religious susceptibilities, two sections held special interest for the Agrarian and Basque–Navarrese deputies: Those concerned with regional autonomy and the position of private property. And in the circumstances these sections too were likely to be approached in part from a religious point of view.

The debate on the powers of autonomous regions was held during the night of 2 5–26 September, and as expected it was the religious aspect of the question that generated most heat. Every attempt by Rodezno, Leizaola and the other Basque–Navarrese, supported by the less liberal members of the Agrarian Bloc, to persuade the Cortes to accept the principle that an autonomous region might regulate its own religious policy was overwhelmingly defeated on a straight left–right division. [95] Firm support for the aspirations contained in the Estella amendment thus came from those attracted by the Vaticanist Gibraltar idea. With its religious amendment now unconstitutional, the Statute of Estella lay dead; Aguirre remained philosophical about the future, since the Constitution would still permit a considerable degree of autonomy, [96] but for the great majority of Carlists autonomy had now lost its main attraction.

Catholic deputies were also broadly agreed in opposing what they regarded as the 'socialistic' orientation of the draft Constitution's clauses on property. Basing their attacks on the Papal Encyclicals of Leo XIII and his successors, they argued that the draft erred in asserting the state to be the original owner of all sources of national wealth, able to pursue its gradual socialization with or without compensation; instead, the state should accept private property as a natural right, expropriable only if blatantly abused and then only in return for just compensation. [97] Although again their efforts to alter the draft met with scant success, support from conservative Republicans, including the Radical followers of Lerroux, suggested the basis of a future alliance on social issues. In the debate, Lamamié emerged as the most ardent Catholic opponent of state interference with the distribution of landed property. [98]

These were emotive issues, yet they paled into insignificance when the question of the Church's position under the Republic was discussed. The anti-clerical clauses of the draft declared that Spain had no official religion, withdrew state assistance from religious Orders and foresaw the nationalization of their property, suspended state contributions to clerical salaries, legalized divorce, and introduced a system of free, obligatory and laic primary education. Taken together, these measures promised to destroy the privileged position enjoyed by the Catholic Church during the Liberal Monarchy, and at the same time to reduce its influence as a pillar of social conservatism.

When the Basque–Navarrese and Agrarians united to resist these clauses during the debate of 8–14 October, the Carlists came into their own. Beunza, accepting with pride the term 'Basque–Roman' applied to his group by the Socialists, argued that the question was

one of coexistence among Spaniards, with the Republicans creating
a religious problem where none naturally existed; instead they should
concern themselves with remedying social injustice, since what
Spaniards needed was not irrelevant and divisive anti-clericalism
but 'work and food'. Why, he asked, should religious Orders be
picked on when the Socialist *Casas del Pueblo* also owned property
and maintained links abroad? His parliamentary correctness deserting him, Beunza concluded one speech with words which Republican
supporters interpreted as threats of violence; persecution, he said,
would force Catholics to invoke 'the dignity of free men against
tyranny . . . our defence will meet aggression wherever it strikes
(Murmurs) . . . If you force battle on that ground, we Catholics
must triumph.'[99]

The climax of the debate was the discussion of Article 24, regulating the position of religious Orders and in particular the Society
of Jesus, which was declared liable to dissolution and its property to
nationalization. The government's case was made by the Minister of
War, Manuel Azaña, who became a national figure in the process.
Defending Article 24 on the grounds that the independence of the
Orders imperilled public safety and threatened the Republic itself,
Azaña incensed the Catholics by stating that 'Spain has ceased to
be Catholic' – not because the faith had lost its grip on the population at large but because it was no longer the principal influence upon
the educated elite. The Catholics did their best to resist the proposals
by means of delays and amendments, but without success; Carlist
deputies were in the thick of the debate and warned of dire consequences should the Article pass. Rodezno prophesied that it would
'open up an abyss between Catholic sentiment and the Spanish Republic', while the more pugnacious Lamamié threatened that if a
sectarian Republic oppressed Catholics 'we shall have no other
remedy than to move against the Republic'. Opposition proved
futile, Catholic amendments receiving only 35–40 votes, and the
Article, which became Article 26 of the eventual Constitution, passed
by 178 to 59. The debate broke up amid uproar and scuffles.[100]

The two Catholic ministers, Alcalá Zamora and Maura, having
voted against the contentious Article, promptly resigned, and the
Republic entered a new phase with the formation of a government
headed by the man of the hour, Azaña. On the same day the Catholic
deputies met and at Lamamié's suggestion announced their withdrawal from the Cortes for the rest of the constitutional debate.
Their press statement spoke of a wish for 'peace and concord',

thwarted by the revolutionary fervour of a majority unaware of popular feeling and unwilling to extend the freedom of conscience of which it made so much to those with whom it differed:

We have arrived at the limit of our transigence. The Constitution about to be approved cannot be ours ... The political Constitution nourished by a sectarian principle does not exist for us.[101]

The Basque–Navarrese issued a separate statement, justifying their withdrawal on the grounds that the Cortes were out of sympathy with the religious sentiments of the Basque and Navarrese people.[102]

In the absence of its only determined opponents the rest of the draft occasioned less debate, and the Constitution finally passed on 9 December. A week later Alcalá Zamora, to the disgust of the Carlists, became the first President of the Republic, Azaña continuing as Prime Minister. The Constitution was accompanied by a law which the Carlists were later to claim made all its supposed freedoms inoperable: the Law for the Defence of the Republic, a sweeping piece of enabling legislation designed by Azaña to counter Catholic efforts to revise or subvert the Constitution. The law permitted the Minister of the Interior, now Casares Quiroga, to detain or fine individuals and to ban meetings and publications considered to have committed or to be likely to commit 'acts of aggression against the Republic'. These could include incitement to resist legislation, incitement of the military, the use of monarchist insignia and the spoken or printed defence of the monarchy. Once the Defence Law was passed there was little effective limitation on the Republic's legal power to deal with those on the right whom its leaders considered their enemies.[103]

Under the Defence Law, Carlist and other Catholic periodicals were suspended and meetings banned, but this was nothing new. Nor was it exhaustive; *El Siglo Futuro* in particular continued to publish vitriolic criticism of the Republic and its leaders, while the Marqués de Villores, making a rare public statement on 1 December, described Spain under the Republic as 'a pathological case of social gangrene'.[104] According to Beunza the Republic was the preserve of democratic fixers (*enchufistas*) who wanted 'liberty for themselves and tyranny for everyone else'.[105] Already, after eight months of the Republic, Carlists were abandoning all talk of 'collaboration'; as Manuel Senante told an audience in Lérida, when the civil power acted unjustly 'it is obligatory to disobey'.[106]

3

The national arena

Autumn 1931 saw the end of the first phase of Carlism's response to the Republic. Both the Basque Nationalist alliance and participation in Acción Nacional involved close co-operation with those who in turn appeared willing to work within the Republic: an inevitably temporary and defensive strategy dictated by general uncertainty about the future and by Carlism's own weakness. As the Republic's orientation and ability to survive became clearer, and as Carlism itself began to revive and to recover its sense of identity and purpose, these early alliances were exposed as unsatisfactory and the Carlists briskly sloughed them off.

The alliance with the PNV lost its chief *raison d'être* once the goal of a clerical Gibraltar was rendered unattainable; even so it was the PNV which made the first move towards dissolving it by accepting a partnership with the Temporary Committees when the latter were entrusted by the government with the drafting of a new, 'acceptable' statute.[1] The Basque Nationalists thus committed themselves to the Republic in the hope of winning some measure of autonomy – a step which Carlism as a party would obviously never take, even if individual Carlists might continue to work within the autonomist camp.

The situation regarding Acción Nacional was somewhat similar. Carlists had joined Acción Nacional as a temporary electoral organization, and as it developed during the summer of 1931 into something resembling an accidentalist political party, they began to pull out. Rodezno continued to sit on Acción Nacional's national committee until early 1932, and many Carlists still voiced sympathy with its general aims. At the same time, however, they were increasingly airing their differences with it; Acción Nacional, *El Siglo Futuro* declared, was 'neither active nor national' while *El Debate*'s 'unctuous and carefully weighed dialectic' was sheer republicanism.[2] Gil Robles' view that Catholics were bound to accept the constituted power was dismissed as 'absurd'; Carlists accepted the Republic simply as a fact 'imposed upon us by reality' and would consistently judge it according to its works.[3] While they would therefore co-operate with Acción Nacional for electoral purposes and in pursuit of constitutional revision, they could not adhere closely to a movement whose programme they regarded as incomplete and whose activity as equivocal.[4]

In effect, Carlist talk of judging the Republic on the basis of its actions amounted to prejudging it, since only inimical actions were to be expected of such a regime. The Carlists' hostility towards the Republic was therefore in no doubt; nevertheless, the time had not yet arrived − if, indeed, it ever would − when they could think of challenging the Republic on their own. Allies were still desirable, and more attractive allies than accidentalists and Basque Nationalists were on hand in the shape of Alfonso XIII's diehard supporters. Although Don Jaime's repeated appeals for the unity of monarchists under his leadership met with little response, leading Carlists and Alfonsists had soon discovered within Acción Nacional that in present circumstances they had much in common. The first fruit of this new-found mutual sympathy was a society for the propagation of integral monarchist ideas, Acción Española. Those involved in this venture included the leading Carlist theorists Víctor Pradera and Marcial Solana; Rodezno, the Carlist who moved most freely in Alfonsist circles; a pro-Alfonso intellectual, Eugenio Vegas Latapié; and Alfonsist activists like General Orgaz and the Marqués de Quintanar who were already sowing the seeds of a plot against the Republic.[5] Financed mainly by Alfonsist aristocrats, Acción Española was founded in July 1931 and the journal of the same name appeared in December. The parallel with Action Française was fully intended, the aim being to reverse the liberalization and de-Christianization of the Spanish intelligentsia believed to have taken place during the previous century.[6]

Most of the Alfonsists involved in Acción Española and some who, like the foppish ex-minister Antonio Goicoechea, were still influential within Acción Nacional, remained utterly loyal to the person of Alfonso XIII. However, as the ideological emphasis of Acción Española demonstrated, they were already beginning to abandon the 'liberalism' of his fallen monarchy, partly as the result of accepting the Carlist critique of liberal monarchism, but more out of deference to the authoritarian spirit of the age.[7] While other former monarchists such as Gil Robles were busy veneering their undoubted monarchist sympathies with accidentalism, none of any eminence showed signs of heeding Don Jaime and becoming Carlists. Among younger members of the Alfonsist rank and file, disillusionment with liberal monarchism did sometimes extend to Alfonso XIII himself, and the Carlist press was able to blazon several cases of defection from the Alfonsist *Juventud Monárquica* to the local Carlists, together with appeals from the apostates to their comrades to follow their example.[8] The Alfonsists' arch-conspirator, Juan Ansaldo, later admitted that this drift, if not enormous, was an appreciable one.[9]

The new blurring of the hitherto sharp ideological line separating Carlists and Alfonsists, their common hostility towards the Republic, and the shared exile of their titular leaders, if not erasing all obstacles to a fusion of the two causes, did tend to weaken objections to the consideration of joint political activity with fusion as a possible final goal. Don Jaime was in his sixties and a resolute bachelor, while his uncle and heir-presumptive, Don Alfonso, was eighty-one and also childless. The result was an acute succession problem, which Rodezno and other leading Carlists felt might best be resolved through a reconciliation with the defeated and discredited 'usurping' branch of the Spanish Bourbon family.[10] The Alfonsists, desperate to grab at anything which might boost the slender chance of a restoration, found the idea even more attractive. Exploratory talks were held late in May 1931 at the Saint-Jean de Luz home of the French legitimist Vicomtesse de la Gironde. Feeling proved broadly favourable towards the creation of a single monarchist front, but it became clear that any further progress depended upon the two 'kings' settling the dynastic issue.[11] Two of the negotiators, Julio Danvila for the Alfonsists and Gómez Pujadas, a former Integrist, for the Carlists, accordingly consulted their respective monarchs and were entrusted by them with the task of drafting a political and dynastic agreement.[12]

Don Jaime was anxious for a settlement, which he believed must be clearly spelt out and involve concessions on both sides. After discussions with Gómez Pujadas he wrote to Alfonso proposing that each renounce his claim to the throne in favour of Alfonso's third son, Don Juan, to whom he, Don Jaime, would give a 'traditionalist education'. Alfonso seems to have been favourably impressed by the proposals, but to have been dissuaded from replying by advisers.[13]

By the beginning of September the Gómez Pujadas–Danvila agreement was complete. After receiving the claimants' approval, it was sealed by its drafters at Territet, Switzerland, on 12 September. Its signatories rejected restoration of the monarchy by force – a less-than-honest intention in view of their followers' activities – and agreed to co-operate in forming a united monarchist party and seeking new Constituent Cortes. These would – though the text refrained from saying so explicitly – be corporatively organized and would decide who was to be king. If Alfonso were chosen, Don Jaime and his uncle would renounce their claims, while in the event of Don Jaime's being selected the Cortes would also name his successor – presumably Don Juan.[14]

Once signed, this relatively sensible agreement, which might have constituted the basis of a powerful monarchist party, passed into a sudden and mysterious oblivion. No machinery was created to publicize or implement it, and it was agreed that rank-and-file monarchists should be told simply that the succession issue had been resolved. In the event they were not even told this. Since neither signatory had consulted advisers before approving the pact, the cause of its abandonment may well have lain in the opposition of those consulted after the event, many of whom had played no part in the Saint-Jean de Luz talks.[15] However, if the detailed provisions of the 'Pact of 12 September' sank without trace, the spirit of accord survived. Later in September Don Jaime joined Alfonso in Paris, and visits were exchanged at the latter's suggestion. Following Don Jaime's visit to Alfonso at Fontainebleau the claimants issued a joint communiqué consisting of amiable generalities as to their wish for closer ties between the two branches of the Spanish Bourbons and 'relations of fraternal friendship' directed towards the greater good of Spain. Don Jaime issued a separate, more specific statement:

We have decided to combine our efforts with the aim of forming a single political front which will struggle in Spain against anarchy and communism . . . Neither my cousin nor I have abdicated our rights, for this is simply a matter of political agreement with no other goal than the happiness of Spain.[16]

No mention was made of the recent pact, of new Constituent Cortes, or of specific plans for a final monarchist settlement, yet those monarchists who desired this could only feel encouraged by the obvious cordiality of the royal discussions.[17]

Their hopes received a setback when on 2 October Don Jaime suf-

fered a fatal heart attack. The Carlist claim now passed to the octogenarian Don Alfonso. A veteran of the 1870–6 war and of the
defence of Rome in 1870–1, the new Pretender lived quietly and
frugally in Vienna with his wife, Doña María de las Nieves of Braganza. The old couple were emotionally much closer to the members
of the Parma branch of the Bourbons than to those of Spain, and although Don Alfonso had conformed to the tradition of Carlist
pretenders by making several incognito visits to Spain, he was
almost totally unknown within the movement he was now called
upon to lead.[18] Nor was much known about his feelings concerning
the now even more pressing problem of the Carlist succession and
relations with Alfonsism. His adoption of the style 'Alfonso Carlos I'
seemed a hopeful portent to the fusionists, carefully calculated as it
was to avoid upsetting Alfonsists by the choice of 'Alfonso XII' or
Carlists through that of 'Alfonso XIV'.[19] This hint at a desire for
continued intimacy between the Bourbon branches was given substance when Alfonso Carlos wrote to Alfonso XIII affirming his
'complete agreement with every part of the pact' of 12 September.
But all was not as it seemed. Perhaps not surprisingly, the old man
had confused the broad principles contained in the Paris press statements of Alfonso and Don Jaime with those of the abortive pact
signed a fortnight earlier. When the details of the Territet agreement
were made known to him some time later, Alfonso Carlos' rejection
was immediate and total. The shock caused by the information was
reportedly so great as to inflict upon him 'acute nervous agitation'
and insomnia.[20] Personal relations within the Bourbon family nevertheless remained warm, and in November Alfonso Carlos and María
de las Nieves paid a successful visit to Alfonso XIII at which it was
agreed to keep negotiations going.[21]

One important consequence of Don Jaime's death was an acceler-
ation of the reunification of the three Traditionalist factions; the
removal of the second principal of the Mellist schism, three years after
the death of Mella himself, destroyed Mellism's *raison d'être*, while
the succession of Alfonso Carlos, who was reputed to be sympathetic
towards Integrism, banished what few remaining doubts Integrists
still nursed as to the desirability of a reconciliation. Both Mellists and
Integrists proved willing to forgive and forget, and joined Jaimists
in celebrating masses for the soul of the Pretender whom they had
opposed.[22] Leading Mellists like Pradera and Esteban Bilbao, who

had continued to resist rejoining Carlism in the months after the coming of the Republic, considered themselves automatically 'reconciled' upon Don Jaime's death; in once more committing themselves to Carlism they brought with them the Mellist organization, largely limited to Álava and Guipúzcoa, and the important psychological factor of, as it were, Mella's posthumous blessing. The return of the Integrists was less automatic but almost as rapid. In moving towards fusion with Carlism the national Integrist leader, Juan Olazábal, received the full support of other prominent Integrists such as Lamamié, Senante and Estévanez, and at local level it was often the Integrists who took the initiative – especially where, as in Málaga, they were the stronger element.[23] A symbolic climax came on 11 January 1932 with a celebration in Pamplona of the renewed unity of Traditionalists in the matrix of Carlism.[24] On 1 February Olazábal resigned from the Integrist leadership, a position he had held since Ramón Nocedal's death, and Integrism thereupon ceased to exist as an independent party.[25] The united movement now became the Carlist Traditionalist Communion, although the title more commonly used was the Traditionalist Communion.

The movement's most crying need at this time was for the erection of the effective national and nationwide organization which Jaimism had so signally lacked during the previous decade, with Don Jaime in exile, Villores ageing and infirm, and regional juntas either non-existent or ineffectually led by elderly and inactive veterans. As membership picked up during 1931, the Communion retained a rickety, decentralized structure wherein authority theoretically descended from above while initiative sprang from below, both processes having in reality ceased to operate.

Villores' illness in the winter of 1931–2 gave Alfonso Carlos, who despite his age was showing a lively interest in his cause, the chance to tackle this unsatisfactory situation. In January 1932 he appointed a Supreme National Junta, with powers to handle matters of 'general importance' subject to the approval of Villores and, ultimately, of Alfonso Carlos himself.[26] The National Junta's composition reflected an attempt to balance the various regional and factional interests within the Communion. Navarre was represented by Rodezno and Beunza, the Basque provinces by Oriol, Catalonia by Juan María Roma, Castile by Lorenzo Sáenz, and the south and east by the *alicantino* Senante. There were two former Integrists, Senante and Lamamié, and a veteran of the 1870–6 war in Sáenz, while the ex-Maurist Oriol spoke for the 'Carlists of 14 April'. A Secretariat, headed by Lamamié, was also created to assist in the stimulation of expansion and the organization of party activity.[27] When Villores died in May 1932, the National Junta became *de jure* as well as *de facto* the chief source of authority within the Communion after the Pretender. Its president, Rodezno, if officially no more than a first among equals, thus became the effective political leader of Carlism.

By now there was no question that Carlism, which had appeared to be on its last legs during the 1920s, was enjoying one of its periodic revivals as the result of swelling Catholic opposition to the Republic. Before the end of 1931 a score of new circles had been formed in Navarre,[28] and a similar if smaller-scale awakening of dormant Carlist feeling was apparent in Catalonia and the Basque region. In the Levant, Carlism's sudden resurgence during 1932 suggested that it was reconquering some of the support earlier lost to the DRV; by June 1932 the city of Valencia possessed six Carlist circles,[29] while in the province of Castellón there were eight circles and eighteen local juntas.[30] Even in historically non-Carlist regions such as Galicia, Extremadura and Andalusia, skeleton organizations came into existence as conservative Catholics started to show an interest in Carlism.[31]

At first, expansion was a largely spontaneous business, as groups of individuals — sometimes, as in Málaga, mostly from a single family — met and formed a local junta or 'delegation', and later, if numbers and resources permitted, a circle.[32] The creation of the National Junta and the Secretariat enabled official help and encouragement to be given to what nonetheless remained a predominantly grass-roots process. During 1932 the network of regional and provincial *jefaturas* was extended throughout the country, and although there remained areas where this organization was purely notional, elsewhere the appointment of young, energetic regional and provincial *jefes* led to the rapid establishment of local organizations. This was above all true of Andalusia, where the ex-Integrists Fal Conde in Seville and Cádiz, José María Alvear in Córdoba, the Contreras brothers in Granada and Jaén, and the remarkable Huelín family in Málaga, achieved outstanding success in implanting Carlism in a region where it was virtually unknown.[33] By the summer of 1932 Carlism was consequently showing signs of succeeding where for so

long it had failed: in breaking out of its confinement in the north
and east to become a truly national movement.

During this phase the Carlist revival was essentially a religious
protest. In the north and east one taste of the Republic was enough
to drive lapsed or passive Carlists back into a cause with which they
had retained strong sentimental associations, while in other regions
converts were mainly Catholic intransigents who saw in Carlism the
most resolute vehicle of opposition to a godless regime. Other considerations were secondary; certainly it is difficult to explain Carlism's recovery in economic terms. Three sectors of Spanish Catholic
society provided the mass of new or returning Carlists: the professional bourgeoisie, the artisan class, and, as always, the middling
peasant farmers of the north and east. [34] Apart from the artisans, who
like the working class proper were feeling the effects of the general
depression, and particular agricultural interests – Valencian fruit-
growers for example – whose sales were hit by the contraction of
markets, these were economically relatively secure elements in the
Spanish population of the 1930s, capable of riding out the depression and the specific effects of Republican economic policies. What
provoked them to become Carlists was not their present circumstances so much as fear of a future viewed through an ultra-Catholic
lens. When those who bracketed republicanism, laicism and moderate social reform with 'communism' saw a Republic in being, the
Church attacked and reform in the air, they logically if falsely concluded that a Soviet Spain lay around the corner. In such a situation,
Carlism's total rejection of everything connected with the Republic,
together with its own offer of an alternative 'system', took on a new
relevance and attractiveness. This development, it must be stressed,
occurred without significant help from the Church's authorities, who
for the most part continued to lend their support to Acción Nacional.
Not a single bishop associated himself publicly with Carlism, though
as always there must have been some who nursed private sympathies.
As had been the case since the 1870s, active clerical support came
exclusively from the parish clergy and members of religious Orders in
those regions with a more or less vigorous Carlist tradition – Navarre,
the Basque country, the Levant, parts of Old Castile and to a lesser
extent Catalonia; here, the lesser clergy were prominent in helping to
revitalize the Carlist movement.

Most Carlists naturally rejoiced at the movement's new vitality, but there were plenty who had their reservations. The rapid absorption not only of erstwhile schismatics but also of former Alfonsists and independents was seen by some as a threat to Carlism's ideological integrity. Typical of this view was *Reacción*, which remarked that with the Communion experiencing a 'crisis of growth', Carlists must ensure that converts knew their Traditionalism and that the movement's intransigence was in no way relaxed.[35]

Carlist meeting places were now emerging from the lethargy of recent years into an unaccustomed frenzy of social and political activity. All circles aspired to create dependent organizations, especially Youth and Women's sections and, where youthful membership allowed, branches of the Requeté and the Carlist students' association, the Agrupación Escolar Tradicionalista (AET).[36] Outside Navarre the Requeté and AET were largely restricted to big cities, and even there most Requeté groups consisted merely of members of the Carlist Youth who donned red berets and khaki battle dress for special occasions. Only in Navarre could anything approaching true paramilitarism be said to exist.[37] As yet, youth sections concentrated upon studying Carlist doctrine in 'conference cycles' and evening classes, while the Women's groups or Margaritas devoted themselves mainly to charitable work.[38]

The highlight of circle activities was a visit from one or more of Carlism's national figures – a deputy such as Lamamié or an extra-parliamentary orator like Senante or the immensely popular woman propagandist María Rosa Úrraca Pastor. Large urban circles received these visits frequently, but most villages were obliged to wait for one of the speaking tours or 'Traditionalist Weeks' which became a feature of Carlist propaganda activity during 1931–2. In the course of a 'Traditionalist Week', virtually all of Carlism's leading personalities would descend upon a region – Andalusia in March 1932, Catalonia in May – and address meetings in up to a score of villages and towns, climaxed at the weekend by a mass rally in the regional capital.[39] Besides these exclusively Carlist campaigns, collaborative meetings continued with Acción Nacional – renamed Acción Popular in April 1932 – and with leading Alfonsists. As time passed, diehard Alfonsists like Goicoechea, the Conde de Vallellano and Pedro Sáinz Rodríguez became increasingly frequent attenders at Carlist meetings, and Gil Robles' accidentalist associates less so.[40]

All Carlist activities were conducted under the close surveillance of the Republican authorities and of the political militants of the left. The early months of 1932 were marked by numerous street clashes between Carlists and leftists. On 17 January in Bilbao, fighting followed a meeting of Carlists in a local *pelota* hall; the disorder was provoked by Young Socialists, but the shots which killed three of the assailants were fired by Carlists. *El Pensamiento Navarro* did not deny Prieto's charge that the shots came from the nearby Carlist circle, merely claiming that they were fired in self-defence.[41] Three months later a gunfight between Carlist and Socialist youths in Pamplona ended with a death on each side and several wounded.[42] During the twenty-four hours after each of these incidents, groups of leftists roamed the cities concerned, attacking Carlist headquarters, Catholic newspaper offices, and the homes of prominent Carlists. In April, violent affrays occurred in Madrid between AET students and members of the Republican students' union, the FUE,[43] while other incidents were reported during 1932 from Catalonia, Aragon, Andalusia and Galicia.[44] In the majority of cases the initial provocation came from the more numerous leftists, but the young Carlists were both well prepared and eager for retaliation, which often – as in Bilbao – took the form of meeting fists with bullets.

The most serious consequence of these incidents from the Carlists' point of view was that they provided the Republican authorities with cause for restricting the Communion's activities. The most frequent sanction was the closure of circles and the banning of public meetings. The Bilbao, Pamplona and Madrid clashes were all followed by the closure of the local Carlist circles,[45] and lesser incidents or merely the public utterance of words deemed to be anti-Republican were used to justify similar measures in Córdoba, Santiago de Compostela, Haro and Calatayud.[46] Although most of these circles gradually reopened, those in Pamplona stayed closed for several months. The bare possibility of anti-Republican rhetoric and provocation of violence was commonly used to justify the advance banning of public meetings.[47]

Individual Carlists also suffered terms of imprisonment for their actual or supposed involvement in violent incidents or for lack of discretion in their public pronouncements. Esteban Bilbao began 1932 with two months of exile in the province of Lugo for unspecified anti-Republican activities,[48] and later in the year the editors of *Reacción* and *Tradición Vasca* were jailed for publishing articles hostile to the

Republic.[49] However, it was the unruly public meetings and street violence which led to most detentions. After the Bilbao incidents in January, forty-five Carlists were held without a hearing for several days;[50] following the brawl in Pamplona several Carlists, mostly Red Berets of the local Requeté, remained in prison for some months. They included the two 'field commanders' of the Navarrese Requeté, Jaime del Burgo and Generoso Huarte. Burgo was released on 25 May and rearrested four days later; not until 14 June were he and another Carlist tried – not with responsibility for the events of 17 April but for illegally importing arms. Although found not guilty, Burgo stayed in prison along with ten comrades until November, an experience which differed from that of numerous other Carlists only in the length of time involved.[51] Being a Carlist under the Second Republic certainly had its risks, but it is necessary to keep a sense of proportion with regard to governmental harassment. For despite the arrests, the fining and suspension of newspapers, the searches and closures of circles and the rest, the vast majority of Carlist activities, dedicated as they were to the eventual destruction of the Republic, took place without any official interference.

The political events of 1932 strengthened the Carlists' anti-Republicanism, if that was possible. In January the Azaña government, besides promulgating the laws secularizing cemeteries and permitting divorce, decreed the dissolution of the Jesuit Order and the sequestration of its property. In the Cortes the Carlists sprang to the Jesuits' defence against what Beunza claimed was masonic-inspired persecution. Lamamié, the most persuasive and accomplished Carlist orator, attacked the decree as inhuman, irrational and unconstitutional. Only a tenth of the Order, he argued, took the crucial 'fourth vow' of obedience to the Pope which ostensibly justified the measure, nor were Jesuits the Republic's enemies.[52] But opposition was, as Beunza admitted in the chamber, a waste of time;[53] the debate was guillotined, the Order dissolved and its schools closed. In Navarre, schoolchildren demonstrated and bystanders wept as the Jesuits left and as crucifixes were carried from the schools.[54]

Another symbol of conservative Spain under attack as 1932 opened was the rural police force, the Civil Guard, known to its admirers as the *'benemérita'*. On the last day of 1931 in the Extremaduran village of Castilblanco, five Civil Guards attempting to enter the Socialist Casa del Pueblo were killed and their bodies mutilated by its members. A week later in Arnedo (Logroño), jittery Civil Guards shot dead six demonstrating strikers. These were far from being the first instances during the Republic of violence committed by and against the Civil Guard, but they were the first to attract nation-wide publicity.[55] Carlist sympathies in the furore lay squarely with the Civil Guard, which they regarded as one of the last surviving healthy institutions in a 'sour and sad regime', society's last line of defence against a corrosive lack of respect for authority.[56] The responsibility for the Civil Guard's widespread unpopularity lay, it was suggested, not within itself but with the liberal governments and local *caciques* who had traditionally employed it to oppress the poor.[57] The poor, for all that, received less sympathy; few tears were shed for the dead of Arnedo, also considered the Azaña government's responsibility.[58] For several weeks, Carlist organizations held special meetings and memorial services in tribute to the dead guards.[59]

Solidarity with the Civil Guard epitomized Carlism's essential conservatism in a crisis. Some of the material interests upon which this conservatism was based rose to the surface during the Agrarian Reform debate which commenced in May. The government's bill, much amended in committee, provided for the expropriation without compensation of aristocratic *señoríos* throughout the country, plus the indemnified confiscation of various categories of estate in the lati-fundist regions of the south and west. The *arrendamiento*, a form of sharecropping conspicuously favourable to landlords' interests and widespread in the Castiles, León and much of the rest of northern Spain, was to be abolished. The peasants and land-workers settled on the newly released land would be able to work it either in-dividually or collectively.[60]

It would have been impolitic for the right to deny the desperate need for land reform. Carlist spokesmen nevertheless argued that the government was going about it the wrong way. The bill, they de-clared, was 'socialistic'; Lamamié regretted that a justified reaction against a century of rural liberalism 'has brought us a worse doctrine, converting us all into slaves of the state'.[61] Where liberal members of the Agrarian group refused to accept any limitation on the enjoyment of private property as currently distributed, the Carlists, Basque Nationalists and social-Catholic Agrarians showed greater subtlety. Countering with the principles of *De Rerum Novarum*, they claimed to be willing to accept expropriation in the interests of extending the smallholders' society typical of northern Spain, whence many of them came. Where the Carlists were concerned, this amounted to a reiteration of policies advocated thirty years earlier by Mella.[62]

In fact, save for the genuinely social-Catholic Basque Nationalists, there was less to divide Catholic landowners than superficially appeared to be the case. Carlist opposition to the bill was led by those deputies with most to lose. Rodezno, owner of a *señorío* in Logroño and extensive estates in Cáceres, defended the *señoríos* and the *status quo* in Extremadura; Estévanez, speaking for the entrenched interests of Burgos, feared that the bill's provisions would lead to an increase in the area under cultivation and thence to a collapse of wheat prices; Lamamié sought the exclusion of his province, Salamanca, from the bill's scope and staunchly defended the system of *arrendamiento*, which he operated on his own estates. It was, he and Rodezno suggested, the best means of exploiting tracts of average fertility, a 'protected' smallholding system in which the proprietor provided the technical and financial assistance which the tenant would otherwise lack.[63] What they did not stress was that the landlords also controlled all sales outlets, the farmers' organizations, and through them much of the political life of the districts concerned.

In other words the Carlists accepted the need for agrarian reform in theory but resisted its practical fulfilment. How their smallholders' society could be brought into being was as unclear as ever, since there could be no reason for supposing that they would greet other reform projects any differently from the present one. Where their own interests were at stake, their social-Catholicism evaporated and they behaved much like their liberal enemies. Perhaps the attitude of Carlist property owners was most dramatically exemplified by the veteran ex-deputy Jaime Chicharro, who in March 1932 sparked off a riot in Soria by proclaiming to a public meeting that he had no intention of surrendering an iota of his land or wealth without a fight.[64]

An even more explosive issue was that of Catalan autonomy, parliamentary discussion of which also dragged on through the summer. The right, apart from the Basque Nationalists, united to oppose the Statute. The Carlists had by now abandoned their initial tactical sympathy for autonomy, incensed at their own treatment at the hands of the Catalonian authorities and generally appalled at what they regarded as the disorderly condition of Catalonia. When a CNT-inspired three-day rising paralysed the Llobregat valley in January 1932, the Catalonian Carlists held Macià and the Esquerra responsible; Macià, they alleged, was in the pay of Moscow, in league with international masonry and in political debt to the CNT – all anti-Spanish and anti-Catalonian forces.[65] In *Reacción*, a pseudonymous columnist asked whether anything could be more ludicrous than that Catalonia should seek the recovery of her historic personality through 'the votes of a labouring mass in the majority not Catalan' and a Statute which, in the Esquerra's hands, constituted a threat to Catalonia and Spain alike.[66] Rodezno considered the Statute 'unrepresentative',[67] while Lamamié spoke for the Carlists of central Spain in emerging as one of its most outspoken critics. True autonomy, he insisted, was impossible under the Republic without implying total separation; to extend the Statute's provisions to Catalonia – or any region – without the unifying bonds of monarchy and Church was to 'imperil the unity of the nation and the sovereignty of Spain'.[68]

The Basque Nationalists considered the Carlists' growing coolness towards Catalan autonomy a betrayal of the Basque–Navarrese Bloc's programme, and relations between the two parties continued to worsen. The issue of Basque autonomy was still very much alive. In January a new round of local council assemblies gave the Temporary Committees the go-ahead for a single, regional Statute rather than the alternative of four linked provincial Statutes;[69] during the late winter and early spring the Temporary Committees, aided by the PNV and the formerly anti-autonomist Basque–Navarrese Socialists, busied themselves with drafting the new Statute and mounting an intense propaganda campaign on its behalf, aimed particularly at areas of southern Navarre where Basque sentiment was known to be weak.[70] On 24 April the new Statute was published. As expected it marked a retreat from the Statute of Estella, not only in its abandonment of religious autonomy but also in its lack of reference to a 'Basque State'. Instead the four provinces were to form 'an autonomous politico-administrative unit within the Spanish State', with considerable power over internal social and economic policy but little or none where security and public order were concerned. Socialist amendments meant that half the regional parliament would be elected on a regionwide basis, with the probable result of concentrating power in the most populous province of Vizcaya, where the Basque left and the PNV were strongest.[71]

From the end of 1931 the Carlists had stood somewhat aloof from the new autonomy campaign, chiefly owing to confusion and internal disagreements regarding the sure prospect of a laic, 're-publican' Statute. The January assemblies showed that autonomist sentiment was still strong within the Carlist rank and file, even in Navarre; some leading figures like Oriol, Oreja and Beunza still waxed enthusiastic, but Rodezno, the single most influential Carlist in the region, was less keen than ever and was now toying with the idea of an exclusively Navarrese Statute, while Olazábal led many former Integrists in outright opposition.[72] The Statute's publication inspired a similar range of reactions. The more convinced autono-mists among the Carlists accepted it more or less willingly,[73] and Rodezno most grudgingly;[74] Olazábal and Pradera, on the other hand, were passionate in their hostility towards a document which they regarded as anti-religious, centralizing and 'un-foral'.[75] All reference to the *fueros* was futile, for by now they meant quite dif-ferent things to the Carlists and the PNV. To the former they were a set of static prescriptions unalterable by government or people, to the latter something dynamic, adaptable and capable of enshrinement within any Statute which met the current majority aspirations of the region. As a Basque columnist wrote: 'The *fuero* is not the will of those who lived long ago, but of those alive to-day.'[76] The Carlist juntas, unable to take a firm stand one way or the other, announced that Carlists might vote according to their consciences in the Pam-plona assembly of local councils which was to pass verdict on the new Statute on 19 June.

As the assembly drew nearer, attention concentrated upon Nav-arre. Álava, Guipúzcoa and Vizcaya were certain to approve the Statute, but local council discussions in Navarre suggested that opinion in that province was moving decisively against acceptance.[77] When the Basque Nationalist deputies arrived in Pamplona, they were greeted with posters and graffiti, written by young Carlists and calling for the Statute's rejection.[78] The assembly confirmed these expectations; Álava, Guipúzcoa and Vizcaya approved the Statute by large majorities, but Navarre rejected it by 123 councils to 109 with 35 abstentions. The proceedings were suspended and the as-sembly broke up in disarray. In rejecting the Statute the Navarrese, though they could not have known it, had postponed the realization of any kind of Basque autonomy by another four years.[79]

The irate Basque Nationalists promptly turned upon the Carlist authorities, accusing them of 'sinning gravely against Navarre and the sister provinces' by not ordering their councillors to vote for the Statute.[80] Three years later Aguirre showed that he had had no second thoughts when, in his memoirs, he attributed the Statute's defeat in Navarre to the machinations of the Communion. True Carlists, he argued, would have supported the Statute if free to do so, but their leaders had instructed them to oppose it; since 1931 Carlism had been subverted by Integrists and Alfonsists to such a degree that the Pamplona assembly marked 'the last stage in the decomposition of an organization which had accomplished its historic mission'.[81]

Whatever his motives, Aguirre's assessment of the Navarrese vote fell wide of the mark.[82] What it actually demonstrated was that opinions within the Communion were genuinely divided, that its Basque–Navarrese leadership therefore found it impossible to give a lead, and that Carlist delegates at Pamplona were accordingly free to vote as they wished. Numerous Carlist-controlled councils certainly did switch to opposition between January and June 1932, but a considerable number continued to support autonomy even on the new terms. What Aguirre conveniently chose to ignore was that the PNV was let down by its new allies as well as by the Carlists, for in Navarre the gamble of relying upon the left to offset ebbing Carlist support had failed. A small increase in support for autonomy from the Navarrese left would have produced a majority in favour of the Statute; instead left-wing opposition, concentrated along the Navarrese *ribera*, strengthened despite the Temporary Committees' propaganda efforts and the official support of the Basque–Navarrese Socialist Federation. In other words, the Statute was rejected in Navarre not because of systematic opposition from the Carlist leadership but through a combination of largely spontaneous right- and left-wing hostility. And as far as Carlist opposition went, the Basque Nationalists' cries of 'betrayal' smacked of hypocrisy when, after all, it was they and not the Carlists who had changed course since Estella. Having dropped the Carlists and embraced the left, and produced a Statute bereft of that element which for many Carlists was the chief justification for the pursuit of autonomy, they had little genuine cause for complaint if the latter then lost interest.

The effect of Navarre's decision upon the Statute campaign was naturally damaging. Although the Temporary Committees decided to postpone further action for the time being, sooner or later they and the PNV were likely to settle for a Statute limited to Guipúzcoa, Vizcaya and Álava, and when that happened the Carlists would have to reconsider their position. Carlist enthusiasts for autonomy like Oriol and Oreja were genuinely saddened at the events of Pamplona,[83] yet this did not mean that they would necessarily support a Statute from which Navarre was excluded. Without Navarre, Carlism would count for little in the autonomous region, especially if its constitution rested disproportionate power in Bilbao. Oriol in particular was acutely conscious of the problems facing rural, thinly populated Álava in a Basque state or region dominated by the more urbanized and densely populated provinces of Vizcaya and Guipúzcoa.[84] Carlist alienation from the cause of autonomy was therefore cumulative; regional autonomy made sense only if it satisfied Navarre, and when it failed to do so Carlist interest flagged. The juntas of Álava, Guipúzcoa and Vizcaya made the position plain by publicly defending Navarre's action and reserving their right to insist that any new Statute resemble that of Estella – in other words, effectively promising to resist any Statute likely to be offered them.[85]

Relations between the Carlists and the Basque Nationalists sank to a new low in the aftermath of the Pamplona assembly. The existence of a Basque–Navarrese parliamentary group had become a farce; Beunza, its leader and the only prominent Navarrese Carlist to display real regret at Navarre's decision, offered to resign his seat now that the Basque–Navarrese Bloc's purpose had been vitiated, but the Carlist-dominated Catholic–Foralist electoral committee turned down his offer.[86] Beunza, Oreja and Urquijo attended a meeting of the Basque–Navarrese deputies and the mayors' committee on 1 August, and left before the end of what Aguirre later described as a 'disagreeable' session. Those remaining declared the Basque–Navarrese Bloc dissolved, and henceforth, though committee representation made its nominal continuation necessary until the next election, it ceased to be more than a convenience.[87] It had collapsed because its two main elements, the Carlists and the PNV, adhered to a different order of priorities; whereas to the Basque Nationalists autonomy was all-important and its specific character secondary, to the Carlists autonomy was attractive only if it served the cause of religion and order. Once its attainment involved dealing with laicism and socialism, the price became too high for most Carlists. Now, in the Basque–Navarrese region itself, Carlist supporters of the Statute maintained an embarrassed silence as the Communion's meetings were led by its opponents, notably Pradera.[88] Violence erupted in Guipúzcoan villages when Basque Nationalists interrupted Carlist speakers with cries of 'Long live the Republic!'[89] and at the end of June Carlists in Pamplona produced and distributed a pamphlet entitled 'Judaism, Nationalism, Communism', which impugned Basque Nationalism as at least the unwitting agent of the international Jewish–Masonic–Bolshevik conspiracy.[90] This turn of events may well have distressed some Carlists, but Rodezno was not among them. Navarre, he announced, could at last proclaim herself 'completely foral and completely Spanish'.[91]

In his fellow-Carlists' eyes, Rodezno was already identified with the late Don Jaime's policy of *rapprochement* with Alfonsism. The succession problem remained intractable. Yet another pact was drafted at discussions held in Bordeaux during December 1931, providing for combined monarchist political action. It also stated that when the appropriate hour struck, Alfonso Carlos would convoke Constituent Cortes which would give Spain a traditionally inspired regime. Again the agreement proved a dead letter, neither claimant actually signing it.[92] The impasse reached in the negotiations on the succession was revealed during January 1932, when both claimants published manifestos indicating that, while both favoured the idea of monarchist unity and spoke warmly of the other, neither would yield on the question of his own legitimacy.[93] As long as this situation persisted, real progress was impossible. Alfonso's new lip-service to Traditionalism cut no ice with the Carlists while he rejected the validity of the Carlist claims – which were, after all, an integral part of their brand of Traditionalism – and refused either to recognize Alfonso Carlos as legal monarch or to abdicate so that one of his sons might do so. Since Alfonso Carlos was every bit as unwilling to accept Alfonso XIII as *de facto* king, much less as legitimate monarch, the result was a dead end.[94]

Dynastic reconciliation was made even more difficult to attain by the existence of opposition within both parties. On the Alfonsist side it came mainly from dyed-in-the-wool liberals like the Conde de Romanones who retained considerable personal influence over Alfonso despite the general drift away from liberalism.[95] Within the Communion uneasiness was more widespread. Official secrecy notwithstanding, all Carlists knew that some kind of accommodation with Alfonsism was in the air, and a great many reeled at the prospect.[96] The reverse side of the simple dynastic, even personalist loyalty to the heirs of Carlos V which remained the hallmark of the politically unsophisticated Carlist masses was an intensely emotional hatred for the line of Isabella II which made them instinctively hostile towards the least sign of a *rapprochement*. The chief spokesmen for this view among the Carlist leaders came from the oldest generation, whose hatred of Alfonsism was almost equalled by their resentment towards the Integrists whom they now saw assuming important positions within the Communion, and whose lack of affection for Carlos VII's descendants they believed accounted for current policies.

The leaders of this small but noisy faction were José Cora y Lira, editor of *El Cruzado Español*, and Lorenzo Sáenz, who early in 1932 resigned from the National Junta and the regional *jefatura* of New Castile rather than continue working alongside Integrists and 'new' Carlists.[97] The Conde de Arana, *jefe* of Vizcaya, also handed in his resignation.[98] The malcontents petitioned Alfonso Carlos to turn away from the usurpers and designate a successor from elsewhere;[99] Cora y Lira rushed out a book in which he argued that any successor must accept *all* the Communion's principles and that female lines of descent need not be excluded from consideration in the quest for an heir – a principle, itself scarcely sanctified by Carlist tradition, designed to allow the succession of the offspring of Don Jaime's sister Doña Blanca, wife of the Habsburg Leopold of Tuscany.[100]

Alfonso Carlos himself nursed growing misgivings about dealing with the Alfonsists, yet could not rid himself of the conviction that the succession rightfully fell upon Alfonso XIII and his sons if only they would fully embrace Traditionalism and deny the legitimacy of their line since 1833.[101] More to the point, however, he was disinclined to tolerate other old men telling him how to run his affairs; after several warnings the National Junta deprived *El Cruzado Español* of official recognition and threatened the grumblers with expulsion from the Communion.[102] The '*cruzadistas*', still protesting their loyalty to Alfonso Carlos, began describing themselves as the 'true Carlists' or the 'Loyal Nucleus' and came out openly against the policies of Rodezno's Junta: 'No . . . our Kings and *caudillos* cannot be succeeded by those alien to our sentiments and convictions, much less those who have fought us in war and persecuted us in peace.'[103]

The rebellion spread. Another newspaper, *Oriamendi* of Bilbao, joined the campaign and was also disowned;[104] the regional authorities of Asturias were removed for disloyalty;[105] three more elderly provincial *jefes* resigned, thus allowing the National Junta to replace them by younger and more energetic figures;[106] and one or two dissident, self-styled 'Carlist' circles were formed, for example in Madrid and Bilbao, but were officially blacklisted and made scant impact.[107]

To all intents and purposes this was yet another schism. But while it inevitably conjured up memories of 1888 and 1919, it was nowhere near as serious – save perhaps in its deeper implications. Actual numerical involvement was negligible, and apart from Sáenz no personalities of national standing were prepared to push any misgivings they may have felt about the National Junta's policies to the point of risking expulsion. The mere fact that the veterans' spokesman could be dropped from the Junta without a major crisis was itself a sign of the times; indeed Sáenz's conduct was patently motivated not least by his recognition that power within the Communion was fast slipping from veteran and old-guard hands. The *cruzadistas'* action, far from stemming this process, only accelerated it.

None of this altered the fact that dissatisfaction, if at a lower pitch than that of the *cruzadistas*, was widespread and increasing at all levels of the Communion. Perhaps sensing this, Alfonso Carlos was reluctant to take the final step of expelling the *cruzadistas* and risking making things worse than they already were. In order to test the feelings of leading Carlists, he summoned an assembly which met on 2 June 1932 at the Château de Mondonville near Toulouse, the property of a French legitimist sympathizer. Over a hundred Carlists were present, and although nothing was decided the general climate of the assembly was plainly averse to anything approaching a complete reconciliation with Alfonsism.[108]

This revelation of how unpopular was Rodezno's policy of *rapprochement* let to a pronounced lessening of emphasis upon the dynastic issue from the middle of 1932 onwards. Sheer frustration at the lack of success probably did as much, along with the increasing influence within the Communion of Integrists who, contrary to the *cruzadistas'* simplistic belief, were for the most part less keen on a settlement than former Jaimists like Rodezno.[109] The National Junta was not, however, diverted from co-operating in other ways with the slowly reorganizing Alfonsist forces. The schismatics' failure to attract much popular support seemed to suggest that most Carlists were amenable to a policy of day-to-day collaboration with the Alfonsists just as long as no surrender of Carlist principles or independence was involved. Furthermore, the veterans' worries were belied by the speeches and writings of Alfonsist politicians, which proved that it was they and not the Carlists who were eating past words, denying former deeds and shifting their position. From February 1932 onwards, joint meetings and guest appearances by representatives of one party at the other's functions became commonplace. Carlist meetings were by far the more numerous, so that leading Alfonsists like Goicoechea, the Conde de Vallellano and the distinguished academic Pedro Sáinz Rodríguez were often to be seen on the Communion's platforms uttering lavish praises for the heritage, ideas and great men of Carlism.[110]

Co-operation was just as cordial, though differently weighted, within Acción Española. From its inception this was a predominantly Alfonsist concern; during 1932 Rodezno, as Carlism's political leader, and Pradera, as its acknowledged intellectual giant, contributed to the review, but otherwise few Carlists were actively involved. This was hardly surprising; Carlist ideology was amply publicized in the Communion's press, as well as in Mella's collected works, publication of which began in 1931, and little benefit was therefore to be derived from more than a token commitment to Acción Española. For the proponents of the new Alfonsism, on the other hand, it offered an invaluable channel for disseminating their *mélange* of neo-Traditionalist and fashionably authoritarian ideas, of delineating their affinities and differences with Carlism, and not least of attempting to bind Spanish Traditionalism, whether in pure or adulterated form, to the struggling cause of Alfonso XIII and his family.

Meanwhile, leading Alfonsists continued to plot against the Republic. During 1932 links were forged with dissatisfied elements in the army through the sympathetic General Barrera, and in the early summer, nourished by growing centralist discontent at the probable passing of the Catalan Statute, the conspiracy coalesced with a parallel right-wing Republican plot. The putative head of the latter was General José Sanjurjo, Director-General of the Civil Guard until February 1932.[111] The most active Alfonsist conspirators included the chief protagonists of monarchist unity, who naturally wished to draw the Carlists into the rising now planned for the late summer. Carlist mass support in northern Spain, if difficult to assess with accuracy, certainly had to be considered a vital asset in any monarchist rising – especially given the army's doubtful degree of enthusiasm. All along, prominent Carlists knew the substance of the conspiracy; Alfonsist security was so poor that many details soon became known to the Republican authorities, and it was therefore inevitable that Carlists like Rodezno, Pradera and Bilbao, who mixed politically and socially with Alfonsist conspirators in the small world of political Madrid, should also be party to what was afoot.

Despite later accounts, however, the amount of actual Carlist 'collaboration' in the plotting was very limited. Villores in January 1932 and the National Junta in the spring shrank from committing Carlism to an adventure, the long-term consequence of which seemed likely to be either a military-dominated conservative Republic or an Alfonsist restoration, and whose chances of success in any case appeared meagre.[112]

Carlist interest in the conspiracy's progress was nonetheless considerable, the more so as the Communion's own military reorganization went slowly ahead and as Alfonsist plotters hopefully kept up contacts. In the spring of 1932, Alfonso Carlos and María de las Nieves arrived in the French frontier village of Ascain, near Saint-Jean de Luz – traditionally the scene of *émigré* Carlist conspiratorial activities. Posing as a Colombian couple named Fernández, they moved unobtrusively into a house paid for by Carlist supporters, and were soon put in touch with Alfonsist plotters. An interparty committee was set up to plan a 'combined monarchist rising'; perhaps significantly, it consisted of three Alfonsists and a single Carlist, Rafael Olazábal. Although it achieved nothing in terms of drawing the Communion into the planned rising, the committee did succeed in increasing the flow of illicit arms across the frontier into Navarre, a supply most of which found its way into Carlist hands.[113] Evidently, the Carlists were determined to have the maximum information concerning the conspiracy, and a measure of indirect benefit from it, with the minimum of actual commitment.

This is borne out by the equally close contacts made between the conspirators and the Carlists within Spain itself. Junyent and the Catalonian Carlists were approached, but despite their favourable reaction they as yet commanded insufficient manpower to think of going further; they also lacked the authority to do so other than as individuals, and the National Junta's permission was not forthcoming.[114] This did not prevent the Catalonian authorities from assuming Carlist implication in the plots which they knew – and imagined – were being hatched. In mid-July leading Catalonian Carlists were arrested on suspicion of participating in a 'monarchist–communist' plot and held until well after the real rising, in which their part was, to say the least, peripheral, had passed.[115]

As the date of the rising approached, the Carlists were represented at some of the meetings of the chief Alfonsist and military conspirators. The Navarrese Requeté instructor, Sanz de Lerín, and a Carlist army officer, Justo San Miguel, attended the final meeting near Madrid on 8 August,[116] but this did not mean that Carlist participation, even in Navarre, was promised or likely. At the Toulouse assembly in June, it had been decided that the Communion would act officially neither in preparing nor in carrying out a rising, but that individual Carlists might join if they wished.[117] Sanz de Lerín's status of instructor gave him no personal authority within the Communion, so that he was in no position to 'promise' the '6,000 Red Berets' of later Carlist legend.[118] Even had the Regional and National Juntas permitted it, effective mobilization of the Navarrese Requeté would have encountered a further problem: the imprisonment throughout most of spring and summer 1932 of Burgo, Huarte and several other *decuria* commanders. This rendered effectively leaderless the Requeté of the only Spanish province where it could be considered a calculable force. Again, this did not stop Basque–Navarrese Republicans feeling sure, in the tense atmosphere of summer 1932, that the Carlists of Navarre were once more scheming rebellion; in June and July their press published a substantially true exposé of the Navarrese Requeté's strength and organization, and reported a less credible Carlist conspiracy involving a pincer movement on Madrid by Red Berets from Pamplona and Valencia. The Carlist press met the true and false reports with equally firm denials.[119]

The final shape of the rising which by July all Spain, and the Azaña government in particular, was expecting, was thus a combined Alfonsist and military affair, with the promised or hoped-for collaboration of other civilian elements – not only conservative Republicans and Carlists but also the JONS (Juntas de Ofensiva Nacional Sindicalista), a small fascist group led by Ledesma Ramos and Onésimo Redondo.[120] The army officers, led by Sanjurjo, commanded virtually all the rising's physical resources, and therefore dictated its forms and goals. It was envisaged that it would follow the classic pattern of the nineteenth-century *pronunciamiento*: after simultaneous, bloodless *coups* had taken place in several cities – Madrid, Seville, Cádiz and Valladolid – other garrisons, it was hoped, would join the movement or at least adopt a position of benevolent neutrality as promised by the infantry commander at Corunna, the up-and-coming Brigadier-General Franco.[121]

The generals lacked any coherent, long-term political plan. In private Sanjurjo and others spoke of an Alfonsist restoration, but this seems to have been wishfulness rather than expectation.[122] The Alfonsist conspirators for their part followed the lead of their general, Barrera, in accepting the consensus view that the movement's 'single and exclusive aim' was to replace Azaña by a provisional junta dedicated to uphold public order. A restoration they viewed as the ultimate but distant outcome of a rising the main purpose of which was to strike the first blow against the Republic from the right.[123]

The long-awaited rebellion occurred at last on 10 August and was a fiasco. In Madrid, after violent skirmishes around the main post office and the War Ministry, it was crushed before most Madrileños knew it had begun. Sanjurjo's control of Seville lasted less than a day, and none of the other intended centres of rebellion saw serious trouble. When Barrera, following the defeat in Madrid, was flown by the Alfonsist aviator Ansaldo to Pamplona, he found the city quiet and neither the garrison nor the Carlists in the least inclined to move. For several hours he tried to persuade the Carlist leaders to join the rising, but without success.[124] Had he succeeded it is unlikely that the outcome of the rising would have been much different.

Carlist involvement in Sanjurjo's revolt was thus not only slight but even less than has since been claimed. Had the rising succeeded in Madrid and sparked off a series of *pronunciamientos* throughout the country, it is quite possible that a belated attempt might have been made to mobilize the Navarrese Requeté in the hope of sharing the fruits of victory. But there was, and could have been, no prior commitment to participate in the vital early stages of the rising. Burgo and his comrades, incarcerated but kept aware of the general lines of the coming rebellion, knew nothing of Sanz de Lerín's alleged promise to the military conspirators, which must therefore be dismissed as sheer myth.[125] Other accounts also exaggerate the Carlist role. Although the Sevillian Carlists and Tejera's *La Unión* naturally welcomed Sanjurjo's fleeting success,[126] tales of 'ninety Red Berets' parading the streets bear little relation to the true state of the Sevillian Requeté in 1932.[127] Two Carlists, San Miguel and a student from the Madrid AET, followed the National Junta's line on individual participation and were killed in the fighting in Madrid's Plaza de la Cibeles.[128] In Jerez, where the Civil Guard briefly assumed control, the local Carlists associated themselves with the rising. In the main, however, the National Junta's unenthusiastic attitude set the tone for that of Carlists in general.

The Communion's air of detachment was not only understandable but also sensible and necessary. Carlism's military organization was still far too weak and localized for the National Junta to be able to feel that there was the remotest chance of turning a successful *coup* into a Carlist restoration. On the other hand the possibility of the movement's succeeding was so slender as to make it unnecessary for Carlism to participate for fear of being swept aside by a triumphant tide of counter-revolution.

The Carlists' relatively discreet behaviour did not make them immune from the governmental repression which inexorably followed the rising. Some like Sanz de Lerín, promptly arrested in Burgos, could scarcely complain,[129] but during the rest of August numerous Carlists, the majority unconnected with the conspiracy, were detained in most regions of Spain. Although many were quickly released, others were left in prison, untried, for three months or more. Among these was Fal Conde, whose three-month stay in a Seville jail was exceeded only by the leaders of the tiny Sevillian Requeté, Luis Redondo and Enrique Barrau.[130] Carlist circles were searched and closed by local authorities and in several places sacked by angry left-wing crowds;[131] the party's press, in common with that of the entire right, was suspended – *La Unión* for three months in payment for its ecstatic reception of Sanjurjo's *coup* – and Carlist judges removed from office.[132]

Within a week of the revolt Azaña's government seized the moment and rushed through the Cortes the expropriation without compensation of the land of 'suspected' conspirators, thereby giving a much-needed boost to the cause of agrarian reform. Among those affected were all the grandees of Spain; Carlists now liable to immediate expropriation included Rodezno, the Valencian Barón de Cárcer, the Chicharros, Juan José Palomino of Cádiz, and Sanz de Lerín.[133] The passing of the Agrarian Reform Act itself was also facilitated by the post-rebellion atmosphere and took place on 9 September, the Carlists abstaining. The same day also witnessed the passage of the Statute of Catalan Autonomy, delayed throughout the summer. To crown the right's dismay, 145 suspected conspirators, mostly army officers of right-wing persuasion, were ordered without trial to an uncomfortable exile in the Spanish Sahara outpost of Villa Cisneros.[134]

In defending his government's legislative attacks upon the conspirators and the social class from which most of them came, Azaña
insisted that he wished to create 'beggars, not martyrs', but it was
with a posture of martyrdom rather than mendicancy that the Carlists
now reacted. Lamamié was typical in belabouring the government
for stepping up its 'tyrannical' behaviour by means of indiscriminate
arrests, suspensions, closures, expropriations and deportations.[135]
Yet over the years Carlists had become inured to such treatment, and
knew that 'persecution' only heightened the resolve of the committed
and fostered proselytization. 'What if fear does reign in the streets,'
wrote Fal Conde from his cell, 'It does not matter – we are on the
way.'[136]

4
Rivals on the right

The rising of 10 August 1932 obliged all the elements on the Spanish right to examine and declare their position in relation to the Republic. Virtually all those who spurned the embrace of overt Catholic Republicanism as incarnate in Alcalá Zamora, whether Carlists, Alfonsists or accidentalists, were agreed that the Republic in anything resembling its present form was unacceptable; their differences centred upon what should replace it and, far more urgently, what course should be adopted in order to transform or overthrow it. To the accidentalists, Sanjurjo's failure proved not the immorality of political violence but its futility in existing circumstances, especially when alternative means were available whereby the Republic's own machinery might be exploited in order to produce a system far removed from the expectations of its founders. The Alfonsists drew the opposite conclusion, arguing that the *débâcle* of 10 August had happened simply because the Spanish right had lacked unity and militancy, and that if the lesson were learned, the failure need not be repeated. The coexistence of accidentalists and open Alfonsists within Acción Popular, increasingly awkward even before the rising, plainly could not continue much longer.

The Carlists accepted the Alfonsists' 'catastrophist' view of general anti-Republican strategy, while remaining critical of the rising. When the Communion's press began gradually to emerge from suspension, it flatly denied Carlist complicity in the revolt, attacked its negative or at best Alfonsist complexion, but applauded it nonetheless as a noble and patriotic gesture.[1] Fal Conde epitomized his comrades' ambivalence in suggesting that it was the 'Sanjurjada's' very failure which made it praiseworthy; if successful it could only have postponed the ultimate disaster inherent in liberalism, whereas in defeat 'it represents a virile pounding upon the doors of a hitherto unchallenged revolution'.[2] As for the Carlist-bred Sanjurjo, Fal Conde later declared with characteristic frankness that although the Carlists had not risen with him on 10 August, they stood with

him on the eleventh when they witnessed and shared in his 'persecution'.[3] Such reactions proved, if proof were needed, that the
Carlists opposed neither the principle nor the reality of anti-
Republican violence, merely that they considered Sanjurjo's revolt
to have been precipitate and ideologically confused. Henceforward
the discretion which they had on the whole displayed during the
Republic's first sixteen months gave way to a more or less open
commitment to long-term violence. Although governmental and left-
wing accusations of conspiratorial and paramilitary activity continued to be publicly denied,[4] Carlist propaganda during 1932–3
resounded with references to the right of an oppressed people to
rise up against 'tyranny'. Ponderously, too ponderously indeed for
many Carlists, but no less decisively for all that, the Communion
was returning to its insurrectionary tradition.

Renewed aggressiveness was fostered by the persistence of governmental repression. By the end of 1932 most of the Carlists
imprisoned in Seville and Jerez had been released and the Seville
headquarters reopened, but four members of the Sevillian Requeté
had to wait until January 1933 for their release while one of its
leaders was held in prison until amnestied in April 1934.[5] In other
regions, too, official restrictions stayed in effect long enough to
overlap with further waves of arrests and closures in the spring and
summer of 1933. In February 1933 Rodezno complained in the
Cortes that the three Carlist circles in Pamplona and nearby Viana,
closed following the incidents of April 1932, had not yet been permitted to reopen, while in the province of Valencia the Communion's
forty-odd circles remained closed and its press silent, despite the
total lack of incident there in August.[6] Throughout most of 1933,
indeed, Carlist circles in the big cities of Madrid, Barcelona and
Seville were closed as much as open. Official harassment was sufficiently widespread and frequent to sting Carlists into protesting,
without being comprehensive enough to render all protest impossible.
Perceptive Carlists like Rodezno's astute young *protégé*, Luis
Arellano, recognized that the very unevenness of this repression was
precisely what a militant movement like Carlism needed. In April
1933 he told *La Unión* that recent 'persecution' had proved invaluable in dragging 'dormant' Catholics, Carlists included, into the
streets in defence of public order and the Catholic faith.[7] Moreover,
official identification of Carlism with the 10 August rebels unquestionably stimulated within the Communion an even greater sense

of fraternity with the rebels than might otherwise have been the case.

During the autumn and winter following the Sanjurjada, Carlist dreams of leading a successful rising against the Republic and of installing the Traditional Monarchy received a boost from the unexpected quarter of Villa Cisneros. Among the 145 sent there were a number of Carlists including the two sons of Jaime Chicharro, the Jerez wine-producer Juan José Palomino, Mier Terán, the Marqués de Sauceda and several students from the Madrid AET.[8] The Carlists appear to have been the only politically organized group at Villa Cisneros; this, combined with the isolation of the penal colony and the understandable hostility of its inmates towards the regime which had exiled them, created an ideal situation for proselytization. Within weeks Alfonso Carlos had received a letter of support signed by forty-two of the exiles, and after two months eighty-four had joined the Communion's Villa Cisneros cell.[9] During December and January most of the exiles left Africa, either returning to Spain to be freed or stand trial, or, in the case of twenty-nine others, escaping by boat to the safety of Salazar's Portugal.[10] Alfonso Carlos, acknowledging yet another message of support from twenty-three of the escapers, all but four of whom were army or naval officers, gave utterance to what he claimed was a long-felt love for the Spanish army against which he had once fought, an army 'unique in the world for its heroism, bravery and suffering'.[11] Many, perhaps most, of the military converts were to lose their enthusiasm for Carlism once away from the unnatural atmosphere of Villa Cisneros, but in the meantime Carlism had struck a propaganda blow of considerable significance.

A less immediately sensational ,but ultimately more lasting and important conversion was that of Colonel Varela, one of the outstanding young officers of the Moroccan War and the intended leader of the rising in Cádiz. Although on the day Varela had sensibly judged it best not to move, he was nonetheless arrested and placed in the same Seville prison which held Fal Conde and several members of the city's Requeté. The debonair Varela naturally became the focus of the young prisoners' attention, yet it proved to be they who influenced him rather than the reverse. Soon Varela, impressed by their enthusiasm and ideas, was devouring the works of Mella, presented to him by the Requeté leader Luis Redondo; in December, Redondo and Varela were transferred together to the prison at Guadalajara, where the latter's conversion to Carlism was sealed.[12] It was to prove permanent.

With leading Carlists now turning their minds to serious thoughts of eventually overturning the Republic by force, these developments could not have been more opportune. Army officers, it seemed, were no longer necessarily immune to the appeal of Traditionalism, and there now rose up the beguiling vision of a Carlist infiltration of, or at least alliance with, the army. During his imprisonment Varela was visited by Rodezno and Fal Conde, both of whom dangled before him the prospect of leading a Carlist rising. Whether out of modesty or pessimism as to the chances of such an enterprise, Varela demurred, discreetly suggesting as a more suitable leader the more senior but non-Carlist Franco. His suggestion was not acted upon. Varela did, however, accept the more down-to-earth offer of the clandestine military leadership of the national Requeté, a great relief to the Carlists, whose first choice among the army leaders, Sanjurjo, was out of the running owing to his Portuguese exile. Varela's immediate tasks were to draft a set of general military instructions, later known as the *Ordenanzas del Requeté*, and to sketch a new, national structure for the Requeté, something without which any hope of successful rebellion could be forgotten. Both tasks were completed before his release from jail.[13] Varela's new role appealed to him as a military man as well as a Carlist, for both he and the chastened Sanjurjo were now convinced that any future rising must possess the popular base which the rising of 10 August had lacked and which Carlism, more than any other element on the right, might be able to provide.

A further symptom of Carlism's abandonment of political discretion was the severing of the few remaining ties with Acción Popular in the immediate aftermath of 10 August. There was nothing very dramatic about this; with only one or two exceptions such as Rodezno and Senante, the Carlists had never played a central role in Acción Nacional and Acción Popular, any collaboration being a mere tactical expedient designed to tide the movement over the difficult period following Alfonso XIII's fall. Effective participation had been negligible since the early months of 1932, and the Sanjurjada merely hastened the completion of gradual withdrawal. For the Alfonsists the situation was entirely different. Demoralized by the catastrophe of April 1931, they had joined Acción Nacional with enthusiasm and had participated wholeheartedly both in it and in Acción Popular. Before 10 August acceptance of accidentalism was convenient and only mildly embarrassing for Goicoechea and his associates; after 10 August it was patently absurd. Those Alfonsists who openly confessed their past – and future – anti-Republican activities could no longer pass as accidentalists, any more than the genuine accidentalists – monarchists as most of them certainly were – could be expected to compromise their gradualism and risk discredit through maintaining their close links with unrepentant plotters.[14]

Goicoechea and the Alfonsists hoped to stay in Acción Popular and to bind it securely to the monarchist cause, but Sanjurjo's failure meant that they were fighting a losing battle. For if the rising temporarily threatened to taint the entire Catholic opposition, it also strengthened the appeal of accidentalism by helping to convince a large proportion of Catholic – and monarchist – opinion that a policy of conspiracy and *pronunciamiento* was less likely to produce results than one of tactical accommodation to the Republic in the cause of gradual, preferably peaceful, but in the long run total transformation of the political system. In order to pursue this goal effectively, a formally constituted accidentalist party would be necessary, and in the view of Herrera and Gil Robles, the logical basis of such a party was Acción Popular.[15] On 22–24 October 1932, a national assembly of Acción Popular accepted a firm accidentalist line.[16] While the decision did not actually oblige monarchists to leave the organization, it made it virtually impossible for those who would neither stifle their monarchism nor repudiate rebellion to work sincerely within it. For the time being Goicoechea and other undisguised monarchists continued to belong to Acción Popular, but from now on it was obvious that they were going to need a different front for their activities.

The way was now clear for the forging of a genuine political party out of Acción Popular and the bewildering variety of regional, provincial, and local Catholic and landowners' organizations which moved in its orbit. Moreover, the time was particularly ripe. By the end of 1932 the rallying of the Republic's supporters which followed the Sanjurjada was already nearing its end; the year 1933 was to see the collapse of the San Sebastian coalition, as the Socialists became disillusioned with their Left Republican allies and the Radicals hungrily pursued power for themselves. With Azaña's grip visibly declining, expectation of a general election became widespread, which in terms of the accidentalist strategy made the rapid marshalling of the right's electoral forces a matter of urgency.

Azaña's protracted decline began with the new year itself, as a consequence of Anarchist risings in Aragon, Catalonia and Andalusia. The bitterness of social conflict and the government's unease in handling it were encapsulated in the events which took place in the Andalusian village of Casas Viejas, where after the crushing of a local Anarchist rising, fourteen villagers were shot dead in cold blood by members of the Assault Guard, a new police force set up by the Republican government as a counterweight to the Civil Guard. Azaña, it was rumoured, had ordered the massacre. The premier denied all responsibility and was subsequently exonerated by an enquiry, but the mud stuck. [17]

Casas Viejas had become a *cause célèbre*. Besides souring relations between the government and the Socialists, it provided fuel for both Radical and right-wing opposition to Azaña. The Carlists were, of course, temperamentally more sympathetic towards the forces of order than towards Anarchists, especially with Casas Viejas only a few miles from the vineyards whose profits helped to subsidize Andalusian Carlism. Nevertheless they could not bring themselves to squander a golden opportunity for attacking the Republic, and thus resolved their dilemma by diagnosing Casas Viejas as a classic symptom of Republican liberalism. Such events, they argued, were the logical and inevitable outcome of combining economic exploitation with softness towards revolutionary agitators. [18] In Sanlúcar la Mayor, near Seville, Úrraca Pastor was fined by the authorities for publicly voicing the general Carlist conviction that Azaña and his government were morally − if not legally − responsible. [19] Even after a month had passed, *La Unión* was still moralizing. 'The whole of Spain is Casas Viejas,' it declaimed, 'for Spain is a Republic.' [20]

With the government still reeling from the shock of Casas Viejas, public attention turned to the proposed Law of Religious Confessions and Congregations. Based on Articles 26 and 27 of the Constitution, the bill asserted the State's ownership of ecclesiastical property and banned religious Orders from participating in industry, commerce, agriculture and education. Catholic sensibilities were affronted on every count, but it was the curtailment of the Church's educative role which provoked the bitterest response. In the Cortes the Agrarians and Basque−Navarrese combined to resist the bill, but their demands for 'freedom of choice' met with little sympathy on the one issue around which the San Sebastian forces could still unite.[21]

The excitement which the issue produced among Catholics did much to encourage Herrera and Gil Robles in their plans for the new party. To help them in the task, they chose Luis Lucía, the ex-Carlist leader of the thriving Catholic party of Valencia, the DRV. Lucía remained strongly influenced by his Carlist past, and in 1929–30 had drafted a blueprint for a national party dedicated to the creation of a corporate state inspired by social-Catholicism.[22] Four months of frenetic activity were climaxed in Madrid at the end of February 1933 with a Congress of 'autonomous right-wing groups' (*derechas autónomas*), at which the presence of 400 delegates allegedly representing 735,000 adherents attested to the birth of the largest political party in Spain's history.[23] The Confederación Española de Derechas Autónomas, or CEDA, predictably emerged as openly accidentalist, prepared to work within the regime while shrinking from an actual affirmation of Republican faith. It claimed to defend 'Christian civilization', and announced that it would combat the Republic's sectarian legislation and pursue the eventual drastic revision of the Constitution. Great stress was also laid upon an 'advanced social programme' which it was claimed would provide an alternative to 'atheistic' socialism. Yet the new party could not convincingly disguise its essential social conservatism, given that the 'autonomous groups' of which it was made up were in the main dominated by large landowners and the Catholic middle class.[24]

The CEDA's programme had much in common with that of the Communion – not surprising in view of Lucía's earlier career, Gil Robles' parentage and upbringing, and the general if not always active espousal of social-Catholicism by most educated Spanish Catholics, Carlists included. During the party's formative period, Gil Robles himself went out of his way to emphasize this community of ideals in public, in the hope of silencing possible Carlist criticism and doubtless of wooing Carlist adherents. The Carlists, he declared in Salamanca in December 1932, held ten fundamental principles, nine of which he and Acción Popular shared: only the question of the regime kept them apart.[25] To the Carlists this point was naturally crucial, and while any evidence of a rallying of Catholic opposition to the Azaña Republic was in theory to be welcomed, its present manifestation in the form of the CEDA was not a little disturbing to them. As things stood they had little reason to suppose that the monarchic principle to which they were bound to cling was more likely to attract Catholics in search of a political home than to deter them; on the contrary, the mere fact of the CEDA's existence, not to mention its supposed three-quarters of a million adherents, demonstrated that Carlism's recent revival, although considerable, had none the less failed to touch an enormous number of Spanish Catholics. The problem was further accentuated by the character of the CEDA's mass base. Besides the prosperous fruit-growers of the Levant who formed the mainstay of the DRV, and the beef and dairy farmers of the somewhat similar Agrupación Regional Independiente of Asturias, the CEDA rested in large part upon the National Catholic Agrarian Confederation (CNCA), an extensive if amorphous association of Castilian and Leonese smallholders dominated, as the events of 1931 and 1932 had shown, by the Church and the wealthy landowners from whom most of their land was leased.[26] These 'middling' men of rural Spain were precisely those from whom a resurgent Carlism needed to recruit in order to aspire to power on a national level.

Once more, therefore, a Catholic party with a less than integralist programme loomed as a threat to Carlism. From its inception the CEDA was bigger, richer, better publicized and outwardly more up-to-date than the Communion, added to which it enjoyed the tacit support of the Spanish hierarchy and, through Tedeschini, the Vatican. There was thus revived the spectre of the loss of potential and actual Carlists to a rival movement which commanded irreproachable religious credentials and duplicated much of Carlism's appeal, while making fewer demands upon the consciences of its members. In the short term, Carlist–CEDA co-operation would be unavoidable if elections and parliamentary votes were to be won, but in the long run any hopes of a Carlist triumph had to hinge upon the failure of the accidentalist tactic and the collapse of the CEDA.

Among the first of the leading Carlists to state his position with regard to the political drift of Acción Popular was Gil Robles' fellow Salamancan, Lamamié. In November 1932 he criticized the reiteration by accidentalist Catholics of the 'lesser evil' thesis so consistently opposed by the Carlists of the nineteenth century;[27] the following month, leading the few but wealthy Carlists of Salamanca out of Acción Castellana, he wrote to Gil Robles that membership of the Communion was incompatible with that of the new-style Acción Popular – a mirroring of the principle laid down at the latter's

October assembly.[28] During the winter of 1932–3 the attitudes of the two now-distinct parties towards each other were identical, both calling for close circumstantial co-operation alongside the maintenance of ideological and organizational independence. The Carlists' advocacy of 'Union of the Right' or a 'Single Front' continued unabated throughout the first half of 1933.[29] The Spanish right, according to *Reacción*, was as rich in shades of opinion as the left, notwithstanding which 'the formation of a Single Front is not just possible, it is indispensable'.[30]

Differences regarding the CEDA did exist, however. Rodezno and the Navarrese notables, impregnably entrenched in the stronghold of Carlism, could afford to be generous. 'Good, very good' was Rodezno's verdict on the founding assembly of the CEDA,[31] and when a CEDA offshoot, Unión Navarra, was formed in Pamplona by the two independent members of the Basque–Navarrese Bloc, Aizpún and Gortari, *El Pensamiento Navarro* remarked that while it was largely superfluous since its essential principles were already well served by Carlism 'its manifesto paints an accurate picture of the situation and we are bound to regard it sympathetically with a view to united action. We therefore salute Unión Navarra with a friendly hand.'[32]

The southern leadership, whose recently founded and burgeoning organization was more obviously threatened by the appearance of CEDA competition, reacted quite differently. A policy of circumstantial co-operation was not rejected, but the gulf separating Carlism from CEDA accidentalism was loudly advertised. Carlists, Fal Conde insisted, would always accept *legitimately* constituted authority – but this did not include the Republic:

... the usurper who gains power by the window, having scaled the wall under cover of darkness, is in the position of a criminal, of a thief who has no legal right over what he has stolen ... To go further: just as it is the duty of everyone to support the restoration of stolen goods to their rightful owner, similarly there exists a serious obligation to support the restoration of legitimate power and not back up the usurper.[33]

Three months later he stated that only maximum programmes really mattered to Carlists, and that it was the liberal and 'adhesionist' Catholics who were willing to settle for less who were the 'immediate obstacle' to their realization.[34] Fal Conde was outspoken enough, but was surpassed by the young *jefe* of eastern Andalusia, Fernando

Contreras, who repeatedly demanded not the recognition of the constituted power but its prompt and violent overthrow. 'Excessive
prudence,' Contreras warned, 'is a fault, not a virtue.'[35]

As yet such differences of outlook between the established and
rising leaders of the Communion had little practical effect. In
Andalusia, although Fal Conde described relations between the
Carlists and the CEDA as cooler than in the north, co-operation for
meetings was as common as in all areas where the two parties lived
side by side.[36] Carlists were nonetheless unanimous in wishing to
advertise the crucial line dividing them from the CEDA; Lamamié
insisted that Carlism would never contemplate collaboration with any
government, however far right, within a Republic or a restored
monarchy of a liberal character.[37] Even Rodezno, the most pragmatic and political of Carlists, claimed to spurn 'tactics'. Power,
he announced, was 'a means for implanting our total thesis'.[38] In
his mouthpiece, *El Observador*, Fal Conde spoke with typically
greater forthrightness: 'Power is violence, power is physical force.
It will only remain to organize resistance adequate to violence and
force . . . and by that route we shall reach our goal.'[39]

The extent of the right's resurgence, and therefore of its under-
representation in the Constituent Cortes, was demonstrated when
partial municipal elections took place in April 1933. Held in 2,478
municipalities where in April 1931 monarchist majorities, many of
them uncontested, had been followed by the interposition of Temporary Committees, they returned some 5,000 Catholic and monarchist
councillors, 5,000 Left Republicans and Socialists, and around 4,200
representing the Republican opposition.[40] Azaña's critics, understandably interpreting the results as embodying a popular repudiation of
his government, demanded his resignation and a general election,[41]
but the premier, dismissing the municipalities concerned as 'pocket
boroughs' riddled with lingering *caciquismo*, refused to be downcast
and totally ignored them. It was true that an anti-governmental
swing was only to be expected in many of the contested districts, yet
the scale of the left's defeat was both surprising and humiliating. The
genuine shift of opinion which it indicated stimulated the militancy
of the Catholic right and the parliamentary gyrations of the Radicals.

Nor did the evident mobilization of Spanish Catholics do anything
to deter the government from its anti-clerical course. On 17 May
Catholic opinion suffered the expected blow when the debate on the

Law of Congregations was guillotined and the Act passed. Lerroux, once more free to pursue his strategy of parliamentary obstruction, predicted that it would be impossible to apply; Carlist reaction was summed up by *El Siglo Futuro*:

We insist that our children ... will listen to no atheist teacher; they will not hear the blasphemous negation of God. Catholic parents! Rather death than consent to our children attending laic schools.[42]

Lamamié contended that the law, having been dictated neither by reason, nor the common good, nor even by a majority of the nation, was 'not a true law' and that, as a law against God, it should be disobeyed.[43] Fal Conde's *El Observador* went further still: the Catholic citizenry, it declared, must defend society 'even with its blood' against an unjust and usurping power.[44]

With the Radicals bent upon bringing down Azaña and the Catholic opposition inflamed by the Law of Congregations, the political climate could hardly have been less propitious for the government's introduction in the summer of 1933 of a bill on Rural Leases. The bill's long-term implications were scarcely less far-reaching than those of the 1932 Act. In seeking to enable tenant farmers to buy land rented for twenty years or more, it ought to have satisfied both the Radicals' desire for a stable, French-style property-owning democracy and the social-Catholics' proclaimed belief in the small-holding.[45] But in present circumstances neither Radicals nor Catholics in the Cortes were in any frame of mind to judge on its merits a piece of legislation which, if successfully applied, would have transformed the land-tenure situation in much of northern Spain; on the contrary, the Catholic deputies mounted a successful delaying campaign in which they received considerable Radical and conservative Republican support. Carlist social-Catholicism yet again wilted when put to the test. The bill was attacked as an assault upon property designed to erode and ultimately destroy a system from which members of the influential Carlist landlords' lobby bene-fited.[46] The voice of the unknown but far greater number of Carlist tenants who stood to gain from the scheme was inaudible. This was all the more true in the CEDA, where landowners' interests were even more strongly represented. Nothing good, it was now widely believed among many Spanish Catholics, rich and poor alike, could possibly come from a government which waged war upon the Church.

While the Carlists waxed indignant at the government's conduct and wrestled with the tactical problems created by the CEDA's arrival on the scene, their relations with two other 'adhesionist' parties, the Lliga and the PNV, continued to deteriorate.[47] When Catalans went to the polls in November 1932 to elect their first autonomous parliament, the right was divided in three of the four provinces. When the Lliga's leaders rejected Carlist proposals for an anti-Esquerra 'single front' everywhere save Tarragona, the Carlists and a sprinkling of Alfonsists formed an extreme right-wing alliance, the Dreta de Catalunya.[48] Carlist feelings against the businessmen of the Lliga were venomous; in their propaganda they assailed it as a nest of Protestants and freemasons, the mouth-piece of capital and oppressor of the Catalan worker, and the betrayer of the 'authentic right'.[49] The election results proved depressing for both sections of the Catalan right. The Lliga came a poor second to the Esquerra, with the Dreta de Catalunya so far behind that the Carlists could not even argue that Catholic unity would have brought victory. On the contrary, the heavy Radical vote in Barcelona suggested that the Lliga's flirtation with moderate Republicans was misguided only in stopping short of a firm alliance.[50] This lesson was unlikely to be lost on Catholics already inclined towards a tactical accommodation with the regime. For the Catalonian Carlists the results provided a bleak reminder of their movement's limitations in one of its historic bastions. *Reacción* gamely tried to raise its readers' spirits by hailing the Dreta's voters as 'the Christian and anti-Republican elite of Catalonia ... the advance of the army of liberation now beginning the spiritual reconquest of our country'.[51] Throughout the length and breadth of Catalonia, however, there were a mere 22,000 of them. *Reacción* concluded that violence might be the only answer; it was, it declared, a 'patriotic and Christian duty' to use all means, force included, to prevent an entire people from committing suicide.

In the Basque–Navarrese region the Communion, like all the political parties, was obliged to re-examine its position in the light of Navarre's rejection of the Temporary Committees' Statute. The leading Navarrese Carlists were unwilling to believe that the whole 'foralist' campaign in their province might have been effectively ex-tinguished and not just diverted. In October 1932 the Regional Junta therefore changed tack and adopted the idea of a Statute limited to Navarre.[52] *El Pensamiento Navarro* defended this conversion to the policy long advocated by its more independent 'colleague' *Diario de Navarra*, reaffirming Navarre's devotion to the *fueros* and arguing that the Carlists merely wished to avoid the perils of too close an association with an overcentralized autonomous Basque region.[53] Desultory talk in the weeks that followed went unaccompanied by action, and the Navarrese Statute remained no more than an idea.

The initiative in the other three provinces now rested squarely with the PNV and its Republican and Socialist allies. Prieto, recently converted to a belief in Basque autonomy, expressed a widely held view when he asserted that with or without Navarre the Statute would be won.[54] In October 1932 the Temporary Committees of Álava, Guipúzcoa and Vizcaya decided to entrust the drafting of a new Statute to an interparty committee, but the project foundered when several parties including the Carlists refused to participate on the grounds that the committee's composition unfairly reflected the distribution of political strength in the region.[55] The Temporary Committees now assumed the task themselves, and after several months of laboured discussion and consultations a new draft Statute was published, substantially the same as that rejected by Navarre but restricted to the three Basque provinces proper. On 6 August 1933 it was accepted by an assembly of the region's local councils and in November was submitted to a plebiscite. Needing a two-thirds majority of the electorate, it was approved overwhelmingly in Guipúzcoa and Vizcaya, but in Álava, where Carlism was strongest, only forty-six per cent of the voters supported it.[56] Yet again the campaign stuttered to a halt.

Prior to both the assembly and the plebiscite the Carlist juntas met but failed to give a clear lead to their followers.[57] Their ambivalence and the Álava vote convinced most Basque Nationalists that the Carlists had sabotaged the autonomy campaign for the second time. By the end of 1933 mutual hostility between the Carlists and the PNV had reached a new peak, marked by vituperative editorials in the rival press and frequent street-fights between supporters. In Basque Nationalist eyes the Carlists had betrayed the *fueros*, whilst even those Basque Carlists who still felt the pull of autonomy had become convinced that the PNV had sold out to socialism. The breach was now irreparable.

Meanwhile, the Spanish right continued to put out new growth. During 1933 Alfonsism finally broke with Acción Popular to form its own organization. This was inevitable following the Acción Popular assembly of October 1932, which brought its internal conflicts into the open and made a formal split between accidentalists and diehard monarchists a mere matter of time. From the Alfonsists' point of view, departure from what was in the process of becoming the CEDA had its dangers, foremost among them the very real possibility that the great mass of 'silent' monarchists within Acción Popular might refuse to abandon accidentalism in order to join a new, Alfonsist party. Should this happen the Alfonsists' influence upon Catholic Spain was likely to atrophy as their party was crushed between the CEDA's numbers and Carlism's militancy. This fear was never far away during the winter of 1932–3 as Goicoechea, Sáinz Rodríguez and their colleagues went about forming an Alfonsist party and publicizing its programme, while simultaneously attempting to keep up links with Acción Popular and the Carlists through a 'Federation of the Right'.[58]

As the outlines of the new party's composition and ideology emerged, it became evident that several of its most prominent personalities, as they drew away from Gil Robles and Acción Popular, were moving correspondingly closer to the position of the Carlists. It was, in fact, at a Carlist meeting on 18 December 1932 that Goicoechea expounded both the fundamental principles of his nascent party and his plan for a permanent Federation of the Right embracing Alfonsism, Carlism and Acción Popular. Goicoechea's fervent praise for Traditionalism in general and the Communion in particular raised fleeting, if not very serious, hopes among Carlists that he and the other Alfonsist luminaries might even go so far as to throw in their lot with the Communion. Introducing Goicoechea, Rodezno claimed him as 'one of us' and described his non-membership of the Communion as 'accidental'. The Carlist press received Goicoechea's address warmly: it could now almost be stated, announced *El Pensamiento Navarro*, that the ex-Maurist minister of Alfonso XIII was 'in the ranks of the Traditionalist Communion'.[59] *El Siglo Futuro* wisely had more reservations, centring mainly around Goicoechea's emphasis upon the 1876 Constitution and his admittedly somewhat ambiguous use of the word 'democracy', but was just as effusive in its welcome of what appeared to be a neo-Traditionalist orientation on the part of Alfonsism.[60]

On 11 January 1933, the same day that Goicoechea at last announced his long-awaited rupture with Acción Popular,[61] there appeared in the right-wing press a letter of support for the Alfonsist leader signed by most of the like-minded Alfonsists and a handful of Carlists, notably the Valencian Cárcer, calling for a 'restoration of the eternal values of the Spanish spirit, realized through a total renewal [*renovación*] of the structure of the State'.[62] Goicoechea's reply sketched the bases of the party he was already organizing: 'In the religious sphere, we are Catholics; in the political sphere, monarchists; in the juridical sphere, constitutionalists and legalists; and in the social sphere, democrats.'[63] Alfonso XIII promptly gave his approval to the party's creation, and by the end of January, under the name Renovación Española, it was a reality.[64]

Although it had soon become clear that Goicoechea's new-found zeal for Traditionalism stopped short of his actually crossing over to the Communion, he continued to express his admiration for Carlism and official relations between the two organizations were close and friendly from the outset. Along with preaching a brand of monarchism which owed much to Carlism and also to fashionable foreign right-wing ideas such as those of Italian Fascism, Action Française and Portuguese Integralism,[65] Goicoechea and his chief propagandists – the poet and playwright José María Pemán, Sáinz Rodríguez and Cirilo Tornos – made much of the 'Federation' idea. At first they hoped for an umbrella organization stretching from Acción Popular rightwards, in which permanence and some form of overall, 'federal' control would be combined with a considerable degree of autonomy for each constituent element. However, any prospect of such a federation was dashed by Gil Robles even before Renovación Española came into existence. As he later wrote, 'federation' amounted to a return to the early days of Acción Nacional, and if realized would have rendered stillborn the efficient, modern party organization which he and Lucía were busy creating. This in turn would have made more difficult, if not indeed impossible, the right's achievement of power by parliamentary means.[66] Gil Robles was perfectly right. The Alfonsists were no more committed to parliamentarism now than in August 1932; despite Renovación Española's political trappings, its founders were chiefly concerned with erecting a façade behind which conspiracies could be hatched and a climate of violence created which would help to discredit the Republic.[67]

Rebuffed by Gil Robles, the notables of Renovación Española stepped up their wooing of the Carlists. Pemán, after the now-ritualistic paean of praise for Traditionalism, unleashed a new scheme in the columns of *El Siglo Futuro* – a federation of monarchists quite distinct from the accidentalist right with which it might still co-operate at elections.[68] This plan also fell upon stony ground, for both Rodezno and Lamamié lost no time in stating that now the Alfonsists had formed their own party, union between it and the Communion could exist only 'for activities relating to concrete and determined ends' – specifically elections.[69] All roads to 'federation' were thus closed to the Alfonsists, who found themselves stranded in a painfully difficult position. Their monarchism made continued membership of Acción Popular impossible, while their loyalty towards Alfonso XIII obstructed an otherwise not unattractive merger with Carlism. This necessitated their founding a separate Alfonsist party, an act which made 'federation' the only alternative to isolation and simultaneously rendered it unattainable owing to the other parties' fear of losing their identity. The Carlists had everything to lose through joining forces with Renovación. In comparison with the new party Carlism possessed tradition, numbers and ideological coherence, with the result that any blurring of the distinctions between the Communion and the tiny, ideologically more eclectic Renovación could only benefit the latter.

The early weeks of Renovación Española were not, therefore, very successful ones. Even allowing for its leaders' primary concern with conspiracy, there was no question that they also hoped for a mass exodus from Acción Popular of those who remained Alfonsist monarchists at heart – a very considerable proportion, as Gil Robles later acknowledged.[70] This failed to materialize. Any slight possibility of its occurring vanished when Gil Robles himself visited Alfonso and managed to persuade the exiled king to resist the desperate entreaties of his supporters that he declare membership of the CEDA incompatible with monarchism.[71] Alfonsist hopes of wooing away either long-standing or recently converted Carlists were as unrealistic as those of drawing off the CEDA's masses. Renovación Española was therefore forced, since neither the CEDA nor the Carlists were prepared to boost its numbers and prestige through a closer association, to soldier on alone as a splinter-group of the Spanish right and, before long, the paymaster of Spanish fascism.

Less intimate and permanent association was perfectly possible, however. Joint meetings of leading members of the two monarchist parties were held in February 1933, and in March they set up an electoral office known as TYRE (Tradicionalistas y Renovación Española), which functioned in the elections of April and November.[72] Speakers offered nothing but mutual praise – a fact especially gratifying to the Carlists, whose historic position now appeared vindicated and who accordingly felt able to respond to Alfonsist encomia with more than a hint of the kind of condescension to which they themselves had become accustomed over the years.[73]

Despite this public *bonhomie*, not all Carlists were happy to see their cause apparently moving towards a position of peaceful coexistence with Alfonsism. The foundation of Renovación Española and the close relations between its leaders and members of Rodezno's Junta injected new life into the groundswell of discontent of which *El Cruzado Español*'s protestations were merely the most open expression. However much hard sense the notion of a permanently or loosely united monarchism, capable of challenging the CEDA, might make, it nonetheless grated upon the sensibilities of an indeterminable but certainly large number of Carlists, whose dissatisfaction with Rodezno's leadership began to surface during the second half of 1933.[74] Before that, the *cruzadistas'* dissent came to a head. On 9 March, their chief spokesmen met Alfonso Carlos and left after a lengthy discussion confident of having won him over to their arguments. These were that the Alfonsist family must be permanently excluded from the succession; that leaving the choice of an heir to 'Traditionalist Cortes' was dependent upon a far from certain – or imminent – Carlist triumph; and that therefore an assembly of Carlist notables should be summoned to decide the succession once and for all.[75] Their hopes were disappointed, for a few days later, having succumbed once more to the advice of Rafael Olazábal and Gómez Pujadas, Alfonso Carlos issued a final demand for obedience. When it went unheeded, the *cruzadistas* stood expelled from the Communion.[76] The Pretender's sternness brought results, however, for the great mass of unsettled Carlists who sympathized to a greater or lesser degree with the *cruzadistas* were sufficiently cowed to fall into line. Beneath the surface, unrest went on simmering; the veteran Larramendi spoke for this feeling in July 1933 when he claimed that the only true supporters of a *rapprochement* with the Alfonsist usurpers were the members of the National Junta themselves.[77]

Revulsion against Rodezno's policy was emotional rather than rational, for despite Carlist suspicions that it was the Alfonsists who were gaining most from close monarchist relations, the establishment of Renovación was actually no bad thing for Carlism.

Although the new party was well financed and possessed prestigious individuals, its lack of popular support merely served to highlight the extent to which monarchist Traditionalism was the preserve of the Communion, which looked vast in comparison. If the CEDA's strength was immediately discouraging for the Carlists, the lack of serious competition from Renovación at least raised the possibility that a failure of the CEDA's tactic might unleash a reaction in their favour. Over this comforting scenario, however, there loomed a dark cloud: the prospect that even were such a reaction to occur, the beneficiary might not be Carlism but fascism.

The assortment of fascist and quasi-fascist groups, all of them insignificant in size, which had blossomed in Spain since Primo de Rivera's fall had been treated by the Carlists with indifference. Foreign fascism was little discussed in the Carlist press before 1933 – in contrast with *El Debate*, which painted it in glowing colours – and considered to have little or no relevance for a country blessed with Carlism. When Carlist commentators used the term 'fascist' in relation to Spanish politics, it was more often to blacken what they regarded as the *étatiste* authoritarianism of the Republican leaders than to describe any group or individual on the political right; in *El Pensamiento Navarro*, for example, a regular columnist wrote in 1932 that Spain was living under a 'fascist' tyranny 'more hypocritical and less gallant' than that of Mussolini.[78]

The one small, radical right-wing party which did attract a measure of both attention and sympathy from the Carlists was the monarchist Partido Nacionalista Español, founded in 1930 by an eccentric, stentorian-toned neurologist, Dr Albiñana. Largely confined to Burgos, where Carlist strength was sufficient to explain this attention, the PNE's 'style' was undeniably fascist, but its leader's ideas inclined more towards a Traditionalism of an officially Alfonsist yet at the same time somewhat personalist character. 'The PNE,' Albiñana proclaimed, 'has no other base than the very broad one of Tradition',[79] and its political and social programmes, if lacking in explicitness, closely resembled those of Carlism. Although the recipient of a disproportionate amount of publicity, the PNE attracted neither financial nor popular support. Albiñana himself was arrested for sedition in 1932, and in 1933 was exiled to the remote and desolate region of Las Hurdes. The Communion, Renovación Española and elements within Acción Popular agitated for his release, but without success.[80]

The activities during 1931 and 1932 of the real founding fathers of Spanish fascism, Ramiro Ledesma Ramos and Onésimo Redondo, were almost totally ignored by the Carlists, perhaps because they were concentrated in two cities – Madrid and Valladolid respectively – where Carlism was weak. Ledesma, a post-office clerk and student of German philosophy, was the moving spirit behind *La Conquista del Estado*, a financially insecure weekly which appeared for six months in 1931. Although Ledesma paid tribute to Carlism, Spanish Traditionalism contributed only marginally to a promiscuous radicalism more obviously influenced by contemporary European fascism and Spanish Anarcho-Syndicalism. Redondo, a former propagandist of Catholic Action and an admirer of Nazism since spending a year in Germany in 1928, formed in August 1931 a minuscule political organization, the Juntas Castellanas de Actuación Hispánica (Castilian Groups for Hispanic Action), the purpose of which was to employ fascist means in order to bring about a Spain Catholic, traditional and characterized by peasant proprietorship and corporative organization – a vision much closer to Carlism's than that of Ledesma. In autumn 1931 the two came together to form the Juntas de Ofensiva Nacional Sindicàlista (JONS), an ideologically confused movement which by the beginning of 1933 had made a negligible impact upon Spanish politics.[81]

The vital boost to Spanish fascism came from abroad. Hitler's appointment to the Chancellorship of Germany at the end of January 1933 was the cue for six weeks of excited discussion of 'fascism' in the Spanish press, culminating on 16 March in the publication of a weekly, *El Fascio*. This was the brainchild of Manuel Delgado Barreto, editor of the *primoderriverista* daily *La Nación*; among those invited to collaborate in the venture were Ledesma and the JONS-ists, a verbose nationalist intellectual, Giménez Caballero, and the late dictator's son, José Antonio Primo de Rivera.[82] *El Fascio* was advertised early in March throughout the right-wing press, and from this point on 'fascism' became a major preoccupation of the Carlists.

Their reactions to announcements of *El Fascio*'s forthcoming appearance closely foreshadowed the complex of attitudes which was later to be adopted towards the far more serious Falange. Since *El Fascio*'s declared targets were more or less the same as Carlism's – marxism, liberal democracy, freemasonry, Jewry, in short all the ideals and interests allegedly enshrined in the Republic – a direct attack upon the new weekly would obviously have been imprudent. On the other hand the Carlists dared not risk ceding to the handful of Spanish fascists the leadership of the extreme right-wing assault on the Republic, especially since there were elements in the fascist *credo* with which they honestly and profoundly disagreed. Early commentators therefore tended to argue that while *El Fascio*'s publication was a healthy symptom of anti-Republican reaction, much of its apparent programme was either wrongheaded or superfluous. *Reacción*, for example, complained that the attempt to create a Spanish fascism artificially would merely divide the forces of anti-marxism; anyone looking for a Spanish *caudillo*, it went on, need look no further than Alfonso Carlos.[83] *La Unión* took a different line, arguing that Spanish fascism lacked tradition, mass support 'and a leader, not because he does not exist, but because he is confined in Las Hurdes'.[84] In other words the PNE, itself a colourful irrelevance, was the Spanish version of fascism, and all further experiments were a waste of time. Other Carlists were less concerned with finding somewhere to pin the fascist label and more with isolating its attractions and disadvantages. The commonest view was that expressed by the veteran Jaime Chicharro: fascism in a general sense was '*simpático*' but its deification of the state was unacceptable.[85]

The left in general and the Republican authorities in particular were uninterested in the nicer distinctions of right-wing ideology. When the day of *El Fascio*'s appearance arrived, copies were promptly confiscated, and among the political centres raided and searched – in this case unsuccessfully – for stray copies was the Madrid headquarters of the Carlist Youth. In Oviedo left-wing youths set upon Carlists with cries of 'Fascists!', a taunt indignantly rejected by the city's Carlist Youth.[86] The left, understandably enough, saw little difference, and there can be little doubt that the increase in the incidence of violence between Carlists and leftists had a great deal to do with the latter's identification of Carlism – and the rest of the right – with the 'fascism' which was crushing the left elsewhere in Europe.[87]

The suppression of *El Fascio* did nothing to inhibit the gradual emergence of a Spanish fascism during the summer of 1933. The initiative in its promotion was now grasped by the idealistic, intellectual José Antonio Primo de Rivera. Together with the aviator Julio Ruiz de Alda, and with the backing of right-wing financial interests, he began to plan the formation of a new fascist movement which would win greater success than the JONS. By now even the latter was showing signs of life; during June and July 'national syndicalist' pamphlets were widely circulated in Madrid, and between 19 and 22 July the Security Section, under pressure from the Socialists, arrested hundreds of alleged fascists in order to forestall what was variously described as a 'fascist–communist', 'fascist–syndicalist' or just plain 'fascist' plot against the Republic. Numerous Carlists, especially in Madrid, Seville and Jerez, were among those detained, and several Carlist centres closed, in a swoop affecting organizations from all parts of the political spectrum.[88]

The Carlists were outraged at being accused of conspiring with fascism, which they claimed barely existed in any case. *El Pensamiento Navarro* believed the whole affair to be a concoction of international masonry; fascism, it declared, was non-existent in Spain and 'nobody speaks of it save those who have seen in foreign fascism a threat to their doctrines and their bastard interests' – a comment unthinkingly applicable to the endless discussion of fascism by Carlists since the previous spring.[89] If the government's move against the supposed plot achieved nothing else, it served to guarantee the germinal fascist movement far greater sympathy from the Carlists than might otherwise have been the case. Nothing, Fal Conde protested, justified the government's 'brutal' treatment of the fascists.[90] He was proved correct, for within a fortnight the police had convinced themselves that no plot had ever existed, and the various suspects were released.

In August José Antonio and Ruiz de Alda completed their plans, in spite of being disappointed in an effort to incorporate the JONS in their movement. The dissolution of the Cortes in October created a suitable air of crisis amid which to launch it. The Falange Española was born at the Teatro Comedia in Madrid on 29 October. On the platform were José Antonio, Ruiz de Alda and the leader of the tiny, allied Frente Español, Alfonso García Valdecasas; prominent in the audience, besides Ledesma and the JONS, were the AET of Madrid and numerous other interested Carlists.[91] With a hectic election campaign in full swing, however, the Carlist press gave the occasion only the most formal coverage and, perhaps calculatedly, withheld all comment.

The possibility of introducing fascism into Spain was regarded with considerably more enthusiasm by the leaders of Renovación Española, still searching anxiously for an identity. In September

Goicoechea, advocating a united right yet again, stated his position with characteristic lack of precision: 'That of a Traditionalist? That of a fascist? Something of both – why deny it?'[92] The following month he visited Germany as a guest of Von Papen, and returned to Spain dazzled by the personality and achievements of Hitler, 'a really superior man, a true political genius', and sanguine as to the feasibility of adapting fascism to the needs of Spain.[93]

There can be little doubt, even though it cannot be proved, that the CEDA, and to a much lesser extent Renovación Española and the young fascist movement, attracted support which might otherwise have gone to Carlism. Yet this did not mean that the Carlist revival which had begun in 1931 was appreciably stayed. Far from it: the first half of 1933 produced evidence that the expansion so apparent in the months before the Sanjurjada was again under way, with news of a wide variety of Carlist activities and the formation of new local organizations, not only in traditional strongholds of the north and east but also in areas of longstanding weakness such as Galicia, Cuenca, Huelva and Ávila.[94] Proof of this advance came with the local elections in April. Of the 5,000 seats won by Catholic and monarchist candidates, Carlists took between 1,000 and 1,300; and even though the majority of these were in Navarre and Álava, where the Communion's success was sweeping, and in Vizcaya and Guipúzcoa, where in general it ran second to the PNV, substantial numbers of Carlist councillors were also elected within Catholic coalitions in Burgos, Logroño, Castellón and Salamanca, and smaller minorities in all but five of the remaining provinces.[95] Carlism still demonstrably lagged behind the CEDA, but by the spring of 1933 it had at least staked its claim as a national movement.

Along with increased numbers went greater militancy and diminished discretion. This was spontaneous rather than officially sponsored, and was understandably concentrated among the Communion's younger elements. When the Madrid headquarters of the Carlist Youth were raided by the police in April 1933, weapons were uncovered for the first time and fifty members detained;[96] in Madrid, Seville and elsewhere, AET members led their fellow-Catholics in fights with Republican and left-wing students.[97] On other occasions it was the left, irritated by the sight of flourishing Carlist centres and successful public meetings, which initiated the attacks against 'fascists'. In June 1933 Carlists leaving a meeting in Zaragoza were assaulted by groups of Anarchists, and a few days later in Fuencarral, north of Madrid, a similar attack was launched against the Carlist circle and the cars and persons of its members.[98] All public demonstrations of Carlist faith had their dangers, evidently, yet they were generally recognized to be vital in disseminating doctrine to new converts and inspiring a euphoric sense of strength through numbers.

The most dramatic developments within the Communion continued to take place in Fal Conde's fief of western Andalusia. Here the aftermath of 10 August was marked by a phase of exceptionally rapid growth, as the zealous young Carlists of Seville and the other provincial capitals exploited the paralysis of the rest of the right in order to found local organizations in several towns and villages where Carlism was at most a faint folk-memory of sporadic nineteenth-century banditry. Much of this success derived from the simple fact of being first in the field, converts coming mainly from sectors of the population which were predictable and elsewhere flocked to the CEDA – the Catholic middle class and the modest landowners threatened by the Agrarian Reform.[99] Not infrequently these were combined in the same individuals, since most of the proprietors concerned – owners of *ruedo* land situated close to towns and villages – lived in the towns. Carlist proselytization in this quarter was soon overtaken by the slower-starting Andalusian CEDA, but as far as can be discerned early converts stayed loyal.

A distinctive feature of Andalusian Carlism as it developed during 1933, and one which gave rise to organizational innovation, was the impact made by its young propagandists upon other Catholics of their generation; so great was this that in many districts of Andalusia Carlism was exclusively a youth movement.[100] Fal Conde soon became convinced of the need for formal links between the local Youth sections in his region, and in April 1933 instituted a federation of Western Andalusian Youth groups for the purpose of maintaining contacts and facilitating central control over further expansion.[101] This attempt partially to remove local Youth Sections from the control of local juntas was a complete novelty in the Communion. Its success demonstrated Fal Conde's gift for organizational innovation and efficiency, and offered a foretaste of the manner in which the entire Carlist movement would be overhauled between 1934 and 1936.

Seville was the scene of another ambitious initiative, namely the establishment of a branch of the Communion specifically aimed at

the urban working class. This was a reflection of the relative sensi-
tivity to social issues which existed among Carlists in Seville, and in
Andalusia generally; awareness of the acute unemployment in the
region, not to mention the constant threat of working-class violence,
inevitably forced Carlists to adopt a more 'social' posture than in the
more stable, predominantly rural areas where the movement was
traditionally strongest. Furthermore, the combination of unemployment and interunion rivalry between the more or less evenly balanced
UGT and CNT rendered the Catholic minority of the Seville
working class particularly susceptible to the blandishments of the
first Catholic party actively to seek its support. That party was
Carlism.[102] The encouraging trickle of what were described as
'workers' joining the local circle early in 1933 persuaded Fal Conde
and the Regional Junta to found a Workers Section which predated
its CEDA equivalent by several months.[103] Most of the actual impetus behind the formation and subsequent operation of the Workers
Section came from a genuine member of the working class, Ginés
Martínez, a railwayman who emerged in 1933 as an unusually
effective orator, propagandist and organizer, and who became president of the Section in July. His organization sought to train
working-class propagandists in the cause of further recruitment, to
furnish labour-exchange facilities for unemployed Catholic workers
as well as various forms of accident and unemployment insurance,
and to nurture within its bosom a rudimentary guild system which
it was hoped would be the germ of Spanish society's reconstruction
and future organization.[104]

In view of the limited number of Catholic workers in and around
Seville, the Workers Section scored a striking success. At the end
of May, Fal Conde, who unlike many leading Carlists was not given
to exaggerating Carlist numbers, announced that it had already
enlisted over 1,000 members,[105] and by August *El Observador*
reported a still-rising membership of 3,000 even though the Section's
work-finding facilities had been closed for some weeks.[106] Hopes of
a breakthrough into the working class indicated that some Andalusian Carlists, at least, grasped the fact that Carlism, like so many
movements of the extreme right, possessed little credibility as a
movement above class as long as it remained the almost exclusive preserve of Catholic bourgeois, small farmers, and a handful of businessmen and latifundists. Yet despite their justified self-congratulation,
the Sevillian Carlists' achievement in attracting the city's workers

was less of a triumph than they liked to believe, and on close examination only underlined the limitations of Carlism's social base. For
recruitment was almost wholly from among insecure artisans and
employees in small concerns, rather than the genuine local proletariat of factory and dock workers. The political conversion of
devout Catholics, especially with jobs as an inducement, was one
thing; the religious *and* political conversion of marxists and Anarcho-
Syndicalists was quite another, and as remote a prospect as it had
ever been. To the majority of Carlists, however, the Workers Section
of Seville was the source of nothing but encouragement, and evidence
yet again of Fal Conde's magic touch.

By this time, in fact, Fal Conde's organizational accomplishments
in western Andalusia were attracting attention and praise from all
sections of the Communion. In March 1933 *El Siglo Futuro* hailed
him as 'a man in whom we rest many hopes, a person of great initiative, crowned with positive successes, a new man of great political judgment'.[107] Two months later it published an interview in
which Fal Conde gave a detailed account of the strength of the
Seville organization.[108] An increasing number of northern Carlists
began to visit Seville and invariably went home impressed, but it
was not until June 1933 that Fal Conde returned their visits when
he led a party of Sevillian Carlists to a rally – in the event banned –
in Zumárraga. For Fal Conde this was a welcome opportunity to
visit Pamplona and meet many prominent northerners for the first
time, as well as to accept a recent royal invitation and cross the
frontier for his first, highly successful interview with Alfonso
Carlos.[109] Fal Conde's was clearly a rising star in the Carlist
firmament.

5

A young man to lead the young

With the right reviving, the Socialists moving away from their former Republican allies, and the Radicals manoeuvring for power, the feeling was general by the summer of 1933 that the era of Azaña's dominance over Spanish politics was nearing its end. The government actually fell in early June, but the delight of the Carlists and Azaña's other critics was cut short by his immediate return at the head of a reshuffled, clearly caretaker cabinet. The Carlists called repeatedly for a general election, and somewhat self-righteously taunted the Republican parties with reluctance to submit themselves to the 'popular will'. These accusations were not unfounded, given the electoral potential of the CEDA and the poor prospects of the Left Republicans should the Socialists, as seemed likely, choose to sever the 1931 alliance.

The *coup de grâce* for Azaña came from an unexpected quarter. In September the first elections took place to the Court of Constitutional Guarantees, the Republic's supreme court which would consider the constitutionality of all legislation passed subsequent to its formation.[1] The contest, which involved the election of fifteen members and alternates by municipal councillors voting in large, regionwide constituencies, aroused little public interest. The Carlists mixed apathy with scorn. '[it is] a body of picturesque activity,' *El Siglo Futuro* sneered, 'and Spaniards know what kind of guarantees it is going to guarantee them.'[2] As in the April local elections, however, Carlist advocates of boycott like Fernando Contreras were overruled in the interests of defending religion and property; candidates were presented in Navarre and the Basque region, the two constituencies where Carlist strength in local government offered hope of success.

The outcome was another disaster for the government and the left. Only five of the fifteen members elected were governmentalists, the other ten consisting of four Radicals, three 'Agrarians', one independent Republican, one Basque Nationalist and one Carlist. This

was Pradera, who won over three-quarters of the votes cast in
Navarre. In the Basque region the Carlist candidature polled almost
a third of the votes and ran a respectable second to the PNV, winning
an overall majority in Álava.[3]

In the light of this defeat, Azaña had no choice but to resign,
and at long last the sixty-nine-year-old Lerroux was called upon
to form a government. The Carlists rejoiced at the departure of
Azaña and his lieutenant Casares Quiroga, described by *El Pensamiento Navarro* as 'these two wicked, vain, inhuman and cruel men'.[4]
They were confident that the 'tyrant' Azaña was finished politically,
but just to make sure *Reacción* advocated a propaganda campaign
to prevent his staging a comeback:

Inculcate children, write on walls, repeat whenever possible what for
a great majority of Spaniards must constitute a sacred and unshakable
oath — AZANA — NEVER![5]

The apparent shift to the right embodied in Lerroux's assumption
of the premiership was nevertheless considered no cause for celebration. Throughout the year the Carlists had viewed the increasingly likely prospect of a Lerroux ministry with undisguised gloom.
True, *El Pensamiento Navarro* had assured its readers that Lerroux,
who over the previous thirty years had evolved from an early career
as an anti-clerical mob orator, through a phase as the monarchy's
'pet' Republican to his present eminence as the great white hope of
Spanish conservatives, had no future in politics. 'He is too old for the
barricades now,' it added unkindly.[6] Not all Carlists were so sure;
Fal Conde expressed a commonly held view in arguing that
'sensible people' could place no trust in the sometime *caudillo* of
the Barcelona crowd.[7] Now the Andalusian leader warned that the
new, predominantly Radical and Radical–Socialist cabinet was
'revolutionary and sectarian' and Lerroux's appearance of respectability nothing but 'senile vanity' which must not be allowed to
mislead conservatives into thinking him one of them.[8]

In the excited pre-election atmosphere now gripping the
Spanish political world, no government could be expected to last
for long. In fact Lerroux survived a mere month, to be replaced after
a week-long cabinet crisis by another Radical, the Sevillian and
leading freemason Martínez Barrio, at the head of an interim government pending a general election. The Carlists reacted with predictable cynicism to the elevation of the 'Grand Master of Spanish

Masonry' and with mixed emotions to the resumption of the electoral 'farce'.[9] In principle they remained as hostile as ever towards parliamentarism and electioneering, but on this occasion optimism as to the right's chances caused such reservations to be swept aside in an unprecedented wave of election fever. The press and the new National Junta, still headed by Rodezno, readily accepted the obligation, forced on them by the Communion's role in the Cortes opposition, to participate wholeheartedly in the election alongside the rest of the Catholic right. The 'Spanish crisis,' they maintained, would never be solved by 'inorganic suffrage', yet all available means must be seized when the Church and the spirit of Spain were under attack.[10]

'Union of the right', an accomplished fact since the local elections, now sprang into life again. Lists of candidates, many containing Carlists, began to take shape at constituency level,[11] and very soon overall co-ordination of the process was imposed through the creation of a national committee based upon the conveniently multiparty Agrarian minority. The Carlists' representative on the committee was Lamamié.[12] The composition of the lists approved by the committee broadly reflected the relative strength of the various provincial parties and the temperature of their mutual relations. In Navarre and the Basque provinces, with the CEDA a negligible force and the PNV opting to go it alone, the Carlists as the largest right-wing group provided most of the candidates.[13] In Castellón, Cádiz, Seville, Valencia and Zaragoza, Carlist strength was sufficient and relations with the CEDA warm enough to ensure two places in the right-wing list,[14] while in ten more provinces (Alicante, Burgos, Corunna, Lérida, Logroño, Madrid-Province, Málaga, Salamanca, Santander and Tarragona) the Communion was allotted one place.[15]

Complications ensued from the CEDA's desire for electoral pacts with opposition Republicans. In Córdoba, Granada and Jaén, the Carlist leadership refused to join such alliances, but urged the rank and file to support the CEDA candidates.[16] CEDA pressure caused the dropping of briefly floated Carlist candidacies in, for example, Almería, Ávila and Orense,[17] and in Burgos, where one seat fewer was at stake than in 1931, it forced the exclusion of Gómez Rojí from the official list. Gómez Rojí, deeply hurt, then joined Albiñana in an extreme right-wing attempt to win the province's two minority seats.[18] Carlist relations with the Lliga continued to be mixed, and in Gerona and Barcelona-Province independent

Carlist candidacies were launched in opposition both to the Lliga and the Catalan left.[19] The final total of Carlist candidates was thirty-nine.[20]

Besides regulating lists of candidates, the right's national committee drafted a common programme which served as the basis for the campaigns of all the right-wing parties. It uttered no call for violence, made no mention of restoring or 'installing' the monarchy, but was nonetheless threatening enough to alarm Left Republicans and Socialists. Bemoaning the anti-clericalism, economic difficulties and social unrest of two years of 'socialism', it called in the name of anti-marxism and anti-masonry for a political amnesty, the defence of the national economy and of agrarian interests in particular, the repeal of laic and socialistic legislation, the reimposition of order and the revision of the Constitution. In social, economic and religious terms, this could only mean a return to the old regime.[21] The right's political intentions were less explicit, yet the columns of *El Debate* and Gil Robles' inflammatory campaign speeches left little doubt that the CEDA, its dominant element, was bent upon establishing some form of authoritarian, corporative system. As a minimum programme this satisfied the Carlists admirably. Their own campaign, far overshadowed by the scale and professionalism of the CEDA's, followed essentially similar lines.[22] As always, Carlist candidates and orators expressed complete lack of faith in the political usefulness of parliamentary institutions, even if controlled by the right, while reiterating that it was the duty of Catholics to vote in the hope, however slender, of defending the Church.[23] Optimism reigned regarding the result, not least because the women's vote, operating for the first time, was expected to help the right.[24] Caught up in this mood, Lamamié predicted the election of between 140 and 150 right-wing deputies including 40–50 avowed monarchists.[25]

The election of November–December 1933, thanks largely to the left's disunity, the abstention of the CNT's members and the effect of female suffrage, brought defeat to the main governing parties of 1931–3 and effective victory to the Radicals and the right. In the Cortes the largest party would be the CEDA with some 115 seats, closely followed by the Radicals with 104. Lamamié's prediction came remarkably close to realization. Thirty-six confessed monarchists were elected, of whom 21 were Carlists and 15 adherents of Renovación Española; in addition, there were ten or a dozen independents who were later to attach themselves loosely to the monarchist forces. Of the Carlist deputies, the four Navarrese and Oriol in Álava were elected as comfortably as expected, but only one, Oreja, was returned from the coastal Basque provinces. In Guipúzcoa, Antonio Pagoaga would probably have been elected had the sole Alfonsist in the right-wing list been anyone but the famous writer Maeztu, who squeezed ahead of him by a mere 70 votes.[26] Three more constituencies – Cádiz, Seville and Zaragoza – returned two Carlists each, while Logroño, Burgos, Salamanca, Santander, Lérida, Tarragona, Castellón, Valencia and Madrid-Province returned one each.[27] There could be no real doubt that most of the Carlist successes outside the Basque–Navarrese region were due to alliances with less extreme parties. In several constituencies successful Carlist candidates trailed their allies sufficiently to suggest that running alone they would have lost; in others the difference was enough actually to produce defeat where moderate rightists were elected. Where, as in Barcelona-Province and Gerona, Carlists ran alone, defeat was humiliating.[28] Reasonably enough, the Carlists themselves chose to gloss over the less encouraging aspects of the results, concentrating instead upon the undeniable fact that they had achieved, by whatever means, their largest parliamentary representation since 1873.

The newly elected deputies vividly illustrated both the changes undergone by Carlism during the previous two years and its enduring characteristics.[29] The sharpest contrast with the Constituent Cortes was provided by the recent injection of youth into the Communion. Fifteen of the twenty-one deputies were totally new to parliamentary life. None of these was past early middle age, with several – for example Joaquín Bau (Tarragona), Cárcer (Valencia-City), Ginés Martínez (Seville-City) and Ramírez Sinués (Zaragoza) in their thirties and two – Luis Arellano (Navarre) and José Luis Zamanillo (Santander) – in their twenties. Also reflected was the unchanging middle-class predominance in the Communion's leading echelons. Bau and Martínez Pinillos (Cádiz) stood out as wealthy businessmen, Juan Granell (Castellón) was a successful engineer, and Juan José Palomino (Cádiz) a producer and exporter of sherry. Palomino had also just purchased a newspaper, the *Diario de Jerez*, thus complementing *La Unión* of Seville which was run by another new deputy, the professional journalist and fanatical scourge of the freemasons Domingo Tejera (Seville-Province). Seven new deputies were qualified lawyers; one of these, Jesús Comín (Zaragoza), occupied a chair in Law at the University of Zaragoza, and another, Martínez Morentín (Navarre) was also a landowner and pillar of Navarrese social-Catholicism. In general, however, direct interest in the land was rather less typical of the new deputies than of those who had sat in the Constituent Cortes.

The lone deputy not of the prosperous middle class or lesser aristocracy was Ginés Martínez, who for this very reason received the most publicity. His rugged, roughly dressed figure was held to testify to Carlism's concern for the working class, and in the press he was commonly described with affection as 'our railwayman deputy'. His impact upon the Cortes of 1933–5 was nevertheless to be slight. It was not Ginés Martínez, the proletarian hammer of the selfish capitalist, who came to speak as the most authentic parliamentary voice of Carlism, but Lamamié, the last-ditch defender of property.

The right's electoral success convinced the Carlists that continued unity in the new Cortes was both logical and morally imperative.[30] Ideally this ought to be embodied in a monarchist-supported CEDA government, dedicated to immediate constitutional revision and the eventual installation of the Traditional Monarchy; if this was asking too much, then a more realistic vision was that of a united Catholic opposition. It quickly became plain, however, that the CEDA's leaders, ambivalent as ever towards the Republic, could scarcely wait to wriggle free from all formal ties with the monarchist parties. Their electoral alliances with conservative Republicans, if in no way casting doubt upon their long-term objectives, had certainly suggested that their means of attaining them might be uncongenial to the Carlists. Between the principal and secondary rounds of the election, the CEDA's manoeuvring continued, and in two provinces, Alicante and Málaga, Carlist candidates were forced out of right-wing blocs in favour of a new alignment of *cedistas* and Radicals. Protests from both monarchist parties were ignored, and the ploy vindicated in CEDA eyes by its success.[31]

The CEDA's 'tactic' was now gathering momentum. As soon as the final results were known, negotiations began with Lerroux concerning possible parliamentary co-operation between the two parties,[32] and on 7 December the CEDA's council announced that since the moment was inopportune for a rightist government it would

support any 'centre' administration which committed itself to legislation 'rectifying' that of 1931–3.[33] The moment undeniably was
inopportune. The right, as Gil Robles realized, had not actually
won the election, and the CEDA's claim to office as the largest single
party was strong but not indisputable. Accidentalism, essential for
the CEDA's unity, bred Republican suspicions, compounded in the
crucial case of Alcalá Zamora by personal pique at Gil Robles' having
upstaged him as the political leader of 'moderate' Catholicism.
Political power was thus unlikely to come easily to the CEDA, and a
permanent monarchist alliance was guaranteed to postpone rather
than hasten it.

Ten days later Gil Robles unilaterally declared the Union of the
Right dissolved.[34] When Martínez Barrio resigned on 16 December,
the CEDA leader was among the political figures interviewed by
Alcalá Zamora, but the premier appointed was Lerroux. In his first
speech to the new Cortes, Gil Robles made clear the use to which his
party intended to put the Republic's machinery. He demanded a
drastic 'rectification' of the errors of the previous two years, including
a new Concordat, an amnesty which would apply, among others,
to those punished after the Sanjurjada, and the repeal or modification
of 'socialistic' legislation. The Constitution, he insisted, was quite
unworkable and must be revised.[35]

These indications that the CEDA's goals remained those upon
which it had fought the election did nothing to prevent an explosion
of Carlist indignation at their 'betrayal' by Gil Robles. Pradera
accused him of deceiving Catholic voters, and warned that in the
unlikely event of the CEDA's ever replacing the Radicals as ruling
party, it would have no allies left.[36] *El Siglo Futuro* likened the
'opportunism' of *El Debate*'s editorial board to that of the *afrancesados*
of the Bonapartist occupation:

> Under the present Republic they are Republicans; if Socialism triumphed
> they would be Socialists; if Bolshevism, Bolsheviks – and Traditionalists
> the moment Traditionalism triumphed, though that is what some of them
> fear most.[37]

The possibility that measurable 'rectification' might come from a
Radical government was scornfully dismissed. Fal Conde, recently
promoted Delegate for All Andalusia, contended quite correctly that
Lerroux was out to consolidate the Republic; in an open letter 'To
our friends of Acción Popular' he complained that by supporting

Lerroux, Gil Robles had cut himself off from his former allies, and that his was no way to defend religion and save Spain. Henceforth, Fal Conde concluded, enunciating for the first time a personal view which was to mature into a dogma, members of the various right-wing organizations had better stick within their own parties.[38]

The only significant absentee from this chorus of Carlist criticism was the movement's political head and parliamentarian-in-chief, Rodezno, who actually went so far as to remark in public that Pradera's attacks on the CEDA had been 'too violent'. Unlike most Carlists Rodezno was confident that the new Cortes would achieve 'some useful things' in the way of 'rectification', not only because of the CEDA's strength but also of the election of what he termed 'new, conciliatory Radicals' who might assist in repealing 'social-istic' legislation and at least halting the application of statutory anti-clericalism.[39] This indulgence towards the CEDA tactic was to prove short-lived, but while it lasted it served as yet further evidence of a difference of outlook between Rodezno and many of his fellow Carlists, few of whom shared his tactical flexibility – or, perhaps as important, his personal contacts with non-Carlist politicians.

Yet another rift in the right's ranks opened up in January 1934 when, amid renewed Carlist protestations, a majority of Martínez de Velasco's Agrarian Party – in effect the liberal rump of the Agrarian Bloc to which Lamamié, Estévanez and Gómez Rojí had once belonged – went a decisive step further than the CEDA and declared itself Republican.[40] But although such differences regarding long-term goals and attitudes towards the regime were both sincere and, on occasions, bitter, right-wing unity remained natural and inevitable where everyday political matters were concerned. Carlist, Alfonsist, CEDA and Agrarian deputies collaborated on parliamen-tary committees, in special bodies such as the social-Catholic *Grupo Social Parlamentario*,[41] and on the floor of the Cortes. If nothing else could have cemented the right, its obsession with public order would have done so, with a serious Anarchist rising throughout Aragon in December 1933, a general strike in Zaragoza in March 1934, and frequent student unrest in several universities. On this issue at least, the right stood squarely behind a government which, after the Radical hard-liner Salazar Alonso took over the Ministry of the Interior in March 1934, echoed its concern.

Right-wing solidarity was also possible on the three political issues which most preoccupied the Carlists during the first half of 1934:

the Basque Statute, the amnesty and the reversal of anti-clericalism. New discussions on Basque autonomy revolved around the question of how Álava's tepid performance in the plebiscite affected her place within the region and the very applicability of the Statute. The Carlist attitude was effectively determined by Oriol, who led a majority of Álava's local councils in announcing for the Cortes' benefit that they regarded the Statute as rejected by, and inoperable in, their province. This view, which was supported by Renovación Española, the CEDA and the Agrarians, implied the death of the Statute, which would be an absurdity if limited to the two coastal provinces.[42] The Basque Nationalists retorted that the Statute, having received a bare majority of the votes cast in Álava, ought to be taken as approved. In the Cortes Statute committee, and then in April 1934 on the floor of the Cortes, the Republican and Socialist majority overrode the mutually incompatible objections of the right and the PNV and recommended that the plebiscite be repeated in Álava.[43]

This decision, part compromise and part delaying tactic, was never to be acted upon. Even so, the public and parliamentary debate proved decisive in the political evolution of Basque Nationalism. Throughout the discussions, Carlist hostility towards the Statute and the PNV intensified. Pradera, as always the Basque Nationalists' harshest critic, damned the Statute as having been born with 'the original sin of being intruders' work' and the plebiscite as 'an electoral farce consistent with the doctrinal farce of [Basque] Nationalism'; as for the PNV itself, it had never possessed 'a single figure whose stature would merit so much as a Civil Governorship . . . they are all mediocrities, petty *politicos*, totally unknown provincials' – and racial *mestizos* into the bargain.[44] In the Cortes debate, the PNV and right-wing deputies spent as much time in insulting each other as they did in attacking the government, and the session ended amid a hysterical clamour of vilification. The Basque Nationalists, vowing never to re-enter the Cortes now that their autonomy had been snatched away yet again, shouted to the Esquerra deputies who had supported them in the debate: 'You are our friends now!'[45]

For the parliamentary right, Carlists included, the Basque autonomy question was much less important than the approval of an amnesty and the opening of a counter-attack upon the anti-clerical enactments of 1931–3. On these issues the monarchist parties combined to press Gil Robles to use his new influence with Lerroux, notwithstanding their open contempt for that CEDA support for the

Radicals without which their urgings would have been pointless. The outlines of the desired amnesty were drafted at the end of 1933 by Gil Robles, Martínez de Velasco, Goicoechea and Rodezno, and covered all prior activities against the form of government, civil and military sedition, strikes and printed offences.[46] Throughout January and February 1934 the monarchists mounted a noisy campaign for amnesty, boosted by AET-organized rallies in Madrid and Seville.[47] As the government vacillated, Carlist impatience rose to fever pitch; Rodezno joined Goicoechea in personally urging Gil Robles to hurry things up, and the Carlist deputies issued a press statement along similar lines.[48] In March the Amnesty Bill was finally published, in terms broadly acceptable to the entire right,[49] and passed the Cortes after a heated debate punctuated by scuffles between Carlists and Socialists during which Rodezno was hit by a flying water-glass.[50] In freeing all those still detained after the Sanjurjada, returning confiscated estates to grandee proprietors like Rodezno, and reinstating army officers such as Varela and the Villa Cisneros converts, it fully justified and explained the Carlists' sense of urgency. It also – though the Carlists were disinclined to admit it – constituted the first dramatic success for the CEDA's policy of attracting Radical support for right-wing measures.

The second success followed swiftly, with the passage on 4 April of a Clerical Property Act which committed the State to paying two-thirds of the clerical salary bill and returned all Church property confiscated since 1931. The Carlists greeted this virtual reversal of a central part of the Constituent Cortes' anti-clerical legislation with jubilation. 'We anti-parliamentarians are feeling pleased with ourselves,' Rodezno exulted, literally rubbing his hands in glee at this parliamentary triumph, paradoxically attainable only via the votes of the historically anti-clerical Radicals.[51]

When to this 'rectifying' legislation was added the repeal or suspension of laws fixing wages and setting conditions of employment, the removal of tenants' guarantees against wilful eviction, the indefinite postponement of the replacement of Church schools, and a cut in educational expenditure, the success of the CEDA tactic seemed plain – at least to its devotees. Support of a Radical administration had helped bring about a significant shift in the Republic's orientation. And although Lerroux's wish to bind Catholics to a 'moderate' Republic undoubtedly enabled him to put aside his past and his instincts in accepting the reversal of anti-clerical legislation, there was also no gainsaying that in both degree and kind the 'rectification' which had occurred owed less to Radical volition than to CEDA pressure. This in turn was sustained in part owing to pressure from the monarchists, who made it difficult for the CEDA to compromise. Thus, indirectly, the Carlists and Alfonsists helped to polarize the politics of Spain during the first half of 1934.

The Carlists' attitude towards the CEDA was nevertheless hardening, despite or possibly because of its tactical success. Little credit was given the CEDA for achieving 'rectification', which although vindicating Rodezno's mild optimism and far exceeding the gloomy prognostications of other Carlists, was now casually dismissed as barely scraping the surface of the Constituent Cortes' 'socialistic' legislation.[52] What genuinely worried the Carlists was the spirit underlying CEDA–Radical 'rectification'; to them it had to serve as the first step in a total dismantling of the Republic, not, as they claimed was actually happening, as part of a more general tactic of rendering the Republic respectable in the eyes of conservatives who might otherwise assist its overthrow. They had little faith in Gil Robles' much publicized three-stage plan whereby the CEDA was supposed to advance from its present position of support for a moderate Republican government to one of sharing power, and thence to the assumption of 'full power' and the revision of the Republic along corporative lines. They believed that even if Gil Robles were ever to win 'full power', he would have become too republicanized to use it in a manner acceptable to them; in any case, 'transigence' was less likely to bring power to the right than to permit the exploitation of the CEDA in the cause of consolidation of the Republic, which in turn implied the ultimate victory of the left.[53] Young Carlists were the most scathing; the militant students of Navarre declared themselves 'fed up with legality and politicking', alleging that while the CEDA was 'obsessed' with parliament the Socialists were abandoning it and working towards the creation of their state.[54]

As for Gil Robles himself, Carlists saw him as becoming increasingly and inevitably contaminated by his close contacts with Republicans. Howls of Carlist derision erupted when the CEDA saved Lerroux's government from collapse early in 1934,[55] and again when in April it voted confidence in a new Radical administration under the colourless Ricardo Samper. Lamamié scoffed that Gil Robles' hope of improving the Republic by supporting the Radicals was an unrealizable dream; one might just as well try, he went on, 'to wash a negro's face'.[56] According to Fal Conde's *El Observador*, participation had already turned Gil Robles into a party leader no different from the rest. In a clear warning to 'parliamentary Carlists', it continued by saying that were Rodezno to triumph as leader of the Communion within a democratic regime, he too would be corrupted by the experience.[57] As if to discount any such possibility, Rodezno himself now joined in the criticism: Gil Robles, he prophesied, would go the way of Alejandro Pidal and be swallowed by the system.[58]

Thus the Carlists happily accepted the legislative fruits of applied accidentalism while refusing to admit that accidentalism had made them possible. Such an attitude was unfair, but was an inevitable consequence of the Carlists' integralist view of their own role. For Carlism the only ultimate political success, at least in theory, was the installation of the total apparatus of the Carlist monarchy, and the only political achievements worthy of applause were those which brought this apocalyptic vision closer. All else, in greater or lesser degree, was failure. And if one thing was certain in the world of Spanish conservative politics, it was that the CEDA, with its essentially Alfonsist mass membership and its fascistic fringes, would never consecrate its efforts to the cause of Alfonso Carlos. If it succeeded by its own lights and presided over an Alfonsist restoration or the introduction of a corporative republic akin to that being set up in Austria by Dollfuss, this was hardly what the Carlists had in mind and might indeed postpone their own triumph indefinitely. On the other hand, if – as the Carlists thought far more likely – the CEDA failed completely or else was sucked into the Republic, then, they believed, the way would be open to a revitalized and perhaps radicalized left. Either way conviction and self-interest combined to convince a growing number of Carlists that their cause had more to gain from the CEDA's failure than from its success, a tendency reinforced by the Communion's own continued expansion and the advance of the more militant elements within it.

Cedistas were acutely irritated by Carlist criticism. In February the Seville CEDA daily, *El Correo de Andalucía*, complained of the anti-CEDA campaign being waged by *La Unión* and *El Observador*, a charge only half-heartedly denied by the latter.[59] Four months later *El Debate* protested against the 'unjust offensive' which it claimed the Carlists were conducting against Gil Robles.[60] Relations between the CEDA and the Carlists were rapidly cooling at all levels. Symptomatic of this was the sudden desire of local Carlist organizations to follow Fal Conde's advice and emphasize their complete independence of the CEDA. The Sevillian Carlists, for example, pulled out of the local Catholic women's association, Acción Ciudadana de la Mujer, and formed their own Women's Section, while in Málaga the Provincial Junta urged all monarchist members of the CEDA to repudiate their betrayers and become Carlists.[61] When in April 1934 the CEDA youth movement, the Juventud de Acción Popular (JAP), towards whose peculiar blend of neo-Traditionalist theory and fascistic posturing the Carlist attitude hovered between scorn and condescending approbation, held its first mass rally at El Escorial, the Carlist Youth brusquely refused an invitation to participate.[62]

Carlist criticism of the CEDA was echoed by leading Alfonsists, who were uncomfortably conscious of the fact that Renovación's embarrassingly scanty support was largely attributable to the unwillingness of monarchists to abandon the CEDA. Renovación was trapped inside a vicious circle: until Alfonso XIII ordered his followers to leave the CEDA, Renovación Española would remain a negligible popular force, yet it was this very weakness which made the king reluctant to take the step. In the spring of 1934, worried by new rumours that Alfonso was about to yield to Renovación's pleas and issue the order, Gil Robles sent the president of the JAP, José María Valiente, to ask the exiled monarch for a further six months' indulgence. Valiente discovered that the king nursed surprising faith in the CEDA's essential monarchism and in its prospects of success — and correspondingly little in what he rather ungratefully termed the 'drawing-room monarchists' of Renovación Española.[63]

Their hopes of taking over the CEDA's monarchist masses thus frustrated once more, Renovación's leaders were compelled to focus their efforts on the extreme right, with the goal of harnessing both Carlists and Falangists in the Alfonsist cause. Even though a deliberate attempt to turn the Falange — recently fused with the JONS — into a quasi-monarchist strong-arm squad was dashed in July 1934, Renovación continued to patronize it for several months more. Goicoechea and Sáinz Rodríguez kept José Antonio in touch with important sources of finance, and even drafted an agreement with him which if applied — it was not — would have curbed the Falange's anti-monarchist tendencies.[64] This marked the high point of Alfonsist–Falangist relations, which then cooled appreciably. When José Calvo Sotelo, the former finance minister of Primo de Rivera, returned to Spain as a result of the April amnesty, he immediately assumed a dominant position within Renovación Española and fixed his sights upon a takeover of the Falange. He actually went so far as to apply to join the Falange, only to be rebuffed by José Antonio, who besides having neither liking nor respect for someone whom he regarded as having betrayed his father the Dictator, fully realized that there simply was not room for the two of them in one small movement.[65] The gulf thus opened up between the Falange and the Alfonsists widened further when the wealthy, pro-Alfonsist Marqués de la Eliseda resigned from the Falange late in 1934 in protest against its lack of religiosity.[66] With the CEDA as well as the monarchist right offering corporativism without radicalism, the appeal of the still weakly Falange for Spanish conservatives began to diminish. From late 1934 its ties with Alfonsism were severed and it was left on its own, free from obligations but short of men and money. In addition to losing the monarchists and their riches, José Antonio was soon to lose the revolutionary *élan* of Ledesma and the extreme National Syndicalists; after an unsuccessful attempt to lead the Falange in a more radical direction, Ledesma was expelled from the movement in January 1935.[67]

Renovación's designs on the Falange were, however, little more than a sideline to a more ambitious plan: the construction of a 'national Spanish bloc' embracing Renovación, the Carlists, the Falange and Albiñana's PNE. The idea, an elaboration of the abortive 'federation' schemes of 1932–3, was first raised at an Acción Española banquet in May 1934 by Sáinz Rodríguez,[68] to be repeated three weeks later by Calvo Sotelo.[69] For the moment, however, the 'national bloc' remained a mere idea. Official Carlist–Alfonsist relations were relatively cordial during the first half of 1934, especially in the Cortes where the two groups met frequently and normally voted together. Further evidence of monarchist fraternalism was provided by TYRE, its organ *La Época*, and Acción Española's society and review. In every case, though, Alfonsist involvement far outweighed that of the Carlists; *La Época*'s editorial board was entirely Alfonsist, while Pradera was the sole Carlist on the large executive board of *Acción Española*.[70] This was, of course, a reflection not of relative strength but of relative enthusiasm. Whereas the

Alfonsists comforted themselves with the illusion that by dominating these collaborative bodies they were equally dominating the monarchist cause, within the Communion the tide was now turning decisively against joint monarchist activity.

By the early months of 1934 it was becoming apparent that three years of continuous growth had produced urgent problems of organization, communication and discipline at all levels of the Communion. According to the Secretariat there were now 540 circles, 803 Youth Sections and a total membership of 700,000.[71] However exaggerated these claims, the Communion's size was certainly now such that its lack of a formalized and efficient structure of command and information could not be permitted to continue. A few tentative steps were taken during 1933 to deal with this situation. The unwieldy and largely ineffectual Supreme National Junta gave way to a smaller and more active Delegate Junta consisting of Rodezno, Pradera, Lamamié and Oriol; the functions of the Secretariat in the spheres of information and publicity were increased;[72] and liaison between the Delegate Junta and *El Siglo Futuro*, now the movement's *de facto* official organ, was improved by the establishment of a *Sociedad Editorial Tradicionalista*.[73] Such changes indicated that Rodezno and other leading Carlists grasped the needs of the moment, but their actual effect upon the running of the Communion was small. The Delegate Junta was admittedly a more manageable and effective body than its predecessor, yet its membership embodied an imprudent reversion to northern control and a stubborn emphasis upon politics and propaganda rather than organization and militancy.[74] Moreover, although the Delegate Junta headed a nominally hierarchical organization which on occasions proved capable of working, albeit creakily, in reality both authority and initiative resided at regional level and below. The true, as distinct from the theoretical, organization of the Communion consequently took the form of a loose confederation of regional hierarchies only intermittently controlled from above. This worked satisfactorily enough as long as Carlism remained a highly regionalized movement, preoccupied with propaganda and locally sponsored expansion, but was grossly inadequate for coping with the problems and potentialities of the national movement thus created.

This situation was complicated by recent changes in Carlism's centre of gravity. Although still strongest in its traditional northern and eastern bases, Carlism was no longer confined there, with inevitably profound effects upon the movements's internal pressures and overall character. Carlist 'new men', especially in Andalusia, were disinclined to accept that the north should automatically dominate the Communion or dictate its strategy. Furthermore, while expansion had occurred among all age groups, it was the Youth Sections of the various local organizations which showed the most dramatic rates of growth.[75] This was true everywhere, but the significance of the phenomenon varied crucially according to region. In areas of traditional strength, whether young converts joined already existing Youth Sections or else created new ones, it was normally as an offshoot of established circles and did little to weaken the position of the usually middle-aged or elderly *jefes* and juntas. In Andalusia and other 'new' areas, on the other hand, the creation of Youth Sections often preceded that of circles and in many districts Carlism remained exclusively a movement of youth.[76] Regional, provincial and local *jefes* and juntas in these areas therefore tended to be considerably younger than their northern counterparts and correspondingly more sensitive to the feelings of their own Youth and Requeté. This took on particular importance when grass-roots dissatisfaction with the Communion's structure and leadership exploded in the spring of 1934.

This dissent, which reached its climax in April, focused on the policies of peaceful conversion, vote-getting, parliamentary activity and accommodation with the Alfonsists which, inspired by Rodezno, had characterized the past three years without visibly shaking the fabric of the Republic. The first and shrillest critics were the Navarrese Youth, chafing against the control of cautious juntas in whose eyes numerical strength was an excuse for inactivity and who above all shrank from 'crazy behaviour' such as attacks on the locals of rival parties.[77] This kind of generation gap was common in 'old Carlist' areas. To Jaime del Burgo and the other young Navarrese who early in 1934 began to publish their own weekly, *a.e.t.*, this restraint was simply a local manifestation of an excessively 'political' and parliamentary policy at the top – a policy, at that, which the CEDA's current course was judged to be proving both unproductive and perilous. When *a.e.t.* declared itself 'fed up with legality', its target was not only the CEDA but also Carlist 'politicians' like Rodezno and the elderly *junteros*.[78] According to *a.e.t.* the past three years had been 'years of inactivity' and the Communion's present condition was 'soporific'. The chief reason for this lamentable state of affairs was its association with 'this refuge of *caciques* and debris of the Alfonsine Monarchy, which has adopted the name of Renovación Española – as if we did not know that the 'renewal' which they offer us is a return to an iniquitous regime repugnant to every honest conscience'.[79] Rather than the elusive and dangerous dream of monarchist unity and the self-defeating course of circumspection, *a.e.t.* called for a total break with Renovación and an overdue return to the militancy of the nineteenth century:

Young Carlists, students, let us imitate our crusaders; let us, like them, form legions of the valiant and raise the immaculate standard . . . Carlism is action, movement, organization, ceaseless struggle, sacrifice and brotherhood.[80]

The intemperate tone of *a.e.t.*'s first two editions shocked the Navarrese Carlist authorities into ordering its young editors to 'calm down', a call brushed aside by Burgo and his comrades with the unheard-of cry: 'We are revolutionaries! Do you hear – revolutionaries!'[81]

The Navarrese Youth made no bones about the strategy that appealed to them – the building up, organizing and arming of the Requeté 'so that it may, on the outbreak of war, destroy the Republican barricades'.[82] War, then, was explicitly on the agenda. Carlism's enemies certainly had reason to think so, for in the early part of 1934 the Requeté in several provinces, besides expanding rapidly, was coming out into the open as never before. On 18 February the Guipúzcoan Youth held a rally attended by 2,000 Red Berets from the Basque–Navarrese region;[83] a few days later what was described as 'the Carlist army' assembled in a Pamplona *pelota* hall;[84] and in April the uniformed Requeté of Vizcaya held military exercises in the sierra.[85] Popular militancy, barely controlled by the incumbent Carlist authorities, was fast becoming the dominant mood within the Communion.

Desire for change was not confined to the Youth, even though nobody else voiced it quite so bluntly. Feeling was now widespread that the time had come for more open aggressiveness and a break with the Alfonsists. In January *El Siglo Futuro* asserted that monarchist unity would eventually be achieved through the absorption of Renovación Española – and the Falange – by the Communion.[86] Fal Conde, addressing the Navarrese, criticized both Renovación and the Falange for being 'disoriented as regards their goals' and insisted that Spain could only reach political salvation through the complete installation of the Catholic Traditional Monarchy.[87] Although the fact was not yet public, this kind of political isolationism and general belligerence, increasingly strong among southerners and former Integrists, was now shared by Alfonso Carlos.

This climate of restlessness was natural enough, for zealous Carlists could not be expected to rest content with electing deputies and passing legislation, however welcome this might be. But the critics were wrong if they believed that the Delegate Junta was in any way averse to violence. Late in 1933 it had sanctioned the holding at Vergara (Guipúzcoa) of a clandestine meeting, attended by Varela, which signalled the effective resumption of serious conspiratorial activity.[88] It was also the Delegate Junta which took the first steps towards improving the national organization, especially that of the Requeté. In January 1934 it took an important stride towards centralization and announced that henceforth presidents of juntas would be appointed by their superior junta rather than elected by their colleagues.[89] This was followed early in April by the creation of a *Frente Nacional de Boinas Rojas* (National Red Beret Front), the first attempt to give the Requeté something resembling a national organization. Its members were forbidden to belong to non-Carlist bodies and were promised an imminent period of 'patriotic activity'.[90] During the preceding months, Varela's schemes for restructuring the Requeté had begun to be applied in Navarre, under the auspices of the Regional Junta, which appointed an ex-Jaimist from the mountain village of Leiza, Antonio Lizarza, to supervise recruitment and training.[91]

As long as Rodezno headed the Delegate Junta, the underlying assumption of such preparations was that the Carlists would join any rising of a recognizably counter-revolutionary character: hence the climax of Rodezno's leadership – the joint monarchist–military mission to Rome in the spring of 1934.[92] On the last day of March, Lizarza and the Guipúzcoan ex-Integrist Rafael Olazábal, with the knowledge and blessing of Rodezno and the Delegate Junta, arrived in Rome accompanied by Goicoechea and General Barrera, hopeful of obtaining Italian financial and material support for a monarchist rising to take place on a date as yet undetermined. Satisfied by the unanimous assurance of the emissaries that the restored monarchy would be 'corporative and organic', and dismissing as no concern of his the dynastic gulf still yawning between Goicoechea and the Carlists, Mussolini promised to back the proposed rising with preliminary aid consisting of 1,500,000 pesetas in cash, 20,000 rifles, 20,000 hand grenades and 200 machine-guns. Further assistance was to follow the outbreak of hostilities. It was agreed that Olazábal should assume the responsibility for receiving and distributing the cash, the first 500,000 pesetas of which were handed over promptly on 1 April, but an awkward situation arose when Goicoechea demanded that both money and material be divided equally between Renovación and the Carlists. The latter retorted unkindly that they commanded enough mass support to put the aid to good use, unlike Renovación. Barrera, whose personal sympathies were torn between the two movements, accepted the Carlists' militarily unanswerable case, and forced Goicoechea to give way. The agreement thus benefited the Carlists *vis-à-vis* the Alfonsists both militarily and from the point of view of morale and prestige, but in provoking ill feeling it did little to further Rodezno's hopes of a monarchist *rapprochement*.

Although to those who knew about it the Rome mission was evidence that the Delegate Junta was in no way dragging its feet where rebellion was concerned, it also showed that Rodezno was as keen as ever on co-operating with the Alfonsists. In the eyes of the great mass of Carlists who were ignorant of recent goings-on, Rodezno and his Junta remained too closely identified, not only with the unpopular policy of monarchist co-operation but also with a wider, almost gradualist strategy, to be capable of a convincing and effective change of gear.[93] For months now the Junta itself had been inundated with letters from Carlists throughout the country pleading for the adoption of 'new orientations', and similar petitions had been reaching Alfonso Carlos. Caught between the popular unrest and the Pretender's own growing impatience at his conduct, Rodezno had come to the conclusion by April 1934 that he could not continue as head of the Delegate Junta, and made it known that he was ready to resign. There remained the difficult problem of who should replace him. No automatic alternative leader to Rodezno existed, but a party led by Lamamié, Senante and Fernando Contreras was soon busy floating the candidacy of Fal Conde. Rodezno was hostile to the idea; Fal Conde, he commented, lacked the necessary 'position' for the job, which he then suggested ought to go either to Oriol or Contreras. At most, Fal Conde might be allowed to serve as political secretary until an acceptable Delegate emerged.

Matters came to a head between 15 and 20 April. On the fifteenth, Rodezno, acting on Alfonso Carlos' instructions, sent a circular to the Carlist regional *jefes*, informing them officially of his resignation and summoning them to a meeting in Madrid. The following day Fal Conde dispatched a letter to Alfonso Carlos, suggesting drastic reorganization of the Communion and a more militant policy generally; the letter, which also proposed de-emphasizing the dynastic issue, was favourably commented on by other prominent figures including Lamamié and Pradera. Whether or not Fal Conde's letter amounted to a bid for the leadership, it appears to have had that effect, for sometime within the next couple of days Alfonso Carlos asked the Delegate for All Andalusia to accept the position of Secretary-General of the Communion.

On 20 April the regional *jefes* assembled in Madrid. The meeting was a milestone in Carlism's history; the first such occasion for over a decade, it brought together for the first time in formal conclave the old and new leaders of the Communion, the middle-aged and elderly ex-Jaimists of the north and the thrusting young ex-Integrists of the south and south-east. From the point of view of the latter the affair could not have been more timely, coming as it did only five days after an unprecedented display of Carlist vigour in Andalusia. At the inauguration of a new centre in Seville, young northerners like Arellano and Zamanillo had been staggered by the 'revelation' of 650 well-drilled Andalusian Red Berets and by the evident success of southern militancy and organizational expertise.[94] *El Siglo Futuro's* reaction was to describe Carlism's growth in Andalusia as an 'explosion' and the man deemed responsible, Fal Conde, as 'the Sevillian Zumalacárregui'.[95]

As expected, the meeting of regional *jefes* accepted the need for 'new orientations'. The entire Delegate Junta took the hint and through Rodezno tendered its resignation to Alfonso Carlos, who accepted it with formal expressions of praise and gratitude for the Junta's past efforts. On 3 May Fal Conde's appointment as Secretary-General of the Communion was made public. His powers, it was clear from Alfonso Carlos' proclamation, would be considerable; all other *jefes* were subordinated to him, and he was empowered to recommend to Alfonso Carlos such additional Delegates, Subsecretaries and *jefes* as he might consider necessary in the total reorganization with which he was expressly entrusted.[96] Not only had the Communion thus reverted to the system of one-man delegated control which had always proved its most effective form of organization, but in addition Fal Conde's brief — and his personal temper —

promised that he would exercise fuller control than any of his predecessors since Cerralbo.

Given the generally accepted view that an organizational overhaul was the Communion's most pressing need, Fal Conde's appointment made sound sense, for although Carlism had expanded throughout Spain it was in Andalusia that this expansion owed most to deliberate and successful organization. In Navarre and the Basque region membership swelled more or less spontaneously in response to the events of the Republic, and within an already existing organizational framework. To a lesser extent the same was true in Catalonia and the Levant, where Carlist tradition was rooted and where such a framework, even if run down, could quite easily be reconstructed. In Andalusia none of these preconditions obtained. To all intents and purposes, the confident and flourishing movement witnessed on 15 April constituted not the renaissance but the birth of Carlism in Andalusia, where every local organization shone as proof of the energy and competence of Fal Conde and his lieutenants.

However logical, the step was both revolutionary and risky. Fal Conde was the first Andalusian to serve as a royal Delegate, was a mere forty in a movement wherein age was customarily revered, as an Integrist had played no part in the Communion before 1931, and was still little known outside his native region. Even granted the case for one-man rather than junta command, his appointment clearly implied the rejection by Alfonso Carlos not only of the four members of the Delegate Junta but also of other Carlists of long-standing prestige, together with the repudiation of Rodezno's policy of attempted *rapprochement* with the Alfonsists. This was demonstrated only three days after Fal Conde's elevation, when Rodezno, as leader of the Carlists in the Cortes, received instructions from Alfonso Carlos forbidding any official union with Renovación Española and the participation of Carlist deputies and office-holders in its meetings, and ordering the suppression of TYRE.[97] Although Rodezno loyally complied, and reacted with outward generosity to Fal Conde's appointment, relations between the two were cool from the start of the latter's secretary-generalship.[98] No open complaints were uttered, yet the baldness of *El Pensamiento Navarro*'s announcement of the change in the leadership veiled but thinly the distress of many older Carlists, especially in Navarre and the north generally, at the news. They, together with all those who still craved close relations with Alfonsism, continued to look for leadership to Rodezno.[99]

The majority of reactions were nonetheless decidedly favourable. *El Siglo Futuro* greeted the promotion of a fellow-Integrist with predictably fervent vows of loyalty,[100] while *La Unión*, recalling Fal Conde's role as the lynch-pin of Sevillian Carlism, contrasted his youth with the 'old age' of everything connected with the Republic.[101] The Secretary-General's youth was also considered highly significant by Burgo and his Navarrese comrades, who by no means shared the coolness of their regional authorities. His appointment, they declared in *a.e.t.*,

opens up new horizons and awakens our slumbering hopes. The illustrious leader will have no wish to lower the confidence of the Navarrese, who are only waiting for the moment of the great battle to fall upon Madrid and put in his rightful place the royal person of Don Alfonso Carlos.

Fal Conde, *a.e.t.* concluded, as the man who 'brought Montejurra to Andalusia', would be 'a young man to lead the young'.[102] Behind all the slogans lay a point of real substance. With Fal Conde as leader, the Communion could present itself as a reinvigorated, youthful movement, unambiguous as to its purpose: the violent overthrow of the Republic and the installation of the Traditionalist state.

6

Traditionalism and the contemporary crisis

In the past, save in such periods of international crisis as 1914–19, neither Carlism as a cause nor Carlists as individuals had displayed more than the most general interest in foreign affairs. The insularity of Spanish politics in the later nineteenth and early twentieth centuries was exaggerated in Carlism's case by the peculiarity of being a mass legitimist movement without close counterparts abroad. Catholic universalism, devotion to the idea of *hispanidad*, and sympathy for foreign legitimist causes lent traces of internationalism to the Traditionalist credo, without seeming to jolt Carlists out of their overwhelmingly inward-looking preoccupations. Ironically, those Carlists most affected by general European currents were the Pretenders themselves, who proved to be continually susceptible to 'liberal' and 'Europeanizing' influences.

During the five years of the Second Republic, all this changed. If the cataclysmic events of the depression era throughout Europe and beyond were not enough to arouse Carlist interest, then perhaps what did guarantee its arousal was the heightened consciousness of foreign affairs resulting from the wider diffusion of international news via agencies, radio and the cinema. What is inescapable is that during the early 1930s, and more particularly from the start of 1933 onwards, Carlist concern for the fate of Spain came increasingly to be expressed in terms of a broader European or even worldwide political crisis, in which left and right were seen to be hurtling towards a collision, crushing democracy between them. In such a situation, press reports and comment on foreign affairs served a purely propagandistic purpose: to highlight the world crisis and stimulate fear of a general left-wing victory: to predict, publicize and applaud the apparently accelerating triumph of the right elsewhere in Europe; and to advertise Carlism as the vanguard of a similar triumph in Spain by pointing out the differences within the right-wing camp. Accuracy was therefore a secondary consideration, if indeed it mattered at all. Readers of Carlist newspapers were certainly less well informed on events abroad

than those of the Republican *El Sol*, of *El Socialista*, *El Debate* or even
the Alfonsist *ABC*, but what they did read strengthened the opinions
and prejudices which most of them already held.

The Carlists believed that the successive collapse of the Dictatorship and the Liberal Monarchy, followed by the introduction of a
democratic Republic, had precipitated Spain into the arena of a global
struggle currently reaching its climax in most of Europe. In a world
tragically riven between capitalism and socialism, revolution, planned
in Moscow, financed by international Jewry and spread with the
assistance of freemasonry, constituted a permanent and ubiquitous
threat, whether in the naked form of communism or the subtler but no
less dangerous guise of social democracy.[1] Great stress was accordingly laid both upon the menace of socialism abroad and upon steps
taken to combat it, the more so when these steps could be interpreted
as undermining democracy in the name of order, authority and,
better still, tradition.

Particular interest was shown in the 1931 crisis in Great Britain,
a country which Carlists considered the sole respectable advertise-
ment for parliamentary democracy, now brought 'to the brink of ruin
by Socialism'.[2] The Labour Party's shattering electoral defeat in
October 1931 was warmly welcomed not only by *El Siglo Futuro*
but also by *El Pensamiento Navarro*, in which foreign news was seldom prominent. The British electorate, it was repeatedly claimed,
had seen the light just in time to prevent the country from plunging
into an abyss. British Socialism was now surely destroyed: 'What a
lesson comes to us from England,' *El Pensamiento Navarro* proclaimed, adding sadly '... but we shall not know how to use it.'[3]
Some months later, Carlist readers' attention was drawn to the
British 'recovery' accomplished as the result of an anti-socialist
reaction and Ramsay MacDonald's patriotism, though *El Siglo
Futuro* regretted that it could not imagine Lerroux leading a similar
movement in Spain.[4] The Labour Party's gradual revival rather
weakened these arguments, but enabled their proponents to draw
further useful conclusions: firstly that 'either England puts an end
to Socialism or Socialism will put an end to England', and secondly
that the latter was the more likely development as long as the British
clung stubbornly to parliamentarism.[5] The message for Spaniards was
obvious enough.

If nothing else, the British experience fortified Carlist convictions that democracy could not in the final analysis resist socialism without resorting to desperate solutions such as the National Government – solutions which might, moreover, portend a retreat away from democracy and towards conservative authoritarianism. And almost everywhere they looked, the Carlists saw democracy in retreat. The evidence adduced to support this belief was varied and sometimes bizarre. Examples cited included André Tardieu's attempts to revise the French constitution in the direction of greater presidentialism;[6] the Parisian riots of February 1934;[7] the alleged anti-parliamentarism of the *Daily Mail* and 'corporativism' of Roosevelt's New Deal;[8] and, wildest of all, the ouster of the despot Machado in Cuba which, according to *El Pensamiento Navarro*, was 'the story of all democracies'.[9] If statements like this seemed to suggest that Carlist definitions of democracy were extremely loose, other outbursts called into question their very comprehension of its foreign manifestations. One of *El Siglo Futuro*'s last sallies against the ramparts of British parliamentarism, for example, contained an analysis of the two historic political parties of that system, the 'Wips and Torys' (*sic*), imaginatively described as 'the advanced and conservative parties which everywhere serve as the wheels of revolution's chariot'.[10]

Acutely sensitive to an omnipresent threat of revolution, and sure that democracy could not contain it, Carlist spokesmen naturally responded warmly to what they regarded as the contemporary political mood of authoritarian nationalism. In 1932 Rodezno defined this reaction as embracing not only fascism and Catholic corporativism, but also Ramsay MacDonald's government and a motley assortment of Latin American dictatorships.[11] Eighteen months later, after Hitler's attainment and consolidation of power, Fernando Contreras confidently asserted that the Spanish Republican regime now stood opposed to a 'world current' flowing everywhere else apart from Mexico and the Soviet Union.[12] During 1934 the advance of fascism in France and Dollfuss' smashing of the Austrian Socialists further assured Carlists that for the first time in a century they now reflected the prevailing European political climate instead of opposing it.

They nonetheless realized that this Continental, even worldwide, reaction against democracy and socialism was itself made up of several not always harmonious elements. The left might label the whole process 'fascist', but Carlists felt themselves to be separated from Italian Fascists and German National Socialists by a gap every bit as wide as that, say, dividing marxists and anarchists.[13] What they, of course, looked for in the 'European reaction' was evidence of a monarchist revival, and although appreciating that the devotees of legitimate monarchy were a minority within the European right, they managed to exhibit a quite extraordinary optimism regarding the possibility of foreign restorations. From the start of 1932 onwards, the return of monarchy was seriously discussed as an imminent prospect in France, Germany, Bavaria and Austria.[14] In 1935 it was even reported that Great Britain, too, was moving towards restoring an 'integral monarchy' which, presumably, had died with Charles I; the development was supposedly backed by a galaxy of right-wing talent including Churchill, Salisbury, Mosley, W. B. Yeats, Sir Charles Petrie, Douglas Jerrold and a mysterious 'Brov'.[15] It must be doubted whether even many Carlists were taken in by speculation of this kind, and it was not until the Greek monarchy was revived late in 1935 that the faith of Carlist publicists in a new Restoration Era was even partially rewarded.[16]

In view of the unconvincing and generally frustrated nature of the above reflections, Carlists were forced to look elsewhere for signs of concrete achievement with which they could more or less fully identify. They found it in regimes and movements which, while not necessarily monarchist, differed from Italian Fascism and German National Socialism in drawing their inspiration from Catholic integralism. During the first biennium of the Republic the sole such regime was that of Salazar in Portugal, although admiration was also expressed for Pilsudski's Poland.[17] However, in March 1933 there commenced in Austria the rule by decree of the man who instantly became the chief foreign hero not only of the Carlists but also of Gil Robles – Engelbert Dollfuss. Carlists found Dollfuss attractive because, set against the Italianate Heimwehr and the Austrian Nazis, he appeared to stand for Austria in the same way that they believed Carlism stood for Spain; his background was that of the devout peasantry upon which Carlism was historically based, his religious faith essentially a simple one, his corporativist programme a home-grown traditionalism.[18] This view of Dollfuss, if romanticized, was fundamentally correct. Like Carlism and the CEDA, in their different ways, the Austrian chancellor upheld the notion of the Christian State and drew his inspiration from the Papal Encyclicals from *De Rerum Novarum* to *Quadragesimo Anno*. Austria's 1934 constitution conformed in broad outline to many

Carlist ideas, monarchy naturally excepted, and even more to the CEDA's.[19] When he was murdered by Austrian Nazis in July 1934, the Carlists granted Dollfuss an honorary place alongside the 'martyrs' of Spanish Tradition. *El Siglo Futuro*'s obituary pronounced him the outstanding political leader of the past half-century, surpassing Bismarck by virtue of his Catholicism and ranking second only to the *'simpático'* Metternich.[20]

It was another two years before Europe threw up a figure capable or rivalling Dollfuss in the Carlists' estimation. Now it was Léon Degrelle, youthful leader of the Belgian Catholic extremist movement, Rex. At its inception Rex represented the kind of Catholic integralism implied by its slogan 'Christus Rex' – the exact equivalent of Carlism's 'Cristo-Rey', while Degrelle's attitude towards the Belgian Catholic Party closely resembled that of Carlism and Renovación Española towards the CEDA.[21] Rex's sudden and dramatic electoral gains in June 1936 were hailed by the Carlists not only as heartening in themselves but also as dealing an exemplary blow at Belgian Catholic 'adhesionism'.[22] What they could not know was that Rex had already reached its peak; that as Degrelle moved closer to outright fascism his movement would rapidly decline. As was so often the case, serious analysis was quite absent. The Carlists saw in Degrelle, as in Dollfuss, precisely what they wanted to see: evidence that Traditionalism was the European wave of the future.

Alone of the Spanish right-wing parties of the 1930s, Carlism was an established movement resting upon a more or less coherent corpus of ideas. Reasonably enough, Carlists felt and said that they had no need to borrow ideas from elsewhere; their new awareness of the outside world consequently had little effect upon the Communion's official ideology and programme, which remained essentially those developed by Mella during the early years of the century. Mella's place as leading theoretician of Carlist Traditionalism was now occupied, unchallenged, by his onetime *protégé* Víctor Pradera. Hitherto overshadowed by his patron and exemplar, Pradera emerged during the years of the Second Republic as the prophet of a Traditionalism similar to Mella's, yet in some respects more rigid, better integrated, and less self-consciously obsessed with making Carlism 'modern'. This last point is perhaps explained not so much by any difference in outlook between the two men as by the fact that, with rightism in fashion, 'modernity' no longer seemed worth searching for.

Eager to encourage the spread of Traditionalism among the Alfonsists, Pradera collaborated from the start in Acción Española, to whose review he contributed a series on 'False Dogmas' during 1932. This series, essentially an attack upon the assumptions of liberalism allegedly derived from Rousseau, formed the nucleus of a more ambitious set of articles in 1934 on the theme of 'The New State'. These, slightly amended, were in turn published as a book, *El Estado Nuevo*, in 1935.[23]

El Estado Nuevo constituted the most intelligent, eloquent and consistent distillation of Carlist ideology ever produced, and was promptly accepted within the Communion as the most authoritative statement of contemporary Traditionalism. The title plainly derived from the fashionable vocabulary of the inter-war right throughout Europe and more specifically from the Portuguese *Estado Novo*, yet in the book Pradera revealed that in his hands the term involved a paradox: since what Spain needed was not simply a New State but also a 'Good State', might it not turn out that this was actually an 'Old State'?[24] That this was the case was implicit in Pradera's definition of tradition as 'the past which survives and has the virtue to make itself future'.[25]

The *leitmotif* of *El Estado Nuevo* was Pradera's highly individual critique of false dogma. There were, he claimed, three basic doctrinal systems of Christian origin: the Pelagian heresy which held Man to be naturally good; the Protestant heresy which regarded human nature as totally corrupt; and the Catholic doctrine which stated that human nature was merely weak, resulting in the mutual dependence of all men and Mankind's dependence upon God.[26] The two heresies, despite their superficial irreconcilability, had intermingled in the Enlightenment, and personified in Rousseau had produced liberalism and, when further distorted, socialism. Pelagianism and Protestantism had in common 'the dissolution or negation of civil society', just as liberalism, notwithstanding all disclaimers, defended not true civil freedom but extreme individualism.[27]

If one element in the thought of the revolutionary era appalled Pradera more than any other, it was its interpretation of 'freedom' and above all its talk of 'the Rights of Man', a notion which since 1789 had 'deranged the world'. It was not that Man possessed no rights, but whereas for the 'revolutionary' rights were boundless and pre-existed duties, to the Catholic they originated in Natural Law and were 'limited by the fulfilment of a duty'. The consequences of this distinction were crucial to a society, for whilst in the former case 'social fellowship' was crushed under a deafening individualistic clamour, in the latter that sense of sociability was nurtured which 'precisely urges men to fulfil their duties'.[28]

Discounting as mere supposition Rousseau's picture of Man's natural state, Pradera declared sociability 'a natural characteristic of Man', a fact recognized, if, in his opinion, ill interpreted, by Marx.[29] Even if originally dispersed, it was 'natural' that men, in furtherance of 'co-operation in the fulfilment of the duties of every man towards God', had collected in groups of families to form townships, municipal guilds, regions and ultimately the nation, 'the major, the concrete and the particular society within which Man attains his temporal destiny'.[30] Pradera's view of the nation as an organically constituted 'major society of societies, not of individuals' clashed with the atomistic nation of Rousseau, made up of theoretically equal individuals but dominated by the 'fifty per cent plus one' worshipped by liberals.[31] As a 'great society of societies' the nation subsumed but did not consume its component elements — the family, the township, the guild and the region.[32] It was indivisible, whether potential sources of division be individuals, political parties, social classes or the pseudo-nationalism of constituent regions. The Spanish nation owed its 'harmonious co-existence' and 'undivided soul' to the Catholic Monarchs, Ferdinand and Isabella; since its creation, each component kingdom and region had contributed something distinctive to Spain, just as each organic nation contributed something special to a common human destiny. Here Pradera reiterated his fundamental argument:

Let not those who feel Spain's sorrow search for a New State. Let them return to tradition. There we shall find it, as we have found the true and legitimate national structure.[33]

Pradera's conception of the Spanish nation as an entity evolved organically, ratified by tradition and hence divinely ordained, led him into a hostility towards Basque and Catalan nationalism more bitter than that of most of his co-believers. When valid, he argued, nationalism was 'constructive and unifying', whereas the Basque and Catalan nationalists 'have one ultimate clear final goal — to sever the ties, centuries old, which bind the Basque provinces and Catalonia to Spain, and to set them up as nations by means of a criminal matricide'.[34] The 'zoological nationalism' of the racially 'hybrid' Basques and the cultural nationalism of the culturally divided Catalans were invalid, Pradera argued, even according to their own criteria of nationhood; to him, of course, the criteria themselves were false.[35] Neither Basques nor Catalans had historically revealed any 'national spirit' comparable with that of which both partook within the unity of Spain. On the other hand, within the foral system which Pradera, like all Carlists, advocated, regional personality and national spirit were seen as complementary and not conflicting.[36]

The organic formation of a national society was perfected by the institution of monarchy, for sovereignty, while resting ultimately in the nation, demanded an incarnation through which to express itself.[37] Either a monarchy or a 'national' republic was capable of providing a head of state of unimpeachable legitimacy, but Pradera denied that the question of regime was a matter of indifference, legitimacy and perfection being far from synonymous. He had no doubt that an hereditary monarch best represented the nation 'in his physical unity'. Such a ruler was dependent neither upon an oligarchy nor upon plebiscite but on fundamental law;[38] he was prepared for the onerous task of kingship gradually within the bosom of that perfect social unit, the Christian family; his private interest and the public interest coincided, while the possible personal deficiencies of an individual could be compensated by the strength and continuity of the institutions surrounding him.[39] Thus Pradera, like Mella, repudiated the theory of Divine Right which Carlism's detractors attempted to pin upon it (and in which innumerable rank-and-file Carlists doubtless believed): 'Sovereignty in a limited being cannot be absolute. The notion of an absolute king is as absurd as that of an absolute nation!'[40] On the contrary, royal authority was limited both by the superior spiritual power of the Church, since all authority emanated from God, and by the 'social sovereignty' of the various regions, hierarchies and corporations of the organic nation, which not only restricted possible royal despotism but also positively supported the king in the conduct of government. The final product was an overall 'picture of insuperable perfection'.[41]

The monarch was the supreme 'representative' of the nation, which Pradera insisted could not be accurately represented by 'delegation' through political parties. These by their very nature lacked national ideals, pursued sectional interests, regarded power as an end in itself and divided a fundamentally cohesive and balanced society.[42] The corporative state envisaged by Pradera acknowledged the existence of classes – but not of class conflict. 'A society without classes cannot be imagined' since the classes are the 'natural organs with which human society affords satisfaction to social needs'.[43] This was the whole point: social classes were not only natural but necessary and mutually dependent, and corporativism was designed to 'establish a concordant alliance across class lines'. Pradera identified six classes: agriculture, industry, commerce, property, the liberal professions and manual labour; besides these there were six 'state bodies' not susceptible to class analysis: the clergy, aristocracy, judiciary, diplomatic corps, armed forces and regions, plus a thirteenth category of 'national bodies and corporations' embracing a wide variety of interests and occupations.[44]

This corporate society would naturally be reflected in the 'true' Cortes, which apart from providing functional representation of the various 'classes', 'corporations' and 'state bodies', would play an active role in the governance of the realm. Pradera's plan for the composition of the Cortes was more specific than Mella's: each of the six classes would send fifty deputies, as would the regions, the 'state bodies' whose combined role was the 'direct' defence, safeguarding and furtherance of the public interest, and the 'national bodies and corporations'. There would thus be constituted a chamber of 450 members divided into nine equal sections, the purpose of this strict parity being to prevent the possibility of one interest's obtaining an advantage over the others.[45]

Pradera saw the Cortes as one element in a tripartite legislative organ, the others being the king and his nominated Council. The Cortes and the Council were described as the king's 'co-legislators' though not as his equals in terms of sovereignty. The legislative process would initially involve the submission of any proposed measure to the king for permission to place it before the Cortes. If this approval were given, the bill would then be discussed simultaneously in all the corporate 'sections' of the Cortes, each one examining the proposal's implications in its own sphere. Finally there would take place a 'full debate' in which each section would be represented by a single spokesman permitted to speak for a limited period. The Cortes' opinion, it would appear, would be arrived at through consensus rather than by a vote; its strict function was the discussion of a proposal's 'necessity and convenience'. If accepted by the Cortes, the bill would then go before the Council which would consider it from a constitutional and juridical point of view, and finally to the king. Although a royal rejection could be followed by a reintroduction of the proposal by the Cortes, in the last resort the royal veto was final.[46] The supposed virtue of this system lay in the alleged repudiation of ideology and class as bases of division, as well as in its requiring deputies to concentrate upon those matters directly affecting them and on which they were presumably knowledgeable, instead of being expected, as in a parliamentary regime, to deal with matters of the majority of which they were probably ignorant.[47]

The fundamental responsibilities of the 'government' – king, Council and Cortes – involved the maintenance of all forms of national and societal unity. National frontiers and, implicitly, internal peace, would be protected by a modern but not inflated army based upon voluntary recruitment, although conscription remained at the government's disposal in the event of war.[48] Even more important was the upholding of the nation's spiritual unity through the pursuit of justice, founded on Catholic Public Law in general and the decisions of the Council of Trent in particular, and the defence of Catholic education.[49] Although Pradera denied that the state should itself assume an educative function, he affirmed its responsibility for 'regulating' education by guaranteeing the educative role of the Church. The 'Catholic unity' thereby ensured would soften and even remove class and regional discord.[50]

While explicit and even detailed on the subject of the organization of the state, Pradera had little to say concerning the resolution of social problems. Like Mella and all social-Catholics, he stressed that private property, although natural and just, was a right limited by religious, moral and social considerations.[51] Throughout, however, he emphasized the interdependence of all forms of labour – and of labour and property – without apparently following some contemporary social-Catholics in advocating governmental intervention in order to confiscate and redistribute unused or abused property. Underlying this casual treatment of the acute social problems currently agonizing Spain was, of course, the assumption that these were the outcome of liberalism and socialism, and would disappear once the system which had created them was destroyed. Yet in providing for no significant readjustment of wealth, Pradera's corporativism left unanswered the question of whether in practice it would be any less socially unjust than liberalism or foreign corporativist experiments.

Pradera's 'New State', which in his conclusion he predictably revealed to be 'none other than the Spanish State of the Catholic Monarchs',[52] was in substance the vision of most thinking Carlists in the 1930s, besides giving form to the vaguer ideas of the majority. As a purely intellectual statement of Spanish Catholic Traditionalism it was coherent and by no means unimpressive. As a political programme or a blueprint for the future it was unrealistic to the point of downright utopianism, an academic vision of an ideal society founded not upon force or the Inquisition — of which there was no mention — but on harmony, interdependence and universal faith. Like all Carlists, Pradera harped constantly upon the inconsistencies and hypocrisy of liberalism while failing totally to realize that Traditionalism, too, was riddled with contradictions. Even assuming that the 'Good State', new or old, offered a desirable form of social and political organization, the vital question was evaded: was it a practicable proposition in twentieth-century Spain? When Carlists described their system as 'authentically liberal', they were voicing a sincere belief in wide civic participation, popular acquiescence in public policies, lack of governmental authoritarianism, and 'representative' monarchy. And yet the very validity of this system rested upon assumptions which paralleled those of liberalism and raised similar questions. Both claimed to be non-authoritarian and thus presupposed the existence of a sympathetic consensus, but even as Pradera wrote, liberal Republicans were in the process of discovering that the absence of a liberal consensus in Spain was pushing them towards ever greater illiberalism. Likewise in a Spain which, even if it had not ceased to be Catholic, clearly also lacked a Catholic consensus, it was to say the least improbable that the Carlist vision could ever enjoy the degree of acceptance accorded to the Republic.

In particular, the 'official' Carlist line as laid down by Pradera offered no solution to class conflict, since its system was dependent upon the prior existence of social peace. Were a Traditionalist regime to be miraculously introduced without there first taking place a drastic redistribution of wealth, then class divisions would be as naked as before in spite of all the attempted concealment of the corporative Cortes; should that regime then erect a repressive apparatus in order to quell social conflict, it would cease to conform to Pradera's Traditionalism. Here lay the central issue of corporativism as it affected not only Carlism but also all those other Catholics who resisted the idea of the all-powerful state. Corporativism and social peace might go hand in hand for one of three reasons. Theoretically, authentic corporativism might flourish simply because the concept of harmony and interdependence on which it rested was accepted by all classes and interest-groups. This was apparently the vision of Pradera and the majority of Carlists who could be bothered to consider the problem, and patently bore no relation to the social realities of the times in which they lived. Alternatively, a genuine corporative system might be introduced after a revolution – presumably from above – had first destroyed serious inequalities of wealth and extirpated the roots of social conflict. This formula, so far untried and probably impracticable, was, as the next chapter will show, the sincere if inadequately worked-out hope of minorities within both the Falange and the Carlist Youth. The third possibility involved the imposition of what, according to Pradera's criteria, could only be a spurious corporativism wherein a dictatorial regime would maintain social peace in the interests of the economically privileged. This, more realistic no doubt, was the way of Mussolini.

Carlists vehemently rejected the imposition and manipulation of a corporate state from the top downwards[53] – yet European experience was already suggesting that it could function in no other way. With a few exceptions, the Carlists no longer sought – or admitted to seeking – the restoration of the Inquisition, thus depriving themselves of a possible means of controlling men's minds and actions; in rejecting *étatisme* they perhaps too readily surrendered another. In fact they were still confronted by the painful choice which they had avoided since the later nineteenth century and which they did not openly recognize until 1936: either to go on hoping for the miracle of mass conversion of marxists and anarchists and the consequent emergence of a favourable consensus, or else to sully the purity of their corporativism by moving towards acceptance of a more modern authoritarianism.

A closely related problem ignored in *El Estado Nuevo*, as it had so often been before, was that of how Carlism might achieve power in the first place without making consensus impossible – a serious question to which most Carlists, content to accept uncritically the social myth of a final, successful Carlist War, gave little thought. The Traditionalism of *El Estado Nuevo* was thus all ends and no means. The connected problems of how power was to be won and a corporative system introduced without self-betrayal were totally ignored; this was particularly tragic since it was these selfsame problems which increasingly governed both Carlism's relations with other right-wing parties and its own internal disagreements.

Those entrusted with the actual running of the Communion were bound to face the issue of 'means' more directly than the theorist Pradera, and it was precisely here that the schools of thought personified by Rodezno and Fal Conde came into contention. What was at stake was far more than a strategic detail: it was the whole conception and future of Carlism. Rodezno was above all a realist, and as such appreciated that the ideal of mass conversions leading to a purely Carlist seizure of power was nothing but a dream. Rebellion on any other terms would inevitably involve alliances – with non-Carlist civilians, with the army, or more probably with both. In these circumstances, which Pradera had actually envisaged throughout his career even though he was silent on the subject now, the installation of the Traditional Monarchy would be far from a foregone conclusion. At most, a 'New State' ushered in by this route might accept parts of the Carlist programme, in which event the faithful would presumably have to settle for second best. Rodezno nevertheless believed that Traditionalism's chances might be increased through maintaining good relations between Carlism and Alfonsism; aristocrat, socialite and politician, he maintained closer personal ties than any other Carlist with leading Alfonsists and with many *cedistas*, and held fewer objections than most, not merely to a dynastic settlement recognizing either Alfonso XIII or Don Juan as Alfonso Carlos' heir, but even to a complete fusion of the two causes.

To Rodezno the fall of the Liberal Monarchy, in vindicating Carlism's historic struggle, had also weakened its *raison d'être* as a separate political organization. This did not mean, as has since been suggested, that he believed Carlism itself need cease to exist,[54] but rather that it ought in future to function as an ideological and spiritual force and not as a 'party'. Now that the ideals for which Carlism had so long militated appeared to be permeating most of the Spanish right, Rodezno felt that questions of organization, leadership and personality ought not to be allowed to obstruct a monarchist reconciliation made easier by Alfonso Carlos' lack of a clear successor.[55] The problem of how the Traditional Monarchy might be achieved was thus solved by accepting the possibility of abandoning a distinct Carlist organization in favour of a wider monarchist movement in which the ideology of Carlism would be the new orthodoxy.

This outlook arose quite naturally out of Rodezno's 'Navarrese' conception of Carlism as a matter of local and family tradition, something fully able to survive the absence of formal organization. Monarchist unity, of course, proved more elusive than Rodezno perhaps expected; nevertheless as a strategy it made sound sense. A single monarchist party would have offered a far more credible and serious challenge to the CEDA for the allegiance of Spanish conservatives than two rival parties were able to do, and might conceivably have been powerful enough to ensure that conspiracy and rebellion would lead rapidly to restoration – or 'installation'.

This view was stubbornly and successfully resisted by Fal Conde and most of the new generation of regional, provincial and Youth leaders. For the new occupants of Carlism's hierarchy, many of them former Integrists and most of them owing their positions to Fal Conde, Carlism as they knew it was the product not of inheritance but of proselytization and organizational efficiency. They had every reason to fear that a dynastic settlement, or worse still a political merger with Alfonsism, would mean the winding up of the Carlist organization which they had done so much to create and within which they enjoyed relative eminence. Navarrese, Basque, Catalonian and Valencian Carlists might expect to dominate a unified monarchism in their respective regions; Andalusian Carlists in particular could entertain no such hopes, given the wealth of Andalusian Alfonsism. For Fal Conde and his supporters, power therefore had to be won without compromise; rebellion, if not an exclusively Carlist affair – and that was the ideal – must at least be unleashed, monopolized and controlled by the Traditionalist Communion in order that the road to monarchical installation might be a straight one. Compared with Rodezno's pragmatic strategy, Fal Conde's was sheer wishful thinking.

One of the strangest experiences enjoyed by Carlists in the 1930s was that of finding their ideas suddenly in vogue. Since the end of the 1870–6 war, amid perennially unfavourable circumstances, the cause of Traditionalism had been upheld virtually alone and unheeded by the Carlists and their schismatic offshoots. During these years most Alfonsists regarded Traditionalism as a doomed relic of the past, and even those of a more conservative, authoritarian disposition were drawn to the writings of the politically non-aligned, basically *pidalista* Menéndez Pelayo rather than to the similar, if

admittedly less dazzling works of Mella. Many adherents of
Alfonso XIII, especially former Maurists, began to abandon liberalism
with the advent of the Dictatorship, although they exhibited singular
uncertainty as to their future ideological position. Confused by
Primo de Rivera's fall and the subsequent collapse of the monarchy
itself, and then horrified by the events of the Republic's early months,
an increasing number of Alfonsists began to divest themselves of the
last few trappings of liberalism; so, for that matter, did the exiled
monarch himself.[56] Although inspired in part by the ideas of Action
Française and Portuguese Integralism, most of them initially
embraced with enthusiasm the notion of Traditional Monarchy as
formulated and expounded by the Carlists.

This was a natural and probably inevitable step. In the first few
months of the Republic, organized monarchist expression was effectively limited to Carlism, whose spokesmen wasted no opportunity
to point out what many Alfonsists had already realized for themselves: that Mella's predictions concerning the fate of the Alfonsine
monarchy had finally been vindicated, thereby bestowing a new
relevance upon the rest of Carlism's ideas. Added to this was the
coincidence that political notions related to those of Carlism, if
not necessarily identical, appeared to be becoming fashionable in
other parts of Europe; Traditionalism's appeal for wavering liberal
monarchists thus rested on a feeling that it represented a distinctly
Spanish version of a general European trend, that it was, depending
upon individual outlook or definition, either a Spanish alternative
to fascism or fascism's Spanish manifestation. Carlism was not, of
course, the sole intellectual inspiration for those who became the
pillars of Renovación Española. The Dictator's Minister of Labour,
Eduardo Aunós, borrowed from La Tour de Pin and from Italian
Fascism; the moving spirit of Acción Española, Vegas, drew in
roughly equal proportions from Carlism, Portuguese Integralism
and Action Française; and the influence of Charles Maurras upon
Calvo Sotelo was even more marked.[57] Carlists were nevertheless
inclined to feel that all these roads led back directly or indirectly
to their own beliefs, freely acknowledging Carlism's kinship with
foreign rightism and considering the broad body of Traditionalist
ideas to possess universal validity even if their detailed application
might vary from one country to another. Thus they could argue that
Alfonsist debts to foreign right-wing publicists were equally owed
to Carlism.

The Alfonsists themselves certainly had no reservations about attempting to validate the neo-Traditionalist element in their ideas by relating them to Carlism. In his book *Cartas a un escéptico en materia de formas de gobierno*, José María Pemán extolled the 'purity' of the monarchism of Donoso Cortés, Aparisi, Nocedal and Mella as compared, for example, with the rationalism and agnosticism of Action Française.[58] Likewise, Vegas and his fellow-editors of *La Época* recognized the Carlist dynasty as the 'spiritual family' from which the future succession must spring – even though they also concluded that this must now reside in the persons of Alfonso XIII and his sons.[59] They, too, acknowledged Mella's predictive accuracy, besides paying special tribute to the doctrinal purity of Integrism.[60] Such recognition of Carlism's ancestry of modern, not necessarily Carlist Traditionalism was commonplace among the chief spokesmen and theorists of Renovación Española and of the Alfonsist cause in general.

To have acted otherwise would have been dishonest in view of the many points of similarity between the programmes advocated by the Alfonsists and that of the Communion. Approaches varied from Pemán's essentially abstract, even aesthetic defence of monarchy to Calvo Sotelo's opinion that the Traditional Monarchy was justified not in doctrinal terms but as a purely pragmatic response to Spain's four crying needs – national unity, supreme authority, Christian spirituality and social peace.[61] For the anglophile, onetime leftist Basque, Ramiro de Maeztu, 'Catholic Monarchy' offered a way of cementing ties of *hispanidad*,[62] while for Aunós it was a step on the road to 'the imperial unity of Europe' formerly known under Charlemagne and the Emperor Charles V.[63] The implications for Spain were all broadly similar and were summed up by Vegas:

It is necessary to forge a new state using the institutions which in the course of centuries have demonstrated experimentally a suitability and aptitude for purifying a good government and a just organization of society.[64]

In Vegas' opinion the monarchy provided a guarantee of 'continuity, competence, and responsibility for the state's good government'.[65] Continuity was equally important to Pemán, who like Pradera made much of the benefits supposedly resulting from a monarch's domestic preparation for kingship, his impartiality and his life-long responsibility for his own actions: 'Kings have the nation as a wife in indissoluble matrimony; presidents, as a mistress in fleeting dissipation.'[66] Calvo Sotelo considered that monarchy combined with the virtue of continuity the equally desirable qualities of efficiency and authority. What was more, it was in vogue: 'We are monarchists because today we wish to Europeanize ourselves, for now to Europeanize is to monarchize.'[67]

All the Alfonsist spokesmen adhered to the now conventional critique of liberalism and parliamentarism, and to the vision of the corporate state as the best means of harmonizing national unity with regional aspirations and social justice. Pemán, Sáinz Rodríguez and, on the whole, Vegas assumed a straight neo-Traditionalist position by accepting almost without modification the Mellist version of corporativism, whereas Aunós and Calvo Sotelo showed signs of a more ready acceptance of modern authoritarianism. Any taste for absolutism was nevertheless unanimously denied. Although employing the terms 'authoritarian' and 'totalitarian' far more freely than the Carlists, the Alfonsists tended to insist that both words referred to the intrinsic strength and cohesiveness of a corporate regime rather than to the manner in which governmental power was to be applied. Pemán, for example, wrote of the 'broad, totalitarian power' of a traditional monarch, but continued that royal power should be limited along the lines drawn by Mella and Pradera.[68] Calvo Sotelo, though attracted by the dubious tool of the plebiscite, affirmed that the 'authoritarian state' of his dreams was not absolutist: 'Nothing within the State against the State; but the State in the service of the Nation.'[69] Even Aunós, who along with Goicoechea was more obviously influenced by Italian Fascism than any of his colleagues, claimed to eschew the idea of a state party and an 'absorbent State' in favour of a genuine, representative, corporate monarchy.[70]

The doctrines of the CEDA, and more specifically of Gil Robles, while drawn principally from Catholic Public Law and recent papal declarations and hence less conscious of any debt to Carlism, nonetheless closely resembled the latter regarding ends, if not means; in particular Gil Robles' vision of the practical application of social-Catholic principles in the Spanish setting benefited directly from Spanish Traditionalist thought. It was no coincidence that Gil Robles had grown up within a Carlist family, while one of his leading lieutenants, Lucía, was actually a former Carlist whose fundamental ideas, despite the equally firm denials from him and from the

Carlists, had largely survived his apostasy. Gil Robles made it plain that his ultimate goal was a corporate system avoiding equally the perils of liberalism and totalitarianism:

true corporativism is a complete system. It embraces the economic, the social and the political order; it has as its basis men grouped according to the community of their natural interests and social functions; and it aspires to the public and distinct representation of such organisms, as the coping and pinnacle of the system.[71]

While preferring to place the CEDA within the sphere of papal-inspired European social-Catholicism rather than that of Spanish Traditionalism, Gil Robles willingly admitted his debt to his Carlist forebears. When in the Cortes the Carlist deputy Toledo interrupted a statement of principles from Gil Robles with the comment 'This is Traditionalism', Gil Robles did not deny it, simply remarking that Traditionalism was not the exclusive preserve of the Carlists.[72]

This was obviously true, but Carlists were entitled to retort that had they not been kept alive by Carlism, many of the ideas now being propounded by both Renovación and the CEDA would have had neither existence nor validity. Had Carlism withered and died in the face of advancing liberalism in the 1870s and 1880s, contemporary corporativism could less easily have been defended as 'authentically Spanish'. It would, in fact, have appeared as 'alien' as its own propagandists claimed fascism to be.

As stated above, the most serious weakness of Traditionalist theory as expounded by Pradera and his contemporaries was its failure to grapple with the practical difficulties and probable contradictions inherent in attempting to apply a non-coercive corporativist programme in a predominantly hostile society. The Alfonsists of Renovación and the *cedistas* had the opportunity and incentive to face this problem more realistically, free as they were of the inherited association of dynastic ties and integralist ideology which stood in the way of Carlist pragmatism.

In general, the Alfonsists resolved the problem by moving beyond an initial neo-Traditionalism to a position closer to fascism in its open authoritarianism and pseudo-radical demagoguery.[73] The latter, somewhat reminiscent of the early stages of more than one frankly fascist movement, stemmed from an apparently greater appreciation of the need to win over hostile and apathetic workers than was normally displayed by all but a youthful minority of Carlists. Maeztu – the only prominent Alfonsist with a left-wing past – considered it a matter of 'evangelizing the revolutionary masses and gaining them for Spain and civilization, for love, education and social solidarity'. A hint of the methods that might be necessary to achieve this followed, with the demand that agitators first be 'reduced to silence'. But 'that is not enough. The people must be won.'[74] Maeztu thus saw the difficulty, but offered no constructive suggestion as to how to overcome it. Similarly, Aunós visualized a development of the Primo de Rivera dictatorship whose *caudillo* would be supported by the Socialist masses and the youth of Spain;[75] though he avoided the conclusion, the experience of the Dictatorship suggested that such a formula could only be imposed from above. The character of Renovación Española's financial and industrial contacts only served to make this all the more likely, as well as to expose Alfonsist gestures towards the working class as the cynical posturings they undoubtedly were.

When facing the thorny problem of the transition from Republic to corporative monarchy, the Alfonsists showed every sign of being less ideologically constricted than the Carlists and began to flirt with the dangerous idea of 'temporary' dictatorship. As Pemán remarked, a monarchy could become a Republic overnight, but the reverse process would inevitably take a great deal longer.[76] Admittedly the Carlists also realized this, both Villores and Rodezno having at various times thought in terms of a brief bridging period during which would be erected the institutions necessary to underpin the monarchy.[77] Jesús Comín's advocacy of a 'National Dictatorship' as an alternative to 'Red Dictatorship' was, however, highly unusual coming from a Carlist.[78] Vegas and his collaborators, if scarcely less vague on details, went much further than most Carlists in accepting the possibility of an unavoidable and perhaps even indefinite postponement of the restoration;[79] Aunós appeared to regard fascism as a transitional stage on the way to genuine corporativism;[80] and Calvo Sotelo eventually came to see the return of the monarchy as a desirable but distant end to a lengthy evolutionary process under an authoritarian regime.[81] Calvo Sotelo, whose views came to dominate Renovación Española from 1934 onwards,[82] frequently denied any personal aspirations towards dictatorship, yet his plans seemed to promise at least a period under such a system.

What the Alfonsists preferred not to consider was the possibility that a dictatorship, whether civilian or military, might prove self-perpetuating and the restoration even more distant than they liked to contemplate. Perhaps this was natural enough, since in one important respect the whole transition problem was less serious for them than it was for the Carlists. Whereas the latter's connections with the army were relatively tenuous, the Alfonsists had increasing reason to believe the army sympathetic to their cause. Assuming, therefore, that force would be indispensable to a change of regime, and that force was likely to be applied mainly by the army, the Alfonsists had less cause than the Carlists to fear the paradoxical possibility that their ultimate goal might be vetoed by an ally necessary to its very attainment. Even so, with Calvo Sotelo, Goicoechea and other Alfonsists openly declaring their sympathy for fascism – and even on occasions for Nazism – the conclusion was there to be drawn that in the New State towards which they were moving the king's position might be that not of a 'traditional' monarch but of a Victor Emmanuel III.

While the Carlists turned their backs on the riddle of reconciling ends and means, and the Alfonsists reacted by allowing monarcho-fascism to supersede neo-Traditionalism, Gil Robles, in his own way, faced it more or less squarely.[83] Hardly less drawn than the Carlists to a nostalgic, romanticized vision of the supposed organic society of the pre-Enlightenment era, and just as depressed by its disappearance since the French Revolution, Gil Robles none the less grasped the enormous difficulties involved in a return to corporativism in the absence of the religiously inspired consensus upon which it had originally been based. It was all very well to argue that corporativism should replace party politics and class warfare, individualistic and *étatiste* excess; yet their very existence made any such reversion problematical. Gil Robles believed it necessary to begin by accepting the arrival of democracy, and then to employ it as a transitory means towards the end of genuine, rooted, popular corporativism. In other words, a mass electorate fragmented materially and spiritually must be persuaded, however gradually, to abandon democracy democratically, in favour of a corporate system. He was by no means sure that this would happen:

Will the peoples return to those immutable and eternal principles, unifiers of consciences, without loss of liberty? I do not know, though I hope so ... Meanwhile, we do not deceive ourselves. In Spain there is in the political sphere no reality other than parties.[84]

Gil Robles recognized the absurdity of proposals such as those offered by the Carlists for a rapid and voluntary return to the organic society and state. Rapidity and voluntarism being incompatible, he claimed to be willing to sacrifice rapidity. The latter he considered possible only through the suppression of political parties in favour of a single party, thereby muffling ideological divisions without destroying their causes. In short, he saw what most Carlists failed to see: that genuine corporativism could not be imposed from above upon an unprepared and largely hostile society. In attempting to do this, the Italian Fascists – perhaps because their corporativism, like that of the Alfonsists, was so shallow – had merely erected a despotism without producing social justice.

On an abstract plane, Gil Robles' strategy of approaching the corporate state by popular consent possessed a logical consistency quite absent from Carlist millenarianism. Since corporativism rested upon consent, and since the electorate at present withheld that consent, then the electorate must be persuaded. In the real world, however, this strategy also had its weaknesses. The patience of Gil Robles' followers was not boundless – nor, for that matter, was that of Gil Robles himself. What attitude ought therefore to be adopted should the process of peaceful persuasion take an unbearably long time or even fail altogether? More urgent still, was there the remotest chance of gradualism succeeding in the face of increasing militancy on the left and more purposeful, if less consistent rivals on the right? The shrill quasi-fascism of the JAP, the presence within the CEDA of military plotters like General Fanjul, and the dangerously weak hold which social-Catholicism and gradualist corporativism in any case had upon a great many *cedistas* meant that should a crisis of this nature arrive, Gil Robles and his party were unlikely to balk at an authoritarian 'solution' to Spain's difficulties.

When a rising figure within the Communion, José María Arauz de Robles, claimed in 1934 that almost all the ideas current on the Spanish right were of Carlist origin, he was guilty of oversimplification rather than exaggeration.[85] Without question both Renovación Española and the CEDA held ideas which, if related to the fascism, authoritarian conservatism, traditionalism and social-Catholicism of

Europe as a whole, nevertheless descended in the Spanish context from nineteenth-century Carlist Traditionalism. Closer examination, however, reveals greater complexity. Carlist-inspired neo-Traditionalism was one crucial element within Alfonsist thought, but tended to weaken as the Republic wore on. This was partly the result of tackling the problem of 'transition' shirked by the Carlists, partly the effect of greater susceptibility to foreign ideas because of the relative newness and superficiality of Alfonsist Traditionalism, and partly the direct consequence of Calvo Sotelo's leadership. The CEDA's official goals were and remained substantially similar to the Communion's, with the significant but not necessarily permanent exception of the monarchy itself, but its view of 'means' was radically different. Even so, the CEDA's dilemma of what to do if its tactic failed was not unlike the Communion's own unrecognized problem of 'means'. The Carlists' antagonism towards authoritarianism and dictatorship depended upon ignoring the internal contradictions of their ideology in the light of modern necessities; were they to be brought face to face with reality, might not they too find authoritarianism acceptable? This failure to face facts and arrive at a convincing strategy was all the more serious since in the Falange there was emerging a possible rival with fewer qualms about forcing its particular distortion of corporativism on an unwilling populace.

7
Carlism and fascism

Unlike the Spanish left – and, for that matter, much of the right – the Carlists were extremely selective in their use of the term 'fascism'. Where the left employed it as a catch-all embracing any expression of militant opposition to itself, and rightists such as Calvo Sotelo, Goicoechea and the JAP's spokesmen casually accepted it as applying to themselves, the Carlists consistently refused to don the label. They believed that fascism was an essentially non-Spanish phenomenon, relevant only in countries where no organized, indigenous Traditionalism existed. In Spain, which was blessed with Carlism, it was simply unnecessary. Within the broad and varied spectrum of right-wing politics, fascism was distinguished from all forms of Catholic corporativism by its secularism and above all its 'Hegelian' worship of the all-powerful state, a notion which the Carlists rejected as a kind of socialist deviation. In both the Spanish and the general European contexts, individuals and groups were regarded as 'fascist' by the Carlists to the extent that they combined *étatisme* with other, more congenial right-wing attitudes.

The largely uncritical acceptance extended by the Carlists to Salazar, Dollfuss and Degrelle was inevitably somewhat qualified in the case of Mussolini and severely so in that of Hitler, although both naturally came in for praise on account of their anti-communism and their destruction of liberal democracy. Of the two, Mussolini received much less attention but was by far the more sympathetically viewed, his state-worship being amply compensated for by his maintenance of the Italian monarchy and his *détente* with the Vatican through the Lateran Treaty of 1929. The veteran Jaime Chicharro summed up the Carlist attitude early in 1933: Italian Fascism was '*simpático*' because it combated 'Judaism, masonry and marxism' (this was five years before Mussolini's introduction of the racial laws), and had 'restored temporal power to the Popes and restored religion'.[1] Carlist admiration for Fascist Italy remained fairly restrained, however until the outbreak of the Ethiopian War in autumn 1935. As war

loomed, *El Siglo Futuro* sprang to the defence of 'learned and populous' Italy's right to 'a place in the African sun' at the expense of
'savage and almost depopulated Ethiopia', a land egregious for the
'barbarity of its social organization'.[2] Subsequent reports on the war
itself made much of the 'humanitarian sentiments' which it was
claimed inspired the advance of Italy's armies and the fulfilment of
her civilizing mission.[3] Italy's critics, clustering in the League of
Nations, consisted of the 'barbarous hordes of the Negus, plus the
hidden forces of Jewish plutocracy, freemasonry, marxism and communism, as well as the diplomacy of the world's most powerful
empire'.[4]

This last remark illustrates how sympathy towards Italy generated
a sudden and violent recrudescence of a Carlist anglophobia last
apparent during the Great War. Britain, it was asserted, was pursuing a purely selfish policy motivated by the needs of her overblown
empire and thinly veiled by her 'hypocritical English puritanism',
while actually playing the game of international communism and
risking world war in the process.[5] Fascist imperialism also helped
to rekindle expansionist ideas which Mella had once held; at the
time of the Stresa conference in May 1935, Rodezno declared in the
Cortes that Spain's interests, albeit as a benevolent neutral, lay with
Italy as 'the leading Mediterranean power' and a fellow Latin nation.
The ultimate objective of this alignment would be the recovery of
Tangier and, implicitly, Gibraltar.[6]

If Carlist warmth towards Mussolini tended to become more
effusive as the Republic's life lengthened, feelings towards Hitler if
anything cooled as evidence accumulated of the wide gulf separating
Nazism from Catholic Traditionalism. When Hitler became Chancellor of Germany at the end of January 1933, comment was wholly
favourable and prognosis optimistic. *El Siglo Futuro*, for example,
attributed Hitler's successful rise to his exploitation of the traditionalism of the German people, and interpreted the not altogether voluntary acceptance of his authority by the Catholic Centre Party as
indicating that the Church could expect an important position within
his regime.[7] *Reacción*, keeping its customary eye on the Catalonian
proletariat, hailed the conversion to National Socialism of a vast
number of German workers, and called upon their Spanish brothers
to act with comparable patriotism.[8]

Greater realism came with the passage of time. For those elements
of the Third Reich common to the general European reaction, ap-

proval was maintained; writing early in 1935, Don Jaime's former secretary, Francisco de Melgar, invited *El Pensamiento Navarro*'s readers to consider how great would be Spain's gratitude towards

the man capable of extirpating socialism in our country, capable of inculcating the entire nation with an ardent patriotism and of making the working class forget the repugnant and suicidal class war invented by the Jew Karl Marx.[9]

In the sphere of foreign policy, Hitler's intentions were considered to be completely pacific and defensive, even after the remilitarization of the Rhineland in March 1936. Then, as before, *El Siglo Futuro* argued that the only threat to European peace came from 'Soviet, militaristic, praetorian Russia', against whose revolutionary designs Hitler offered a bulwark.[10]

Other aspects of Nazism, however, provoked criticism and even bitter hostility from Carlist commentators. Respect for Hitler nose-dived when Austrian Nazis assassinated the Carlists' great hero, Dollfuss, in July 1934. Protested *El Siglo Futuro*:

And this gang of murderers who killed [Dollfuss] in so ruffianly a manner are *Nazis*? What guarantees of order do these *Nazis* offer? ... What dictatorship is not justified against these and other bandits?[11]

Early illusions concerning Hitler's Catholicism had been quickly and brutally shattered. Indeed, nothing bewildered the Carlists so much as the religious policies of Nazism, and they were uncertain whether to be more revolted or amused by the neo-pagan dabblings of leading Nazis such as Darré and Rosenberg. Darré's plan to reorganize the calendar in line with Teutonic mythology stung *El Siglo Futuro* into remarking somewhat sweepingly that the Germans were evidently gifted neither in theology, philosophy nor sociology, and more safely that such absurdities were hardly calculated 'to provide evidence of racial superiority'.[12] *El Pensamiento Navarro* appeared to take these matters more seriously, and described Nazi neo-paganism as the partner of Soviet atheism in a pincer attack on Catholic Christianity.[13]

The Carlists had no time for Nazi racism, which they flatly condemned as a blasphemy. Emilio Ruiz Muñoz, a priest who wrote regularly in *El Siglo Futuro* under the pseudonym 'Fabio', suggested that nobody but a lunatic could believe himself a member of a master race and that the only thing proved by racist writings was the inferiority of the supposed intellectuals responsible for them.[14] What Carlists objected to was not, it must be emphasized, anti-semitism, which they regarded as one of Nazism's virtues, but the 'pure race' concept which elevated Germans above other Europeans, Latins certainly not excepted. *El Siglo Futuro* cited scientific research to prove the invalidity of the 'pure race' idea, concluding that 'German racism is a myth . . . without historical basis', and its bible, Rosenberg's *Myth of the Twentieth Century*, nothing but a collection of 'unintentional jokes'. What mattered to a nation was not race but national tradition, not the colour of skin, eyes and hair but 'that the material be unifiable and that it unite and vivify itself through an independent spirit'. Thus, even though Nazism had achieved incidental good through its war on socialism and democracy, it was held to be far removed from Traditionalism. The latter, it was argued, was a true 'concept' not a 'myth', a 'historical reality', a movement securely rooted 'in a people's history . . . in facts, in the law'. Compared with Carlism, Nazism was 'a contradiction of Traditionalism expressed as a ridiculous caricature'.[15]

When 'Spanish fascism' began to be taken seriously during 1933, the Carlists were quick to attack it as an unnecessary foreign import, and a doctrinally dubious one at that. It was generally conceded that fascism was a mixture of good and bad elements, but argued that since all the good ones could be found in Carlism, it was therefore an utter irrelevancy. 'It is a political conception which I do not share,' Lamamié commented, 'since I believe that what is appropriate for Spain is the Traditionalism which I profess.' The qualities in fascism which he found attractive, its emphasis upon hierarchy and combativeness, were, he pointed out, unchallengeably represented by the Requeté.[16] The absurdity of importing 'foreign' ideas to do a job for which Carlism was ideally suited was also stressed by the head of the Madrid AET, Aurelio González Gregorio, who went on to say that fascist corporativism was actually a Traditionalist axiom.[17] Nor was it only the Carlists themselves who took this view; Albiñana, deftly side-stepping *La Unión*'s attempt to boost him as the rightful – perhaps because harmless – *caudillo* of Spanish fascism, obligingly predicted that fascism would get nowhere in Spain because its cause and appeal had already been cornered by Carlism.[18]

The main fault of fascism as far as most Carlists were concerned was what Fal Conde described as 'the fascist political socialism of "everything for the state"";[19] so disturbing did it seem that both Fernando Contreras and Marcelino Oreja concluded that there was little to choose between living under fascism and communism, both systems being equally despotic.[20] The leadership principle was just as alien to members of a cause based on hereditary monarchy; it was repeatedly stated that the role of the superhuman leader in the regimes of Mussolini and Hitler might be the ideal thing for the countries which spawned them, but that to graft a similar system on to Spain would be as wildly exotic as it was unnecessary.[21] When the Falange was founded in October 1933, Pradera wrote in *Acción Española* that José Antonio's speech contained nothing of substance that was not already familiar to any Carlist.[22] Once having been laid down, the official Carlist line on 'fascism' continued essentially unchanged through 1934, although like the rest of the right the Carlists paid the subject rather less attention as the Falange's fortunes seemed to be foundering. Truth to tell, they virtually ignored the spoken and written outpourings of José Antonio, Ledesma and Ruiz de Alda, merely taking it for granted that Falangism was nothing more or less than a Spanish version of Mussolinian Fascism.

A classic statement of the orthodox Carlist case against fascism came early in 1935 from a student propagandist, Francisco de Soto Oriol, later to become president of the Seville AET. In an essay 'Traditionalism and Fascism', which was awarded a prize by the Communion's Council of Culture, Soto Oriol accused fascists of opportunism in their selective use of those aspects of Traditionalism which appealed to them and total rejection of the remainder. Above all, where Carlism stood for the devolution of power, fascism meant 'totemization' of the state and its absorption of corporations, regions and individuals. Apart from acceptable variants in Portugal and Austria – Soto Oriol, it must be admitted, was less than orthodox in classifying them as even loosely fascist – fascism lacked the vital Traditionalist postulate of 'God before everything' or Catholic unity; hence, even if the fascists were the sons of Traditionalism 'let us agree that they are degenerate sons'.[23]

Soto Oriol was perfectly representative of Carlism as a whole in his refusal to treat Falangism as a distinct political phenomenon in its own right, preferring to damn it through an implicit association with Italian, and to a lesser extent German, fascism. Closer examination of Falangist ideas and propaganda would have made such comparisons more complicated, and contrasts less neat. Like most of the movements on the 'new' European right, Falangism was highly eclectic, especially after the fusion with the JONS early in 1934. From then on, and even after Ledesma's expulsion a year later, at least four different strands were discernible: the initially powerful conservative influence, based largely upon old supporters of Primo de Rivera's Patriotic Union and boosted by Alfonsists like Eliseda and Ansaldo who wished to use the Falange as a tool of monarchism; the austere, Castilian, Catholic authoritarianism of Redondo, which while not actually inspired by Carlism certainly shared common spiritual ground with it; Ledesma's strident, radical National Syndicalism; and José Antonio's own distinctive brand of elitist regenerationism, of politics through 'poetry'. Of these four strands, Redondo's was never likely to become that of the Falange as a whole, while 'monarchist Falangism' largely vanished from the middle of 1934. Nevertheless, until José Antonio succeeded in placing his stamp on the movement in 1935, any generalizations seeking to encapsulate the principles of Falangism were highly dangerous, the Carlists' included.

The elements of 'fascism' most distrusted by Carlists were to be found in the ideas and plans of Ledesma, which went on coursing through Falangist veins even after his expulsion. Ever since 1931, Ledesma had employed Mussolini's formula 'All power belongs to the state'; his admiration for the Duce and for Hitler was quite open, and his National Syndicalism bore more than a passing resemblance to both the early programme of the Italian *fasci di combattimento* and that of the Nazi 'left'.[24] The fusion of the JONS and the Falange, and Ledesma's position as triumvir, lent substance to Carlist belief not only in the Falange's *étatisme* but also in its derivativeness.

The characteristic tone of Falangism was not really that of Ledesma, however, so much as that of José Antonio, who consistently shrank from the full-blown 'state totemism' which the Carlists reasonably regarded as central to fascism. Midway through 1934, José Antonio visited Germany and returned to Spain much less enthusiastic about Nazism than Goicoechea and Gil Robles on their return from similar trips. From then on he began to drop favourable references to fascism and even to deny altogether that the Falange was fascist – a complete turn-around from his position of a few months before.[25] His political ideas, hitherto little more than vaguely exciting abstractions, began to assume somewhat greater clarity, one result being a lessening of the Falange's deliberate identification with foreign fascism and totalitarianism. Particularly striking were the clashes of emphasis between José Antonio's developing outlook and the views of Ledesma. Where Ledesma proclaimed 'All for the State', José Antonio insisted that the State must not engulf the individual;[26] where Ledesma increasingly condemned every manifestation of regionalism, José Antonio was careful to draw the line only at separatism;[27] where Ledesma and the dedicated National Syndicalists were staunchly anti-clerical, José Antonio now affirmed that the Catholic interpretation of life was both true and 'historically Spanish' and that any reconstruction of Spain must therefore 'bear a Catholic meaning'.[28] This was not quite good enough for Eliseda and the coterie of clerical Falangists, who for the most part gradually pulled out of the party, but it satisfied a great many practising Catholic Falangists, including the pious admirer of Torquemada, Redondo.

On the pivotal issue of the state's role, a measure of doubt thus exists as to whether the Falange of José Antonio merited the amount of Carlist criticism it received. On the other hand, as Falangist *étatisme* diminished, the cult of José Antonio bloomed, thereby confirming the Carlists' second big objection to fascism. Yet perhaps what really kept their criticism alive, aside from sheer political rivalry, was simply the great difference in style between the two movements. Whatever the *content* of José Antonio's argument, and that was never easy to pin down, its presentation, with its irrationalism, empty hyperbole and 'poetic' fancies, was utterly unlike the rather stodgy, churchbound propaganda of Carlism. Inability or unwillingness to penetrate the fog of Falangist rhetoric prevented the vast majority of Carlists from recognizing how much their movements actually had in common. This was all the more true as the Falange became less radical following Ledesma's ouster, and as evidence began to accumulate that not all Carlists unquestioningly accepted the doctrinal and policy positions of the Communion's leaders.

What divided the Falange from the majority of the monarchist and *cedista* right was less its supposed totalitarianism – to which not all Catholic conservatives were as theoretically ill disposed as the Carlists, especially once Calvo Sotelo assumed the political leadership of Alfonsism – than its display of social radicalism and the manner of its expression. From Ledesma's lips this had involved a sincere belief in 'national revolution', wherein land would be expro-

priated, private property nationalized, and both handed over to municipalities and to syndicates of workers and peasants.[29] In spite of the
embarrassing fact that few workers — and fewer real proletarians —
could be persuaded to embrace this programme, it was every bit as
revolutionary as its proponents claimed, and permitted conservatives
of every stripe to regard Ledesma, the JONS and then the Falange
as advocating a perverted form of socialism. Ledesma and the
National-Syndicalist Falangists, for their part, seemed perfectly
happy that this should be so.

Under the single leadership of José Antonio, the Falange kept up
its verbal allegiance to 'revolution', and those National Syndicalists
who chose not to follow Ledesma out of the movement continued to
mean it. But while conservatives' suspicions lingered, José Antonio's
conception of 'revolution' was more limited than Ledesma's, if anything approximating more closely to the state-run reformism of
moderate Socialists like Prieto. It involved the nationalization of
credit, state-imposed agrarian reform the details of which would vary
according to the needs of particular regions, state sponsorship of
new industries, profit-sharing schemes for workers and employees —
and, of course, the establishment of the Falangist variant of the corporate state.[30] What this amounted to was a radical-nationalist
programme intended to modernize a backward country. As such,
it would have raised few eyebrows in the developing nations of the
post-1945 world; owing to the political fashions of the 1930s, however, it inevitably came to be expressed and interpreted within the
capacious framework of fascism.

Even though José Antonio's outspokenness on social and economic
matters did not approach that of Ledesma, it made more impact
because of the higher social circles in which the Dictator's son moved.
It was certainly more than sufficient to disturb conservative leaders
in the 1933–5 Cortes, among them the most determined Carlist
opponents of Republican agrarian reform, Lamamié and Rodezno.
The impression was thus created of the Falange as a radical, and
Carlism as a conservative movement of the right — a picture seemingly
acceptable to the leaders of both. But it was a misleading impression;
on one side, numerous Falangists could not have cared less about
social radicalism, while on the other a vague but genuine radical
impulse was stirring in the Communion, not all of whose members
were satisfied with a policy of charity and condescension towards
the poor. The modish blending of ultra-nationalism with social

radicalism was widespread among young rightists, affecting not only the Falange but also the JAP and the Carlist Youth and Workers Sections.

If in the past Carlists had shown inadequate understanding of social problems, the reason was not so much selfishness born of sympathy with the rich as ignorance produced by sheer lack of contact with the poor. Indeed, Carlism's relative independence of financial and industrial capitalism and, admittedly to a lesser degree, of large landowning interests, meant that its spokesmen, in criticizing the socio-economic *status quo*, did so genuinely if seldom knowledgeably. Like other Catholic parties, Carlism officially approved of the capitalist system but not of its so-called 'excesses' and 'abuses'; the Carlist grass-roots remained for the most part set in the countryside and the smaller towns, as out of tune as ever with city life and large-scale capitalism. In the 1930s, the same improvement in communications which brought news of European events into the Spanish home also heightened a more general awareness of the condition of Spain itself. With Carlism now represented in most Spanish regions, the relatively comfortable Carlists of the north were no longer as cut off from the social distress of the south and the big cities. The result was an intensification of Carlist social protest, often extremely confused but nonetheless sincere, which perhaps brought its utterers closer to the 'modern' right.

This development became marked during 1934, as class conflict grew more bitter both in the cities and in the southern countryside. According to Ginés Martínez, conditions in rural Andalusia were at their worst ever, with hunger and unemployment increasing at an alarming rate.[31] Ginés Martínez, as well as other, less plebeian Carlists, were quite obviously upset by the sight of such misery, yet naturally saw its cure as lying not in short-term legislation or a change in governmental social and economic policy, but in a total replacement of political and economic liberalism by the principles of the Encyclicals. All the prevalent social evils of the 1930s – unemployment and underemployment, falling wages, strikes and lock-outs, eviction, malnutrition and downright starvation, and their end-product, class war – were considered by the Carlists to be the logical and inescapable consequences of liberalism, remediable only through the destruction of the system which produced them.[32]

By taking this line, Carlist critics were freed from having to con-

sider the responsibility for social distress of the wealthier members
of their own cause, who had, after all, prospered under liberalism,
and had recently supported the 'rectifying' legislation which had
contributed something, at least, to present hardship. Fierce criticism
certainly was levelled at employers guilty of wage-cutting and lock-
outs, not only liberals but also Catholics who had been so seduced by
liberal economics as to forget or ignore the Christian obligations of
ownership; but these were not believed to include Carlists.[33] Attacks
on employers were commonest in Seville, where class conflict, interunion rivalry and *pistolerismo* were unequalled and where Carlism
had most pretensions towards being a workers' movement. The
speeches and newspaper articles of Ginés Martínez, the chief would-
be scourge of the bosses, invariably contained attacks on economic
liberalism and more often than not on 'un-Christian employers'. Even
within a liberal system, he charged, there was no excuse for Catholic
employers ignoring the Encyclicals while paying them lip-service,
filling their own pockets while cutting wages, and loudly defending
public order when it was they who were the real authors not only of
pistolerismo but of the 'red wave' now threatening to swallow them.[34]

Ginés Martínez, if more outspoken than most Carlists, was essentially orthodox in his social criticism. Not so the Navarrese Youth,
whose characteristically shriller assaults on the 'economic right' led
them to step out of line with the Communion's general policy. Their
newspaper *a.e.t.* followed the pattern of the radical, rather than the
conservative right of interwar Europe, in using both the critiques
and, on occasions, the language of socialism in support of conspicuously unsocialist solutions. It was time, *a.e.t.* thundered, to end
the situation whereby a chasm yawned between

an enormous mass of miserable beings who clench their fists menacingly
against cold and paralysed machines, and a privileged section of politically
dominant potentates who, protected by their vast resources, bar the way to
the multitude in order to squander their wealth in orgies and banquets
before the wide-open eyes of the proletariat.[35]

The 'economic right', it was argued, had produced no social reforms
of its own, but had attacked every proposal of the Socialists 'without
thinking that in the greater part of them there resides a fund of justice'.
Unlike their superiors, the students of *a.e.t.* fervently endorsed the
Agrarian Reform which they claimed was being obstructed by 'the
feudal egoism of the odious grandees of grain', by no means all of

whom were to be found outside the Traditionalist Communion. They went still further, urging an immediate limitation of private wealth and a 'regularization' of profits, all in the name of the Communion's 'proletarian mass' which they, like all Carlists, contrasted with the riches and aristocratic connections of Renovación and the CEDA.[36]

The dream of the radical students was an intoxicating one: the 'Carlist Revolution', carried out with 'the genuine representatives of the people, not with well-heeled politicians'; a revolution, moreover, which would be the absolute opposite of 'cedism'.[37] Here again they saw a brighter side to socialism. Might not 'a good clean-up of society' be exactly what was needed? Might not the threatened socialist revolution thus prove to be 'the crucible in which will be purified such avarice, such obstinacy, such seigneurial despotism?' This speculation, wisely perhaps, was not pursued very far. In particular, the highly relevant question of what would happen to the Carlists, young or old, should the left carry out its purifying task, was prudently skirted.[38]

The details of the Carlist Revolution were left unclear too, save that its physical arm would be the Requeté which, apart from going 'up to the palaces that the powerful may atone for the misery of the starving', would apparently be the agent whereby the sceptical lower classes would be converted to Carlism via a kind of 'going to the people' movement:

We, the Carlist Requeté, must go to the fields, the factories, the slums. We must go up into the mountains and down into the plains, to wherever there may be a peasant, a worker, a proletarian, in order to convince him of the truth of our regenerative doctrines.[39]

Here, *a.e.t.* moved back into line with official Carlist policy, for the 'regenerative doctrines' in question were, there could be no doubt, those involving the restoration of the guild and corporation under the aegis of the Traditional Monarchy.

The students' talk of going to the people was never translated into serious action, but it is in any case hard to imagine that action would have been crowned with much success in view of the firm political allegiances of most of the Spanish working class. The mere conception, however, demonstrated the awareness of some of the younger generation of Carlists that the Traditionalist form of corporativism must rest upon consent, and that this could only be achieved through a Carlist—proletarian *rapprochement* and *some* kind of revolution. This in turn led them to appreciate that their most urgent problem was that of attracting uncommitted workers and peasants, and more important of reconquering the far greater number at present committed to Anarchism, Anarcho-Syndicalism and marxism. There was rather more to this than crude demagoguery; though the radical young Carlists undeniably failed to grasp the complexities and contradictions inherent in mixing social radicalism with religious and ideological conservatism, nothing was further from their minds than serving the interests of Spanish capitalism.

However genuine the Carlists' concern for the working class and however intense their hatred of liberalism, not even the tortuous arguments of *a.e.t.* could disguise the fact that at bottom its authors shared the general horror of Carlists at the prospect of successful left-wing revolution. Towards the libertarian left, Carlists did display a modicum of understanding and even sympathy, based upon a common heritage of opposition to and 'persecution' by all the governments of the past half-century, a shared desire for decentralization and rejection of bureaucratic control, and a vague sense of common *hispanidad*. In Seville especially, where the Carlist Workers Section enjoyed some small success in attracting former Anarchists,[40] the tightening grip on the workers' movement of the UGT and the Communists, and that of the Radicals upon local government, allowed the Carlists to pose as the Anarchists' fellow victims of state repressiveness. *La Unión* published lengthy comparisons of the two causes, and actually claimed that 'if the Syndicalists only believed in God, they would be Traditionalists for life'. According to Tejera, most Anarchists were not gunmen but honest and contemplative, if misguided souls.[41]

No such sympathy was extended towards marxism. Although many Carlists were prepared to acknowledge that marxist socialism was a natural by-product of liberalism, they also agreed with Ginés Martínez that in the final analysis it was even worse than the system against which it protested.[42] Even the exuberant students of *a.e.t.* combined their penchant for revolution with a frank hatred of its marxist form. The aspect of socialism which Carlists claimed to find most repellant, apart from its godlessness, was the excessive centralism and *étatisme* which they believed it had passed on to fascism. In embryonic form, these abominations were observable in the professionalized leadership of the Socialist Party and the UGT, whose alleged remoteness from the workers was frequently contrasted with the genuine proletarian status of that epitome of the Catholic worker, Ginés Martínez.[43] Faced with the regimented and apparently unconvertable Socialist masses, even *a.e.t.* lost sympathy. No longer ingenuous seekers after social justice, 'today they are nothing but herds of degraded serfs in the service of tyrants and bosses . . . hordes of incendiaries and assassins' spurred on by hatred to commit infamous crimes.[44] Were marxism to triumph and the Socialist state to become a reality, the worship of 'the god Capital' would simply be replaced by that of 'the god State', with freedom destroyed, humanity bestialized, and the workers themselves turned into automata.[45] The result would be 'a condition of unbearable slavery in which every tinpot leader would be a tyrant protected by the shadow of the most odious of all despotisms – the despotism of the State'.[46]

It was thus plain that the Navarrese students' scorn for the 'economic right', while sincere enough in its way, went nowhere near as deep as their detestation and fear of the left. Like the foreign fascists and the Spanish Falangists whom they so criticized but with whom they shared their radical-nationalist outlook, they were sooner or later going to have to decide where they stood in the event of open war between the 'economic right' and a working class which ignored them.

Despite the existence of common ground between the Falange and the radical elements in the Carlist Youth, pronounced differences persisted as to the kind of polity ultimately desired. The radical young Carlists' heterodoxy lay in the realm of means, not of ends; their goal was essentially the same kind of corporative system as that envisaged by Pradera and the Carlist establishment, but erected upon a society first drastically transformed. However dimly, they perceived that some sort of 'revolution' might be a necessary prerequisite for the survival of a system which spurned the coercive apparatus of contemporary totalitarianism. Once society had been revolutionized and social justice effected, then the Traditional Monarchy, Catholic Unity and the rest of the Carlist programme could be introduced without the need for repression or the defence of gross social and economic inequality.

Whereas the protagonists of 'Carlist Revolution' hovered between the imposition of revolution from above, difficult to achieve without a powerful state machine, and the more stirring vision of a mass rising under the standard of Alfonso Carlos, the Falange under

José Antonio was more frankly elitist. Indeed, it is arguable that for José Antonio himself, with his admiration for the elitists of the Spanish 'Generation of '98', his liberal intellectual debts and continued friendship with liberals, an authoritarian, nationalist movement such as his, led by a narrow 'revolutionary' elite, was necessary precisely because Spain had proved to be incapable of producing a wide, liberal, middle-class, modernizing elite along British or French lines.[47] In insisting that the Falangist state would be 'totalitarian but not all-absorbent', José Antonio was using the word 'totalitarian' in the Traditionalist sense of embracing a single and consistent ideology, rather than in the more 'modern' sense of subjecting the individual and corporation to an all-powerful party and state.[48] Even so, it would be the Falangist elite which would pull Spanish society into the required shape, which would compel sacrifice from the rich and elevate the lowly. It is difficult to see how such a policy was itself practicable without very considerable coercion, probably necessitating recourse to the methods and institutions of contemporary totalitarianism, yet José Antonio admitted to no contradiction. If his increasingly vehement denials of 'fascism' and of the all-powerful state, and his emphasis upon the importance of Catholicism are accepted as genuinely reflecting his state of mind, then what emerges is a movement less alien to Carlism in general and its Youth in particular.

Thus the Falange became less raucously radical even as the steady influx of youth into the Communion strengthened the radical minority in Carlism. To the left, neither José Antonio's new disavowal of fascism nor the consistent and sincere denials of the Carlists were worth taking seriously; both, along with Renovación and the CEDA, were manifestations of Spanish fascism. Now, as then, 'fascism' is largely a matter of definition, not of objective truth. If any organization inspired by extreme nationalism and dedicated to resisting the liberal and socialist conceptions of progress is accepted as 'fascist', then the Spanish left's sweeping use of the term was perfectly reasonable. Certainly, in the heated political climate of the 1930s, it was understandable, not least because the fate of the left itself was likely to be much the same whichever right-wing group eventually prevailed over the rest. If, on the other hand, 'fascism' is taken to refer to a particular form of nationalistic, anti-liberal, anti-socialist organization, a form characterized above all by a leaning towards centralization of power, glorification of the state, and the probable dictatorship of a charismatic leader, then Carlist denials were quite justified and those of José Antonio deserved more serious consideration than either right or left was prepared to give them.

What the impatient Carlist Youth were preaching from the mid-point of the Republic onwards, and the Falange during 1935, was not so much fascism, save in the very broadest sense, as two variants of something perhaps better categorized as populism.[49] In calling for workers, peasants and students to 'close ranks', the Navarrese students and young Carlists in other regions were in effect demanding that Carlism build on its tradition and potential as a movement of all modest men directed against a predominantly 'liberal' oligarchy of land and money. Even after the departure of Ledesma, the bourgeois, student-dominated Falange showed something of the same character. The two parties employed their populism in different directions, to answer different needs. Carlism, still overwhelmingly rural, religiously inspired and backward-looking, appealed to and attracted those anxious to cling to a way of life which now, even more than in the nineteenth century, was disappearing; Falangism was moved by a more secular nationalism, displayed far greater acceptance of urbanism, and laid stress upon modernization and industrial development – two things of which Carlists seldom spoke with enthusiasm. It sought to offer, in effect, a means whereby the patriotically minded might embrace and celebrate a 'modern' Spain.[50] In each case, an overwhelmingly middle-class leadership offered the poor hope while continuing to withhold from them political power. In as much as for the entire Spanish right the problem of 'means' was more difficult than the more distant one of 'ends', Falangist espousal of revolution from above and frank willingness to force the Spanish people to be 'free', was more convincing than the perhaps more genuine populism of the Carlist Youth – if for no other reason than that the former policy was José Antonio's own whereas the latter struck few sympathetic chords in the upper levels of the Communion.

Despite the foregoing remarks, it has to be admitted that the Carlists were not always entitled to complain at the taunts of 'fascism' hurled at them by the left. For ironically, even while much of the Spanish right absorbed the influence of Traditionalist ideas and confessed to doing so, and while the Carlist leadership for the most part held fast to orthodox Traditionalist doctrine, some elements within the Communion, probably out of a mixture of impatience, frustration and insouciance rather than in a conscious and deliberate quest for new ideas, were uttering statements and adopting positions which made the label of 'fascist' less inaccurate than previously. The aforementioned radicalism and verbal violence of an increasing section of the Youth, AET and Requeté could be seen by more orthodox rightists as tainted by fascist crypto-socialism, and certainly by the left as typical fascist demagoguery aimed at misleading the working class for the benefit of its exploiters. There was no question that it was quite unprecedented in the history of Carlism, and for this if for no other reason invited comparisons with the 'new' radical right. Moreover, Carlist propaganda in general was taking on a different tone. The words 'dictatorship' and 'totalitarian', if used less freely than by the more or less open authoritarians of Renovación Española, were becoming quite common; even if dictatorship was regarded by Comín and others as at most a very temporary expedient, and 'totalitarian' as implying intrinsic strength rather than coercion and state control, most of those who were now using the terms gave little sign of having bothered to work out such nice distinctions. Other unusual turns of phrase were creeping into Carlist rhetoric. To quote just one example: late in 1934 Arauz de Robles called for 'a new spirit ... to ventilate and purify the sources of life';[51] there was nothing conclusively un-Carlist about this and other expressions like it, yet their tone was closer to that of José Antonio than to that of traditional Carlist propaganda.

Far more significant, probably, was the place of racism in Carlist public statements. Anti-semitism was nothing new, of course, nor was it by any means confined to Carlism. Most of the Spanish right had traditionally exhibited a vague, religiously-inspired anti-semitism, based on dogma and myth rather than biology and the actual – and negligible – doings of Jews in Spain. In the 1930s the CEDA and Renovación Española, as well as the Carlists, were openly anti-semitic.[52] Paradoxically, this contrasted with the outlook of the Falange, which was the least anti-semitic of the principal right-wing parties. Redondo, it is true, subscribed to essentially the same brand of Catholic anti-semitism as the rest of the right, but Ledesma regarded it as a peculiarly German phenomenon, albeit a justified one,[53] while José Antonio evinced no interest whatsoever in the 'Jewish question'. Unaffected by a religious antipathy towards the Jews, José Antonio and Ledesma presumably recognized that anti-semitism, however fashionable and successful a political weapon elsewhere, had no relevance to the affairs of Spain.

This was not the case with the Carlists. Indeed, it was particularly ironic that Carlist suspicion of Nazism should hinge largely upon its racial doctrines, for as the Republic wore on the Carlists' own emphasis on race increased appreciably. At the birth of the Republic a great deal was made of the supposed Jewish blood of Alcalá Zamora, Miguel Maura and Fernando de los Ríos, and of an imminent 'invasion' of Sephardic Jews from Morocco and points east.[54] Already it was claimed that the Republic was the visible manifestation of a Jewish conspiracy against Spain. Late in 1931 and during 1932, *El Siglo Futuro* serialized *The Jewish Conspiracy*, a work by one Robles Delgano who argued, with grateful references to Henry Ford and the *Protocols of the Elders of Zion*, the standard, not to say hackneyed case concerning Jewish undermining of western society through a monopoly of finance, commerce and the communications industry.[55] Also in 1932 *La Unión*'s daily column of political comment ran a series on 'The Jewish Problem', a typical headline of which was 'Our Enemy the Jew'.[56]

The actual physical threat of 'Jewish invasion' continued to give the Carlists nightmares throughout the Republican period. An influx of Jewish refugee doctors during 1933 was considered to threaten the very lives of Spanish patients, and it was hinted with no great subtlety that Jews had been responsible for the deaths of both Don Jaime and Primo de Rivera.[57] The constantly rumoured arrival of floods of Sephardis and the possibility of their being granted Spanish citizenship provoked bitter comment in the Carlist press, surpassed only by the horror at the prospect of Spain's welcoming Jewish refugees from Hitler's Germany.[58] *El Siglo Futuro* unsympathetically described it as suicidal to create a racial problem in this way: 'They are wandering peoples with no homeland, and for that very reason they are undesirable in the homelands of others.'[59]

A Catalan Carlist, Llanas de Niubò, graphically expressed in 1935 the fundamental case against the Jews as accepted by virtually all Carlists. The Jews, he claimed, had throughout their history shown treachery towards each other and towards God, the climax coming with their responsibility for the Crucifixion. Judas Iscariot's thirty pieces of silver symbolized the Jewish obsession with money. Cursed by God and dispersed, they took 'rapacity and treachery' wherever they settled. In Spain's case they betrayed the Visigothic kings, invited the Moorish invasions, and then enriched themselves by battening upon Moors and Christians alike. Only when they were expelled by the Catholic Monarchs did the 'era of national prosperity' begin. In the modern age the Jews provoked the Sarajevo assassination and through it the Great War; theirs were the doctrines of Karl Marx and hence the class war; and in spewing forth 'American modernism' they had brought about the moral degeneration from which the western world was now suffering. The undermining of the west was still being pursued by the Jews Trotsky and Bela Kun, and it was up to the Spaniards to 'reaffirm national sentiment' by taking appropriate steps along the lines laid down in Germany.[60]

The Carlists were utterly convinced of the existence of a Jewish-led world conspiracy, and of the authenticity of the *Protocols of the Elders of Zion*. The Communion's leading expert in Jewish affairs, the Marqués de Santa Cara, disclosed that the conspiracy was engineered by the 'Supreme Sanhedrin' from its base in New York,[61] in which city was also to be found a 'Green International' headed by no less a figure than Einstein.[62] Apart from the pincers of international socialism and North American capitalism, the conspiracy's main weapon was freemasonry. According to Domingo Tejera, the Carlists' chief masonophobe, freemasonry played Celestina to the 'libidinous concupiscence of international Jewry'.[63] *El Pensamiento Navarro*'s columnist Emigdio Molina called for a crusade against masons and the exposing of 'all their intrigues, all their secrets, all their shame and all the evil arts which they command and exploit towards the achievement of their unmentionable ends'.[64] These were, apparently, extraordinary varied; at the height of the Ethiopian War, *El Siglo Futuro* described freemasonry as 'a branch of the secret service of the British Crown'.[65] The network did not end there, for rotarianism, too, was considered 'an instrument of Judaism for the infiltration of materialism into the upper class ... a levite 'masonry'.[66] The campaign of what Llanas de Niubò called 'the four Horsemen of the Apocalypse' − Judaism, communism, freemasonry and death − had brought such countries as Britain, France and Australia under Jewish control, and as far as many Carlists were concerned Spain appeared to be heading in the same direction.[67] In January 1936, *El Siglo Futuro* reported that New York Jews were fastening their grip on the Spanish economy, and some weeks later it published a full-page revelation of an alleged Jewish plot to take over the country.[68] Evidence in support of these charges, it need scarcely be pointed out, was non-existent.

Such opinions were perfectly consistent with traditional Carlist anti-semitism, and could also be found in only marginally less strident form in, for example, *El Debate*. After 1933, however, the anti-semitic rantings of Santa Cara, Llanas de Niubò, Tejera and others took on a more disturbingly contemporary tinge. Llanas de Niubò harped upon the physical repulsiveness of the archetypal 'wandering Jew';[69] Santa Cara declared that Jewish blood, admitted to the body politic by the early Bourbons, was denationalizing the Spanish spirit and that the time had come for a new expulsion.[70] Increased concentration on race was boosted by the racial overtones of the Italo-Ethiopian War and was now pushing Carlist propaganda to unprecedented excesses. Thus, in the spring of 1936, *El Siglo Futuro* attempted to provide a racial explanation of communism, commenting on 'the inferiority – racial – of almost all the oriental peoples of today ... Chinese, Indians, Arabs, Abyssinians and Soviets' (*sic*).[71] This kind of intuitive racism obviously differed in both nature and degree from the calculated, institutionalized variety characteristic of Nazism and of northern and eastern European fascism, and failed to make the leap from stressing the inferiority of Semitic, Asiatic, African and Slavic peoples to erecting a corresponding cult of biological *superiority*. Nevertheless it did approach blasphemy as Pradera and other Carlists had only recently defined it, and lent at least some credence to those who accused Carlists of fascism.

The gap between Carlism and Falangism was thus wide at some points and at others almost non-existent. More to the point, with Falangist 'fascism' being diluted during 1935 and some Carlists deviating from Traditionalist orthodoxy in a markedly 'fascist' direction, the gulf was arguably narrowing. Relations between the leaders of the two movements were negligible before 1936, but this was not always the case at grass-roots level. The chief driving force of rank-and-file Carlists continued to be ultra-Catholicism, that of Falangists ultra-nationalism, but the shared attitudes, enemies and social origins of members ensured some degree of contact. By the very nature of things it was the Carlist Youth, AET and Requeté who had the closest day-to-day dealings with the equally youthful Falange. In some areas, Seville for example, relations tended to be formal to the point of coolness, but in the main young Carlists and Falangists got along affably enough. In Santander, the future national head of the Requeté, Zamanillo, was on the best of terms with the Falange's provincial *jefe*, Manuel Hedilla, himself a former Carlist, and this warmth was reflected in their organizations.[72] Relations were also good in Navarre, where save in some predominantly left-wing *ribera* villages the Falange was overwhelmingly outnumbered by the Carlists, and where it exhibited a significantly more Catholic face than anywhere else in Spain.[73] In the universities, too, Carlist and Falangist students drew together during 1934–5.[74] As the Falange shook itself free of its ties with the Alfonsists, and as the new leadership of the Communion prepared to do likewise, the ground was being laid, however unconsciously, upon which Carlism and Falangism might later meet.

8

The politics of counter-revolution

Since the coming of the Republic, the Carlists had never faltered in their belief that such a regime – at least in Spain – could, if permitted to do so, only end in a full-scale social revolution. Incidents like Castilblanco and Casas Viejas fortified their conviction that Spanish liberalism, by breeding socio-economic injustice while blindly allowing its manipulation by the propagandists of revolution, was self-defeating. After the 1933 election these utterances assumed a new stridency, and a mere article of faith was transformed into an acute, visceral fear as revolution seemed to loom closer. Carlist speakers now began to refer repeatedly to the revolution which they expected the left, backed by Jews, freemasons and the Comintern, soon to unleash upon an unprepared Spain.[1] Given the characteristic Carlist belief in attack as the best form of defence, Fal Conde's assumption of the Secretary-Generalship suited this mood perfectly.

The new sense of urgency was well founded, for to the innate revolutionary activism of the CNT, expressed in the unsuccessful but nonetheless ominous risings of winter 1933–4, was now added the adoption of a revolutionary posture by an increasing number of Social-ists. To the right and the bourgeois Republicans alike, the CNT was a threat which could be contained; the prospect that the tradi-tionally bureaucratic, reformist Socialist Party and the UGT might be about to devote their vastly superior organizing abilities to the revolutionary cause was infinitely more alarming. The drift left-wards had begun before the November election, as Socialists grew restive at the slow pace of social reform and the emergence of a revived and threatening right. Their withdrawal of support con-tributed to Azaña's downfall; their refusal to renew the 1931 electoral alliance facilitated the Centre–Right victory in 1933. As the temper of the new government became apparent, the drift became a lurch; early in 1934 the former Minister of Labour, Largo Cabal-lero, inaugurated the Alianza Obrera, a tentative and scarcely con-vincing step towards revolutionary unity on the left, whilst he and other Socialists, the more moderate Prieto not excepted, began to talk with ever greater frequency about a future revolution.[2]

The condition of Spain in 1934 provided revolutionaries with excellent fuel. Under the Radical governments of Lerroux and Samper, many of the achievements of the previous biennium most prized by the left were being nullified. These included not only the anti-clerical and minimum-wage laws, but also the Mixed Jury system of wage arbitration and the Municipal Boundaries law, the operation of which had done much to increase Socialist patronage and membership in rural areas. Although the application of the Agrarian Reform was belatedly picking up speed, the advantage in rural Spain now rested once more with the proprietors, a development symbolized by the return of confiscated estates to mostly monarchist owners as part of the 1934 amnesty. Not without reason, left-wing Spaniards feared a general reversion to pre-Republican levels of rural exploitation. Notwithstanding that economic prospects were actually the best for years, the government's 'blind-eye' policy and a continued labour surplus brought a sharp fall in rural wages and a marked deterioration in workers' conditions. As the situation in southern and south-western Spain became more volatile, revolutionary Socialists took over the leadership of the UGT-affiliated Land-Workers Federation, and in the early summer prolonged strikes of agricultural workers, provoked by landowners in the hope of breaking working-class resistance, were accompanied by the occupation of estates.[3] If conditions in the cities were less bitter than in the countryside, industry's considerable recovery from the trough of depression did not lift wage levels appreciably; indeed, Socialists complained that the industrial workers' lot was no better than under the monarchy. All in all, they had good reason to conclude that after three years of Republicanism, the socio-economic power-structure of the old regime remained essentially intact.

This alone would probably not have driven the Socialists to revolution in 1934, however. For them the most frightening aspect of the situation following the 1933 election was the very real possibility of power passing to Gil Robles and the CEDA. Even as they watched, a government inspired by the selfsame ideas which drove the CEDA's leaders, and which was constantly lauded in the CEDA's press and propaganda, was in the process of crushing Austrian Socialism and erecting a corporate, authoritarian system; small wonder, therefore, that the Spanish Socialists were apprehensive of similar developments at home. Determined to avoid the fate of their Italian, German and Austrian comrades, they thus fell for the appeal of prophylactic revolution, just as fear of revolution fed the belligerency of the extreme right, each side convinced that a shaky democracy could not withstand the attack of the other.

Although, as has already been pointed out, not all Carlists were insensitive to the deteriorating situation in the rural south and the increasingly bitter urban class conflict, those like Ginés Martínez who responded with anything more than conservative reflex-actions were a tiny minority. Faced with the spectre of left-wing revolt, the Communion behaved with the same dedication to the cause of law and order which had led its deputies to support the government during the Anarchist disturbances of the previous winter. In March 1934 Rodezno grandiloquently proclaimed that 'the shock troops of Carlism' could be relied upon to defend society against the 'marxist' threat.[4] Others saw social upheaval as providing Carlism with a golden opportunity. As Arellano put it, 'If they start a revolution, we shall end it.'[5] As always the Youth were more graphic. Predicting their presence at 'the death-rattle of Karl Marx's ideas', they warned that Marx's latter-day disciples 'will whimper beneath the military leather of our boots'.[6]

Parallel with intensifying social unrest went a resurgence of militant regionalism, fanned by Radical and CEDA coolness towards the autonomist causes. In the Basque region the PNV and the left launched unofficial local elections in an attempt to concentrate local frustration at the lack of progress towards autonomy. The Carlists unequivocally condemned as rebellion what they now regarded as the PNV's opportunistic willingness to reverse the 1931 policy and turn the region into a kind of 'Azañist' Gibraltar.[7] In Navarre and Álava Carlist resistance helped strangle the movement; in Guipúzcoa and Vizcaya it went ahead in a minority of towns and villages despite the government's sending troops to Bilbao and San Sebastian and the subsequent arrest of several mayors. Bellicose meetings of the PNV and the left followed, together with mass resignations of local councils.[8] These too were boycotted and attacked by the Carlists, who voiced particular disgust at the sight of Prieto intoning the Basque anthem 'Gernikako Arbola' during one such meeting.[9]

Every stage of the renewed Basque disaffection was abetted by the

Esquerra, whose own differences with Madrid were even more acute. A crisis erupted when Samper's government accepted the Court of Constitutional Guarantees' rejection of the Generalitat's Leases Act, designed to enable the Catalonian *rabassaires* − sharecropping viticultors − to purchase land cultivated for fifteen years. In protest the Esquerra and the PNV walked out of the Cortes and the Generalitat's supporters began to prepare for armed resistance.[10] In the Court of Constitutional Guarantees, one of the votes against the Leases Act was cast by Pradera; in defending the central government, he and the rest of the Carlist leadership once again demonstrated their hostility to left-wing autonomism, and more important their support of Catalonian landlords against the *rabassaires'* aspirations. When a delegation of Catalonian landlords flocked to Madrid to lobby the government they were escorted by the Catalonian Carlist deputies, Bau and Sangenís, and fêted at the Secretariat's offices. In their stand on behalf of the sacred rights of property, they were assured, the Carlists were behind them 'to a man'.[11]

During the troubled parliamentary recess of 1934 it became plain that when the Cortes reassembled Gil Robles would bring down the Samper government by withdrawing CEDA support. That this was the next stage in the CEDA's conquest of power was stated, if a trifle ambiguously, at the CEDA's rally of 9 September, held at Covadonga in symbolic commemoration of the Christian Reconquest of Spain, and in defiance of local Socialist-led protest strikes.[12] Tension mounted during the next fortnight as the CEDA's council finally decided to overthrow Samper, as *El Socialista* threatened revolution should the CEDA enter the government, and as illegal arms consignments were discovered on the north coast.[13] With revolution apparently inevitable, the Carlists attacked Gil Robles with unprecedented venom. The well-organized threat of revolution, the government's pusillanimity in facing it, and the right's lack of unity, vigour and resolution were all, according to Lamamié, the result of Gil Robles' policy of 'collaboration and transigence'.[14] In reality, the reverse was if anything the case; the revolutionary situation had come about because Gil Robles had made no serious attempt to convince the Spanish left that he and his party were any more 'transigent' than those whom they admired abroad.

When the Cortes reconvened early in October, the expected happened. Samper, deprived of CEDA support, resigned and was replaced by yet another predominantly Radical government under Lerroux. This time, however, there was a difference, for the cabinet also included three *cedistas*, though not Gil Robles himself.[15] The Carlists were derisive at what the CEDA hailed as a further 'tactical' success, heaping scorn on Gil Robles and recalling with denied but ill-concealed satisfaction their predictions that he would never be handed power. According to Lamamié the CEDA had spinelessly accepted 'a minor role under the command of one of the leaders of the opposing army', an error likely to have 'fatal consequences'.[16] Three portfolios, Domingo Tejera sniffed, amounted to nothing but 'alms'.[17]

The left took a very different view, agreeing with the CEDA itself in seeing its entry into the government not as 'alms' but as a crucial step on the way to bigger things. In the Socialists' eyes especially, it was the thin end of a fascist wedge. While Azaña and other Left Republican leaders announced their 'non-conformity' with Spain's existing institutions, the Socialists decided on an immediate general strike. In most of the country local strikes quickly collapsed thanks to lack of CNT solidarity, but in two regions strikes became revolutions. In Asturias proletarian unity, sealed for the first time, brought social revolution to Oviedo and the mining districts, and in Catalonia Macià's successor, Companys, was manoeuvred by his more extreme colleagues into declaring 'the Catalan State within the Federal Spanish Republic'. The Catalonian rising was swiftly overcome with only slight loss of life, but that in Asturias lasted a fortnight, cost thousands of lives, and was defeated only by means of a full-scale military operation involving the use of Moorish troops. In the event the rising's extreme localism and wider half-heartedness suggested that the revolutionary talk of the Socialist leaders had been talk and nothing more; certainly, during the entire October crisis they did everything possible to restrain the more militant rank and file.[18] Just the same, Spanish conservatives had had their first, nightmarish glimpse of organized social revolution and henceforward were to show less and less inclination to accept the Republic which, they believed, had made revolution possible. Overnight the commander of the counter-revolutionary troops, General Franco, became their hero.

Throughout the troubles the Communion adopted its customary position of backing the authorities in the interests of public order.[19] In Madrid, Andalusia and the Basque country, young Carlists co-operated with JAP-ists in driving and conducting trams, working on the railways and in gas and electricity supply stations, protecting cars carrying food and 'black' workers, and selling right-wing newspapers on the streets.[20] Their Catalonian counterparts, whose activities had been hampered for much of the summer by the Generalitat,[21] were now prevented from combating the revolution by the arrest early in September of almost one hundred Red Berets, accused of planning an improbable and certainly suicidal 'march on Barcelona' from the Sierra de Montserrat.[22] In parts of the Basque region the general strike turned violent, and three Carlists died. In the Guipúzcoan industrial town of Mondragón, the deputy and factory-owner Marcelino Oreja was killed in the Casa del Pueblo by some of his own Socialist employees, and a Red Beret, Eugenio Echurra, died of wounds inflicted by strikers who attacked him on his way to work. The third Basque fatality was the leader of the Requeté of Eibar, Carlos Larrañaga. Two more Carlists were killed by the Asturian revolutionaries, one an octogenarian veteran of the war of the 1870s.[23] The Republican authorities in Asturias rejected Carlist offers of help, in spite of which the Asturian Requeté lost no time in lending its support to the relieving army.[24]

The Carlists' natural concern over their 'martyrs' was reinforced by the spine-chilling effect of the atrocity stories which swamped the right-wing press after the crushing of the Asturias rising. Carlist editors accepted unquestioningly every allegation of murder, rape and mutilation committed by the revolutionary miners;[25] an investigating committee consisting of Rodezno, Arellano and Martínez Morentín visited Asturias but issued no statement either confirming or denying the reports.[26] Few Carlists doubted their accuracy, which helped add volume to the Communion's cry for vengeance on the 'social-Azañist' revolutionaries and the Basque Nationalists whom it charged with having been their allies.[27] The Carlist deputies demanded draconic punitive measures: strict application of the law against all those involved in the risings; the withdrawal of parliamentary immunity from deputies guilty of revolutionary activity; the dissolution of all Socialist and 'separatist' organizations; the outlawing of politically motivated strikes; the enforcement of the veto of the Catalonian Leases Law; and the indefinite suspension of the Catalan Statute.[28]

The call for revenge and a 'cleansing' of Spain of all vestiges of socialism, anarchism, 'separatism' and freemasonry was just as enthusiastically taken up by the Carlist press.[29] In defending their demand, Carlists insisted that 'the revolution' had not been conclusively defeated but had merely suffered a setback, and that were every trace of revolutionary organization and propaganda not ruthlessly eradicated, it would quickly return more dangerous than ever.[30] As for the right, they continued, its choice was now clear. Either it could sit back, or even 'collaborate', and allow the Republic to resume its inexorable slide towards bolshevism, or else it could seize the moment and act resolutely to defeat, or better still forestall, revolution.[31] For the Carlists themselves there was no choice. henceforward, though differences of strategy and personality persisted, no Carlist questioned the need for a rising against a Republic which had now passed its climax and was heading for catastrophe.

The emotionally charged atmosphere which followed the October Revolution provided new encouragement for Calvo Sotelo's hitherto thwarted scheme for a united movement of those now calling themselves 'counter-revolutionaries'. In November he therefore invited Fal Conde to lead the Carlists into a 'national counter-revolutionary front' which, without prejudicing the independence of the Communion, would ensure concerted action in times of crisis against parliamentarism, democracy and revolution, with the long-term aim of installing a new, organic, authoritarian order. Fal Conde, who quite apart from his habitual suspicion of alliances had good reason to fear that he, like Goicoechea, might suffer a personal eclipse in the shadow of Calvo Sotelo's charisma and undoubted ambition, openly declared himself antagonistic towards the idea.[32] Nevertheless he could not afford to risk discrediting Carlism as lacking in patriotic solidarity at a time of crisis. He accordingly gave his reluctant approval, to which was soon added that of Alfonso Carlos, and promptly passed to Rodezno and Pradera the task of representing Carlism in negotiations with the Alfonsists.[33] Thereafter, Fal Conde's personal involvement was nil.

Rodezno and Pradera, assisted by Lamamié, pressed on enthusiastically. When an executive committee of the new organization was formed it included Lamamié and Pradera, as well as Calvo Sotelo, Sáinz Rodríguez and Ansaldo. The National Bloc's manifesto was released early in December 1934, copies being distributed in the streets owing to the censoring of its publication in the press.[34] The text opened with a conventional attack on the Republic, stressing the twin perils of marxism and separatism and the probable re-emergence of revolution. From a total rejection of the ideological foundations of Republicanism, the document went on to outline the New State: foral, corporate, authoritarian – in short 'integrative'. Although in the conclusion the question of forms of government was explicitly avoided, the glorification of Spain's monarchic past, together with the monarchist sympathies of all but a handful of the manifesto's signatories, left it in no doubt that ideally the New State would also be a monarchy.

Among the manifesto's 142 signatories were all the Carlist deputies save Esteban Bilbao, as well as Pradera and individual Carlists such as the academician González Amezúa, the Bilbao engineer and propagandist Pilar Careaga, and the Marqués de Santa Cara. Neither Fal Conde nor any of the regional *jefes* signed what was patently an overwhelmingly Alfonsist document. On 8 December the Secretary-General issued a note affirming Carlism's collaboration in 'a coming together of the authentic right and of independent personalities for ends which coincide with those of our Communion'. The Carlists, he admitted, could not stand aloof from any 'authentically national and counter-revolutionary movement' without betraying their own heritage. On the other hand he pointed out that the manifesto was not solely Calvo Sotelo's work, and re-emphasized the obligation on all Carlists to labour unflaggingly for the advance of the Communion.[35] His endorsement of the National Bloc could hardly have been more grudging.

In the event, membership of the National Bloc made few serious demands on the Carlists – or indeed on anyone. Parliamentary collaboration between the monarchist parties was already the normal thing, and the Bloc's only effect upon it was to enhance still further the prestige of Calvo Sotelo. Republicans now regarded him, much to the Carlists' irritation, as leader of a combined monarchist opposition.[36] In the country at large, although formal National Bloc organizations were created in one or two places such as Oviedo and Palencia where Carlist numbers were relatively low, the new body's impact upon the still-growing Communion was negligible. Numerous public meetings took place under Bloc auspices, yet even these served only to advertise the lukewarmness of most Carlists towards its affairs. Carlist contributions to its propaganda came mainly from Rodezno, Lamamié, Pradera and Calvo Sotelo's close personal friend Joaquín Bau; the only others to play a significant part in Bloc activities were Arellano, Comín, Palomino and Toledo. The remaining deputies, once having signed the manifesto, and the notables of the organizational hierarchies, were conspicuous by their absence.[37] Fal Conde considered that Carlists helped to 'raise the doctrinal level' of the meetings in which they participated, but gained nothing themselves;[38] in private he was wont to dismiss the Bloc as 'Rodezno's business' and attempt to dissuade relative enthusiasts such as Arellano from getting involved.[39] It very soon became obvious that the National Bloc posed no threat to the Carlist independence so prized by Fal Conde; it was, he commented in April 1935, 'just another alliance'.[40] From then on it became simply irrelevant to the organizational and military concerns which more and more preoccupied him.

The National Bloc was barely born before heated public disputes broke out between its leaders and Gil Robles.[41] To the latter, already smarting after a year of monarchist sniping, the prospect, however remote, of a united monarchist front led by the aggressive Calvo Sotelo, was immediately annoying and potentially dangerous. Criticizing the Bloc for dividing the right, Gil Robles now made the extraordinary charge that it was not he but the monarchists who had broken the 1933 electoral pact, since which they had selfishly attacked him and his party in the most scandalous terms. More reasonably he reminded Calvo Sotelo, the chief target of his complaints, that he owed his very presence in the Cortes, if not indeed in Spain itself, to the CEDA's good faith in pushing through the amnesty and to the success of the 'tactic' in making this possible. The Bloc's executive committee denied all Gil Robles' accusations, protesting that recent monarchist criticism of the CEDA was motivated by the purest patriotism, and was fully consistent with their attitude towards accidentalism well before November 1933. Gil Robles, they riposted, was now using his influence with Lerroux to turn the censorship with discriminatory rigour against the monarchists. What 'mysterious formula', they enquired, made possible the CEDA–Radical alliance, one between 'Catholic spirituality and incredulous positivism'?

The flavour of the increasingly common internecine quarrels within the right was admirably exemplified by the public debate which occurred early in 1935 between Lamamié and Gil Robles' Salamanca daily *La Gaceta Regional*. The newspaper started the ball rolling by urging Lamamié's expulsion from the provincial Agrarian

Bloc, which he had helped to found, in the cause of 'purifying' the Salamancan right. Under the headline 'Bloc of the Bilious' it excoriated the National Bloc and reviled Lamamié as a member of its executive committee for nursing pride, envy, selfish ambition and cirrhosis of the liver. He had, it sneered, grovelled before Gil Robles in 1933 in order to grab a place on the provincial right-wing candidature, only to betray him once elected.[42] Counter-attacking spiritedly, Lamamié readily admitted owing his present seat to Gil Robles but fairly pointed out that this was a just return for his own introduction of the then little known Gil Robles to Salamanca in 1931. Moreover he, Lamamié, had remained squarely behind the right's election programme 'without crossing over to the enemy, either to parley or to collaborate with him'.[43] When Gil Robles shrugged aside these latest attacks as 'insignificant' and hinted darkly at the discomfiture awaiting many monarchists should he decide to publish their correspondence with him, *El Siglo Futuro* twice challenged him to publish and be damned.[44] The gauntlet was not taken up; the letters stayed a mystery, and for the time being Lamamié remained a member of the Salamanca Agrarian Bloc.

Underlying these petty exchanges were more substantial differences regarding the CEDA's role as a governing party in the aftermath of a revolution. The Carlists and Renovación Española were now obsessed by a wish to exploit the post-revolutionary atmosphere in order to prepare the way for the Republic's destruction; this was to be done by ending Catalan autonomy and politically eliminating everything and everybody from Azaña leftwards. From November 1934 until the summer of 1935 they persistently nagged Gil Robles to use his leverage with the government in the interest of ruthless repression. As in the previous year, Carlist critics had nothing to lose. If the CEDA obliged, the left would be destroyed; if, as they expected, it failed to do so, then they could feel entitled to step up their attacks on it.

Most *cedistas* were no less repressively minded, but their ability to implement their wishes was limited by their party's junior role in the government. Gil Robles realized that the Radicals, while prepared to accept a number of exemplary executions and a host of arrests, would never pursue repression on the scale that the monarchists demanded; by so doing they would sour the political atmosphere still further, either destroy or completely alienate the left, and end up the prisoners of the right. None the less, within the coalition the CEDA took a relatively hard line. It urged the indefinite suspension of the Generalitat's powers and the Catalan Statute, approved that of hundreds of Socialist-dominated local councils and mixed juries, and abetted the imprisonment of over 30,000 assorted leftists.[45] In February two Asturian revolutionaries were shot, but during the following weeks death sentences passed on twenty October rebels were commuted against the wishes of the CEDA ministers. When the Socialists Menéndez and González Peña, together with seventeen other members of the Asturian revolutionary committees, were reprieved, Gil Robles pulled the CEDA out of the government in protest.[46]

Throughout the months of repression, the Carlists had complained at what they considered its slowness and mildness. Even though, as Alcalá Zamora and Lerroux appreciated, the process had by the spring of 1935 gone as far as was compatible with the Republic's survival, this consideration was unlikely to weigh heavily with those who viewed repression as a means of undermining the regime. As their demands for the total withdrawal of the Catalan Statute, the dissolution of the Socialist Party, and more and faster executions, fell upon increasingly deaf ears, the Carlists' frustration grew. What angered them most of all, however, was the government's failure to pursue the political death of Azaña, of whose involvement in the October Revolution they claimed to possess irrefutable evidence.[47] Early in 1935 the monarchists took the initiative themselves and launched a parliamentary campaign to have both Azaña and Casares Quiroga tried by the Court of Constitutional Guarantees with responsibility for importing arms in the summer of 1934. Theoretically the charge was one of encouraging arms shipments for use by anti-Salazar rebels in Portugal, but there was no doubt that his accusers were simultaneously seeking to saddle Azaña with blame for the Asturian and Catalonian risings, as well as – yet again – for Casas Viejas. This time, the CEDA gave its support to the monarchist case, and it was indeed a CEDA proposition which eventually led to the setting up of a parliamentary committee of investigation.

In the Cortes debate, the Carlist spokesman was Esteban Bilbao. Presenting the flimsiest of cases, he harped upon his own exile at the hands of Casares, thus casting doubt upon his claim to be speaking 'with all sincerity, without any sort of passion'.[48] Far more convincing was Azaña's self-defence, by which the Carlists nevertheless refused to be impressed. *El Pensamiento Navarro* commented, 'He is a poor advocate, as he is a poor dramaturge, as he was a very poor ruler and as he is a very poor Spaniard.'[49] But already the process was under way whereby the spitefulness and emptiness of the campaign against Azaña would produce a reaction in his favour and make possible his political come-back. One Carlist only foresaw such a development: Domingo Tejera recalled the career of Antonio Maura in warning that in Spain 'there is nothing like the systematic persecution of one man' for guaranteeing him political potency.[50] The rest, tirelessly howling for Azaña's blood, showed little sign of grasping that their campaign – and indeed the repression as a whole – might prove counter-productive. If they did, it failed to give them pause.

For a minority within the CEDA there was more to governing than mere reaction. When Gil Robles pulled the CEDA out of the cabinet in March 1935, one of those obliged to resign was a special target of Carlist snipers, the Minister of Agriculture Giménez Fernández. A Professor of Canon Law, former leading light of the short-lived PSP, and a spokesman for the CEDA's small but sincere social-Catholic wing, Giménez Fernández sought as Minister of Agriculture to put his principles into practice. In doing this he aroused the opposition of most of the landowners within his own party, as well as that of the Carlists and Alfonsists, and succeeded only in exposing the true strength or weakness of social-Catholicism on the Spanish right.

During his brief occupancy of the Agriculture ministry, Giménez Fernández introduced two bills which provoked Carlist hostility: in November 1934 a bill to protect the short-term position of the *yunteros* of Extremadura, placed during Azaña's premiership in occupation of small areas of *latifundia*, and in February 1935 a new Rural Leases bill.[51] To the majority of Carlist deputies, at least, their devotion to the precepts of Leo XIII wilting still further under the influence of the October Revolution, proposals which might have been barely acceptable in the name of justice a year earlier, now smacked of appeasement. They regarded the Yunteros Act, passed in December 1934, as inspired by the same 'revolutionary principle' as the Act of 1932. Tejera acknowledged that there might be no practical alternative to accepting the yunteros' *de facto* occupancy, but protested that this did not excuse the minister's using Catholic doctrine to defend legalized robbery.[52] Indeed, Giménez Fernández's public justification of his legislative proposals in terms of the Encyclicals incensed the Carlists even more than the bills themselves. Lamamié, the Carlists' arch-defender of large-scale property, complained that the small group of advanced social-Catholics was 'playing with the Encyclicals' in expecting Catholics to accept their subtle interpretations of the advice of Leo XIII and his successors.[53] Eventually Lamamié grew so furious that he interrupted:

If the Minister of Agriculture keeps on quoting the Papal Encyclicals in order to defend his plans, I assure him that we shall end up by becoming Greek schismatics.[54]

Lamamié, backed up by his fellow landowners Rodezno and Estévanez, renewed his attacks during the Rural Leases debate. Improving the situation of the tenant was all very well, they argued, but this bill would actually place him in a privileged position *vis-à-vis* the landlord; what was more, Giménez Fernández's projected rent control was nothing but creeping *étatisme* and yet another blow against the suffering landowning class.[55] Lamamié and Estévanez protested again when the minister proposed cutting the minimum price of wheat in the face of an unprecedented glut. Blaming speculators, they swallowed their dislike of state interference and urged the government to buy up the wheat surplus, a policy adopted later in the year.[56]

Carlist hostility towards Giménez Fernández was understandably strongest amongst the large landowners, who nevertheless found their less fortunate brethren willing enough to back them up. Gradually, the parliamentary pressure from Lamamié, the monarchists and the CEDA right forced Giménez Fernández to dilute his bill's provisions, in particular by inserting a clause permitting proprietors to 'cultivate directly' – a common euphemism for eviction – rather than meet the new rental terms.[57] The outcome was the reverse of the minister's original intentions; instead of enjoying greater security, tenants found themselves caught in a new wave of evictions. Later in the year Lamamié claimed that 'direct cultivation' was the only realistic course open to Salamancan landowners and that he himself was struggling to avoid evicting his tenants.[58]

The CEDA's departure from the government proved to be a victory for the 'tactic', for within six weeks the Radical–CEDA alliance was renewed with the latter now holding five portfolios.

To the alarm of the left and the annoyance of Alcalá Zamora, Gil Robles himself moved into the War Ministry. The CEDA press was naturally ecstatic at this evidence of further progress towards 'full power'; a broader conservative feeling that the political situation was now resolving itself satisfactorily was reflected in a reviving stock market and, more ominously for the monarchist parties, a withdrawal of financial backing from the National Bloc.[59]

The Carlists, who had reacted to the CEDA's surrender of office with a mixture of gratification at Gil Robles' stand on behalf of repression and relief at being rid of the 'socialistic' Giménez Fernández, were unimpressed by its return. Although Rodezno expressed the hope that the CEDA might seize the opportunity to undertake the 'final work' against revolution,[60] the general Carlist verdict, based upon the CEDA's governmental role to date, was that it was the Radical and not the CEDA tactic which was succeeding; the now more balanced Radical–CEDA alliance was the fruit of Lerroux's desire to bind Catholics to the Republic rather than the fulfilment of Gil Robles' ambition to take over the Republic and transform it into something very different.[61] Gil Robles' accession to the War Ministry, which to the left seemed to herald a *coup d'état*, looked to the Carlists more like an attempt to calm potentially rebellious elements in the armed forces who might otherwise precipitate a rising. Emilio Tarduchy, a retired army colonel who linked Carlism and the Falange by organizing the latter's social propaganda while writing a pseudonymous column on military affairs in *El Siglo Futuro*, described Gil Robles' initial addresses to the Madrid and Burgos garrisons as those of one more Republican Minister of War.[62] *El Siglo Futuro* actually criticized the choice of this ministry, which it argued would surely mean the CEDA's helping to consolidate the regime; instead, Gil Robles ought to have demanded the Ministry of Education in order to 'save many generations' of Spaniards through the re-Catholicization of the educational system.[63]

Carlist suspicions that the CEDA was losing sight of its antiparliamentary goals were strengthened in June, when Lerroux attended a CEDA banquet in Salamanca. The sight of Gil Robles and Lerroux embracing in celebration of their mutual indispensability convinced *El Siglo Futuro* that the CEDA leader, whatever his assurances to those on his right, was now content to play Cánovas to Lerroux's Sagasta.[64] In the Cortes two days later the CEDA deputies joined the Radicals and the left in crushing a combined monarchist attempt to hold Azaña and Casares Quiroga responsible for Casas Viejas. [65] With the report due from the Cortes committee of investigation into Azaña's alleged role in the October revolution, it was now evident that Gil Robles was unlikely to provoke another cabinet crisis over the issue.

By late July, when the debate opened, the impetus had gone from the 'liquidation' campaign. Azaña was now back in the political arena and riding a new wave of popularity; Lerroux, protecting his left flank, felt it wise to refer to him as 'a worthy public figure' who might again lead a united Republican left. In the circumstances the Carlists accepted that their final attack on Azaña was doomed to failure, and consoled themselves with the thought that his escape was the logical consequence of parliamentarism. [66] The attempt to send Azaña before the Court of Constitutional Guarantees did indeed fail, for although supported by a majority of the Cortes rump actually present at the debate, this was considerably less than the necessary majority of the Cortes' full membership. Most of the Radicals opposed the proposal or abstained, and while a majority of the CEDA deputies voted for indictment, this time there were no resignations and no cabinet crisis. [67] The disgusted Carlists, watching Azaña's revival accelerate, grumbled that once again the CEDA had sacrificed itself for the Republic. [68]

With the monarchists convinced that governmental softness towards the left had resurrected the threat of revolution, Carlist–CEDA relations now sank to a new low. The CEDA's alliance with the Radicals appeared firmer than ever, now that it was turning its attention to a new, if ill-named Agrarian Reform law, a policy of stringent governmental economy advocated by the non-party Finance Minister, Chapaprieta, and most important the much-mooted question of constitutional revision. By this time the Carlists felt certain that the CEDA, as they had predicted, had become a Republican party unprepared to do more than tinker with the existing constitutional fabric. The publication of the cabinet's constitutional reform plans appeared to confirm this belief. Although abandoning the socialistic elements of the 1931 Constitution, the proposals, which reportedly had the support of the entire cabinet, gave no indication of imminent surrender on the issue of laicism. [69]

The Carlists regarded the whole scheme as inadequate, but reserved their most scathing comments for the CEDA's apparent refusal to make a stand against anti-clericalism. If this was only to be expected of Lerroux 'who for us hasn't changed since the Semana Trágica', how absurd that a party claiming to be the genuine interpreter of pontifical thought should acquiesce so meekly in the maintenance of an 'atheist state'.[70] Carlist propagandists now dropped all talk of constitutional revision, which they had previously supported *faute de mieux*, and followed Pradera in urging that the Constitution be 'consigned to fire and ashes'.[71] Carlist advocacy of the corporate state, hitherto phrased in somewhat visionary terms, now began to sound more like a plan of action.[72]

The new Agrarian Reform Act was passed in July and gave the Carlist landowners some consolation for what they continued to complain was the lamentable state of the countryside.[73] The Act, sponsored by the Agrarian Minister of Agriculture, Velayos, rejected social-Catholicism; as Gil Robles pointed out, it amounted to a 'rectification' of the 1932 law.[74] Its most disputed provisions were those suppressing expropriation without indemnification and further improving the position of the proprietor in relation to the *arrendatario*;[75] ironically, it was precisely this doctrinaire economic liberalism which endeared the Act to the Carlists. Their defence of landowners' rights contrasted starkly with the radicalism of José Antonio's Cortes speech. From the point of view of the Communion's internal discipline it was perhaps as well that the outspoken *a.e.t.* no longer appeared.

However gratified by the Velayos Act, the Carlists did not relax their attacks on the CEDA. All through 1935 they had been claiming that the CEDA was turning Catholic Action against Traditionalism – something, given the close interpenetration of Catholic Action and the CEDA leadership, which if true was superfluous.[76] Now they added allegations that the CEDA was conducting a smear campaign against the Carlist press, and began to indulge in vitriolic personal attacks against individual *cedistas*. The favourite victim was the Carlist apostate Lucía, described by *La Unión* as 'a wingless butterfly – all appetite'. Priests and seminarists sympathetic to the CEDA were, it was claimed, circulating false rumours of imminent ecclesiastical censure upon Carlism.[77] Whether justified or not, accusations of this type indicated the extent of Carlist annoyance at the inescapable fact that the Spanish Church, apart from the parish clergy of Navarre and parts of the Basque provinces, was giving them little assistance in the crusade against godless liberalism. From the point of view of the Church's authorities,

Carlist – and Alfonsist – extremism threatened to frustrate their efforts at reaching a *modus vivendi* with a Republic which, given the CEDA's important role, was becoming increasingly conservative and therefore increasingly palatable.

Besides complaining at the links between the CEDA and the Church, the Carlists did their best to play up internal dissent within the CEDA – from which, as the next-largest and most right-wing Catholic party, the Communion naturally stood to gain. And there were signs, however slight, of such a drift. In February, amid nationwide Carlist rejoicing, two CEDA circles, one in Logroño and the other in Toledo, voted unanimously to join the Communion.[78] No more followed, but optimistic Carlists saw the news as a straw in the wind.

Now, in the summer of 1935, there were more grumblings in the CEDA. Especially irksome to Gil Robles was the rebelliousness of the JAP. Its members' impatience with the Radical alliance, their excited calls for 'full power', and their general quasi-fascism were acutely embarrassing to a Gil Robles currently anxious for political respectability. In the past the Carlists had exhibited mixed feelings towards the JAP, at times identifying it closely with CEDA accident-alism, at others praising its radicalism in the hope of accentuating its differences with its elders.[79] On the whole they were sceptical as to the sincerity of this radicalism, in view of the JAP's adulation of its *'Jefe'*, Gil Robles; *El Pensamiento Navarro*'s columnist Emigdio Molina believed that like the CEDA itself the JAP was simply 'playing out a role'.[80] The greatest irritant to the Carlists, always short of funds, was the sight of the JAP's lavish expenditure on its activities – 'chasing the flies with honey' in *El Siglo Futuro*'s words.[81] When Gil Robles suspended the JAP's newspaper in June 1935, the Carlists openly sided with the young *cedistas*.[82] They got their reward when the JAP's ex-president, José María Valiente, resigned from the CEDA and, amid a blaze of publicity, joined the Communion. Valiente's earlier Alfonsism made his decision doubly pleasing;[83] he now became a regular speaker at Carlist and National Bloc meetings, inveighing with a convert's passion against his old party.[84]

The National Bloc, meanwhile, staggered on without much success. Its rallies and meetings, although enlivened by Calvo Sotelo's oratory and the dialectic of Pradera, were vastly out-numbered by those of the CEDA.[85] And whereas relative size was not a major preoccupation to the Carlists, it mattered a great deal to the Bloc's leaders, who more obviously sought to challenge the CEDA on its own ground. As 1935 wore on, some more militant Alfonsists, frustrated at the excessively 'political' character of the Bloc, began to desert it and Renovación Española and turn their attention once more to the Falange.[86] As the National Bloc stumbled and as the succession question continued to nag at Carlist–Alfonsist relations, monarchist tempers frayed. Alfonso's tenacious defence of his own position and tendency to regard the Bloc as embodying monarchist unity under his banner were upsetting enough to the Carlists, but when Maeztu indiscreetly claimed that Renovación Española had been founded 'because somebody had to defend monarchy', Carlist wrath boiled over. As the rising young Navarrese propagandist Jesús Elizalde brutally remarked, Renovación, 'a General Staff without an army', was hardly equipped to offer much of a defence.[87]

Renovación Española's now incurable weakness and the National Bloc's lack of impact, both only partly obscured by the personal stature of Calvo Sotelo, mingled with Carlist anticipation of the imminent collapse of the CEDA tactic to generate a growing buoyancy and 'go it alone' feeling within the Communion. By August 1935 Fal Conde felt confident enough to announce that the first phase of reorganization was virtually complete and would be followed by 'an overwhelming movement of Traditionalist propaganda' distinguished by 'exclusiveness and decisiveness'. Both Fal Conde and Alfonso Carlos, never happy with Carlism's role in the National Bloc, were now determined that the Communion could and must go forward alone

so that alone we may speak the truth and the whole truth to public opinion ... [and] cry out that not one step further can be taken along perdition's road: the road of dealings with liberal institutions, be they monarchist or republican.[88]

The intended departure from the National Bloc was postponed on account of the prolonged political crisis which opened in September and, by raising the prospect of a general election, made a precipitate rupture with Alfonsism unwise. On 20 September the Lerroux government, weakened for some time by the CEDA's opposition to Chapaprieta's economy drive, fell when its Agrarian members withdrew over the progressive relaxation of restrictions on Catalan autonomy. When a new government was formed by Chapaprieta himself the CEDA representation was back to three. Once again Alcalá Zamora passed over Gil Robles who, gambling on an election victory in the not too distant future, appeared not to have sought power.

On this occasion the Carlists were correct in seeing the cabinet change as the beginning of the end of the CEDA's tactical success. The continued closeness of Lerroux and Gil Robles therefore outraged them more than ever: the latter, they concluded, was now irredeemably lost in a world of tactics.[89] The coalition leaders had let their hour pass, and while they appeared to have forgotten October 1934 the left was reorganizing around Azaña for an electoral alliance which could only be the preliminary to renewed revolution. Although an enormous mass rally addressed by Azaña outside Madrid on 20 October demonstrated, according to *El Pensamiento Navarro*, 'Azaña's total intellectual decay', *El Siglo Futuro* viewed it as a threat of revolution and issued dire warnings of what another Azaña government would mean for Spain.[90]

The following week there exploded the political bombshell of the 'Straperlo' scandal, involving the alleged bribing of prominent Radicals and Lerroux's own nephew by the Dutch promoter of a variant of roulette. This was followed in December by the 'Nombela' affair, in which personal friends of Lerroux were accused of malversation of government compensation for cancelled military supply contracts in Spanish Guinea. Parliamentary investigation cleared Lerroux of personal complicity, but the scandals broke him politically and with him the Radical Party. In so doing, they also dashed once and for all the complementary tactics of Lerroux and Gil Robles.

The Carlists seized on the scandals as proof of the Republic's moral decay, an increasingly dominant theme of their recent propaganda. According to the Carlist press, Spain was the unfortunate recipient of a wave of written and cinematic pornography, released by the Comintern and international Jewry for the express purpose of undermining her civilization. The Republic, which shirked moral censorship and encouraged immorality through coeducation and the legalization of divorce, was all too obviously an accessory in this campaign.[91] The priest 'Fabio' wrote in *El Siglo Futuro* that the Straperlo affair showed how the regime's lack of concern for private morality also affected morals in the public domain.[92] In the Cortes the Carlists hounded Lerroux as they had recently done Azaña,

and were scornful when the CEDA refused to join them.[93] Zamanillo, now leader of the Requeté, voiced the general disapproval; 'We
are surrounded by asphyxiating gases.'[94]

The winding up of the Nombela debate coincided with the
expected resignation of Chapaprieta, whose stubbornly advocated
expenditure cuts and other budgetary reforms remained un-
implemented. Out of office with him went Gil Robles and the other
surviving CEDA ministers Lucía and Salmón. Alcalá Zamora, who
had been considering a dissolution for most of the year, at last
decided that the time had come. Faced with the need to appoint a
premier to preside over the dissolution and general election, and
anxious for a result unfavourable to either political extreme, the
President was less inclined than ever to call on Gil Robles. The task
was eventually given to Portela Valladares, a former Civil Governor
of Catalonia and Minister of the Interior. No *cedistas* were in the
predominantly right-of-centre cabinet.[95]

Despite their revulsion at the sight of a ministry headed by
Portela, a leading freemason,[96] the Carlists could not help feeling
delighted at the apparent collapse of the CEDA tactic. Jesús
Elizalde spoke from the heart: 'Why not admit it – it fills us with
joy.'[97] For two wasted years, the Carlists declared, the CEDA had
allowed itself to be used by Lerroux – but they had always known
and argued that Gil Robles would never be given power within
the Republic. Gil Robles, of course, still had one more card to play.
Election victory, which there was no reason to think impossible,
might even yet bring him the 'full power' which had so far proved
elusive. Carlists claimed to wish him well in this ambition, while
hoping that in pursuing it he would see the light, repudiate the 'men
and parties of the Pact of San Sebastian' and return like the prodigal
son to the bosom of the counter-revolutionary family to which he
truly belonged.[98]

The permanent pre-election atmosphere which had existed during
1935 meant that when on 6 January 1936 the Cortes were finally
dissolved and a general election called for 16 February, the Carlists
were psychologically as well prepared for the contest as they were
ever likely to be.[99] From the moment that Portela assumed the
premiership, TYRE, notwithstanding its supposed suspension, resumed its operations, while the Carlist press, which earlier in the
year had demanded an election so that those who had voted for the
CEDA in 1933 could pass judgment on its conduct,[100] put such feel-

ings aside and called once again for Union of the Right.[101] Gil Robles' departure from office was followed by his reavowal of loyalty to the constituted regime, yet when it came to an election the CEDA and the monarchist parties were as necessary as ever to each other. Active monarchist support was so thinly spread that it was doubtful whether, outside the safest Carlist strongholds of Navarre and Álava, either monarchist party could hope to return a single deputy save in alliance with Gil Robles. Conversely, while the CEDA could bank on winning a large number of seats even against monarchist as well as left-wing opposition, unity with the monarchists was vital if it was to have the remotest chance of the 300 seats euphorically demanded by the JAP, or even the 240 necessary for the overall majority which would ensure Gil Robles the premiership. This was all the more true now that the Radicals were in such disarray as to be useless as allies in all but a few provinces. Besides, whereas in 1933 the right's success had been assisted by the left's fragmentation, this time the left would be united again. On 15 January 1936 a year's manoeuvring and negotiation were consummated by the conclusion of the Popular Front, binding together the Republican Left, the Esquerra, the Socialists and the Communists on a minimum programme of return to the policies of 1931–3.[102] On this occasion it was also to be expected that the Anarchists, most of whom had abstained in 1933, would turn out in strength to support an electoral programme which included the release from prison of thousands of their comrades held since October 1934.

Whatever the right's internal frictions, which were certainly no greater than those within the Popular Front, a resuscitation of the 1933 electoral pact was thus generally recognized to be indispensable. In pursuing his personal 'reopening to the right', Gil Robles faced dissent from his own left wing, led by Lucía and Giménez Fernández, who would have preferred forming with the various conservative Republican parties what Lucía termed 'a loyal and sincere union of the right'.[103] Gil Robles succeeded in overriding this opposition, which if successful might actually have dragged the CEDA across the threshold of the Republic, and instead made contact with Fal Conde and Goicoechea. Several meetings were then held, but no formal liaison committee emerged as it had in 1933.[104] Fal Conde, assisted by Lamamié, negotiated directly with Gil Robles regarding the number and distribution of Carlist candidates, while exercising his personal right to approve or veto individual

Carlist candidacies submitted by provincial organizations.[105] Predictably, he went out of his way to deny any electoral role to the National Bloc.[106]

It was finally agreed that the monarchists should provide a total of sixty-nine candidates, thirty-nine coming from Renovación and the assorted independent monarchists and thirty from the Carlists.[107] On the whole, negotiations proceeded quite smoothly, despite Carlist indignation at the CEDA's exclusion of Carlist candidates in Murcia, Alicante, Logroño and Santander. Here Carlists stood alone, save in Santander where an alliance was made with the similarly excluded Falange.[108] A separate Carlist candidature in Seville was only averted by the timely withdrawal of the Alfonsist Luca de Tena, which permitted the inclusion in the right's list of Ginés Martínez.[109] In Catalonia, unlike the rest of Spain, Carlist candidates swallowed their pride and principles and joined the CEDA, the Lliga and the Radicals in 'Law and Order Fronts'.[110] The Communion finally presented thirty-four candidates, five fewer than in 1933.

Once again the geographical distribution of candidates illustrated Carlism's continuing advance, a challenge being offered for the first time in Almería, Granada, Jaén, Murcia, Orense and Toledo. Among the new candidates were the convert Valiente (Burgos), Rada, the National Inspector of the Requeté (Almería),[111] Elizalde (Navarre) and the brother of the 'martyred' Oreja (Guipúzcoa).[112] Notable absentees were Esteban Bilbao and Fal Conde. The former stood down, he announced, out of hatred for parliamentarism;[113] Fal Conde, despite the firm offer of a place on the Jaén list and pressure from within the Communion, including the Pretender himself, to consider seriously the benefits of parliamentary immunity, equally declined to involve himself in the Cortes' affairs.[114]

The right's campaign was monopolized by the lavish propaganda of the CEDA, outstanding for its unrestrained boosting of the person of Gil Robles.[115] The Carlist campaign was conducted separately and dwelt almost exclusively on two related themes: the threat of renewed revolution offered by the Popular Front and the imperative counter-revolutionary responsibility of the right's electoral alliance. No effort was spared in recapturing the horror of October 1934 and in linking the Popular Front with revolution. Its electoral function was dismissed as a mere façade and its manifesto as irrelevant since in the event of victory its true programme would be imposed by 'secret organizations';[116] its real leader was not Azaña but Largo Caballero, who in turn was a puppet of Moscow. A left-wing triumph at the polls would consequently be followed by a Left Socialist–Communist takeover, a return to the 'bloody scenes of barbarity' witnessed in 1934 and the ultimate imposition of the dictatorship of the proletariat.[117] Nor would this even be a Spanish revolutionary regime, since the Jewish–marxist–masonic conspiracy now at work would assuredly turn Spain into a Russian colony.[118] No solution was to be found in voting for political moderates, whether they be the Basque Nationalists or the Centre Party recently formed by Alcalá Zamora and Portela in the hope of preventing political polarization. The latter was an 'inconceivable absurdity' since to occupy the centre without resolutely opposing marxism was to encourage revolution – as might be expected from a party manipulated by freemasons.[119] As for what Rodezno described as 'the parochial and poverty-stricken' PNV, it was considered to have revealed its true revolutionary colours in 1934 and no longer to merit the votes of sincere Catholics.[120] The PNV retaliated with diatribes against Carlist conservatism as displayed on agrarian issues.[121]

Convinced that the future held revolution whatever the election result, the Carlists insisted that the present 'counter-revolutionary' alliance must differ crucially from that of 1933. They urged that it continue until its programme – a vague but threatening one of 'anti-laicism, anti-separatism and anti-marxism' – had been carried out. More explicit pronouncements like those of Pradera demonstrated that this implied nothing less than the complete Traditionalist system, since 'all else is revolution'.[122] Remarks like this could only embarrass Gil Robles, who remained under pressure from his own moderates and was no more inclined towards a lasting monarchist alliance now than in previous months. He was further irritated by the tone of the monarchist campaign, which exceeded the agreed minimum programme in urging the electorate to 'Vote for the Monarchy'.[123] Since the Carlists rightly suspected that Gil Robles had no intention of allowing the alliance to survive for long after the election, their proposals possessed the double attraction of committing the Communion to nothing whilst providing it with an almost guaranteed future weapon against the CEDA.[124]

Perhaps carried away by the all-pervasive optimism of the CEDA's propaganda, the Carlist press approached election day in a crescendo of confidence in the right's victory.[125] However, the results which unfolded during the days after 16 February showed a Popular Front success sweeping in terms of seats, albeit narrow – or according to some accounts non-existent – in terms of popular votes.[126] After the second round on 1 March, thirteen Carlists stood elected within a fairly steady right-wing total of around 150.[127] The political centre was effectively obliterated, and the Popular Front had won an overall majority.

In the face of this cataclysm the Carlists looked around desperately for consolation, and found it in the failure, and, in their eyes, discrediting of the CEDA, which far from 300 seats had won only 96. *El Siglo Futuro* argued defiantly that in exposing the futility of 'tactics and opportunism' the so-called triumph of the left carried within it a moral victory for Carlist advocates of resolute opposition to the Republic.[128] Fal Conde agreed: the Popular Front's success, he wrote, was an object lesson in the just rewarding of intransigence.[129] Believing that revolution was now inevitable, the Carlists and others on the extreme right concluded that they must strike first – the course towards which Fal Conde had in fact been devoting his organizational energies for almost two years.

9
Preparation for rebellion

In the months and years which followed his assumption of the Secretary-Generalship of the Traditionalist Communion, Fal Conde's personal appeal and political judgment were often to be called into question by fellow Carlists. Never, however, did anyone doubt his powers as an organizer.[1] Within days of taking up his new post, Fal Conde threw himself into the work of giving Carlism a completely remodelled hierarchy of command designed to carry a minority cause into political power by what seemed the only possible route: war. First to be announced, late in May 1934, were three Special Sections or Delegations of the Communion: the Special Delegations of Youth, the Press, and Propaganda, headed respectively by Arellano, Manuel González Quevedo of Editorial Tradicionalista, and Lamamié. Later in the year two more were added, the Special Delegation for the Requeté under Zamanillo and that of Finance under the Barón de Sangarrén.[2] At the beginning of June the Carlist press blazoned the imminent appearance of the *Boletín de Orientación Tradicionalista*, a weekly to be issued by the Secretary-General's office as compulsory reading for all Carlists. It would transmit information and orders, and 'be able to fix standards in more concrete and precise terms than our press is capable of doing'.[3] The *Boletín* was first released on 15 July 1934 and for the next two years served as Fal Conde's official mouthpiece and the principal organ of communication within the Carlist organization. Although not strictly speaking a newspaper, it satisfied as the two main dailies, *El Siglo Futuro* and *El Pensamiento Navarro*, could not do, the perennially frustrated Carlist longing for a national organ. Moreover, it helped to affirm and enforce the Secretary-General's authority and to create within the Carlist ranks a general atmosphere of pride in the movement's past and confidence in its future.

Other initiatives of the early months of Fal Conde's leadership included the setting up of a Council of Culture, the holding of a 'census' and the meeting of a Grand Council (*Junta Magna*) of the

Communion. The Council of Culture was inaugurated in June under the presidency of Pradera and included among its eighteen members Rodezno, Bilbao, Senante, Tejera, Junyent, Fernando Contreras and Comín. Its task was described as the 'synthesis and diffusion' of Traditionalist ideology, which it was to study, discuss and disseminate, and upon the finer points of which it would be in effect the final arbiter. The Council exercised little real power, but served a useful purpose in bringing together eminent Carlists of differing geographical and generational origins.[4] The 'census' was held in September 1934, its purpose being to apprise the new leadership of all Carlist organizations, together with details of their membership. Detailed results were never published, although the returns formed the basis for surveys of provincial organizations which appeared intermittently during the next year in the *Boletín*. It was, however, very rashly announced that the census proved the Communion to be 'the most numerous political party in Spain' – a claim which was quickly buried once reason reasserted itself.[5] The Grand Council assembled in November 1934, and consisted of representatives from all the aforementioned Delegations and sections of the Communion in a vague semblance of the Traditional Cortes. Like the Council of Culture, the Grand Council was a largely decorative body with a measure of influence but no executive role; its irregular meetings nevertheless provided an opportunity for the mingling of disparate and often contending groups and individuals for the purpose of discussion.[6]

Apart from establishing the Secretary-General's authority, subject only to the distant and, where Fal Conde was concerned, amenable Alfonso Carlos, the aim and effect of the new organizational structure were to improve communication in all directions, stimulate militancy, and introduce into the Communion an unprecedented degree of centralization, uniformity and regimentation. This was to be achieved through the assumption by the Special Delegations of functions previously exercised, often in a distinctly lackadaisical manner, by the various juntas. These bodies had hitherto run the Youth and Requeté, more often than not without any permanent ties with neighbouring districts, much less anything seriously resembling a national organization. This situation was intolerable to Fal Conde, and indeed made no sense in the light of the civil war mentality now running through the Communion. The Youth and Requeté were both vital and, on occasions, overexuberant, and in Fal Conde's opinion needed a structure which would combine rigid discipline with opportunities for releasing aggression. They were now therefore largely removed from junta control and placed within quite separate organizations, each with its own hierarchy of regional, provincial and local *jefes* appointed from above. The Delegations of Press and Propaganda also possessed their own hierarchies of *jefes*, but unlike those of the Youth and the Requeté continued to operate in close liaison with the now largely 'administrative' traditional juntas.[7]

The roles of the Special Delegations, all responsible to the Secretary-General and headed, significantly, by young men in their twenties and thirties, were sharply defined. That of the Press was entrusted with improving and publicizing the Carlist newspapers and reviews in collaboration with the Council of Culture, particular stress being laid upon increasing circulation and guaranteeing financial security.[8] The related but more important Special Delegation for Propaganda concentrated on the organization of meetings, study courses and political campaigns at all but the most local level.[9] The Delegation of Finance was responsible for running the so-called 'Treasury of Tradition': in other words, attempting to improve the Communion's eternally delicate financial position by means of appeals and, for the first time since the wars of the nineteenth century, the imposition upon adherents of what amounted to a system of taxation.[10] Essential as were the functions of the Press, Propaganda and Finance Delegations to the Communion's future, however, it was the Delegations of Youth, incorporating the AET, and of the Requeté, which were the most central to its 'new orientation'. Luis Arellano, Delegate for the Youth, defined its role as 'the cultural and physical formation of young people' and the promotion of a manly and resolute spirit.[11] The 'crazy behaviour' so recently frowned on by many timorous juntas was now officially accepted as desirable and was accordingly given rein within the Youth, which was regarded as a 'novitiate' whose most combative elements were drawn off into the Requeté.[12] The latter's duty was clearly laid down in the *Boletín*. It was to recruit from the young and especially from among 'workers', requiring above all people with technical ability and others inclined towards 'heroic' activism. Special attention was paid to the need for military discipline, ideological rigour and an efficient national organization 'without which modern necessities would be poorly observed'.[13] No attempt was made to disguise or deny what was now accepted as axiomatic: that 'modern necessities' involved striking a physical blow against the Republic.

Within six months, the Communion's structure was thus transformed and Carlism, however reactionary its ideas, was well on the
way to becoming organizationally a movement of the 'modern' extreme right. The changes, generating a vast flow of information and
instructions, naturally created new work for the occupants of the
Carlist hierarchy. Interviewed in January 1935 Fal Conde commented on this, adding that he personally was giving up journalistic
work in order to devote himself more fully to the task of organization.[14] The Communion's nerve-centre was now the busy office of
the General Secretariat at Marqués de Cubas 21, Madrid. Here the
Secretary-General, the Special Delegations, the Treasury of Tradition
and the Council of Culture had their headquarters, the *Boletín de
Orientación Tradicionalista* was edited, and a file was kept of the
Communion's membership.[15] In April 1935 the General Secretariat
announced that the Communion now possessed over 700 local juntas
and delegations, 350 circles, 250 Youth sections, 300 women's
groups and 80 local Requeté sections; unlike the absurd claim made
after the 1934 'census', this was probably a fairly accurate statement of Carlism's strength after four years of the Republic and a year
under Fal Conde's leadership.[16]

Hand in hand with organizational innovation went continued
expansion. In December 1934, for example, members of the new
Regional Junta of western Andalusia went to the people once again,
touring the region and inaugurating Youth sections in six *pueblos.*[17]
During 1934 and 1935, Arellano and Zamanillo continuously travelled the country setting up new Youth and Requeté organizations,[18] and throughout its existence the *Boletín* continued to report
these and other new foundations even in such unlikely areas as
Albacete, Ciudad Real and the Canaries.[19] By late 1935 every
Spanish province possessed at least the skeleton of a Carlist organization and several a complete structure with numerous circles or meeting-
places. Among these were Navarre, the Basque provinces, the four
Catalonian provinces, the three provinces of the Levant, western
Andalusia and Zaragoza.

At local level, Carlist organization had come a long way since
1931. Instead of being little more than somnolent clubs for the
elderly and middle-aged, Carlist circles now provided the growing
numbers of Carlists with a kind of counter-culture to what they considered the decadent, permissive and godless world of Republican
Spain. Like many Spanish Catholics, Carlists were fearful of the

effects upon their children of laic and sometimes sexually mixed education. They insisted that the sexes were equal but different; Romualdo Toledo, Carlist educational spokesman in the 1933–5 Cortes, argued that despite the educational radicals 'the intellectual differences which Nature has created between the sexes will always persist' and that mixing the adolescents of both sexes at school was educationally harmful and morally dangerous.[20] Worse, *El Siglo Futuro* claimed that the Republic's schools were encouraging sensitively raised Catholic children to read 'pornography and erotic rubbish' churned out by the Jewish and Communist Internationals 'like a poison which will surely lead our nation to a terrible end'.[21] The perils during out-of-school hours were even greater, thanks to the cinema, 'a Jewish–masonic' enterprise whose creations spread immorality and in certain cases defamed the good name of Spain.[22] In Seville the Carlists launched a campaign on behalf of 'moral cinema'; *La Unión*, berating the CEDA press for advertising the film of *Les Misérables*, declared that it refused to give publicity to such obscenities 'for the same reason that no decent newspaper advertises brothels'.[23] In these circumstances the Carlist circle became a haven of traditional family life, conservative Catholicism and stern morality, into which Carlists fled to escape an alien outside world and scheme its destruction. No effort was therefore spared to provide a rich texture of political, social, cultural and recreational activities, designed to occupy the spare time of the entire Carlist family, and above all the young. Circles now offered libraries of approved literature; orchestras, choirs and folk-dance societies; 'decent' film shows; dramatic societies which performed melodramatic interpretations of Carlist history or tributes to Carlist virtues, written by home-grown playwrights like Jaime del Burgo; and indoor and outdoor sporting facilities. In Navarre a full Traditionalist Football League was founded in order to avoid the danger of moral or political contamination through sporting contacts with the infidel.[24] The evident wish to create a hermetically sealed Carlist world went even further than this; not only were Carlists urged by their newspapers to restrict their drinking activities to the 'Traditionalist' products of the firm of Palomino-Vergara, but also to be sure to spend their vacations in hotels run by fellow Carlists.[25] Even the very youngest children were now liable to be enrolled in the service of the cause, with the creation of the Pelayos, uniformed groups clad in imitation of the Requeté and 'armed' with toy rifles.

All these activities took place against a backcloth of fervent veneration for Carlist traditions and the Carlist royal family, and in an atmosphere of all-pervading religiosity quite different from that, for instance, which reigned in most Falangist organizations. Where Carlist roots went deep, or where the Church was intimately connected with the social strata from which most Carlists came – in Navarre, the Basque region and Old Castile for example – at least one parish priest was usually in attendance to provide religious guidance and keep a watchful eye on the circle's affairs; in Andalusia and other regions where Carlism had developed or revived with little clerical patronage, this was relatively rare. Certainly, with the exception of Navarre, the interpenetration of Carlism and a Church now torn between Alfonsism and the CEDA was a thing of the past. The episcopate in particular did nothing to reciprocate the support which Carlism gave the Church.

More important, perhaps, than priests in helping to give Carlist circles the desired atmosphere were the Margaritas: the Carlist women. During 1934 and 1935 attempts were made to construct a national women's organization on the lines of the Special Delegations. For undisclosed reasons – conceivably the lack of enough suitable officers – little headway was made, but in other respects the Secretary-General, supported by the *de facto* leader of the Carlist women, María Rosa Úrraca Pastor, went out of his way to encourage the foundation of new women's groups and generally to exalt and define the role of women within the Communion. According to the *Boletín*, the Carlist woman was entrusted with a 'Great Spiritual Crusade'. Her chief task lay within the home and family: by raising children – and *ipso facto* new Carlists – she would 'propagandize our sacred ideals'; at the Carlist circle she would take part in study groups, run night schools for workers, pursue charitable activity on behalf of the poor and unemployed, and run the *Socorro Blanco* organization for the relief of 'persecuted' and imprisoned Carlists and their families. She it was who would exemplify the principles of piety, modesty and self-sacrifice and who would provide her menfolk, especially the young, with help, advice and encouragement in peace and war. Despite this essentially conventional view of the woman's role, Carlist male chauvinism was far from total, however. Professional women, especially teachers, were respected and considered to have added opportunities for proselytizing.[26]

By 1935 an increasing number of circles were following the

examples of those of Seville and Barcelona in founding a Workers Section or *Agrupación Gremial* (Guild Group) as it was now more likely to be called.[27] Success was uneven – in aristocratic Jerez only one worker could be found to sit on the circle's committee even though three places were set aside[28] – but far from negligible. It was true that most so-called workers were still artisans, yet even this compared favourably with other right-wing organizations.[29] In Seville, where the Carlist Workers Section continued to flourish, that of the Falange was later described by its own founders as 'minuscule'.[30] Carlists boasted of the egalitarian atmosphere of their meeting places; the officers of the Seville circle claimed that in its rooms could be found members of classes not even admitted to the city's other right-wing centres.[31] Sevillian Carlism was certainly socially democratic compared with the local branch of Renovación Española. When the latter named a council for 1936, aimed at getting the stagnating movement off the ground in Seville, the forty-eight names included ten marquises, three counts and several others related to aristocratic families.[32] No local Carlist organization in the entire country even remotely resembled this. Most juntas and delegations were still dominated by professional men and modest landowners, most of the mass membership coming from the households of peasant proprietors, tenant farmers, artisans and a minority of the Catholic middle class.[33]

Without question the prevalent note in Carlist circles as 1935 wore on was the greatly increased emphasis upon the Requeté. To the customary mood of political protest was now added one of military preparation only thinly disguised as social activity. Local leaders, their former control of the younger generation now exercised by the officers of the relevant Special Delegations, took something of a back seat wherever the Requeté prospered, and gradually the circle's whole life was liable to be adapted to fit in with military needs. Burgo describes the Pamplona headquarters as 'like a barracks' by the end of the year; here, as in most large circles, the Requeté occupied the strategically important ground floor and kept a twenty-four hour guard on the main entrance. On the other hand, where Requeté 'supplies' were stored on the premises, it was more often, as in Seville, on the top floor in the hope of avoiding search and confiscation by the authorities.

The greater stress upon military matters showed itself in other ways. Whereas a year or two earlier, instruction of young Carlists within the circle had mainly centred around Traditionalist theory, social problems and so on, attention now shifted to the kind of theoretical and practical military instruction given by Burgo to the NCO's of the Pamplona Requeté. Exercises and examinations were now necessary for promotion from the ranks, while Requeté officers were required to attend daily instruction. Outdoor week-end exercises involving practice in marksmanship, field combat, strategy and tactics – as well as fundamental physical fitness – were by now commonplace, especially in Navarre, whence 120 Red Berets actually went to Italy and Libya to receive training under the Rome agreement.[34] At mass rallies such as those which took place during 1935 at the Catalonian monasteries of Poblet and Montserrat, the ranks of the Requeté stood as testimony of Carlism's intentions.

All the aforementioned activities needed financing, and although the Communion counted some extremely wealthy individuals among its members, it was not, in comparison with Renovación Española or the CEDA, a rich movement. Indeed, the *Boletín* and Fal Conde himself were in the habit of referring to Carlism's 'poverty' as a kind of corollary of its classlessness and doctrinal austerity.[35] Unprecedented attention was therefore paid to fund-raising during 1934 and 1935. The Special Delegation of Finance introduced its taxation system at the end of 1934. It involved the payment by all Carlists into the Treasury of Tradition of a sum at least equal to that paid in direct taxation to the state; those – and given Spain's archaic tax system there must have been many – who paid no taxes were required to examine their consciences and pay what they could afford. The 'very poor' were taxed at 50 céntimos (about 3d.) per annum. On top of this, Carlists were asked to pay a kind of tithe, actually two per cent of their income, into a special fund for the financing of the Youth. Anyone failing to pay his due was liable to expulsion from the Communion.[36] Apart from systematic taxation and the secret, voluntary contributions from wealthy members and sympathizers, the Communion also had resort to exceptional measures such as a Mussolini-style appeal for gifts of gold and jewellery, which to judge from the long lists of donors published in the *Boletín* was a considerable success.[37] What everyone knew, but even now could not publicly admit, was that besides its normal running costs the Communion had additional 'invisible' expenses. There is no question that a large proportion of the money collected was spent on the purchase and importation of arms.[38]

'Either the Communion is disciplined and efficient,' wrote Fal Conde in his *Boletín*, 'or it is not the Communion.'[39] Up to a point his reforms were successful in imposing discipline upon the Carlist ranks. His own energy and efficiency in carrying out his responsibilities were generally acknowledged, while within the Requeté hierarchy and among his fellow southerners he inspired genuine devotion. There could be no serious grounds for public complaint when in December 1935 Alfonso Carlos raised Fal Conde's status to that of *Jefe-Delegado* (Delegated Leader) of the Communion. Appointed to assist him was a new body, the Council of the Communion, consisting of Bilbao, the veteran Larramendi, the ex-Integrists Lamamié and Senante, and the new regional *jefe* of Catalonia, Lorenzo Alier.[40]

Private dissatisfaction with Fal Conde's leadership nonetheless continued to simmer among those who still preferred Rodezno's style of leadership or who looked for something else again. Since Carlism possessed a royal *caudillo*, albeit an octogenarian exile, the Communion's political chief was under no pressure to project the image of a charismatic fascist leader. Even so, Fal Conde's refusal or inability to cut any sort of dash irritated many Carlists who considered him utterly uninspiring, a colourless, mediocre figure compared with, say, José Antonio and Calvo Sotelo or even the eloquent and gregarious Rodezno. The more pragmatically minded also doubted his political acumen, shrouded as it was beneath a veil of aloofness and political isolationism. For his part Fal Conde, although content to let Rodezno lead Carlism's National Bloc operations, was far from pleased when numerous Carlists, especially of the older generation, continued to seek out the Navarrese aristocrat for the benefit of his political experience and contacts.[41]

Meanwhile, one problem in particular still provoked restlessness among the rank and file – that of the succession. Alfonso Carlos was now eighty-five, and the urgency of the situation created by the possibility of his death was only increased by the growing feeling that a monarchical restoration need not, after all, be an empty dream. It was now over two years since serious talks had been held concerning a dynastic reconciliation with the Alfonsine line, but despite the known lack of enthusiasm of the Communion's present leadership, the existence of the National Bloc seemed to the staunch band of Carlist 'fusionists' to keep the prospect flickeringly alive. The *El Cruzado Español* schismatics believed that this was what the National Bloc was all about. It was, they claimed, the fruit of an 'Integrist–Alfonsist–Traditionalist–Juanist' conspiracy, engineered by Calvo Sotelo with the enthusiastic help of Rodezno, Pradera and Bau, and covertly backed by Fal Conde and the Integrist *camarilla* surrounding him.[42] This was, to say the least, a somewhat idiosyncratic view of Carlism's internal politics.

For some months now *El Cruzado Español* had been pushing the decidedly tenuous claim to the succession of the late Don Jaime's youngest nephew, Karl Pius of Habsburg, son of Doña Blanca's marriage to Archduke Leopold of Tuscany.[43] The putative 'Carlos VIII' had written to Alfonso Carlos late in 1934, enquiring about the validity of his claim; upon being told that he was firmly excluded from consideration by the Salic Law, Karl Pius discreetly contacted Fal Conde in order to disown his advocates' campaign.[44] The *cruzadistas* did not give up as easily, however, and while anxious loyalists petitioned the Secretary-General's office for a resolution of the succession question, the rebels set about resolving it to their own satisfaction by convoking a pale shadow of the 'Carlist Assembly' which they had earlier tried to foist on Alfonso Carlos. This met in Zaragoza in May 1935, and in the brusquest possible denial of the Salic Law proclaimed Doña Blanca 'heiress'.[45] The Communion's leaders went to great lengths to discredit the Assembly, which *El Siglo Futuro* stated was encouraged by the Zaragoza Republican authorities in order to split Carlism.[46] Its official condemnation by Alfonso Carlos represented, according to *El Cruzado Español*, 'the sinister triumph of the Juanist conspiracy'.[47]

Fal Conde, meanwhile, was increasingly the target of loyal Carlist agitation for a solution of the problem, yet he too was forced to wait upon the Pretender's decision. Calmly, Alfonso Carlos assured him that God was assisting him in the task.[48] In August 1935, while Carlist circles put on special religious services to help the Pretender further, the *Boletín* leaked the news that a solution would soon be announced.[49] To the troubled Carlist masses, the suspicious *cruzadistas* and the ever-hopeful Alfonsists alike, this seemed to presage the long-delayed recognition of the succession either of Alfonso XIII or of Don Juan. Prominent Alfonsists still insisted that this was the only way out of the deadlock, though many felt sufficiently con-

vinced of Don Juan's greater acceptability to the Carlists to hint at
the need for Alfonso's abdication. Any such possibility was dismissed
by Alfonso himself, who reiterated his own inalienable right to
succeed Alfonso Carlos as Carlist claimant.[50]

In August 1935 Alfonso XIII visited Alfonso Carlos at Puchheim,
his Austrian home; both the Pretender and Fal Conde hastily denied
rumours of a settlement and yet again repudiated the 'pact' of September 1931, to which Alfonso XIII continued to refer with approval.[51] Taken together with the *Boletín*'s earlier statement, these
reactions hinted that a decision on the succession was indeed imminent – but one not, after all, pleasing to the Alfonsists.

The generally accepted urgency of the succession question reflected
the now prevailing feeling among Carlists that political events were
rushing towards a moment of decision, and that Carlism could ill
afford to be nagged by problems which might blunt its resolution.
Since Fal Conde's elevation to the Secretary-Generalship in May
1934, the Communion's public tone had changed from one of largely
negative anti-Republican outrage to one of threatening violence, the
threat becoming more and more open as time passed. Even before
October 1934 Carlist orators began to praise the right-wing rebels of
1932 and to demand 'heroic' remedies for Spain's condition;[52] rank-
and-file members wrote in still more belligerent terms to the press,[53]
which in turn gave great prominence to *El derecho a la rebeldía* (*The
Right of Rebellion*), a much discussed book by a canon of Salamanca,
Castro Albarrán.[54] Like Castro Albarrán himself, the Carlists were
careful to point out that this right ought not to be invoked lightly,
that violence should be the response to extreme conduct on the part
of others. The kind of conduct held to justify violent rebellion was,
however, defined very loosely. When Tejera wrote of 'a defensive
civil war' in the face of persecution by an illegitimate power, he made
it clear that he regarded that power as inherently persecutory, and
rebellion as therefore justified by its mere existence. The Republic
being 'illegitimate in origin and practice', rebellion against it would
always be licit.[55]

After the revolution of October 1934 and the failure of successive
governments to pursue the kind of repression which they advocated,
the Carlists abandoned all equivocation. Where previously they had
insisted that only the excesses of the left could drive them to take
up arms, now that these excesses had actually occurred they could

regard the Republic as being in a permanently pre-revolutionary state
in which rebellion was an obligation; the Asturian revolt, in other
words, while not turning Carlism into an insurrectionary movement,
provided it with the justification for rebellion upon which it was
already bent. Since it was generally believed that the right could
not afford to wait for the left to strike first again, the Carlists' attention now turned to pre-emptive rather than retaliatory action, no
attempt being made any longer to conceal or deny the Communion's
increasingly military character and violent intentions. Quite the
reverse: overt militancy was the outstanding feature of the Carlist
press and the speeches of the movement's leading personalities. In
the press, led by the *Boletín*, there was a sudden flowering of editorials, articles and series dealing with Carlism's past military glories,
evidently calculated to stimulate a new pride, optimism and aggressiveness. Great publicity was given to surviving veterans of the war
of the 1870s, whose photographs and short biographies appeared in
several issues of the *Boletín*. Besides running other, similar series such
as 'Episodes from our Wars' and 'Carlos V in Spain', the *Boletín*
concentrated upon the inculcation of Carlists with the military virtues
of discipline, obedience and activism, as contrasted with the 'sins' of
downheartedness, inactivity and 'grumbling'.[56]

Coincidentally, 1935 marked the centenary of the death, during
the First Carlist War, of Carlism's greatest war-hero, Zumalacárregui. This created an opportunity for reviving a somewhat
flagging cult of veneration towards him and all Carlist 'martyrs'.
The celebration on 12 March 1935 of the annual 'Feast of the
Martyrs of Tradition' was surrounded by publicity of a quite unusual
intensity, not least since in the recently murdered Marcelino Oreja
there was now a new name for the Carlist pantheon. In *El Siglo
Futuro* a correspondent from Oñate (Navarre) demanded:

The name of Zumalacárregui must be vindicated; he was our hero and is
a national figure . . . Requetés! Let us not forget the red of our beret . . .
the blood we must offer the Cause. More, we have our martyrs and, with
God's help, martyrs we shall be ourselves.[57]

Between the Feast of the Martyrs and the Zumalacárregui centenary
in June, *El Siglo Futuro* carried a series on 'Zumalacárregui's Art of
War',[58] and on centenary day itself Alfonso Carlos proclaimed his
certainty that the martyred *guerrillero* was even now 'imploring the

Lord for a happy final success' for the Cause whose troops he had once led.[59]

At Carlist assemblies, and especially the Aplecs or mass rallies, openly violent language became increasingly common during 1935. The standard theme, the need for preparedness against the not too distant day of battle, was repeated by representatives of all sectors of the Communion, from Fal Conde and his loyal Requeté Delegate Zamanillo to Rodezno and his friend Arellano, from the aged Larramendi and Díaz-Aguado Salaverría to the Navarrese Youth leader Elizalde. Bloodshed was freely predicted. Salaverría called for the Requeté to be 'ready with weapons in hand for the morrow',[60] Arellano and others urged willingness to 'give life for the Cause',[61] and Fal Conde demanded 'death before renunciation and struggle before death'.[62] At a rally in San Sebastian at the end of 1935, Zamanillo whipped up an already excited audience by telling it that he came before it 'not to utter words of peace but cries of war!'[63]

On occasions, speakers reverted to the old position that the call to arms would follow a move by the left. But at the Aplec of Poblet, Fal Conde left it in no doubt that any time-lapse would be infinitesimal – 'When you hear "Young leftists – to arms!", take as given the order to . . .' His final words were drowned by a roar of approval from the 30,000 present.[64] By the end of 1935, however, there was no question that the Carlists were so determined on a prophylactic strike that they might well hear the left's cry before it was actually uttered. 'Fabio', in arguing that 'moral violence' was just as bad as physical violence, seemed to imply a right to take up arms against a regime, or an element protected by that regime, guilty only of a moral violence which, it was to be presumed, the insurgent himself would define and recognize.[65]

Carlist rebellion was obviously dependent upon the satisfactory development of the Requeté. In order that the Carlist militia should become a credible citizen army, four broad conditions needed to be fulfilled. A national organization had to be constructed; an effective military structure and discipline imposed; means obtained whereby the force might be armed, clad and equipped with additional necessities of modern warfare such as motorized transport and wireless; and lastly, a coherent and practicable strategy of insurrection drawn up and accepted. Varela's assumption of overall military command in 1933 marked the start of this process, which gathered speed and

seriousness after the change in leadership of May 1934. By the end
of 1935 the first three conditions were on the way to being satisfied;
only the fourth remained to plague Carlism until the very outbreak of
war.

The new organizational framework, heralded by the creation of
the National Red Beret Front, was introduced under Zamanillo's
delegacy during the second half of 1934. For the first time in Carlist
history the Requeté now possessed a separate and nationwide hierarchy far removed from the fragmented, local units typical of former
days. If Navarre remained the core of the movement and possibly
retained a bare majority of the country's Red Berets, the new national
leadership had nonetheless driven a wedge between that province's
establishment and its Youth. Even so, the nature of Navarrese Carlism was such that Fal Conde, Zamanillo and their associates had no
chance, whatever the new Requeté structure implied, of totally separating the young Navarrese militants from their erstwhile leaders
and bringing them securely under their own control. Admittedly the
Navarrese Youth had welcomed Fal Conde's appointment, just as
their elders had privately deplored it; yet what characterized their
outlook, like that of the Youth throughout Spain, was not so much
unconditional loyalty to Fal Conde's person as activism, impatience
and a belief that the new leadership would drag its feet less than the
old. What no one foresaw was the emergence of a situation in which
the Navarrese leaders would after all prove less hesitant than Fal
Conde in committing Carlism to a revolt. When this happened, it
would become plain that Fal Conde's national organization was less
independent of Navarre than at one stage seemed likely.

This is not to suggest that the national Requeté hierarchy created
by Fal Conde and Zamanillo was a sham. Where most of Spain was
concerned, the new structure stimulated recruitment, improved communication both vertically and laterally, fostered militancy, discipline
and ideological consistency, and most important gave the most
isolated Requeté *patrulla* the confidence derived from belonging to
a large and well-organized movement. What it could not and did not
do was place Navarre on the level of other provinces and bring it fully
under centralized control.

Navarre was nevertheless fully affected by the military rationalization wrought within the Communion from well before Fal Conde's
assumption of the Secretary-Generalship. In the months preceding his
return to active service under the 1934 amnesty, Varela, under the

nom de guerre 'Tío Pepe' or 'Don Pepe', toured Requeté detachments in all parts of Spain and set in motion the grand reorganization which he had been appointed to execute.[66] Varela's plan involved replacing the existing system of small groups – *decurias*, *patrullas* and so on – by a more genuine military structure. The *patrulla* remained the smallest unit, consisting of from four to six men under a corporal and forming the equivalent of an army squad. Three squads plus their corporals and an overall *jefe* constituted a *grupo* or platoon of around twenty men; three *grupos* and their *jefes* a *piquete* or section of almost seventy; three *piquetes* a *requeté* or company of just under 250 men; and three *requetés* a *tercio*, approximating to an army battalion of between 700 and 800.[67] A *jefe de tercio* was thus the equivalent of a major and the highest rank actually allowed for, although there was no reason to suppose that should the concentration of numbers permit it, 'regiments' might not be formed and 'colonels' appointed to command them.

With minor variations, Varela's system was introduced throughout the Requeté between 1933 and 1935, giving it a convincingly military character which it had previously lacked. Naturally many villages had to be satisfied with just one or two squads; for training purposes, where constant communication between local detachments was difficult, the *patrulla* remained the basic unit while the existence of those above *grupo* level was often purely notional. In larger towns and the more strongly Carlist areas the system flowered more impressively. Most Navarrese towns of any size possessed at least a *requeté* by the start of 1936, and some like Pamplona and Corella as many as three.[68] If such numbers were rare outside Navarre, many towns and cities did manage to form the nucleus of a *requeté*; Zaragoza, for example, possessed two *piquetes* by the middle of 1935.[69]

Within the Requeté organization Zamanillo, as Delegate, was primarily responsible for appointments, policy decisions and liaison with Fal Conde and the other Delegates, while the effective military leadership continued to be held by Varela, theoretically acting in lieu of the absent Sanjurjo. The latter was wooed persistently during his exile by Carlist friends and acquaintances, among them Fal Conde; after October 1934 he began to show welcome signs of returning to his Carlist origins and was eventually persuaded to accept the titular military leadership of the Communion's forces.[70] Heartening as this was, Sanjurjo could give little practical help as yet. For that matter, once Varela resumed active service full-time commitment to Carlist affairs became out of the question for him too. Zamanillo's appointment was therefore quickly followed by the designation of a retired Andalusian infantry colonel, Ricardo Rada, as National Inspector of the Requeté – to all intents and purposes Varela's deputy. As a retired officer Rada, while often subject to official surveillance, was able to move around more freely than Varela and hence to execute the task of organization and co-ordination which the latter found it impossible to combine with his official duties. Other retired officers were given important positions at regional or provincial level. Early in 1936 Lizarza, now *jefe* of the Navarrese Requeté, secured the appointment of an ex-colonel of cavalry, Alejandro Utrilla, as Regional Inspector of the Requeté for Navarre, while Zamanillo himself named a former commandant of artillery, Alejandro Velarde, to lead the Requeté of Santander and Vizcaya.[71]

Once the idea of rebellion began to be taken seriously within the Communion during 1934, the need to arm the Requeté became pressing. The problem was basically twofold, consisting firstly of the need for sufficient funds to purchase arms and ammunition, secondly of assuring the passage of *matériel* acquired abroad into Carlist hands and its storage until required. The Rome mission had been the first serious step, and Italian funds formed a welcome basis for Carlist arms purchases. Aid was also promised by the Portuguese government, with whom the Carlists were in touch through Sanjurjo. No details are available as to the fruits, if any, of this arrangement, but it seems unlikely to have helped the Communion significantly.[72] The second important source of finance was the voluntary contribution of considerable sums by wealthier members of the Communion itself, among them Oriol, the Baleztenas of Navarre, Miguel María Zozaya and Fernando Contreras.[73] Help may also have been forthcoming from rich rightists outside the Communion who subsidized most right-wing parties to a greater or lesser extent, but firm evidence on this is lacking. Finally, the aforementioned taxes, tithes and appeals levied by the Delegation of Finance provided the means whereby the Carlist rank and file might do their bit towards improving the Requeté's military potential.

Rather more difficult were the actual acquisition and importation of arms. In the event, the Rome mission proved more fruitful in providing money than in furnishing the promised *matériel*, little of which ever reached Spain and that too late to benefit the Requeté directly.[74] A significant proportion of the arms and ammunition obtained was purchased by Lizarza, who was appointed in 1935 to head a committee specifically entrusted with the obtaining, importing, storage and distribution of military equipment. During the next year Lizarza toured much of western Europe in search of all kinds of *matériel* and in particular the rifles and machine-guns most urgently required. From the Mauser firm he bought 1,000 rifle-butted revolvers and a large quantity of ammunition, while further substantial purchases were made through eager agents in French frontier towns and villages like Hendaye and Saint-Etienne de Bigorre.[75] Individual Carlists also did what they could. Oriol, for example, was able to arrange the charter of a ship for the conveying of 6,000 rifles, 150 heavy machine-guns, 300 light machine-guns, 5,000,000 rounds of ammunition and 10,000 hand-grenades from Belgium. At the last minute the ship was prevented from sailing by officials, and in spite of the successful intervention of the King and Queen Mother of Belgium, reached Spain only after the outbreak of hostilities. The machine-guns, however, were first diverted to Spain and found their way into Carlist hands. Also deeply involved was Alfonso Carlos' nephew-by-marriage Prince François Xavier of Bourbon–Parma, who obtained another 300 machine-guns in Belgium, while the Basque industrialist Agustín Tellería effected the 'exchange' of seventeen cases of assorted arms through a business agreement in Brussels.[76]

The goods obtained abroad had, of course, to be introduced into Spain covertly, and from 1934 onwards Navarrese, Basque and Catalonian Carlists operated a more or less continuous system of weapon-smuggling across the Pyrenean frontier, especially into Navarre. Again Lizarza worked frenetically, making innumerable trips by car to Saint-Jean de Luz and other French border villages and returning to Navarre with hidden cargoes of small arms. Other Carlists took advantage of visits to France to import illegal arms into Spain on their return. On one occasion Zamanillo crossed the frontier with a load of 400 pistols which were later distributed to the Requeté of Madrid and Andalusia.[77] Once in the country, weapons and ammunition were conveyed by shuttle-service across Navarre and the Basque country and then stored in farms and private houses, and even down wells. In view of the large quantity of *matériel* and the number of people involved, as well as the constant watchfulness of the Republican authorities, it is astonishing how few discoveries of arms *caches* there were; indeed, more publicity was given to the uncovering of Carlist arms before 1934 than after.

As an adjunct to the arms-purchasing committee, another group was set up in Navarre to supervise the domestic manufacture of explosives. As a result of this, two small secret 'factories' came into being in the Navarrese towns of Caparroso and Mañerú, specializing in the manufacture of hand-grenades which were then stored in another village, Traibuenas, and secret consignments of dynamite were moved from Vizcaya to Pamplona. Radio equipment was also obtained on a fairly small scale and carefully concealed – in at least one instance in a church tower.[78]

The size of the Requeté at the start of 1936 is extremely difficult to estimate. All official figures have disappeared, while published estimates appear unreliable. Detailed figures available for Navarre suggest that early in 1935 there were already about 6,000 Red Berets in the province;[79] by 1936 the number was almost certainly above 8,000 with a much larger reserve. This was by far the greatest concentration of Red Berets in Spain, but considerable numbers, spread more thinly, also existed in Álava, Guipúzcoa, Catalonia, the Levant and parts of Andalusia. Any attempt to give a total figure must be liable to considerable error, but in the light of later events an estimate of around 30,000 seems not unreasonable. Of these, however, a large majority fell into the 'reserve' category, while arms were available for only a small proportion of the total force. In all probability, the number of fully trained, adequately armed Red Berets as 1936 opened was no more than 10,000.[80] Figures for other right-wing militias are equally hard to obtain, yet it seems certain that as the Republic entered what were to be its last months, the Requeté was the most effective, and probably the most numerous paramilitary body on the Spanish right. More important than mere numbers, however, was the Requeté's distinctive character. The militias of the left, the JAP, the Falange and Renovación – the last of which was a pathetic affair – were all urban-oriented action groups primarily accustomed to street fighting and *pistolerismo*. In contrast the Requeté, by virtue of its traditions, present-day roots, distribution and whole ethos, was a rurally based, genuine citizen army, well trained in the conduct of war in difficult terrain. Small wonder, then, that of all the civilian militia organizations, the Requeté was taken most seriously as a possible ally when army officers began to contemplate a *pronunciamiento*.

The Carlists on their side became increasingly sympathetic towards the armed forces as the Republic's life lengthened. Not that they were ever as hostile towards, or even as suspicious of the army at any time in the 1930s as they had been throughout most of the nineteenth century; but during the early part of the Republic the political complexion of the officer corps was so mysterious as to force them to maintain towards it an attitude of studied detachment. This survived even Azaña's army reforms of 1931–2, which aroused great indignation among other sectors of the right. Sympathy was naturally awakened by Sanjurjo's rising, but in this as in other areas it was the Asturias revolt which proved the turning point. During 1935, as the press and propagandists of the left responded to the post-revolutionary repression with accusations of brutality against the army in Asturias, the Carlists joined the rest of the right in springing to the army's defence. *El Siglo Futuro*'s argument was typical: the campaign against the army was being waged by the lackeys of Moscow and of international Jewry; the brutality and atrocities were wholly on the side of the revolutionaries, while the army's conduct had been entirely 'benign'.[81] After Asturias the army was frequently hailed as the saviour of Spain and, in Bilbao's words, 'the sword of the Fatherland', an apolitical institution concerned only with national integrity and the 'greatness of Spain'.[82]

In crushing revolution, the army removed most Carlist doubts as to where its heart lay. As a body it was obviously not Carlist, but at least its patriotism was now beyond question. From this point onward, it could do little wrong in Carlist eyes. If it was less than perfect and its morale was low, then this was attributable to the internal corrosion of masonry and the external undermining by successive unsympathetic and parsimonious Republican governments. During 1935 the Carlists strongly supported a motion in the Cortes to declare freemasonry incompatible with the holding of commissions in the armed forces,[83] and took the most generous line of any parliamentary group towards military estimates. Although the military allocation for 1935 showed an increase over the previous year, Cárcer, the Carlists' parliamentary spokesman on military affairs, derided this as woefully inadequate. The army, he complained, had been morally and materially destroyed by four years of Republican government, so that it was totally unprepared to fight a modern war. Moreover, he went on, Spain's air force was pitifully small; in vain he demanded an extraordinary budget to repair what was in truth a serious deficiency.[84]

Desire to increase the strength and raise the morale of the army reflected the general conviction among Carlists that a physical clash with the forces of revolution was not far away, that they themselves would be in the thick of the fight, and that the army's sympathy would be invaluable. If a rising were to be the preface to the advent of the Traditional Monarchy, then sooner or later it would be vital to define precisely the relationship between Carlism and the army. For the moment, such details were laid aside. Even Fal Conde, whose attitude towards all forms of collaboration suggested that he would be particularly keen on a carefully spelt-out treaty, was content simply to accept that partnership was likely if not absolutely necessary. At the Aplec of Montserrat he called publicly for the Requeté to march alongside the army 'to bar the way to revolution'.[85]

Unfortunately for the Carlists, the climate within the upper ranks of the officer corps during 1935 was unsympathetic towards the idea of rebellion. The plans of a monarchist officers' clique for an Alfonsist *coup* were frustrated by the moral support given the army by successive governments during and after the Asturias rising. During the following year Lerroux and Gil Robles judiciously rewarded potentially dangerous senior officers with promotion and executive positions within a programme of military reorganization and conciliation towards the armed forces. The troublesome generals Goded and Fanjul were temporarily silenced in this way, while Franco was made Commander-in-Chief in Morocco in February 1935, and three months later Chief of the General Staff and the Superior War Council. As such he became in effect the partner of Gil Robles in the latter's military policy, and despite widespread rumours of a *coup* involving them both, remained averse to political intervention.[86] Varela's own promotion to brigadier brought him added responsibility and a further lessening of his activities within the Communion; on the other hand it ensured him increased communication with Franco, Goded and other top officers.[87] And however quietist the officer corps under Gil Robles' administration of the War Ministry, changed circumstances were still liable to make such contacts crucial for Carlism.

Many lower-ranking officers held fewer reservations than their superiors regarding conspiracy and rebellion, and began to come together in the clandestine *Unión Militar Española* (UME). Founded in 1933 by active and retired officers including Tarduchy and Captain Barba Hernández, the UME officially existed to 'protect order and justice' and defend military virtues and interests against the depredations of Republicanism. It claimed to be apolitical, but quickly evolved into an organization inclined towards an authoritarian solution to Spain's problems.[88] From its foundation, and more particularly after Fal Conde's assumption of the Secretary-General-ship, the UME aroused a lively interest among the Carlists. Fal Conde himself, as well as Zamanillo and Rada, met several times with Barba and other UME activists.[89] Indeed, Rada was active in the UME himself, and like Tarduchy, who by 1935 was moving away from his earlier pro-Falangism in the direction of Carlism, proved an invaluable link between the Communion and the conspir-ing officers. In the Pamplona garrison the UME won a considerable following, and its leader Captain Barrera was the first representative of the military to set up conspiratorial ties with the local Carlists.[90] Until 1935 the UME remained numerically weak and totally lacking in support from among senior officers. After Asturias its membership grew appreciably, and late in 1935 its activities began to attract the sympathies of Goded and Fanjul, though not of Franco or any other high-ranking officers. By this time more formal contacts had been made not only with the Carlists but also with Falangist and Alfonsist conspirators.[91] The Carlists, furthermore, were helping to finance it.[92]

Despite its clandestinism the UME could not remain entirely secret, and during 1935 rumours of its existence and activities began to leak out. Gil Robles hastily claimed that no such organization existed, but the Carlists, far from doing likewise, loudly applauded all steps in the direction of 'cementing unity' within the army. Not sur-prisingly, Tarduchy's column in *El Siglo Futuro* came out especially strongly in support of 'close union in the body of the officer corps'.[93]

Carlist dealings with the UME were inevitably of limited value as long as it met with so little response from senior officers. Contact was necessary if only because of competition for military favours from the Falange and the Alfonsists, but it neither brought rebellion much closer nor significantly increased the number of officers favour-able to the installation of the Traditional Monarchy. In all probab-ility, as even Fal Conde and the Requeté hierarchy were bound to recognize, a Carlist rising would need the army's assistance if it were to succeed; similarly, as Sanjurjo, Varela and other officers ap-preciated, a military revolt would require Carlist support in order to avoid a repetition of the 1932 fiasco. For the Carlists, and above all for those most eager to avoid compromise, one problem was to dominate all others: how to ride the military tiger without being devoured.

Adveniat Regnum Tuum

The election of 16 February 1936 returned Azaña to power at the head of a government consisting entirely of non-Socialist Republicans and pledged to execute the Popular Front's minimum programme. Rumours of a military *coup* intended to annul the election were unfulfilled but not groundless. Calvo Sotelo and other worried rightists considered such a move and even approached Franco, but the plans foundered through lack of wide enough civilian support and the refusal of Portela and Alcalá Zamora to countenance them.[1] The Carlists, who had their own ideas as to how and when to use violence, also stood aside. They were, however, perfectly clear in their own minds as to the significance of Azaña's return to office: it represented the first important stage in the realization of their pre-election prophecies of revolution, a new offensive, as *El Siglo Futuro* put it, on the part of international communism and freemasonry.[2] Azaña, they were sure, would soon be brushed aside by the far more radical forces currently to be seen and heard parading in victory demonstrations ominously different from those of 1931.[3] According to Rodezno, Spain was 'in a pre-revolutionary period';[4] to make matters worse, revolution when it came would not even be home-grown, but planned to the last detail by Moscow and financed by the Jews. The living incarnation of this deadly combination, Bela Kun, was persistently but falsely rumoured to be touring Spain's cities as the Comintern's revolutionary co-ordinator.[5]

So fixed was the attitude of the Carlists and the rest of the extreme right towards the new situation that it is doubtful if anything could have held them back from rebellion. Gil Robles remained more circumspect. The Carlists were shocked when he reaffirmed the CEDA's loyalty to the constituted power and its claim to be the 'sole bulwark of the right', promising to pursue the legal struggle as a 'serene, reasoned and firm' but not systematic opposition to Azaña.[6] They were also contemptuous; in losing the election, they believed, the CEDA had been justly punished for squandering two vital years in tactics and was now finished as the hope of the right.[7] Fal Conde said that he now expected Gil Robles to be inexorably drawn by the laws of parliamentarism closer to Azaña and into collaboration in the name of 'the lesser evil'. This, Fal Conde warned, was 'the politics of perdition'.[8] Up to a point his analysis proved sound. *La Unión* soon reported the CEDA's impending decomposition, as Lucía and Giménez Fernández led a majority of its deputies along the path of conservative opposition within the regime, while parts of the JAP and the party rank and file flirted with a suddenly expanding Falange.[9] Lucía's home base in particular was now deserting him; during February 1936 advocates of anti-Republican violence took over the DRV and began to organize an armed militia.[10]

The position of Gil Robles, desperately trying to hold his forces together, was now agonizingly difficult. The 'tactic' had been a gamble and had failed, and in alienating those likely to be most centrally involved in a right-wing *pronunciamiento* or rebellion, it had ensured that should they ever succeed Gil Robles would be a forgotten man. His chief hope of personal success and the resurrection of the tactic now lay in attempting to play an ostensibly moderate conservative role in opposition to Azaña, perhaps even helping to 'save' the Republic from the extreme left by joining or supporting a government of 'national concentration' ranging from himself to Prieto.[11] At the same time, he made sure of keeping open as many options as possible by staying closely in touch with a conspiracy which was now getting well under way.[12]

The CEDA's severance of its electoral ties with the monarchist parties was by no means unwelcome to Fal Conde, though it would have been impolitic of him to admit it in so many words. At last he was free to implement his policy of 'exclusiveness', placed in abeyance since the previous autumn. 'The Traditionalist Communion', he announced even before the election results were complete, 'will fully recover its personality and freedom of movement. Coalitions, fronts and blocs are done with.'[13] When the reduced Carlist parliamentary party met for the first time in mid-March, Fal Conde, although not himself a deputy, took the chair, a sure sign that he was eager to extend his personal control over this hitherto semi-autonomous body. Rodezno, his policies of close collaboration with the Alfonsists and attempted dynastic reconciliation utterly out of favour, stepped down from the parliamentary leadership. The position was assumed by Lamamié, the Carlists' best parlia-

mentary orator and someone who, in this as in other instances, could
be relied upon to bridge the gap between the Communion's old and
new establishments. [14]

A final rupture with the Alfonsists was now a mere matter of time.
The first stage came on 6 April, when the Carlist masses and the
nation at large learned what leading Carlists – and Alfonsists – had
in fact known since January: that Alfonso Carlos had at long last
reached a decision regarding the succession. The solution was an odd
and inconclusive one. Instead of naming a direct heir, Alfonso Carlos
appointed as Regent of the Communion his nephew, Prince François Xavier of Bourbon–Parma. [15] In a letter to the prince on 10
March, Alfonso Carlos had stated that Alfonso XIII and his sons
were barred from succeeding him by their refusal unequivocally to
deny the legitimacy of Isabella II and her branch of the Spanish
Bourbons. He now hoped that upon the restoration of the monarchy,
'truly constituted Cortes' would bestow the right of succession upon
whatever prince best satisfied the demands of dual legitimacy. The
succession of Prince François Xavier himself, far from being excluded,
was declared to be Alfonso Carlos' ideal. [16]

The announcement of the Regency, while not arousing much
opposition within the Communion, equally failed to excite much
enthusiasm or to resolve the succession question to everyone's
satisfaction. As a Frenchman who had spent relatively little time in
Spain, the Regent, henceforward known as Don Javier, was scarcely
known among the Carlists. His claim to the succession, although
strong enough to merit a better defence than any offered on its behalf, was widely regarded as laughable, and in some quarters was
believed to rest as much upon his aunt's influence with her husband
as upon 'blood', 'practice' or any other personal attribute. [17] Although
Don Javier's efforts on Carlism's behalf during the coming months
were to be considerable, [18] it quickly became evident that many
Carlists had not really accepted him and still yearned for a fusionist
solution. Nevertheless, as long as Fal Conde headed the Carlist
organization Don Javier's 'succession' was assured.

On 16 April there followed Fal Conde's long-postponed an-
nouncement of Carlism's withdrawal from the National Bloc. All
Carlists serving on committees of the Bloc were instructed to resign
forthwith, and the decision was transmitted personally to Calvo
Sotelo and Goicoechea. Again no open opposition rose from the
Carlist ranks. Disillusionment with the never very popular National

Bloc had increased steadily in recent months, and Fal Conde's decision was backed up by numerous petitions from provincial and regional organizations demanding withdrawal from what was generally felt to be just another political party, and one in which Carlism provided the 'army' while a 'general staff' led by the ambitious Calvo Sotelo garnered the publicity.[19] Even among the deputies, who were used to everyday dealings with the Alfonsists and might be expected to have been more 'politically' minded, the Bloc had few keen supporters. Rodezno stoutly continued to believe it 'a useful instrument of counter-revolution' and Bau proclaimed his faith in it, but they were in a minority.[20] They and others who had personal ties with Alfonsists were left perfectly free to maintain them and did so.

Parliamentary co-operation between the Carlist and Renovación groups inevitably survived the effective dissolution of the National Bloc, yet by now Carlist interest in what went on in the Cortes, at times in the past greater than it was ideologically consistent to admit, was genuinely dying. From the moment they witnessed the Socialist and Communist deputies, fists clenched in salute, singing the 'Internationale' in the chamber, the Carlist deputies' worst fears for the future received ever stronger confirmation. Three of their number very soon lost their seats, their election invalidated by the left-wing majority on the Cortes Credentials Committee. The newly appointed secretary of the parliamentary minority, Arauz de Robles, lost his seat when the elections in Granada and Cuenca were annulled on account of alleged irregularities; Lamamié and Estévanez were excluded by virtue of their positions in the National Catholic Agrarian Confederation and consequent involvement in the negotiation of government grain contracts. Estévanez was indeed president of the Burgos branch of the organization and therefore strictly speaking 'incompatible'; in the past, however, the principle had been largely ignored, and the impression was strong of left-wing vindictiveness. As for Lamamié, he had actually resigned his presidency of the Salamanca branch some weeks before the election, so that his exclusion was purely political – a punishment, nobody doubted, for his role in the debates on agrarian policy during 1934 and 1935.[21] The Carlist minority was thus reduced to ten; the parliamentary leadership reverted to Rodezno, but the deputies' disgruntlement and apathy were now so great that they were on the whole content to let Calvo Sotelo speak for both monarchist parties.

The new government's legislative course offered further proof to the Carlists that the pace of revolution was quickening. Political prisoners arrested in 1934 were amnestied; governmental orders suspended evictions, reconfiscated estates restored in April 1934, formalized the spontaneous occupation of Extremaduran estates, and declared the Catalonian Leases Law valid. Not only was the Generalitat handed back the powers which it had exercised before October 1934, but, worse to the northern Carlists, Aguirre was given leave to resubmit the 1933 Statute, incorporating the protesting province of Álava. With the support of Prieto and much of the left, its passage seemed assured despite a spirited campaign of opposition led by Oriol's *El Pensamiento Alavés*. Also resumed was the policy suspended in 1935 of substituting laic for religious education; although both Republicans and Church now behaved with markedly more discretion than in 1931–3, on 20 May Church schools were ordered to be closed.[22]

The right was impotent and frustrated in the face of the Popular Front's overwhelming parliamentary majority. Twice, over the annulment of the Granada and Cuenca elections and the relaicization of education, the monarchist and CEDA deputies staged walk-outs; on the latter occasion *El Siglo Futuro* voiced the opinion of many Carlists in urging that they never return.[23] When the left united to eject Alcalá Zamora from the Presidency, officially on account of his 'unconstitutional' dissolution of the Cortes in January, in reality out of revenge for his admission of the CEDA into the government, the Carlists abstained; the President, they argued, deserved his fate for having 'served revolution', even if the manner of, and pretext for his dismissal were absurd.[24] They abstained again from everything to do with the election of his successor, and when Azaña was elected President saw this as another step on the direct route to revolution, especially since another of their *bêtes noires*, Casares Quiroga, now took over from Azaña as premier.[25]

The Cortes, and indeed all conventional politics, were now quite irrelevant to the Carlists. The deputies and the press naturally continued to express hostility to the government's legislation and what they described as the Popular Front 'dictatorship', yet they perceived that parliamentary politics bore an aura of unreality. In the first biennium of the Republic, the business of the Cortes had been of vital importance even to the bitterest enemies of parliamentarism, for while Carlist determinism held that reformism would lead inevitably to social revolution, this was seen as a relatively distant prospect. There was thus every reason to oppose parliamentary reformism both because of its immediate impact upon religion, property and public order, and because there might still be time to head off its disastrous long-term consequences. But by the spring of 1936 the Carlists looked on the field of legislation as possessing nothing more than symbolic significance, certain as they were that social revolution could erupt at any moment and must be met on its own ground.

The Carlists therefore paid little heed to the gestures made in the direction of isolating the political extremes by means of a broad coalition acceptable to at least part of the CEDA and the Socialist Party as well as to the bourgeois Republican parties. Such comments as were passed were cynical – and perhaps reasonably so. The two key figures in any scheme of this kind, Gil Robles and Prieto, were in similar positions; as an individual each was willing to keep alive his chances of political success by dealing with the other, yet neither could actually do so for fear of splitting his party and strengthening the respective enemy. The Carlists drew attention to the Socialists' internal conflicts but considered them far less important than they undoubtedly were. Both Largo Caballero, openly preaching social revolution and hailed by his followers as the 'Spanish Lenin', and Prieto, were regarded as revolutionaries equally deserving of censure. It was even suggested that 'Prietism' was the more dangerous brand of Spanish Socialism because its 'dormant, anaesthetic quality' encouraged complacency in its enemies while its end-result would be identical with that of the Socialist left and the Communists. Doubt was in any case uttered as to whether either Socialist leader could much longer hope to control his masses.[26] Only *La Unión* struck a slightly discordant note in predicting that the eventual victor within the revolutionary camp would be the CNT, by virtue of its *hispanidad*.[27]

For tangible evidence of imminent revolution the Carlists believed that they need look no further than the undoubted unrest of the first half of 1936. Whole areas of Spain – for example Catalonia – were, it is true, unusually quiet; individuals such as the middle-of-the-road intellectual Gregorio Marañón and the admittedly pro-Republican U.S. ambassador, Claude G. Bowers, declared that tales of disorder were grotesquely exaggerated.[28] Even so it remained true that in parts of the country the spring of 1936 was marked by strikes, shootings, bomb outrages, attempted church-burnings, street fighting and violent talk, all on what was widely taken to be an unprecedented scale. The propaganda of the right, whose own militant elements were contributing their share to any breakdown of law and order, made the most of the situation, thereby helping to create a climate which would justify the actions upon which it was already determined. Between February and June, all the Carlist newspapers, in common with those of the Alfonsists, the Falange and the CEDA, devoted as much space as the censorship permitted to news of disorders; typical of this was *La Unión*, which carried regular columns headed 'Social Conflicts' and, with ponderous irony, 'Public Order'.[29] The condition of Spain, the Carlists complained, reeked of 'anarchy'; in the more imaginative words of Arauz de Robles, 'the beast is in the streets'.[30] No distinction was drawn between different kinds of 'disorder'; between, for example, land seizures which would cease if ratified, and the calculatedly 'political' strikes of the early summer – all were 'revolutionary'. After Calvo Sotelo made a bitter parliamentary speech on law and order in April, *El Siglo Futuro* published an itemized list of violent incidents which it alleged had occurred since the election. It was five pages long and dwelt almost exclusively upon violence employed against the persons and property of the right, including those of a number of Carlists.[31]

The Carlist press and propagandists chose largely to ignore two aspects of this troubled atmosphere: firstly that the right, through its past conduct especially in the agrarian sphere, bore at least part of the responsibility for the intensification of working-class militancy and for political polarization in general; secondly that at least one group on the right, the Falange, was deliberately employing violence on the streets in the hope of precipitating a political crisis. Little coverage was given to Falangist excesses, which multiplied as the Falange itself suddenly expanded in the wake of the CEDA's electoral disappointment, and despite the detention in jail of José Antonio and most of the movement's leaders. In a three-month period as many liberals and leftists lost their lives as rightists, something that no one who limited his reading to the Carlist, or even the wider right-wing press, would ever have realized.[32]

This censorship was wholly self-imposed, since the Republican authorities held no objections to publicizing cases of right-wing violence; it pandered to Carlist readers' certainty as to the overwhelming culpability of the left, and perhaps also reflected a degree of concern at the Falange's overnight emergence as a serious competitor on the extreme right. As the CEDA's disillusioned masses began to desert Gil Robles, many followed the example of the prominent JAP-ist Ramón Serrano Súñer and threw in their lot with the Falange.[33] A lesser number, it is true, became Carlists, but there was no escaping the realization that for the majority of disgruntled *cedistas* the new wave of 'fascism' was more attractive than the old one of Carlism. The latter's press thus had good reason to withhold unnecessary publicity from the Falange.

At grass-roots level relations between young Carlists and the Falange nevertheless grew warmer, as official 'exclusiveness' produced a relative cooling of those between their elders and the Alfonsists. In Santander, Zamanillo maintained particularly close contacts with Hedilla and the local Falange.[34] In the University of Madrid, AET students, led by Pradera's son Juan José, collaborated with those of the Falangist SEU (*Sindicato Español Universitario*) to the extent of planning a single organization of 'nationally' minded students.[35] One AET activist, Juan José Olano, was shot dead while assisting Falangists in a Madrid street battle.[36] In several other cities such as Murcia, Santander and Ciudad Real, Falangists and Carlists demonstrated and suffered imprisonment together.[37] A similar joint rally was held in Pamplona in March, following the violent death of a Falangist in the CNT stronghold of Mendavia, also one of the few Navarrese towns with a sizable Falangist nucleus. Twenty-four Red Berets and one Falangist were detained after a baton charge by Assault Guards.[38] Arrests like these, together with repeated searches and closure of Carlist circles, allowed the Communion to raise yet again the cry of 'persecution' and even to claim its Falangist rivals as brothers in oppression.[39] As the Falange went on growing, the time was approaching when Carlists would be obliged to give more serious thought to their political relations with the new movement, just as they had earlier been preoccupied by those with the CEDA. In the meantime they disdained to share the Falangist penchant for acts of gratuitous violence. Against the revolution which by June they were convinced lay only weeks away, they had other, more carefully laid plans.

As spring turned to summer and as rumours of Moscow-inspired proletarian revolution vied with those of military *pronunciamiento*, the febrile tone of the Carlist press subsided somewhat, due only in part to the rigours of censorship. Recruitment of disenchanted *cedistas* led to expressions of confidence that widespread awakening to the accuracy of Carlist analyses of contemporary problems was about to generate a sudden and vast influx of new members into the Communion, thus injecting it with an irresistible impulse to power.[40] Excited by this and other, less printable convictions, *El Siglo Futuro* treated its readers on 19 June to an unusual and, to those acquainted with Carlist vocabulary, significant cartoon. Instead of the customary gibes at the Republic and the left, it merely portrayed an armed Red Beret gazing expectantly at a rising sun. On its rays were inscribed the legend: '*Adveniat Regnum Tuum*' – Thy Kingdom Come.

Whether or not the right's talk of impending social revolution during the first half of 1936 was justified remains in some doubt. Without question the impulse towards revolution existed within both the CNT and the *caballerista* wing of the Socialist Party; agreement between these forces proved as difficult as ever to cement, however, whilst Largo Caballero's own behaviour at times suggested that as with many a putative Lenin, his taste for revolution stopped short of actually unleashing one. As for the Spanish Communist Party, its numbers and influence were growing, especially among the young, yet the right's rumour-mongering of revolution brewed in Moscow bore little relation either to the conduct of the Spanish Communists themselves or to the current policy line of the Comintern. Any revolutionary process in the Spain of February–July 1936 was at most piecemeal and pragmatic, dependent upon sustained rank-and-file militancy and the *caballeristas'* retention of the initiative within the Socialist Party; by the end of June there were signs that both were waning. Even Calvo Sotelo told an interviewer on 11 July that revolution was further away than it had been in February.[41] One thing now seems certain: no precise plan or timetable of revolution existed.[42] This was emphatically not the case on the right. After the February election, a right-wing blow against the Republic in its present form was not probable but certain; all that was in doubt was the scale of its support and the degree of its success.

The left's return to power threw the Carlists into a frenzy of preparation for their rebellion. This new sense of urgency was inspired not only by fear of imminent social revolution, but also by the realization that more or less open military preparation might soon become more difficult. Any such activity was bound to centre heavily

on Navarre, both because it was there that by far the greatest concentration of Red Berets was located and because during 1935 the
Carlists had enjoyed there a freedom of action unavailable to the
extreme right anywhere else in Spain. At the end of 1934 the Navarrese Temporary Committee was finally withdrawn, and in the
Diputación elected in January 1935 the Carlists and their allies
won control.[43] Combined with their dominance in a majority of
Navarrese local councils, this gave the Carlists an influence over
local and provincial government which, if falling short of complete
control, was invaluable in allowing preparations for rebellion to pro-
ceed relatively unhindered.[44] The new government, with the enthusiastic support of the Navarrese left, was sure to attempt at the earliest
opportunity to replace the Diputación and the right-wing councils of
Navarre by their own nominees. The left was certainly well aware
of what the Carlists were up to; soon after the election, *El Socialista*
warned that the Requeté was armed and dangerous, and urged that it
be broken up without delay.[45] Obviously from the Carlist point of
view the more that could be achieved before such steps could be
taken, the better.

The election over, the emphasis within the Carlist hierarchy therefore moved still further towards militarization. Don Javier, now
throwing himself wholeheartedly into organizing a rising, set up his
residence near Saint-Jean de Luz, while Zamanillo moved from his
home in Santander to that of relatives in Elizondo, strategically
situated in the Navarrese Pyrenees some fifteen miles from the
French frontier.[46] In Saint-Jean de Luz, Don Javier and Fal Conde,
the latter now spending as much time in France as in Spain, established an important new body, the Carlist Supreme Military Junta.
Composed entirely of ex-officers, it was headed by a one-time
follower of Primo de Rivera, General Muslera, and also included
Rada, Utrilla, Lieutenant-Colonel Baselga, Captain Sanjurjo –
son of the general – and other regional inspectors of the Requeté.
In its role of co-ordinating the plans of rebellion, it was immediately
responsible to the Regent and Fal Conde.[47]

As the energies of Don Javier, Zamanillo, Oriol and others were
turned more and more towards the acquisition of arms and ammunition, Lizarza received from Utrilla instructions to place the Navarrese Requeté on what amounted to a state of permanent war-readi-
ness. This was on 22 February, less than a week after the election.[48]
Utrilla also underlined the need to make and maintain contact with

other 'counter-revolutionary' forces — implicitly the army, the Alfonsist conspirators and the Falange.

All the leading Carlists recognized the need for these contacts, whether from the point of view of simply ensuring access to information regarding parallel and possibly conflicting conspiracies, or from that of actual co-operation. By early March the Carlists of Pamplona were in touch with the local UME cell through a go-between, Félix Maíz,[49] and a similar association had been cemented in Seville by Luis Redondo.[50] In Madrid, Varela was personally embroiled with conspiring senior officers;[51] liaison with plotting Alfonsists was guaranteed by Rafael Olazábal's acquaintanceship with Ansaldo and Joaquín Bau's friendship with Calvo Sotelo;[52] Fal Conde himself had entered into talks with José Antonio before the election;[53] and during March the Carlists of Álava followed Oriol in approaching the provincial Falange with a view to eventual collaboration in the event of a rising.[54]

By the middle of March 1936 the Carlists were thus involved in a complex network of anti-Republican conspiracies at both national and provincial level. What was still lacking was a generally accepted policy within the Communion concerning the purposes and limits of co-operation with other right-wing elements, the main differences tending to reflect the division which had existed among Carlists since Fal Conde's assumption of the Secretary-Generalship in May 1934. Fal Conde himself, Zamanillo, some of the ex-Integrist leaders of the south, Don Javier, and to a lesser extent Lamamié, nursed a longing for a purely Carlist rising, or at the very least one led and dominated by the Carlists, the aim of which would be to impose upon Spain the entire, unsullied programme of the Communion. Their extreme reluctance to compromise on any important item of this programme made them, if by no means unwilling to deal with other groups as common sense dictated, nonetheless preoccupied with extracting from these potential allies explicit terms ensuring effective Carlist dominance within a transitional regime leading to the eventual installation of the Traditional Monarchy.

The alternative strategy found its strongest support in Navarre, above all in Rodezno and the regional establishment led by José Martínez Berasáin and the Baleztena family. Believing, more hardheadedly than their national authorities, that a successful, exclusively Carlist rebellion was a ludicrous dream, the Navarrese group and their supporters in other regions concluded that patriotism demanded above all the overthrow of the Republic and the prevention of social revolution; they therefore favoured continuous and friendly contacts with other conspirators, especially the army, even at the risk of compromising Carlism's independence and some aspects of its maximum programme. Both alternatives had their dangers: the first that 'Carlist Revolution' might fail for want of allies, or else that would-be allies, if spurned, might win power themselves and push the Carlists aside; the second that the Carlists might commit their forces to a collaborative rising, and sacrifice young blood only to find themselves gradually excluded from power by Alfonsists, Falangists and generals.

Early in 1936 it was Fal Conde's strategy which held sway, thanks in large measure to the lack of unity and resolution within the officer corps. Following the abortive plans for a *coup* in the hours after the February election, Azaña's new government reshuffled the senior command in the hope of cancelling out any military threat. Franco's rapid rise came to a halt when he was packed off to the Canaries to spend a semi-exile in the pleasant but not normally influential post of military commander of Tenerife. To Pamplona went General Emilio Mola, sometime Director General of Security and Commander-in-Chief in Morocco.[55] None of this was sufficient to discourage the truly dedicated military conspirators for long. Fanjul and Orgaz soon set about planning a *pronunciamiento* to take place in Madrid in April. Among the serving officers drawn into this plot was Varela, while others such as Franco and Mola knew all about its existence. Although Varela's involvement meant that the Carlist authorities were kept informed of the plot's progress, the Communion itself was not a part of it. Indeed, Varela's personal view of the *coup's* likely course was at variance with official Carlist strategy and hinted at a division of loyalties in which his Carlism came second to his professionalism. For whereas Mola seemed sceptical regarding the plot's chances of success, Varela shared the belief of Orgaz that a *coup d'audace* in Madrid would spark off a spontaneous rising of the Requeté. This was the complete opposite of what Fal Conde had in mind, but not a totally unfounded supposition in view of later developments.[56]

On 14 March, while Varela was busy conspiring in Madrid, Mola arrived in Pamplona to take over the Military Governorship. Although his fairly moderate background did not at first sight suggest him as a probable ally of Carlism, he was soon told of Carlist activities by Félix Maíz and Captain Lastra of the UME.[57] Somewhat to his surprise, however, Mola as yet received no visits from Carlism's national or regional leaders.[58] For the time being the national leadership's wish to go it alone stood in the way of Carlist–military contacts. By now, indeed, a detailed plan for Carlist rebellion had crystallized. Drawn up by Muslera and Baselga, it envisaged two *focos* of rebellion in western Spain. The Andalusian Requeté was to assemble under the command of Luis Redondo in the Sierra de Aracena, a low but sparsely populated range of hills in the north of the province of Huelva, while those of Castile, León and Extremadura gathered in the Sierra de Gata, hard by the Portuguese frontier in Cáceres. With these risings occupying the attention of the civil and, conceivably, military authorities, another bold blow would be struck in Madrid, where key ministries and communications centres would be seized by the city's Red Berets. A vital part of this latter plan was the capture of the War Ministry by a detachment of Red Berets disguised as Civil Guard and admitted by complaisant officers within the ministry building. Amid the ensuing confusion, the more numerous Requeté of Navarre, the Basque region, Catalonia and the Levant would descend upon Madrid, reinforced as they advanced by their comrades from Logroño, Aragon and eastern Old Castile.[59]

Elaborate planning went into this ruritanian adventure. Sevillian Red Berets spent several feast days familiarizing themselves with the terrain of the Sierra de Aracena, and a hundred Civil Guard uniforms were illegally manufactured in Zaragoza and then stored over a Madrid shop.[60] In the meantime, Fal Conde continued to woo Sanjurjo in Estoril through intermediaries such as Esteban-Infantes, the general's former adjutant, and González Gregorio. Fal Conde knew that the last thing he could afford to do was to ignore the army altogether. What the Carlist Military Junta was planning was, in effect, a kind of multiple 'March on Madrid' in which the army's attitude would be absolutely crucial. Since a confrontation between the Requeté and the army, although allowed for in the plan of rebellion, could only mean defeat for Carlism, and since there was no prospect of the army's loyally and spontaneously aligning itself with, and committing its forces to, the Carlist cause, Fal Conde was left to hope and pray that the rebellion would at worst divide the army against itself or, preferably, that the army would act as its Italian counterpart had acted in 1922 and adopt a position of benevolent neutrality towards a virile expression of civilian patriotism. In short, by rising first and alone, the Carlists would stamp their imprint on the entire anti-Republican movement which would then accept the *fait accompli* and with it the triumph of Traditionalism. In this strategy Sanjurjo's role might well be the deciding factor, for if he could be persuaded to join or even lead the rising, his prestige among his fellow officers might ensure their acquiescence.

Fal Conde therefore devoted a great deal of his time during the early part of 1936 to tightening the still naggingly vague tie between Sanjurjo and the Communion. Like Varela, Sanjurjo was as aware of military plots as of the Carlist project; pulled in both directions, he was naturally unwilling to close either option by committing himself fully to the other. In March, however, Fal Conde visited Estoril and won Sanjurjo's promise that he would lead the Requeté in revolt if the army did not rise first. In return Fal Conde conceded that the Carlists would support an army rising provided that it was led by Sanjurjo – presumably on the assumption that due deference to Carlist wishes would then be assured. If the Carlist rising took place, it was agreed that Sanjurjo would enter Spain and lead the northern Requeté in its march on the capital.[61]

In accepting this part in the Carlist plans, Sanjurjo may well have been understandably sceptical as to the chances of their ever being implemented and hence have felt that he could lose nothing by appearing amenable. The objections were obvious enough; even supposing that the rising were to take place, the Requeté was more likely to face defeat by or absorption into the army than to receive its meek acceptance of Carlist leadership. A further problem scarcely even considered was the attitude of the left; it was simply not to be contemplated that the organized workers of Madrid, Barcelona, Bilbao, Zaragoza and Valencia would stand idly by while armies of Red Berets mustered for their advance on Madrid.

In the event the plan collapsed not long after receiving Sanjurjo's blessing, when the authorities' discovery of the *cache* of Civil Guard uniforms forced a postponement which was to prove permanent. It was probably just as well for Carlism that this happened, since any degree of success was, to say the least, unlikely, and a premature defeat might have meant the end of the Communion. The details of the planned rising were later revealed with a fair amount of accuracy in the left-wing press. *El Siglo Futuro*, with an unconsciously apt choice of adjective, dismissed the 'rumour' as 'picturesque'.[62]

By the end of April, not only had the Carlist Military Junta's plan been placed in cold storage, but the army plotters in Madrid had also been found out and dispersed, Varela being arrested and placed in the military prison in Cádiz.[63] Despite Varela's Carlism and his constant communication with Sanjurjo, the two plans, which could have been complementary, lived and died in total mutual isolation. Much the same was true of the Falange's plan of rebellion, initially formulated in July 1935 and now revived. This involved the concentration of several thousand Falangists on the Portuguese border of Salamanca province, in the hope that a rising there would spur the army into abandoning all reservations and joining in.[64] Before his imprisonment by the Republican authorities in March, José Antonio had become convinced that there was a lot to be said for a paramilitary alliance with the Carlists, and had made contact with Fal Conde. The latter, to judge from his subsequent behaviour, felt that some such agreement was worth considering, but nothing serious was achieved as yet. As a result the Carlist, Falangist and military projects for rebellion passed together into limbo.

The breaking up of the Madrid conspiracy took place on the same day – 19 April – as Mola's acceptance of the role of 'Director' of the hitherto small-scale conspiracy based on the UME of Pamplona and other northern garrisons, and perhaps helped to inspire it. After a month in Pamplona, Mola had concluded that the military advocates of intervention against the Republic were correct; a meeting with the UME lodge in the garrison sufficed to raise him to the leadership of the northern conspiracy.[65] From the Carlist point of view, Mola's decision coincided providentially with the shelving of the Military Junta's plan of rebellion and the removal of their main working link with the officer corps, Varela. Mola was known to have urged on the Madrid conspirators the need for civilian co-operation in any military movement and it was therefore to be expected that he would now make an approach to the Carlists. It was also more than likely that he would get in touch with Sanjurjo. A three-way relationship would then come into being which the Carlists, or at any rate Fal Conde, would be forced to clarify if the Communion's interests were to be protected. The best course of action seemed to be to take the initiative by attempting to bind Mola and his conspiracy to the Carlist cause; thus, however mixed their feelings about Mola, Fal Conde and his circle were obliged to consider overtures towards him.

The obvious route via which to inveigle Mola into lending Carlism military support was through Sanjurjo. Early in May the Carlists made yet another move towards ensuring Sanjurjo's attachment to their cause and at the same time persuading him to influence Mola in a similar direction. This time it was Don Javier who travelled to Estoril to meet the exiled general. Sanjurjo continued to insist that his first obligation was towards his fellow generals, but at last agreed to make a 'statement' on behalf of Carlism. He also accepted the Carlist proposal that he preside over a 'Provisional Government for the Restoration of Monarchy' once the rising had succeeded. In this way Fal Conde and Don Javier hoped to solve the problem of transition, which circumstances were at last forcing them to face, by sealing Sanjurjo's loyalty to Carlism and gambling on his leadership and example being followed by the rest of the officer corps. If the gamble succeeded, then the Traditional Monarchy might be installed without it first being necessary to erect a dictatorship which might prove to be self-perpetuating; if, on the other hand, the coolness of most army officers towards Carlism were to outweigh Sanjurjo's warmth, the Communion was still liable to find itself the impotent client of a military regime.

Don Javier returned from Estoril bearing a letter for Mola, in which Sanjurjo asked him to act as his representative inside Spain.[66] At the end of May, Mola replied through an emissary, Raimundo García, the proprietor of the newspaper *Diario de Navarra*, an independent Catholic deputy, and a close friend both of Sanjurjo and of most of the leading Navarrese Carlists.[67] As a result of this approach, Sanjurjo acknowledged Mola as Director of the conspiracy, while Mola in return recognized Sanjurjo's overall pre-eminence and his right to head a provisional regime.[68]

Mola's relationship with Carlism was still far too vague for the comfort of Fal Conde and the Military Junta, a problem all the more worrying as the northern conspiracy began to take shape and to pull in senior officers from other regions of Spain. For his part Mola was eager to make contact with Carlism's national leadership in order to secure that civilian support which he considered vital, especially since he was reportedly uncertain of the loyalty of his own troops, many of whom were suspect as Asturians.[69] Neither the national Carlist authorities nor the Navarrese Regional Junta had approached Mola directly when Isidro Arraiza, a member of the Regional Junta and also a confidant of the general, arranged a meeting between Mola and the Carlist *jefe* of Álava, Oriol, at the latter's request.[70] On 3 June, before this meeting could take place, Pamplona and the

surrounding district were the target for a swoop by the Republican
security chief, Alonso Mallol, and a large force of Assault Guards.
Forewarned, both the military conspirators and the Carlists performed miracles of concealment; Mallol returned to Madrid without
the weapons or other evidence of conspiracy which he had been sent
to find, and convinced that rumours of impending rebellion in the
north were exaggerated.[71]

Mola and Oriol met near Leiza on 4 June, with the military rising
now about a month away. Since the postponement of the planned
Carlist rising, no real progress towards rebellion had been made by
the Carlists themselves, and the question was now becoming urgent:
what were the Carlists to do if the army rose before they did?
Oriol's conversation with Mola suggested that some powerful Carlists were all for throwing themselves into the fight alongside the
army without imposing conditions; Mola left Leiza cheered by
Oriol's offer of the useful Álava Requeté and of his personal financial
support.[72] More important still, Oriol also put Mola in touch at
last with Fal Conde, who sent Zamanillo to meet him in Pamplona
on 11 June for the first in a difficult series of negotiations.

For Mola the purpose of talks with the Carlists was to attach the
Requeté, and specifically that of Navarre, to his conspiracy; what
mattered to Fal Conde was that the Requeté's participation be made
conditional on Mola's acceptance of a set of conditions intended to
guarantee that the rising would be the overture to the installation of
the Carlist monarchy. These were placed before Mola by Zamanillo,
and included the use of the red and gold bicolour of the monarchy in
the rising, the immediate derogation of the Republican Constitution
and of all laic legislation, and a commitment to reconstruct the state
along corporate lines. The Carlists also demanded the creation of a
temporary directory headed by Sanjurjo and including two civilian
councillors acceptable to the Communion. One would be concerned
with education, propaganda and relations with the Church and would
be a Carlist; the other would be primarily responsible for local
government and corporations and might be José Antonio, with whom
both Fal Conde and Rodezno remained in close communication.[73]

Mola was shaken by the Carlist demands, not so much because
their content clashed with his own ideas, which had of late become
bitterly anti-liberal, as because of their detailed character and the
aggressive manner in which they were made. After an interval of
two days, he replied that the Carlist terms were 'inadmissible' and

amounted to the mortgaging of the new state to sectional interests –
precisely what Fal Conde was after.[74] A meeting between Mola and
Fal Conde himself was now essential, and took place at the monastery
of Irache, near Estella, on 16 June. On this occasion Mola took the
initiative by handing Fal Conde a list of points agreed upon by the
mostly non-monarchist officers involved in his conspiracy. A broad
statement of good intentions aimed at placating as many sections
of opinion as possible, it conflicted directly with several of Fal
Conde's conditions: Church and state would remain separated; the
Republican regime would be transformed but not destroyed; there
would be no corporate state; new Constituent Cortes would meet,
the process of election being left unspecified, and in the meantime
power would rest firmly in military hands.[75] The confrontation
ended with the two sides further apart than ever as a result of having
clarified their positions. This was to be expected, given Fal Conde's
view of the rising as serving the particular ends of Carlism, and
Mola's unwillingness to alienate possible collaborators by making any
but the vaguest concessions to the Communion.[76] An additional
irritant was unquestionably the element of personality, for in Mola
the stubborn Fal Conde had come face to face with someone as inflexible as himself.

July arrived with Mola's military conspiracy nearing completion
and the date of the rising fixed for the fourteenth of the month, but
agreement with the Carlist leadership no nearer. This was not for
want of trying on the part of Mola. On 2 July he again met Zamanillo, whose demands, though now described as 'minimum guarantees',
were virtually unchanged; the Carlists, he declared, would not
move on the flag issue, on the need for a civilian share in power within
the provisional regime, or on the corporative character of the new
state. Zamanillo defended his rigid position by arguing that the
Carlist masses would only follow Fal Conde and himself if these
conditions were upheld – a claim, as things turned out, far removed
from reality. Mola again held his ground, accused Zamanillo of
playing politics, and leaving in one of the fits of depression to which
he was prone, talked for the second time in a month of committing
suicide.[77]

During the next few days Mola tried a different approach: that of
using Gil Robles and Zamanillo's Falangist friend Hedilla to persuade Fal Conde to relax his demands. Gil Robles, who by now had
agreed to subsidize the coup with the CEDA's election funds, visited

Fal Conde in Saint-Jean de Luz, but there made the diplomatic
blunder of hinting that after the rising power would pass into
cedista hands — hardly a strong probability but the last thing calculated to make Fal Conde more compliant.[78] Between 6 and 9 July an
ill-tempered correspondence passed between Fal Conde and Mola.
Fal Conde passed on Gil Robles' hints and reiterated the Carlist
demands that Mola accept their conditions concerning the nature
of the transitional and 'new' regimes. Mola, in reply, denied that
he was serving the interests of discredited conservative politicians
and ended by saying that he and Fal Conde were clearly wasting their
time. Carlist intransigence, he complained, was proving as harmful to
Spain as the excesses of the Popular Front. 'You may,' he warned Fal
Conde, 'have cause to repent.'[79]

Fortunately for Mola's peace of mind, during the previous ten
days he had opened up a new channel of communication with the
Carlists. At the end of June, Raimundo García arranged his first
interview with leading Navarrese Carlists — Rodezno and the
president and secretary of the Regional Junta, Joaquín Baleztena and
José Martínez Berasáin. For Mola, whose discussions with Oriol
must have suggested to him the potential usefulness of dealing direct
with the Communion's provincial officers, it was a prudent move.
For although all the Red Berets of Spain would be welcome allies,
it was the more numerous, more densely concentrated and relatively
well prepared Requeté of Navarre which was central to his plan, and
if the Navarrese Carlist authorities could be brought into the conspiracy, Fal Conde's obstructive attitude might not after all prove
decisive. Mola's meeting with the Navarrese coincided, happily for
him, with a sharp rise in the political temperature of Navarre. On
29 June the news reached Pamplona of the government's decision
to replace the Diputación yet again by a Temporary Committee.
When the three Carlists met Mola, they informed him that the
Diputación was contemplating demonstrations or even rebellion
and that the Communion was capable of mobilizing 7,000 men in the
cause of the *fueros*.[80] Even though Mola would not agree to back a
foralist rising, he could not but be cheered by the evident lack of
inflexibility among the province's leading Carlists. On 5 July he had
a further interview with Rodezno, who deemed it politic to urge him
to maintain contact with Fal Conde but again conveyed an impression of reasonableness and of a desire to join the rising.[81]

By 8 July Mola, the national leadership and the Navarrese Junta were all searching for a way out of the impasse. Fal Conde, believing his trump card to be Sanjurjo, sent Lizarza to Estoril to enlist the exile's help in persuading Mola to make concessions. [82] While Lizarza was away, however, the Navarrese Carlists took the initiative. At another meeting with Mola outside Pamplona, Rodezno openly suggested that in all matters concerning Navarre, Mola should deal directly with the regional authorities, and with Fal Conde where the rest of Spain was involved. [83] Since Mola's interest was overwhelmingly in the Navarrese Requeté, Rodezno's proposal implied his effectively by-passing Fal Conde, or at any rate his forcing Fal Conde's hand, by means of an agreement with the more pragmatic Navarrese. For the latter, and especially Rodezno himself, the vista now opened up not merely of joining the military rising as they genuinely wished to do, but also of reasserting their once dominant influence within the Communion.

From this point onward the Navarrese leaders, with the possible exception of Lizarza, whose official position made independent activity difficult, were determined to join Mola even at the cost of a showdown with Fal Conde. Not only were they now on good terms with Mola, but through Rodezno, Raimundo García and Bau they were also in increasingly close touch both with Calvo Sotelo and the Falange. [84]

Lizarza arrived back from Portugal on 11 July with messages from Sanjurjo to Fal Conde and Mola exhorting them to reach an agreement. Sanjurjo now made his promised 'statement', pressing Mola to allow the Carlists to use the red and gold flag on condition that the army units to which they were attached used no flag at all. The provisional government should be 'apolitical', include civilian members and set about dismantling the Republican regime, abolishing political parties, rectifying Republican legislation and introducing a genuinely 'new' state. [85] Sanjurjo's memorandum went a long way in supporting Fal Conde's demands, and Mola realized it. Receiving his copy on 12 July, he refused to accept it as genuine on the pretext that it was not correctly counter-signed. Lizarza, who by this time was travelling almost continuously between Pamplona and Saint-Jean de Luz, conveyed Mola's refusal to Fal Conde who declared negotiations at an end. [86] But Fal Conde's position was becoming hourly more difficult. The rising, though subject to repeated postponement, was due to take place within the week; the Navarrese authorities were determined to join Mola, and the national and foral crises were now such that the Requeté was more likely to follow those whom its spokesmen had once thought too passive than the man whose elevation to the Secretary-Generalship it had welcomed as evidence of greater militancy. Not only in Navarre but also in Álava, Barcelona, Santander, Galicia, Granada, Seville and Valencia, representatives of the Requeté were in close touch with army and Falangist conspirators. [87] The Carlist troops-to-be, in other words, were eager for action and unconcerned, whatever was claimed by Zamanillo, with detailed political guarantees.

As relations between Fal Conde and Mola sank to their nadir, the Navarrese moved to force the issue. On the afternoon of 12 July, as Gil Robles and the Alfonsist Luca de Tena tried vainly to persuade Lamamié to use his influence with Fal Conde,[88] the Baleztenas, Martínez Berasáin, Arellano and Arraiza drove to Saint-Jean de Luz to seek Don Javier's authorization for their participation in Mola's rising, now expected on the fifteenth. In reply to the Regent's enquiry regarding guarantees, they told him that Mola had conceded the use of the red and gold flag by the Requeté and had promised that the provincial and local administration of Navarre would be left in Carlist hands. Don Javier remarked that this hardly seemed a fair return for compromising the past and future of Carlism, that he could not give permission and must write to Alfonso Carlos in Vienna. Pressed by the Navarrese as to what they should do if, as was to be expected, the army rose before the Pretender's reply arrived, Don Javier gave in and agreed to accept responsibility for their participation. [89]

The absent Fal Conde had thus, in effect, lost the wholehearted support of Don Javier for his policy of 'no concession', and for the next few days was struggling to maintain his control over the Communion. On 13 July he sent Lizarza back to Pamplona with instructions that the Navarrese Requeté was not to rise save on his express orders, and was now to participate only in an exclusively Carlist movement which would presumably have to begin quickly in the slender hope of forcing the army to follow. [90] This order was an empty gesture, however, for Joaquín Baleztena and Martínez Berasáin were almost simultaneously promising Mola 7,000 volunteers whom they were confident of mobilizing in defiance of Fal Conde. Mola, while overjoyed, remarked that this was actually more than he needed at this juncture, if only because there were not enough arms for them all. [91]

The spontaneous desire for action on which the Navarrese leaders were relying received its final stimulus on the same day, when the news arrived in Pamplona that Calvo Sotelo had been assassinated by Assault Guards. The act was carried out in retaliation for the killing of an Assault Guard officer by Falangists a few days before; with José Antonio safely in prison, the assassins had toured Madrid looking for a prominent right-wing victim, settling on Calvo Sotelo after failing to find Gil Robles, Goicoechea and Rodezno at home.[92] The conspiracy now had a pretext and a justification, and things began to move quickly. Fal Conde's attitude now appeared unreasonable to almost all those Carlists who knew of it. Rada was visibly chafing at the delay caused by Fal Conde's obduracy,[93] whilst Utrilla aligned himself firmly with those committed to rebellion when he accepted Mola's orders to assist in co-ordinating the mobilization of the army and the Requeté.[94] Fal Conde's position had become untenable.

According to Lizarza it was he who finally broke the deadlock between Fal Conde and Mola by meeting three of Mola's UME officers on 14 July, as a result of which Mola wrote a note accepting Sanjurjo's points of five days before.[95] This certainly occurred, yet by now Mola had nothing to lose. The Requeté's participation was already assured thanks to the actions of the Navarrese Junta, so that a vague, eleventh-hour acceptance of Sanjurjo's recommendations would serve merely to make official what was now certain. This was indeed its effect. Lizarza and Félix Maíz drove separately to Saint-Jean de Luz, Lizarza sent by Mola and Maíz summoned by Fal Conde. Both returned to Pamplona on 15 July with the agreement of Fal Conde and Don Javier to the Requeté's mobilization on the basis of Sanjurjo's memorandum. The rising in Pamplona, having been postponed yet again, was now fixed for the morning of 19 July, and Utrilla proceeded to draft the order of mobilization.[96]

The effect of Lizarza's meeting with the UME officers was thus not to ensure the participation of the Navarrese Requeté, which was achieved by the Regional Junta's visit of 12 July to Saint-Jean de Luz, but to produce a formula which allowed Fal Conde to save face, avoid a head-on collision with the Navarrese and escape the risk of precipitating a new and possibly fatal schism within the Communion. At one stage Fal Conde considered sacking the entire Navarrese Junta;[97] had he tried to do so he would probably have failed, since unwritten convention still placed Navarre somewhat beyond the writ of the national leadership.[98] It is unlikely that Don Javier, who despite his sympathy for Fal Conde's general outlook also appreciated the independent influence of the Navarrese, would have agreed to what would have been an empty and disastrous move; empty, since the bellicose Carlist masses would under any circumstances have followed those most willing to give them their head, disastrous because it would have split Carlism at a decisive moment in Spanish history.

At the last minute the unity of the Communion and its commitment to the military rising which began in Morocco on 17 July were saved. Fal Conde remained *Jefe-Delegado* and retained the loyalty of the Youth and Requeté who knew nothing of the behind-the-scenes machinations which had just ended, but at tremendous cost. His relations with the Navarrese leaders were soured even more than before, while those between the Carlists and the army were to remain cursed by the mutual mistrust which had permeated the negotiations. The one hope of holding Mola to Sanjurjo's recommendations lay with Sanjurjo himself. The degree of his devotion to Carlism will always be in doubt; what is beyond question is that the future of the Communion and of Fal Conde in particular suffered a grievous blow when the aircraft bearing him to lead the rising crashed as it took off from a Portuguese aerodrome, killing its distinguished passenger.[99]

The Fourth Carlist War

On 17 July 1936 a repentant ex-Radical deputy, Joaquín Pérez Madrigal, arrived in Pamplona in order to assist at the start of the rising with which he had decided to identify himself. Met by Rodezno and Arellano, he was escorted by them to the Carlist circle in the Hotel La Perla, situated in the city's main square, the Plaza del Castillo. Later he recalled the profound impression which the scene made upon him:

There I was! In the deepest recesses of the cavern. The dreadful former 'wild-boar', installed that afternoon in the lair of the fearsome cave-dwellers ... A host of young men moved hither and thither, issuing and receiving orders. Impatient exclamations, exhortations to action, wise calls for prudence, bellicose clamour and cries anticipating victory ... Young priests in the patriotic calling of their rural ministry spend today helping the warriors of tomorrow, while the latter wait their turn to confess. [1]

On a smaller scale this scene was re-enacted in Carlist circles throughout the country, save where, as in Madrid and Barcelona, they had been closed by government order. As the Requeté of Pamplona and the surrounding district mustered in the circle, messengers were sent to Estella, San Sebastian and Bilbao with the final orders for mobilization. [2] News of Fal Conde's agreement with Mola was simultaneously handed to the Andalusian *jefe*, García Verde, who was in Pamplona waiting for a decision. Immediately he flew to Seville, where the local Requeté under Luis Redondo, Enrique Barrau and 'Pepe' Westermeyer had just learned that the rising there would be led by General Queipo de Llano, commander of the frontier-guards. [3]

The military rising began in Morocco on the afternoon of 17 July and thence spread northwards. The first Carlists involved were those of Andalusia, which rose on the eighteenth. Unlike most of the Navarrese, the Sevillian Requeté possessed few adequate weapons; when the army rose in the city, Redondo and twenty-five Red Berets therefore placed themselves promptly under its orders and received rifles from the Soria barracks. Together with Queipo's small military force, fifteen Falangists and a handful of Civil Guard, they then took possession of the city centre.[4] Later the same evening a well-organized detachment of Red Berets under José García Barroso helped the military commander of Jerez to control the town with some thirty troops, while other Carlists assisted in the seizure of Cádiz, Algeciras and La Línea, where the Requeté sustained its first death of the Civil War.[5] In Málaga the rising failed, whilst in Granada, where there was stalemate within the military command, and in Jaén, where the Civil Guard stayed loyal to the Republic, the Requeté waited in vain for orders to rise.[6]

Meanwhile, the much more numerous Requeté of northern Spain impatiently awaited its turn. In Pamplona the order to move came late on 18 July, to take effect the following day. At 6 a.m. on the nineteenth, the Requeté and the smaller Falange flooded into the Plaza del Castillo, and quickly occupied the rest of the city without encountering significant opposition. The whole of Navarre soon went the same way, and within hours more than 6,000 Red Berets had been mobilized; during the next week they continued to pour into Pamplona.[7]

Early on 19 July, Fal Conde and Zamanillo were flown back from France into Spain by Ansaldo, having first issued the final order to rise for which the Carlists of Álava, Santander and Barcelona, among others, were still waiting.[8] The order was given in the name of Alfonso Carlos, and an emissary flown to Vienna to obtain his confirmation; by the time it arrived, the rising was everywhere under way or already defeated. In Álava, Burgos and Zaragoza the local Carlists mobilized rapidly and in considerable numbers. Two *tercios* of the Álava Requeté helped the army to seize control of Vitoria, another occupied the strategically important passes of the Sierra de Orduña, linking the province with Santander, and a fourth took over the town of Llodio. In all some 3,000 Red Berets were mobilized in Álava on the first day of the rising.[9] Burgos also fell to the insurgents without effective resistance; the Carlists of the city promptly went into the streets, and having commandeered a fleet of lorries were soon shuttling in largely unarmed Red Berets from the surrounding countryside.[10] In Zaragoza the army, commanded by a former Radical, still Republican general, Cabanellas, seized control of the city and handed out rifles to the local Requeté under José María

Resa.[11] This pattern, though with numerically less Carlist involvement, was repeated in the other provincial capitals of northern Spain where the rising succeeded: Logroño, Huesca, Soria, Segovia, Ávila, Palencia, Salamanca, Zamora, León and, on 20 July, the four provinces of Galicia. Also on 20 July Granada finally rose, with the well-drilled Requeté prominent.[12]

Elsewhere the outcome was less joyous for the rebels. The rising in the north failed in Santander, throughout all Asturias save Oviedo, in Vizcaya and, to the amazement and disgust of the Navarrese Carlists, in Guipúzcoa. From the isolated strip of Republican territory thus created, Carlists and other right-wing refugees began to cross the *sierra* into the insurgent zone.[13] Catalonia and the Levant were also held for the Republic. After CNT workers seized arms from several depots, Barcelona erupted with the fiercest fighting of all. Two hundred Carlist volunteers reported to military headquarters; some were disarmed and held by loyalist officers, while most of those lucky enough to report to rebel units were forced to accept an auxiliary, non-combatant role.[14] When loyal army and Civil Guard units, together with armed workers, crushed the rising, many Carlists died at the hands of a vengeful populace already tasting the first delights of political power.[15] As Mola had feared all along, the rising in Madrid never got off the ground. After a day of hesitations during which the premiership passed from Casares Quiroga to Martínez Barrio, and from Martínez Barrio to Azaña's friend José Giral, arms were at last distributed to the capital's predominantly Socialist workers.[16] In Madrid few rightists died as yet; many however, Carlists included, were thrown without delay into the city's Model Prison.

The military conspirators' hopes for an expeditious and bloodless *coup d'état* along the lines of the classic *pronunciamiento* as last executed by Primo de Rivera were thus soon disappointed. By any reckoning, things had turned out badly. For one thing the armed forces in peninsular Spain, far from being unanimously favourable towards the rising, had divided almost equally for and against; the most reliable military force was unquestionably Franco's Army of Africa, and while it remained stranded in Morocco there was a serious chance of the rising's fizzling out and dying from sheer lack of momentum.[17] In the event it was the timely intervention of Italy and Germany which made possible the air-lifting of the African Army to Andalusia. This gave the rising a life-saving injection which ensured the securing of western Andalusia as a base for the subsequent advance on Madrid from the south-west. The possibility of early defeat was thus averted, but swift victory was as unlikely as ever. Already Spain had divided into two zones, very roughly corresponding to the left–right geographical division apparent during the past five years: the Republican zone containing most of the large cities and industrial resources of Spain, the rebel zone the food-producing regions which in the long run were to prove the more valuable. Perhaps most significant of all in ensuring that the struggle would be a long and bitter one was the strength, within the area controlled by the Republic, of the popular will to resist 'fascism'.

During the early weeks of what was now inescapably a civil war, the Carlist volunteers played an invaluable military role in three regions: the north, radiating from Pamplona; the Guadarrama front immediately north of Madrid; and western Andalusia, centring on Seville. The Navarrese and Álava Requeté had not only numbers but also, until increased recruitment outstripped equipment, weapons. Within four days of the start of the rising, approximately 20,000 Navarrese volunteers were drawn up in the Requeté or the Falange militia, or were awaiting formal enrolment.[18] This was vital for Mola, who besides lacking complete confidence in the loyalty of his own troops, was still faced with *focos* of left-wing resistance in Logroño and lower down the Ebro valley. The first task of the Navarrese Requeté, indeed, was to flush out enclaves of Republican support in Navarre, Álava and Logroño, which it did with speed, efficiency and the use of summary execution.[19] Fierce opposition was met in parts of Logroño and the Navarrese *ribera*, but in general the left was overcome with astonishing ease.

This was not enough, however. Although the rendering secure of Mola's base of operations was urgent, his overall strategy demanded the deployment of considerable manpower in an advance on Madrid, which he had never expected to fall instantly. Since Mola's military forces were in themselves inadequate for this operation, the Requeté and the Falange militia were crucial, as indeed they were to the two lesser campaigns which he was obliged to mount: that against the coastal Basque provinces and that against the Catalans on the Aragon front.[20] The Navarrese *tercios* were therefore immediately split into three main groupings. The *Tercio* of Pamplona was reorganized so that two of its *requetés* – a total of some 500 men – joined different battalions of the 1,600-strong García Escámez column which on the first day of hostilities in the north left to relieve Guadalajara and advance on Madrid from the north-east. A further 1,200 Red Berets from eastern Navarre, grouped around the *Tercio* of María de las Nieves and commanded by Utrilla, were sent to Zaragoza to boost Cabanellas' meagre forces in the stronghold of Aragonese Anarchism; after helping in the 'mopping up' of adjacent villages, most of these Carlists were then transferred to the Huesca and Teruel fronts.[21] A week after the start of the war, on 25 July, another Navarrese *tercio* was formed and departed for the Guadarrama front where it was placed under the command of Rada.[22]

The largest numbers of Navarrese Red Berets were committed to the Basque front. Like the detachments sent out to the south and east, they were attached to army units and placed under overall military command. In this way several columns were formed under army colonels Beorlegui, Ortiz de Zárate, Cayuela and Los Arcos; fighting across a wide front over mountainous terrain, they were placed in August 1936 under the overall command of the Navarrese general, Solchaga.[23] During August and September these units, which formed the basis of what later became the Navarrese Brigades, conquered Guipúzcoa after incurring heavy losses in the exceptionally bitter fighting against the Basques.[24]

The Requeté of Andalusia was simultaneously undergoing the same experience of gradually increasing absorption into army units. At first the Red Berets of Seville, Jerez and the surrounding region, and those of Córdoba and Granada, performed the useful role of 'flying columns' employed in crushing pockets of mainly working-class resistance, first in the workers' districts of Seville and the other capitals, and then further afield.[25] Outstanding in this capacity was the Redondo column of Seville, which was largely responsible for bringing about the submission of the Sierra de Ronda and the province of Huelva, including the Socialist-controlled Río Tinto and Tharsis mining areas.[26] Once this was achieved, such semi-independent activity diminished and Carlist volunteer detachments were grafted on to the armies fighting on the Málaga, Córdoba and Extremadura fronts. Under Major Castejón and the sole Carlist general, Varela, many Andalusian Red Berets took part in Franco's advance through Extremadura in the summer of 1936, a campaign which reached its climax in September with Varela's relief of the beleaguered Alcázar of Toledo and the beginning of the battle for Madrid.[27]

As the war progressed through the summer months of 1936, the Communion and in particular the Requeté expanded at an unprecedented rate. Throughout the insurgent zone of northern Spain, and above all in Navarre, recruitment to the Requeté continued unabated. By the middle of August 1936 the Requeté's official bulletin claimed that 20,000 Navarrese were fighting at the front, and according to Fal Conde no fewer than 50,000 Red Berets were now enlisted in the Carlist *tercios*. These claims seem reasonable; others do not. In January 1937 the Requeté bulletin claimed 100,000 fighting Carlists, a quite unacceptable figure in view of the fact that Fal Conde and other Carlists were in the habit of stating that 100,000 would have been reached if only the Red Berets of Catalonia and the Levant had been in a position to enlist.[28] The most generally accepted maximum number of Carlist participants at any one time appears to have been about 70,000.[29] Of these, perhaps 40,000 were Navarrese.[30]

Other centres of Nationalist Spain in which Requeté recruitment was feverishly pursued during the summer of 1936 were Burgos, Zaragoza, Valladolid, Orense and Santiago de Compostela. By the end of August 1,500 Red Berets had been signed up from among Catholic families in and around the Falangist stronghold of Valladolid, whilst the assembling of a similar force in Santiago de Compostela indicated successful proselytization among the many Alfonsists of Galicia.[31] The conquest of Guipúzcoa made possible the eventual formation of four Guipúzcoan *tercios*,[32] and a high proportion of escapers from the Republican zones of the north and east also joined the Requeté. The number of such refugees from Catalonia and the Levant by August 1936 was so great that it was possible to organize the predominantly Catalan *tercio* of Our Lady of Montserrat under the leadership of José María Cunill, who had also led the Carlist volunteers in Barcelona on 19 July and had narrowly escaped being shot dead. A Valencian *tercio* was shortly after formed on a similar basis.[33] These acquisitions from the Republican zone may only have numbered hundreds, but they gave substance to Carlist claims that another 30,000 or more potential recruits lay on the wrong side of the battle lines.

The expansion of the Requeté was the tip of an iceberg, for during the early months of the Civil War the entire Communion was growing at a dramatic rate.[34] Any latent or passive Carlists who had not committed themselves wholeheartedly to the cause before

July very soon did so, but even more striking was the influx of converts from other right-wing sources. Foremost among these were the CEDA and the JAP; although both maintained a spectral, independent existence within Nationalist Spain, their membership was draining away into the Communion and, still more, the Falange. The flow of *cedistas* and JAP members into the Communion has been attested by several independent observers; an outstanding but far from isolated example was that of the flourishing JAP of Toledo, which crossed *en bloc* to Carlism in October 1936.[35] Many members of Renovación Española, now more than ever a mere notables' pressure group, also joined the Requeté. In the Canary Islands the two monarchist movements actually fused, and their volunteers went to the front wearing the Carlist Red Beret together with the Alfonsists' St James' Cross.[36] Early in 1937 Carlism's prestige received a new boost with the announcement that the Spanish Nationalist Party, whose founder and leader, Albiñana, had been assassinated in the initial phase of the war, was to merge with the Communion.[37] A less likely source than any of these was the PNV, but in Navarre, Álava and the more rapidly conquered districts of Guipúzcoa, a considerable number of Basque Nationalists, whether out of sincere conviction or discretion, hastened to affirm their loyalty to Spain and hostility to the PNV's 'marxist' allies by turning back to the cause out of which Basque Nationalism had formed. In many parts of Navarre and Álava, the PNV's installations were taken over by the Carlists.[38] In Andalusia, 'conversion' followed the Carlist flag. To cite a single example: in Arriate, near Ronda, where before the rising there had been no Carlists, the Redondo column 'liberated' the village and promptly set about organizing branches of the Requeté, Margaritas and Pelayos.[39]

It is probable that only a minority of new recruits to the Requeté had been active Carlists before July 1936. Of the Catalan *tercio*, fewer than one in three Red Berets appear to have come from a Carlist family or organization; out of 316 fatalities, 93 were long-standing Carlists, seven were Falangists, four had previously belonged to Renovación Española, three to the CEDA or the JAP, and three to the Lliga. The remaining two-thirds came overwhelmingly from devout but politically non-active Catholic backgrounds. This is admittedly a very rough sample; Catalonia was not typical of Spain, much less of Nationalist Spain, and the refugees who joined the Requeté were not typical of Catalonia. It is unlikely, even so, that in any province of Nationalist Spain, Navarre not excluded, a majority of wartime Red Berets had been Carlist activists before the outbreak of war.[40]

Not all Red Berets were even Spanish. In a war which gradually became more and more international, the already colourful Requeté was given an extra dash of colour by the arrival of foreign volunteers. The largest group consisted of 'white' Russian *émigrés*, a full company of whom were recruited by Carlist agents in Paris and one of whose fatalities was the former Tsarist general, Anton Fock. The next most numerous were the French legitimists, followed by a sprinkling of Italians, Portuguese and Latin Americans.[41] One member of the Bourbon dynasty was killed in Guipúzcoa while keeping up his family's tradition of fighting in Carlism's wars: Carlo Maria, son of the Count of Caserta.[42] Not surprisingly, perhaps, the Requeté held little appeal for Anglo-Saxons. Only two Britons were recruited, one of whom – Peter Kemp, a right-wing Cambridge contemporary of the poet John Cornford, who died fighting for the Republic – later moved on to the crack Legion;[43] the South African poet Roy Campbell certainly developed a marked sympathy towards Carlism but, contrary to at least one account, almost certainly did not fight in the Requeté.[44] Apart from the non-Spanish combatants, a number of sympathetic foreigners were awarded honorary membership of the Requeté, among them the war correspondents of the London *Daily Mail* and *Daily Telegraph*.[45]

The Requeté at its height at the end of 1936 offered the best evidence that by no means all 'the people' of Spain were on the side of the Republic. In November 1936 Fal Conde told an Italian journalist that over three-quarters of the Requeté were 'peasants and workers', only between ten and fifteen per cent being middle-class and from five to eight per cent upper-class.[46] The propaganda intention behind this statement is obvious; moreover, Fal Conde's criteria of classification were unstated and any systematic check of his claim is impossible. Nevertheless there seems little reason to doubt its broad veracity. A sample drawn from the Catalan *tercio*, which might be expected to have been above-averagely bourgeois, suggests that according to Fal Conde's probably broad definition around sixty per cent of Red Berets were 'workers or peasants'. To be precise, wealthy urban and rural proprietors made up some eight or nine per cent, priests around two per cent – a high proportion, as might be expected among political refugees – with the remaining nine-tenths divided evenly among three categories: the urban middle class, small and medium rural proprietors and tenants (i.e. 'peasants'), and urban workers and 'employees'.[47] It would be logical to assume that in and around Seville the proportion of workers may well have been higher, partly as a result of the nature of Andalusian Carlism, and partly of Queipo de Llano's extension of financial inducements to workers joining the Requeté and the Falange militia.[48] In Navarre, Álava and much of the rest of Nationalist Spain, on the other hand, there is little doubt that the proportion of 'peasants' would be considerably higher than among *émigré* Catalans.

A distinctive feature of the Navarrese Requeté was its ability to recruit whole families of fathers and sons, or even in some cases three generations of males. This capacity, unquestionably genuine, was actually enshrined in Carlism's own mythology and propaganda. A leaflet released in 1937 contained a conversation between a Falangist and a Red Beret; asked who is to be informed should he die in battle, the Red Beret replies: 'Tell José María Hernandorena, of the *tercio* of Montejurra, aged 65. He's my father.' And if he should prove to be . . . unavailable? 'Then tell José María Hernandorena, of the *tercio* of Montejurra, aged 15. He's my son.'[49] Strictly speaking, neither the eldest nor the youngest José María ought to have been fighting, since enlistment was officially restricted to men between the ages of eighteen and fifty. In practice, however, Red Berets of over sixty and as young as thirteen were far from rare. Several instances were reported of families of up to eight volunteering for the Requeté, and some Navarrese villages were virtually emptied of men. The most impressive performance was probably that of Artajona, which sent 775 out of 800 eligible males into battle.[50]

Many new recruits, besides being unavoidably deficient in their grasp of the essentials of Traditionalism, were militarily raw. Red Berets hastily enlisted around Burgos were rushed to the Guadarrama front totally untrained, while others enrolled in the Navarrese *tercios* had to learn the rudiments of gunmanship *en route* to the Guipúzcoan front.[51] At first an annoyance, this was to become far more serious in view of the high casualty rate in the battles against the Basques and the left-wing militiamen of Madrid. Within weeks there developed a lack of actual and potential officer material so acute that Requeté chaplains were increasingly taking command of Carlist troops in the field.[52] The spirit of the Cura Santa Cruz, it seemed, lived on.

The Carlists' enthusiastic commitment to the rising was epitomized by the conduct of many leading prewar personalities. Most of the younger generation fought in the Requeté, including Arellano, González Gregorio, Cárcer, Ramírez Sinués, Comín and Elizalde, as well as, of course, Rada and Utrilla;[53] some, like the ex-*jefe* of Córdoba, José María Alvear, were killed in action.[54] Even those such as Rodezno, Fal Conde and Zamanillo who, by virtue either of age or hierarchic position, did not actually fight, spent considerable time at the front visiting Carlist combatants. Precisely how dangerous this duty could be was proved by the death of the ex-*jefe* of Ávila, the Conde de Acevedos, slain by a stray Nationalist bullet or, according to a less official version, shot in mistake for a 'red' militia-man.[55]

For the first six months of the war, both zones witnessed a wave of violent repression against those unfortunate enough to find themselves on the wrong side of the lines. It is impossible to state with confidence or accuracy how many lives were lost; the destruction of the myth of 'one million dead' has cast doubt upon virtually all available statistics, among them those referring both to Carlist deaths in Republican Spain and to leftists killed by Carlists.

At the very least, several hundred Carlists died in the Republican zone. Out of between 800 and 900 civilians killed in the coastal Basque provinces, about 350 were Carlists. Among them were Víctor Pradera and one of his sons, shot by militia in San Sebastian on 5 September 1936; Beunza, executed in Fuenterrabía on the same day; and Juan Olazábal, shot in San Sebastian in January 1937.[56] Several Carlists died in the aftermath of the attempted rising in Barcelona. Tomás Caylà, former *jefe* of Tarragona, was seized in Barcelona, taken to the Tarragonese town of Valls and there executed; according to Carlist reports he was publicly beheaded and his head used as a football. A crowd entered the house of the leading Catalonian Carlist, Miguel Junyent, who died of heart failure before there was time to shoot him, while the former deputy Casimiro Sangenís was executed after a kangaroo trial.[57]. In Toledo the provincial *jefe* and Carlist deputy Jesús Requejo was imprisoned along with his son on the outbreak of war, and both later shot;[58] and in Málaga no fewer than five members of the Huelín family met their deaths before the city was taken by the Nationalists in February 1937.[59]

Although these losses were sorely felt within the Communion, apart from Pradera the Carlist cause lost no crucially important individual in the Republican repression. This was in sharp contrast to the Falange, which lost two of its former leaders, Ruiz de Alda and Redondo, at the hands of the Socialist militia early in the war. Ledesma, expelled but still a force to be reckoned with, died in November 1936 in a massacre of political prisoners who had been held in Madrid's Model Prison since July. José Antonio, after nearly six months in jail, was finally tried by a people's court in Alicante for conspiracy against the Republic. Found guilty, he was shot on 20 November alongside four more political prisoners, two of them Carlists.[60]

Carlism's account was balanced by the action of the Requeté. The Spanish Civil War was an unusually passionate conflict, and Carlism an irrationally passionate cause; for five years, rank-and-file Carlists had been told that the Republic was made up of the hordes of Antichrist and encouraged to look forward to the day when it would be possible to crush them, and now that that day had come, restraint was hardly to be expected. More than any other element on the Nationalist side, the Carlists saw the war as an event transcending normal civil or even ideological conflict: in short, as a religious crusade. It was natural, therefore, that from the start of hostilities Carlism's fighting arm should display an excess of zeal for which it became famous, or in the eyes of its enemies, infamous, throughout Spain and beyond. There is little point in regurgitating specific atrocity stories; some are no doubt true, some false, yet apart from the aura of religious fanaticism invariably surrounding them they differ little from those circulated by the Carlists themselves about their left-wing enemies. Suffice it to say that at the front the Requeté earned itself a reputation as the most exaltedly violent element within the Nationalist armies, a reputation which has perhaps been most effectively perpetuated in the novels generated by the Civil War.[61] In the rearguard, during the first year of the war, the Requeté, enthusiastically supported by Carlist civilians, assiduously devoted itself to 'cleansing' Navarre, Álava, Logroño, western Andalusia and parts of Zaragoza, of leftism and Republicanism. The scale of the carnage remains uncertain. In the perfervid atmosphere of the war both supporters and opponents of Carlist repression were inclined to exaggerate it, and figures of from 7,000 to 11,000 deaths in Navarre alone were commonly claimed.[62] Modern Carlist sources seek to play down the repression, and basing their arguments on statistics which would be dubious enough in peacetime but are even more so against a wartime background, admit to only 700.[63] The Republic's own, incomplete estimate of some 2,000 executions in Navarre is probably as reliable as any; such a figure would certainly be high enough to explain the shock and worry of the Carlist authorities themselves at the extent of the killings during the summer and autumn of 1936, and their largely vain efforts to control the fervour of their own forces.[64]

The forging of the Nationalist alliance had been so fraught with difficulties that it was not surprising if the military leaders' initial public declarations appeared distinctly uncertain as to precisely what the rising was intended to achieve. Franco's first call to the armed forces of metropolitan Spain amounted to little more than a general appeal for patriotism;[65] Mola, after declaring martial law in Pamplona, and now sure of Carlist co-operation, showed himself willing to risk arousing Carlist suspicions with the lukewarmness of his advocacy of corporativism — not to mention his talk of religious toleration and the separation of Church and state.[66]

A week after the rising began, a semblance of overall command was assumed by a National Defence Junta, nominally headed by Cabanellas, actually dominated by Mola, and consisting in addition of three retired generals and two colonels on active service; a representative of the navy was co-opted a few days later, and Franco was added early in August.[67] Rumours that the Junta would be broadened to included civilians proved groundless. Military control of the Nationalist cause was already secure enough to make any such concession unnecessary and even, in view of the possibility of factionalism, unwise. The Junta's military complexion conformed closely with the wishes and advice of leading Alfonsists like Goicoechea and Vallellano, who were anxious to prevent too much power from passing into the hands of their Falangist and Carlist rivals.[68] The first manifesto issued from Burgos by the Junta was studiously designed to avoid alienating those relatively moderate Spaniards whose dedication to the rising might be less than wholehearted; stressing the restoration of order, the destruction of bolshevism and anarchy, the guaranteeing of social justice and the general salvation of Spain, it made no reference to religion or to a possible return of the monarchy.[69] Already it was evident that the Carlist programme on behalf of which Fal Conde had so stubbornly haggled was sacred neither to Mola nor his army colleagues.

The Carlists uttered no protest, however. Whereas in Republican Spain the advent of civil war intensified political activity by highlighting the differences between the advocates of liberal democracy and those of immediate social revolution, in Nationalist Spain an official blanket of silence smoothly descended upon all political discussion of a potentially divisive character. Although protected by the Defence Junta's powers of censorship, assumed under the State of War declared at the end of July,[70] this outward cohesion was also based upon the genuine existence of a consensus, less concerning the system ultimately to emerge from the war than the simple priority, never accepted unanimously in the Republican zone, of military victory. Carlists and Falangists each possessed recipes for a New Spain which went far beyond anything the generals had in mind, and a minority of each nursed vague but exciting dreams of a social order revolutionized through war. Neither, however, were prepared – or able – to pursue this chimera at the possible expense of victory, or to argue that victory was dependent upon its attainment, as were the revolutionaries within the Republican camp. Hard military sense was reinforced by the very nature of militarist, Traditionalist and Falangist ideology, the lowest common denominator of which was, after all, the affirmation of patriotism and 'national unity'.

For several weeks, therefore, the Carlists played down the details of their programme. Their early pronouncements, like those of the military leaders, were more explicit regarding what they had taken up arms to prevent than what constituted their long-term objectives. Above all they were convinced that the rising had narrowly forestalled a social revolution: 'It is impossible to calculate what the military movement has avoided,' *El Pensamiento Navarro* asserted, 'since no one knows the magnitude of the catastrophe with which we were threatened...' Perhaps not, but Carlists were perfectly willing to guess: 'an anarchic communism which would have eliminated all those Spaniards offering opposition, just as it was already eliminating them in daily acts of cowardly aggression ... Soviet vandalism ... a terroristic and bloody communism ... the tyranny of a foreign power'. All these horrors had been prevented in the nick of time by a movement of 'honourable, decent and free' Spaniards.[71] In other words, Spain stood face to face with anti-Spain, the mass support of the latter consisting of workers deceived by their leaders. The enemy, liberals and Anarchists included, were more often than not described as 'the marxists'.[72]

El Pensamiento Navarro went further in considering the rising to be not purely pre-emptive but also aimed against the very heart and essence of the Republican system. Its laws, 'unjust and arbitrary', designed by sectarian cliques in the service of hidden powers, had enslaved and crushed good Spaniards; the Republic had been 'laic' and 'persecuting' and its men 'masons and despots' who had defied the national will and made a mockery of their own legislation. Finally, all authority having been lost, drastic steps had been necessary.[73] Thus while the military leaders prevaricated about their attitude towards the Republic, the Carlists left their detestation of that regime in no doubt whatsoever.

In continuing to reflect the views of the Navarrese establishment, the province's press displayed an understandable tendency to look at the war as a peculiarly Navarrese conflict, or at least one led by Navarre. The concept of 'Reconquest' sprang automatically to the minds of those steeped in Spain's Christian past; but where it had once been Fal Conde's dream that the second Reconquest would begin in Andalusia, to northerners there was no gainsaying their knowledge that the new Covadonga was to be found in the Pyrenean valleys of Navarre.[74]

A side-effect of this conception of the war was that the Carlists' hatred of Basque Nationalism rose to a new pitch. They found it impossible to comprehend how the Catholic Basques could have sided with the Republic. Vizcaya and Guipúzcoa, they felt sure, would have been won for the rising but for the shameful conduct of the PNV's leaders; having joined with 'the sempiternal adversaries of the Basque country, the enemies of God and the Old Laws', the Basques, it was claimed, now deservedly groaned under a 'tyranny' instead of being 'free and happy' like Navarre. Basque Nationalism, in fact, was committing suicide by accepting a concept of Euzkadi – the Basque nation – as inventive as 'the tales of Jules Verne' and effectively abandoning Catholicism.[75] The frightful violence of the war between Basques and Navarrese was thus paralleled in the quite extraordinary antipathy now felt by the Carlists towards their erstwhile allies. Its most extreme and bizarre manifestation was a brief outburst of Navarrese expansionism during August 1936, when both the press and the Diputación of Navarre seriously discussed the possible annexation of a strip of Guipúzcoan territory extending along the French frontier and including the coastal towns of Irún, Fuenterrabía and Pasajes. Both historical tradition and the right of conquest were cited to justify a Navarrese corridor to the sea, but with the end of hostilities in Guipúzcoa and in the face of pronounced military apathy, the campaign died a natural and peaceful death.[76]

The views of Fal Conde and the ruling circle of the Communion were temporarily deprived of official outlets at the start of the war by the disappearance of the Madrid-based *El Siglo Futuro*, whose offices and plant were taken over by the Republican Left, and the winding-up of the *Boletín de Orientación Tradicionalista*. Eventually on 8 August the latter was replaced by a new sheet, the *Boletín de Campaña de los Requetés*, which thereafter expressed the opinions of Fal Conde and Zamanillo. From its creation the Requeté's bulletin went out of its way to emphasize the special role being played by Carlism in the present struggle:

the Traditionalist Communion is the only [organization] to have preserved the doctrinal spirit and historical custom, pure and immaculate, of the religious, moral, social, political and economic unity of Spain the Great.

As such the Communion 'has priority by right with regard to the representation of secular Spain'.[77] For the moment, at least, Fal Conde chose to gloss over the recent differences between himself and the army; addressing Red Berets in Seville, he painted a decidedly imaginative picture of his role in establishing a partnership with the army and in organizing the Navarrese Requeté for war. Specifically, he referred to his re-entry into Spain from France where he had been 'organizing, with elements of the army, the Nationalist movement' – scarcely an accurate depiction of the prewar situation.[78] All in all, the vision during the summer and early autumn of 1936 was one, which few army officers could have accepted, of a Carlist–military alliance between equals. In a speech commemorating the opening of the Carlist radio station in Guipúzcoa in September, Fal Conde declared that 'the Spanish army and the Requeté are reconquering the national soil'. In this alliance, Fal Conde found room for the Falange only as a junior partner whose assistance was somewhat condescendingly welcomed.[79]

By the middle of August, early concentration upon the preventive aspects of the rising was gradually giving way to thoughts for the future which lay beyond military victory. Here, too, marked differences were discernible between the statements of Rodezno and his circle, whose co-operation with the army was sincere and unconditional, and those of the group around Fal Conde, Don Javier and Zamanillo, who perforce proclaimed a similar degree of co-operation which actually existed neither in fact nor in spirit. Rodezno's view of the war's purpose and possible long-term consequences was sweeping and unspecific; the 'National movement' was fighting for

our sacrosanct religion ... the liberty of our outraged consciences; the dignity of our family ... ; our blessed foral institutions ... ; the rights of Western Christian civilization; a whole moral and spiritual patrimony which is worth more than life itself, for without it life is vile ...[80]

And when the fight was over — what then? A new life, a new concept of life, austerity and 'efficient bases' enabling Spaniards to feel 'the pride of recovering our historical personality and imperial happiness'.[81] Rodezno thus preferred not to speculate on the form of regime likely to follow the war, on the possibility of installing the Traditional Monarchy, or on Carlism's long-term relationship with the army. In all probability this reticence was the combined product of discretion and genuine uncertainty as to the future succession. Although Rodezno remained silent on the question of the succession when Alfonso Carlos died on 28 September, *El Pensamiento Navarro* was all but forced to make a statement. Monarchies, its editorial declared, do not perish even though kings may die. Nonetheless it was not until the Feast of St Francis Xavier on 3 December that the same newspaper unequivocally recognized Don Javier's Regency.[82]

The national leadership of Carlism was both franker and more demanding. In general it was admitted that while the eventual installation of the Traditional Monarchy remained central to Carlist expectations, the now-dominant role of the army in the struggle and the need for post-war reconstruction within an authoritarian framework suggested a continuation of military rule for some time after the coming of peace. By far the least sanguine concerning prospects for an early return to monarchy was Don Javier himself, who told a journalist that Carlist participation in the war was not conditional upon a restoration, that a 'strong military government' would be necessary for some years to come and that afterwards 'if the people believe that we offer a solution, we shall serve Spain from the throne with complete loyalty'.[83] Thus, however judicious his phrasing, Don Javier made explicit his claim to the throne. Zamanillo echoed the

Regent's acceptance of the need for – and presumably the sheer inevitability of – a post-war military dictatorship 'in order to consolidate victory' and as 'the only form of government capable of reconstructing the New Spain'. He insisted, just the same, that the Carlists held firmly to every point of their programme and that sooner or later it would be necessary to satisfy the wishes of the people, who he was confident would in the majority favour monarchy. Although no precise period was mentioned, this seemed to imply an interim stage shorter than the 'some years' referred to by Don Javier.[84]

Don Javier and Zamanillo had thus come some distance in accepting the inevitability of army dominance in a post-war Spain, while still clinging to the belief that a transition to the very different kind of state desired by Traditionalists would remain possible. Compromise with military authoritarianism was recognized to be necessary in order to win the war, without in any way being permanent. As usual Fal Conde was less flexible than either his king-presumptive or his Requeté Delegate. He too denied that the return of monarchy was actually a condition of Carlist commitment to the Nationalist cause, yet speaking in Jerez amid general expectation of the fall of Madrid, he left no doubt that for him the end of the war and the installation of the Traditional Monarchy should be simultaneous:

This is a religious war and a war of Reconquest, for in Spain everything was conquered under the protection of the Cross and was preserved by the Cross. Therefore this war of reconstruction will end as so great an enterprise as ours *must* end – with the triumph of a glorious and sovereign institution, the model and prototype of all things Spanish.

This, of course, was the Church, with which in the Spanish context the monarchy was indissolubly bound; the king, Fal Conde was sure, would return by popular demand 'and will delay his arrival not one day longer than it takes for Spain to seek him and complete the Reconquest'.[85] Exactly how this process was going to be executed, Fal Conde did not say.

Entry into the war was bound to have profound effects upon the internal affairs of the Communion, especially in view of the machinations of the weeks preceding the rising. The early course of the war and the regional variations within Nationalist Spain worked to the benefit of the Navarrese rather than the national leadership of Carlism. Fal Conde might have saved face and with it his leadership, but his awkwardness in negotiation had alienated Mola and the other generals without, as it transpired, winning the desired concessions. His most important supporter, Don Javier, was still in exile and cut off both from the thick of the fighting and, to a considerable extent, the internal politics of Carlism. In Fal Conde's personal power-base of Andalusia, Queipo de Llano's establishment of a semi-autonomous regime and the dispersal of the Requeté among the many Andalusian and Extremaduran fronts set in motion that very erosion of the regional Carlist organization which he, Fal Conde, had always seen as the likely result of collaboration but in the last resort had been unable to avoid; the creation of new Carlist organizations like those of Arriate was poor compensation for this deeper and more far-reaching development. Yet another inconvenience for Fal Conde was the siting of the Nationalist headquarters in Burgos. Dignity demanded that the Carlist national authorities base themselves in the Nationalist 'capital', despite Carlism's only modest strength in and around Burgos; the result was to increase still further Fal Conde's isolation within a movement whose centre of gravity had suddenly shifted back to Navarre.

In contrast to the weakening of Fal Conde's position, that of the Navarrese was enormously enhanced. Whereas in most of Nationalist Spain military control was almost total, in Navarre the utter dependability of the majority of the population and the warm relations between Mola and the local Carlists made it possible for civilian government to continue alongside the military authorities. Naturally, that government was substantially in Carlist hands. Without reference to Fal Conde, who was annoyed but powerless to resist, the Navarrese Carlists who had dealt with Mola set up a provincial Carlist War Junta under the presidency of Martínez Berasáin.[86] This body, as well as the Regional Junta, liaised closely with the Carlist-dominated Diputación, and with the military *comandancia*. In their turn, all these administrative organs maintained constant contact with the operational columns in the Basque mountains and the Ebro valley.[87]

The leaders of Navarrese Carlism thus found that Mola's promises to the Regional Junta were fulfilled, and confident in their political control of the 'kingdom', they proceeded with measures calculated to turn it into a model of applied Traditionalism. Within days of the outbreak of war, Catholic education returned to Navarre in strength. Religious schools, colleges and extra-mural educational centres, closed under the Republic, were reopened, and amid great celebration the crucifix was ceremonially reaffixed to the walls of schools. In mid-August the Diputación issued the eagerly awaited decree re-admitting the Society of Jesus to all the activities banned under the 1931 Constitution and the 1933 Law of Congregations.[88] The ultra-clerical atmosphere of Navarre, difficult enough to escape even under the Republic, was now reaching a new peak, typified by an official, Church-supported war on so-called political and sexual pornography in print and on film.[89] In many parts of the province the popular exodus to join the Requeté meant that priests and members of religious Orders were just about the only able-bodied men left; as such, they were to be seen out in the fields helping the women-folk of farming families bring in the 1936 harvest. The total identification with the rising suggested by this kind of action was characteristic of wartime Navarre; when the Diputación considered an emergency tax to support families placed in economic difficulties by the absence of volunteers, the necessary funds were quickly raised by local banks, savings institutions and private citizens.[90]

The Navarrese Carlists' enthusiastic use of their new power made obvious what had been concealed before the war: that what interested them was not so much the total victory of Carlism — attractive as that was in an abstract sense — as the obtaining of certain minimum gains, namely the strengthening of clericalism, the guaranteeing of public order, and their control over their own corner of Spain. With numbers and organization based on family and regional tradition, they had much to gain through compromise, where Fal Conde had everything to lose.

For Fal Conde, the resurgence of Navarre within the Communion and unavoidable placing under military command of the Red Berets — still his most fervent supporters — posed a serious threat to the cohesiveness of his organization and, indeed, to his very authority. On 1 September 1936 he therefore announced the introduction of a new organizational structure especially designed to satisfy wartime needs. At its head was the National War Junta, dominated by its president, Fal Conde himself. Immediately under him came two loyal adherents, Zamanillo as Delegate-General of the Requeté and head of the 'Military Section' and the slightly less dependable Lamamié as Secretary-General. Alongside the Military Section, but with a largely subordinate role, was the section of General Affairs which included Valiente (Religious Affairs), Rodezno (Political Delegate) and a little later Arauz de Robles (Guilds and Corporations). The new Junta forthwith assumed 'full powers' and 'all the faculties of existing organizations'; the latter – *jefaturas*, juntas and delegations – were suspended and replaced by regional commissioners (*comisarios*) and war juntas.[91] The National War Junta projected the appearance of a 'shadow' government and in theory represented an even greater degree of centralization than the 1934 reforms. In reality, however, it laid bare the weakness of Fal Conde's position, for there proved to be no alternative to accepting the existence and independence of the Navarrese War Junta and naming its president, Martínez Berasáin, as commissioner for Navarre.[92] Although Fal Conde would never openly admit it, the inviolability of the Navarrese authorities was thus tacitly recognized.

The new structure reflected not only Fal Conde's need to reassert his authority within the Communion, so seriously undermined in the days before the rising, but also his wish to affirm, within the bounds of prudence, Carlism's individuality within the Nationalist coalition. In this it was necessary, as the next chapter will show, to tread warily; in general, Fal Conde's public utterances continued to stress the closeness and equality of Carlism's relationship with the army, for whose leaders, Franco, Queipo de Llano, 'the glorious General Mola' and 'my childhood friend General Varela', he offered nothing but praise.[93] In this respect, at any rate, his example was followed by all his fellow Carlists. Benevolence was also the keynote of Carlist statements regarding the Falange, notwithstanding that the latter was now a larger movement than the Communion.[94] If its emergence as a competitor worried the Carlists, few of them yet said so publicly.[95] The Carlist press gave prominence to Falangist affairs and the joint activities of the two parties;[96] Carlist speakers stressed comradeship and co-operation;[97] and at the front Fal Conde and Zamanillo visited Falangist as well as Carlist militiamen and were rewarded with generous Falangist applause.[98] This political climate could only be temporary, however. The time was drawing near when Nationalist Spain would have to assume a more clearly defined and permanent political shape, and when this happened the three-way relationship of army, Carlism and Falange was certain to be subjected to considerable strains.

I 2

The New State

Carlist loyalty towards the military leadership of the rising received its first serious test at the end of September 1936. For some time now it had been widely recognized in the political circles of Nationalist Spain that drastic military and political changes were necessary. A unified military command was obviously going to be needed before the great assault upon Madrid which, it was hoped, would all but end the war; perhaps more important still was the desire to give the Nationalist cause a more positive form of political leadership than was to be expected from the Defence Junta. Quite apart from domestic considerations, the requirements of dealing with Nationalist Spain's fascist patrons and of impressing the non-intervening democracies made change urgent. By September there existed behind the façade of the Defence Junta's leadership a *de facto* triumvirate consisting of Mola in the north, Queipo de Llano in the south, and Franco effectively dominating the centre. Of the three it was Franco, whose invasion had saved the rising from stagnation and possible defeat and who alone was conducting a dynamic campaign, who had the look of a Generalissimo. In much of the foreign press it was already 'Franco's rising', while German agents in Spain were informing Berlin of Franco's effective ascendency. 'The Commander-in-Chief,' wrote one of them, Seydel, on 16 August, 'is definitely Franco.'[1]

The issue was finally forced by a cabal of mainly Alfonsist officers led by Orgaz and an air-force general, Kindelán, who apparently believed Franco to be the most likely of the leading generals to favour a restoration. It was Kindelán who during late September succeeded in persuading the entire Defence Junta, apart from the staunchly Republican Cabanellas, of the urgent need for a single command, and then in obtaining their agreement and that of other important officers like the Falangist Yagüe to Franco's leadership. On 28 September in Salamanca, Franco accepted the positions of Generalissimo of the armed forces and 'Head of the Government of the Spanish State' with 'all the powers of the New State'. This latter status, engineered by the grey eminence of the affair, Franco's brother Nicolás, was sprung on the other generals by Kindelán and encountered some resistance from, among others, the upstaged Mola before finally winning acceptance.[2] The decree was published on 29 September,[3] and within days Franco was officially referring to himself as 'Head of State'.

While matters were reaching their climax in Salamanca, the leading Carlists were otherwise engaged. On 28 September Alfonso Carlos, at the age of eighty-six, was hit by an Austrian army vehicle while crossing a Vienna street and died a few hours later. The news reached the Burgos offices of the National War Junta on the afternoon of 29 September and the Carlist party, led by Fal Conde, left Spain for the funeral in Vienna on the afternoon of 1 October.[4] The news of Franco's elevation was by now public, so that it is untrue that, as is sometimes stated, the Carlist leaders were absent from Spain when the decree was issued. Not that it made much difference, for they were no less powerless to offer protest or opposition. There was absolutely no alternative but to accept and formally welcome the Salamanca *coup* – for such it was. From a military point of view it made very good sense, and even if Franco's new political powers appeared even more excessive to the Carlists than they did to some of his own colleagues, complaint or outright opposition might have been interpreted as sabotaging the war effort and have proved highly damaging to the Communion. The Carlist press accordingly extended a dutiful if hardly ecstatic welcome to Franco's leadership, while the Navarrese authorities promptly announced their adhesion.[5] On 1 October Franco named a 'Technical Junta' to perform the administrative tasks of government; among its members were two of the more 'collaborationist' Carlists – Joaquín Bau in the Commercial Section and Romualdo Toledo in that of Education.[6] After an appreciable delay, representatives of the Carlist National War Junta finally paid a visit to Franco, who responded with eulogies for Traditionalism when assured that the Carlists in general and the Requeté in particular were solidly behind him.[7]

Although the Navarrese, more concerned with winning the war and running Navarre than with the future of the Communion's national organization, seemed not unhappy with the new situation,[8] there was no reason to suppose that it would mean any favours for

Carlism. In the past Franco had been regarded as apolitical, albeit decidedly conservative; such contacts as he had established during the Republic had been mostly with *cedistas*, while his present intimates were mainly Alfonsists and 'new' Falangists, evidence of an authoritarian temper no doubt nurtured through his reading of *Acción Española*, to which he had been a subscriber.[9] Certainly there was not, and had never been, anything to link him with Carlism. It was therefore not surprising that the Carlists, once having formally acknowledged his leadership, refrained from giving him more attention or praise than was absolutely necessary. On the contrary, Alfonso Carlos' death provided them with an opportunity for concentrating even more than usual on internal affairs. In mid-October, Don Javier assumed the full powers of the Regency,[10] a step which the Requeté's bulletin treated as of far greater importance than Franco's recent apotheosis. Described by Zamanillo as 'a new *caudillo* for the old standard of Spanish Tradition',[11] Don Javier ascended to the Regency in the warming knowledge that Alfonso Carlos had bequeathed to Fal Conde a testament all but calling for his succession to the throne itself.[12] Within days, Don Javier, to no one's surprise, confirmed Fal Conde in his position as *Jefe-Delegado*.[13] The dissatisfaction of the Navarrese establishment was almost audible; now, as had been the case almost constantly since 1934, there were those who wished to replace Fal Conde once more with Rodezno.[14] Don Javier and Fal Conde remained too close for this to be more than a wish, but the gulf between them and the Navarrese was again revealing itself.

For Fal Conde and his supporters on the National War Junta, the events of September and October inside and outside the Communion had cleared the decks for a new phase of action. From late October they launched a series of initiatives which together created the impression of an attempt to assert the distinctiveness of Carlism, to increase its independence within Nationalist Spain, and to influence the political complexion of the new state. One singular feature was the sudden irruption of a Fal Conde personality cult in the columns of his own organ, the *Boletín de Campaña de los Requetés*. Although doubtless aimed in part against his rivals in the Communion, this campaign, the opening blast of which hailed Fal Conde as 'a man sent us by God', also struck implicitly at the pre-eminence of Franco.[15] Indeed, for all the notice paid him in the Requeté's bulletin, the new Head of State might not have existed.

Besides attempting to boost his own position, Fal Conde chose the last two months of 1936 to inaugurate two ambitious projects: the *Obra Nacional Corporativa* (National Corporative Effort) and the Royal Carlist Military Academy. From September 1936 increasing attention began to be paid to the mobilization of popular support through the publication of Carlist policies, especially in the social sphere. The aim was threefold: firstly, to satisfy those Carlists who felt that the Communion's social policy had in the past been inadequate;[16] secondly, by attracting additional support among all social classes, to place Carlism in a more powerful position when the day arrived for the erection of a permanent regime for the new Spain; and thirdly, to supplement mere mass support through a programme designed to construct 'from the bottom upwards' a corporative framework inspired by Traditionalist principles, thereby going some way towards resolving in Carlism's favour the eternal problem of transition. If such a scheme worked – and was permitted to work – then the generals might for a time exercise executive power while the Carlists concentrated on broadening their power-base and both creating and manning the infra-structure of the New State.

The first hint of this new direction came even before Franco's elevation and Alfonso Carlos' death. On 10 September the National War Junta's Delegation of Propaganda issued a press statement, wisely avoiding all reference to the army and the institution of monarchy, but reiterating the main lines of Carlist social policy as developed during the Republic. Carlism, the statement insisted, did not lack social conscience; liberalism in the socio-economic sphere must go – but not to be replaced by any 'Germanic' form of *étatisme*, whether it be socialist or, implicitly, fascist. The New State must be strong but not all-absorbent, not 'indifferent' but reduced to its essential functions. Not only was fascism thus indirectly criticized, but also the 'syndicalism' advocated by the Falange. Carlism, it was declared, rejected *all* forms of syndicalism in favour of the traditional guilds and corporations.[17] A week later words were translated into action, when the National War Junta created a new Delegation for Guilds and Corporations headed by Arauz de Robles.[18]

Finally, in November 1936, the Carlist press announced the inauguration of the *Obra Nacional Corporativa*, also under Arauz de Robles' direction and with its headquarters in Burgos. The *Obra Nacional Corporativa*, which was the object of great attention in the Carlist press, and particularly the Requeté's bulletin, for the next four months, represented something conspicuously absent during the Republic – the creation of a national organization encompassing the numerous Workers Sections and *Agrupaciones Gremiales* attached to Carlist circles. Its minimum goal was the incorporation of all Carlist employers and employees into a rudimentary corporative structure within which the principles and function of the guild would be revitalized and social-Catholic ideas put into practice. In the long run it was designed to attract the adherence of non-Carlists in order that a skeletal corporate state might arise independent of military dictates.[19] An important sub-division of the *Obra Nacional Corporativa* was the *Movimiento Nacional-Agrario*, which sought to restore harmony to the countryside through the protection of all existing forms of individual and communal landed property, the encouragement of local and corporate self-government, of an efficient system of credit and of co-operative buying and selling, and a general renaissance of rural spirit. Carlism, it was pointed out, was after all 'essentially a rural and agrarian movement'.[20]

On paper the *Obra Nacional Corporativa* was an ambitious attempt at using the new situation created by the war in order to achieve that transition towards a non-coercive form of corporativism which had been unattainable during peacetime.[21] Some success was registered during its brief existence. Branches were set up in most of the provinces of Nationalist Spain, and some headway made in attracting non-Carlist interest in what remained essentially a Carlist enterprise.[22] By far the greatest single success was the adherence early in 1937 of the 500,000-strong *Confederación Española de Sindicatos Obreros*, a *coup* which seemed to presage further advances.[23] Yet in reality the appearance of spontaneity and lack of coercion was illusory, since the coercion was obligingly applied at one remove by the military government. When it chose to do so, or rather chose not to do otherwise, the army acted as a detached guarantor of Carlist proselytization. Coercion of this kind, however, was capable of being exercised in more than one direction, against Carlism as well as on its behalf. The affair of the Royal Carlist Military Academy showed just how true this was.

The need for improved training facilities for prospective Requeté subalterns became obvious to all sections of the Carlist leadership very soon after the beginning of the war, as trained 'officers' fell in battle to be replaced by others equally zealous but markedly less expert. During the late summer, members of the National and

Navarrese War Juntas discussed the idea of instituting a Carlist military academy with each other and with Mola, who it appears approved it.[24] The creation of the Academy was eventually announced from Fal Conde's new military headquarters in Toledo on 8 December. It was to be sited in Cáceres, and would be headed by a retired artillery officer, Hermenegildo Tomé, assisted by Colonel Ortega Basso, the former *jefe* of the Madrid AET, González Gregorio, and the Sevillian Requeté commander Enrique Barrau.[25] Besides receiving all kinds of military instruction, trainees would be rigorously educated in Traditionalist ideology – by no means superfluous in view of the large number of non-Carlists now enrolled in the Requeté.

As formulated, the Academy project was almost certain to prove unacceptable to the army leadership. True, the Falange had already been allowed two small military schools, but their scale was sufficiently unambitious not to upset military susceptibilities; moreover, they were opened discreetly, in glaring contrast to the ballyhoo surrounding the foundation of the Carlist Academy.[26] In all probability the intentions behind the scheme were as innocent and patriotic as Fal Conde and Zamanillo later claimed – and as militarily justified. Although part of a long-term strategy aimed at strengthening Carlism's position within Nationalist Spain, it presented no immediate threat to Franco's ascendency. The impression conveyed, nevertheless, was that the Carlists were seeking to play up the differences between army and militia, to remove the latter from military control and possible absorption, and in short to reverse the process of the past months whereby the militias were treated as a subordinate appendage of the army. A specific point which can hardly have commended the scheme to the military command was the stated intention to produce qualified artillery officers, something hitherto unknown in the militias and which threatened to poach upon one of the regular army's most jealously guarded preserves.

What absolutely guaranteed the collapse of the Military Academy scheme was Fal Conde's characteristic decision to consult Franco only after his decree announcing its establishment had been published. Immediately, Fal Conde found himself summoned to Franco's military headquarters in Salamanca to explain his action. Arriving accompanied by Zamanillo, he was received not by the Head of State himself but by the president of his administrative junta, General Dávila, who presented him with the stark alternatives of instant exile or court-martial for what was apparently being interpreted – or more properly misinterpreted – as an attempted Carlist *coup d'état*. Before issuing this ultimatum, it later emerged, Franco had approached Rodezno and obtained his assurance that he did not favour the Academy project – at least in the terms in which it had been publicized. Now, at a hastily arranged meeting of the National War Junta presided over by Rodezno's ally, the Conde de Florida, it was agreed that in the interests of national unity Fal Conde must leave the country.[27] Perhaps the *Jefe-Delegado*'s life was also at stake; some time later Franco told the German ambassador, von Faupel, that he had seriously considered ordering Fal Conde's execution and might actually have done so but for the likely effect on front-line Red Berets.[28] Given Fal Conde's continued popularity with the Requeté, Franco's prudence was well founded; his choice of clemency was more typical of him than the consideration of execution, a step which would have been out of all proportion to the sin committed.

Within hours of the National War Junta's emergency meeting, Fal Conde was ensconced in his chosen place of exile, Lisbon's Avenida Palace Hotel, still *Jefe-Delegado* in name, but obliged to witness from a distance the accelerated revival of Rodezno's fortunes. With Fal Conde went what faint chance existed of an independent Carlist organization capable – and desirous – of resisting the ever-tightening control of Franco.

So effective was the censorship, and so complaisant most of the Carlist authorities, that the drama of Fal Conde's exile went unmentioned in the Carlist press – and for that matter the entire press of Nationalist Spain. If the Carlists at the front got to know about it, they did so only in the form of rumour or else through hearing the broadcasts of Republican radio, which vainly sought to persuade them that Franco's treatment of Fal Conde had made their efforts useless. As late as February 1937, Jesús Elizalde and two more Carlists tried to persuade the Navarrese Juntas to seek the lifting of Fal Conde's exile 'before the affair can leak out'. Unknown to them, moves had already been made. Some two weeks earlier Rodezno had led a deputation to Franco; assuring him of the Communion's utter loyalty and of their disapproval of the way in which Fal Conde had gone about the Academy scheme, they nevertheless admitted to having considered the idea of the Academy reasonable enough, and argued that the punishment of Fal Conde was excessive considering that the Falange had escaped more lightly with greater sins. Having thus demonstrated their willingness to act disinterestedly, the Carlist collaborators got the answer which they probably expected: the Head of State was not prepared to change his mind.[29]

Silence also surrounded the official vetoing of the Military Academy itself, though this was glaringly implicit in measures decisively taken by Franco to ensure army control over the militias; before the end of the year, detachments of the Requeté and Falange militia were compelled to accept junior army officers into their midst,[30] militia members belonging to the 1931 reserve were ordered to transfer to the army,[31] and a new decree was published defining the relationship between the army and militias.[32] Besides stating explicitly that the militias might not form corps of artillery – a direct blow at the dead Carlist plans – the decree brought them more closely than ever under military supervision and control, to such an extent that little independent activity would henceforth be possible. The intention to depoliticize and, as it were, 'militarize' the militias was contained in provisions for the education of militiamen in military schools, with the condition that officers qualifying by this route would then receive priority for promotion within the militias. These plans were quickly put into operation. By February 1937 an increasing number of Falangists and Red Berets were undergoing instruction not only in military techniques but also in military values,[33] while in the same month stricter limitations were imposed upon independent recruitment by the militias.[34]

In spite of the Fal Conde affair, this tightening of army control over the militias and the war effort in general was a relatively brisk and painless business, especially when seen in relation to the agonies of the parallel process in Republican Spain. The Carlists accepted it dutifully. Officially Fal Conde's functions were now exercised by Valiente and Lamamié, but the substance of power and influence was more and more reverting to those personalities with a secure base in Navarre and the Basque country. Ever since the Salamanca *coup* which gave Franco power, the Carlist press of Navarre, Álava and 'liberated' Guipúzcoa had been respectful if not exactly effusive towards him;[35] after Fal Conde's exile, even the more pro-Fal Conde *La Unión* and the Requeté's bulletin perforce carried the odd grudging reference to Franco as Spain's *caudillo*. The 19 December issue of the bulletin was the first to display the slogan, borne by *El Pensamiento Navarro* for several weeks, '*Una Patria, Un Estado,*

Un Caudillo'. The Fal Conde cult of personality did not die with his exile, however; on the contrary, it was if anything stepped up during the early months of 1937 and at times went to quite indiscreet lengths. Fal Conde was unambiguously proclaimed 'the most characteristic and genuine figure of the new Spain', while the now obligatory slogan *'Una Patria, Un Estado, Un Caudillo'* was often craftily juxtaposed with a photograph of the exiled *Jefe-Delegado.* References to Franco, in contrast, remained few, brief and as often as not tucked away on inside pages.[36] In the Requeté's bulletin, the campaign was extended to embrace Fal Conde's most loyal lieutenant and the popular leader of the Requeté, Zamanillo.[37] Evidently Fal Conde and his closest associates were not inclined to submit to Franco without a measure of indirect verbal protest.

By the beginning of 1937 the Falange had arrived at a position in some respects similar to that of the Communion. Both, within the framework of the Nationalist cause, were attempting to make the best of their own opportunities, to emphasize their own individuality, and to insinuate their particular political prescriptions into the emergent edifice of the new state. Where the more independently minded Carlists cautiously talked of the desirability of the Traditional Monarchy and the devolutionary corporate state, the Falangists respectfully offered National Syndicalism.[38] Both movements, moreover, were struggling with problems of growth and leadership. The Falange, having overtaken the Communion in terms of membership, was now a vast, amorphous party, even more ideologically confused than before July as the result of having welcomed refugees from all parts of the political spectrum into its midst. At one extreme, like the Communion, the Falange absorbed large numbers of former members of the CEDA and the JAP; unlike the Communion it also recruited ex-Socialists and Anarcho-Syndicalists who saw in it the only vehicle in Nationalist Spain capable of giving them both physical safety and the continued hope of social radicalism. More complex still was the tendency of liberal and conservative Republicans in Carlist-dominated areas such as Navarre and Logroño to join the Falange in the hope of strengthening the only political 'opposition' to Carlism.[39]

The Falange's increased power through numbers was largely cancelled out by the dearth of leadership following the loss of José Antonio, Redondo, Ruiz de Alda and Ledesma. Nominally the leadership rested with a 'temporary' junta headed by Zamanillo's friend, the one-time Carlist Manuel Hedilla. His position was challenged, however, by a faction led by Sancho Dávila, Agustín Aznar and Rafael Garcerán, and by an assortment of 'technocratic' new Falangists of mainly Alfonsist and CEDA background.[40]

At leadership level and at the front, relations between the Carlists and the Falangists remained on the whole good. This was not always so in the rearguard, where late in 1936 there erupted a series of petty but potentially dangerous clashes between rank-and-file members of the two movements. In Seville, where the two parties competed for recruits and engaged in a poster war, scuffles were frequent, culminating in a gunfight during the celebration of the Feast of the Immaculate Conception in December.[41] Relations also grew strained in and around Burgos where, as in Seville, the Falange was now indisputably the larger party. Falangists obstructed co-operation with other militias, and when Úrraca Pastor, now serving as a nurse, tried to address a meeting in Aranda de Duero, her words were drowned by whistling Falangists.[42] At the front, Red Berets and Falangists alike deplored such goings-on.[43]

In Navarre, where despite the Falange's dramatic growth the Carlists' dominance was not seriously challenged, relations were generally better. The Carlists, it is true, tended to regard the Navarrese Falange with a justified scepticism, feeling like *Diario de Navarra*'s columnist Eladio Esparza that the Falange's ideology could hardly have convinced so many Navarrese so quickly.[44] The Navarrese Falange was certainly heterodox even by the undemanding standards of that movement. Its distinctive ideological colouring was essentially the contribution of a bizarre young priest, Fermín Yzurdiaga, who founded and ran *Arriba España*, a newspaper distinguished by its extreme religiosity, its identification of Falangism with 'tradition', and its reverence for the memory of Mella, described in its columns as 'our prophet'.[45] Other, more direct references to Carlism were conspicuously few, and outwardly the two movements chose to coexist in a totally unreal atmosphere of deliberate mutual neglect. There was, however, little actual friction and, on a personal level, a great deal of amiable contact.

As both Carlists and Falange became sensitive to increased military pressure, as both movements fell prey to factionalism, and as broad mutual sympathy was imperilled by local antagonisms, the idea began to be aired in various quarters of fusing the two main civilian organizations of Nationalist Spain. Given the creation of the Headship of State, it was a logical enough step to consider building the new Spain on the foundation of the kind of 'single party' employed by Franco's allies. Few on the Nationalist side were now disposed to advocate a resumption of party politics after the war, although some liberal monarchists may have nursed the wish privately. Franco had already made it plain that his own inspiration was a 'totalitarian' one; on 6 October, mindful of the desirability of politically disarming the Carlists and Falangists, as well as of providing a single and coherent ideological justification for his crusade, he spoke to a German emissary of a possible physical union of political forces;[46] although the point is unclear, there is no reason to suppose that the idea was not the Caudillo's own. Later in the month Goicoechea urged some kind of political unity at a speech in San Sebastian, doubtless sensing that such a system might more easily be manipulated in the Alfonsist interest than one resting largely upon two large non-Alfonsist parties.[47] Around the same time, one of Hedilla's rivals within the Falange, the Sevillian Sancho Dávila, began to toy with the notion of the Falange's fusion with, or preferably absorption of the Communion.[48]

Although Fal Conde still resisted anything which smacked of a fascist-style single party and a concomitant party dictatorship, preferring to envisage the simultaneous installation of the Traditional Monarchy and withering away of all parties, not all Carlists agreed with him. Many of the confident and flexible Navarrese in particular appreciated that the nature of the Nationalist cause demanded, sooner or later, the resolution of political divisons, and that this could be achieved either spontaneously by the political parties themselves or else forcibly by Franco and his military colleagues. The first public discussion of union from either side came from this quarter. In mid-December 1936 the Carlist diplomat and writer Román Oyarzun published in *El Pensamiento Navarro* an article headed: 'An idea: REQUETÉ AND FASCIO'. Arguing that two such powerful, opposed parties could not survive in a New State, Oyarzun went on to delineate the resemblances and differences between Carlism and Falangism. Those things of which he disapproved in the Falange were mainly external features — flags, colours (the red and black of Anarcho—Syndicalism), uniforms and the use of the term 'comrade'. Against this, 'Both forces are rooted in the people; both nourish their ranks from the masses; in neither of them do great plutocratic interests hold privileged status or positions of command . . . Both forces are believers and put their trust in God.' Oyarzun suggested that it should be possible to smooth out any differences in the inter-ests of so patriotic a goal, and to reach an acceptable formula for union — especially since the probable alternative was a widening of the gap.[49]

The first response from Yzurdiaga in *Arriba España* was sur-prisingly hostile.[50] Why is uncertain, although it is logical to sup-pose that, like the Andalusian Carlists, the Falangists of Navarre feared becoming the junior element in any local fusion. No similar fear was apparent when Hedilla commented on Oyarzun's suggestion on 6 January 1937. A single organization was inevitable, he agreed, but it would come about by means of the Falange's absorbing other elements, Carlists included, and 'assimilating those points of Tradi-tionalism which are compatible with the needs of the moment'.[51] Hardly a tactful statement; this process of selective assimilation was precisely that of which Carlists habitually accused fascism, and in the Falange's case had already been partially carried out.

Hedilla's reaction illustrated how the outlook of leading Falan-gists, euphoric at their movement's expansion, differed from that of even the most fusion-minded Carlists, whose opponents within the Communion were both justified and strengthened as a result. This was only temporary, however. The idea of union refused to die quietly; the Academy crisis and Fal Conde's exile helped to clear the way in two respects: among Fal Conde's own confidants it created such dissatisfaction with Franco's leadership as to render them more amenable to Falangist overtures than would otherwise have been the case, while at the same time it improved the hand of the Carlist prag-matists under Rodezno, whose revival was daily more apparent. During the early part of 1937 numerous conversations took place between Falangist fusionists — or absorptionists — and Carlists favourable or open-minded towards union. The first approach to Rodezno came from Sancho Dávila,[52] his efforts being backed up by two rising new Falangists of Alfonsist origin, Pedro Gamero del Castillo and José Luis Escario, who themselves discussed the pos-sibility of fusion with, among others, José María Oriol, Arauz de Robles, Antonio Iturmendi and the Valencian Puigdollers.[53] Dávila, who in his own words had had 'fruitful contacts' with Fal Conde before July 1936, now wrote to him in Lisbon hinting at the attrac-tions of union, but appears to have received no direct reply.[54]

Fal Conde was nonetheless being manoeuvred into agreeing to talks. At the start of February 1937 he received a visit in Lisbon from an unknown 'senior member' of the Carlist War Junta, who afterwards wrote to Gamero informing him that Fal Conde now wished to meet Dávila as soon as possible; presumably Fal Conde had come to realize that there was no choice but to discuss the question of fusion with the Falange however little he liked the idea.[55] Gamero and Escario promptly left for Lisbon, picking up Dávila on the way, and arriving deliberately to coincide with an assembly of leading Carlists.[56] This event took place at a palace in the Portuguese village of Insua on 13 February, and brought together such figures as Fal Conde, Rodezno, Valiente, Lamamié, Arauz de Robles – all members of the National War Junta – and Martínez Berasáin, under the chairmanship of Don Javier. The purpose was to discuss the present and future position of Carlism in relation to the politics of Nationalist Spain and the country's post-war development. Perhaps because of Don Javier's presence and the fact that the assembly was held on Fal Conde's new home ground, it was their views that prevailed. Against the many reservations of those present, it was 'agreed' that the Communion should 'affirm its personality' *vis-à-vis* the Franco regime and that the question of 'installation' should ultimately be settled by institutionalizing Don Javier's Regency pending a definite decision as to the identity of the monarch. Despite this apparent success, Don Javier formed the definite impression that he and Fal Conde were in a virtual minority of two in their enthusiasm for the Regency, and that the rest of those present wanted a dynastic reconciliation which would permit the succession of Don Juan.[57] With the war now making impossible the kind of rank-and-file pressure which had led to Fal Conde's promotion and the abandonment of the pursuit of monarchist unity, the men and policies out of favour for the past three years were back again in the running.

The Carlists were thus only superficially united when discussions with the Falangist representatives began in the Avenida Palace Hotel on 16 February.[58] The Falangists opened with their suggestions for unity. These involved the Communion's entering the Falange in return for the latter's agreeing to install 'at the appropriate moment' the 'new' but Traditional Monarchy, and Don Javier's delegation of his powers to the party on the understanding that he would be consulted when the question of the throne's occupant eventually arose. The Carlists, naturally balking at what amounted to a total absorption of the Communion by the Falange and the no doubt deliberate vagueness concerning the timetable for 'installation', countered with a set of bases of their own. These were less demanding than those of the Falangists, but just as unlikely to inspire an agreement: union without absorption under a new, composite name; declarations of the monarchic principle and the pre-eminence of Traditionalist values; the supreme authority of Don Javier, with active executive powers delegated either to a single political leader or to a triumvirate consisting of heads of sections of Culture, Militia and Politics; and finally the dissolution of the single party the instant the installation of the monarchy made it unnecessary.

The Carlist proposals clearly represented the views of Fal Conde and Don Javier, and although involving some slight compromise, seemed to require the immediate acknowledgement by the Falange of Don Javier's Regency and eventual succession. Where the Falangist points called for the immediate disappearance of the independent Carlist organization in return for the dim and distant prospect of long-term 'installation', the Carlists were asking the Falange to accept the dissolution of the single party as the price of even flimsier guarantees in the way of National Syndicalism. The gap was sufficient to ensure the breakdown of negotiations, though in an amicable atmosphere and not before a minimum agreement had been reached. This stated that neither party would accept interference in their relations by a third, recognize any civilian government not monopolized by themselves, or establish alliances with other groups.

In view of the venue of the conversations and the conclusions reached by the Insua meeting, it was almost inevitable that the more inflexible line of Fal Conde and the Regent should prevail within the Carlist leadership, in as much as those like Rodezno who were less than devoted either to Don Javier or his exiled Delegate still had no alternative to accepting their authority. The moderate Carlists were not satisfied, however, and had good reason to feel that once away from Lisbon and the dead hand of Fal Conde they might yet find agreement with the Falange possible. As Don Javier feared, several of the Carlists present at Insua and at the Avenida Palace talks did continue to be tugged towards a 'Juanist' escape from the succession problem, and could hardly fail to be aware that Gamero's and Escario's background inclined them, too, towards an agreement based on a Juanist compromise. Many years later, Dávila wrote that it was the Falangists' respect for Franco and the Alfonsine branch of the royal family which made a pact with Don Javier and Fal Conde impossible.[59]

As the various participants left Lisbon, Rodezno therefore undertook to keep up contacts. When he returned to Salamanca he resumed negotiations, this time with a Falangist from Jerez, Julián Pemartín, and with Pemán acting as a kind of honest broker – further evidence of the Juanist character which the schemes for political union were now assuming. Neither Fal Conde nor Hedilla was informed of these latest talks, or of Rodezno's continuing correspondence with Escario.[60] The Carlist case for union had thus fallen completely into the hands of known sympathizers towards a dynastic settlement: Rodezno, Arellano and their supporters. Just as Rodezno had shown willingness in the past to come to terms with the Alfonsists, so now he was prepared to consider a merger with a multi-faceted Falange capable of accepting important elements of the Traditionalist creed and the eventual succession of Don Juan. In Navarre the Carlists stood to gain from any such agreement, for whatever happened in the rest of Spain, there they could rely on dominating the single party and monopolizing provincial and local government.

By March 1937 the general situation in Nationalist Spain had altered in such a way as to make Carlist–Falangist negotiations more urgent than ever. Madrid, thanks to the determined resistance of its workers and the stiffening effect of the International Brigades, had not fallen and evidently was not going to fall in the immediate future. In the north and on the Málaga front the war was going well for the Nationalists, but the end was still nowhere in sight. The case for political unity was therefore regarded as stronger than ever; friction between Carlists and Falangists and the internal differences within both movements might have their uses for Franco, but these were more than outweighed by the actual or potential damage done to the Nationalist war effort and to the desired image of patriotic unity. The idea of unification by decree, which Franco had been turning over in his mind for some considerable time, was now being encouraged by his new chief adviser, his brother-in-law Serrano Súñer. A former *cedista* who had moved on to the fringes of the Falange after the 1936 election, Serrano Súñer was imprisoned in the Republican zone at the outbreak of war, avoided a firing-squad through the intervention of Gregorio Marañón, and escaped into Nationalist territory in February 1937. Straight away he replaced

Nicolás Franco as the chief influence upon the Head of State, and took up the idea of unification with enthusiasm. Personal contacts were made with leading Falangists, Carlists and Alfonsists, including Rodezno and Hedilla, and rumours of impending unification by fiat began to circulate freely in Burgos and Salamanca.[61]

Don Javier and Fal Conde, cut off from the quickening pace of events inside Spain, were also increasingly out of tune with the feelings of large numbers of Carlists. By the middle of March a climate of crisis pervaded the entire leadership of the Communion, from the National War Junta through the Navarrese Juntas to the various provincial commissioners. The National War Junta, never fully accepted in Navarre, was now losing the confidence of many commissioners through its apparent identification with a Fal Conde whose popularity was on the decline. The true situation was rather different; the National War Junta, which had never been a particularly effective body, was simply decomposing under the pressure of recent events, and rumours were abroad that it had either resigned or was about to do so. Fal Conde's critics now decided to seize the initiative, and summoned a 'Council of Tradition' to discuss the matters dealt with at Insua and to offer a challenge to Fal Conde's faction which, it was believed, still controlled the National War Junta. On 22 March the Council, consisting initially of the commissioners of most of the Nationalist provinces – and, in exile, of Catalonia and Valencia – met in Burgos in a tense atmosphere and 'guarded' by a contingent of Navarrese Red Berets. They were soon joined by Valiente, Zamanillo and Arauz de Robles, who arrived to represent the National War Junta but not, it turned out, to obstruct proceedings. The Council began by dispatching a message of loyalty to Franco, and then went· on to discuss relations with the Falange. Valiente declared that the Lisbon talks had indicated that the Falange fundamentally accepted the Catholic state and the Traditional Monarchy, and that agreement ought to be possible through the Falange's embracing the Carlist programme within a totally new party 'with a mixed name'. Although shades of opinion varied, the Council agreed unanimously that political unity, desirable or not, was an inevitability. With Valiente and Zamanillo present, even on the sidelines, the support for Fal Conde's hard-line position was crumbling. The Council, uncertain as to whether or not the National War Junta was still in office, sent it a message urging it to resign in order to dispel any doubts in Salamanca as to the Carlists' patriotism.[62]

In the days immediately following the Council meeting, a number of commissioners began to have cold feet and wrote to Fal Conde pledging their loyalty and explaining their conduct at Burgos as the result of threats by the Navarrese Red Berets. This was all the comfort available to Fal Conde. On 29 March he received a deputation from the Burgos Council led by Martínez Berasáin, which told him of the strong support now existing for a voluntary union with the Falange. Angry words were exchanged and on the following day Fal Conde refused to see the deputation again. Instead he sent it a note protesting against the intimidation allegedly employed at Burgos.[63]

Control of the Carlist movement was slipping from Fal Conde's hands. Political circles in Nationalist Spain were agog by the beginning of April with expectation of an imminent decree of political unification. Prominent Alfonsists like Sáinz Rodríguez and José María Areilza were now taking a hand, pressing both Falangists and Carlists to unite spontaneously and offer their combined forces in a patriotic gesture to Franco.[64] Alfonsist motives were not altogether selfless, considering that a Juanist compromise might well be the only way in which a voluntary fusion could be achieved. Be that as it may, even Hedilla was gradually abandoning the view which he had so far held that talk of imminent unification from above was exaggerated. Suddenly panicked into action, he entered into conversations at Villarreal de Álava with two of the most persistent fence-sitters on the Carlist National War Junta, Lamamié and Arauz de Robles. Like Hedilla, who was supported in his attitude by many of the Falange's northern leaders, Lamamié and Arauz de Robles were unenthusiastic at the notion of union but convinced that spontaneous unification on terms broadly acceptable to the two parties was preferable to a military *diktat*. At Villarreal, Hedilla urged voluntary unification as quickly as possible; the Carlists could only agree, but insisted on consulting Don Javier and Fal Conde. It was also agreed that, in the event of a forcible unification, those present would accept no office in the single party.[65] The result of approaching Don Javier and Fal Conde was predictably negative, but the incident served to demonstrate how the Regent and his Delegate now stood virtually alone in seeing any point in resisting one or another form of union with the Falange.

The revolt within the Communion now gathered pace. On 4 April the Navarrese War Junta held an extraordinary meeting, also

attended by other prominent Navarrese including Arellano and the
latest regional Requeté leader, Esteban Ezcurra; it decided that the
incumbent national leadership of Carlism must give way to one more
in step with the views of the Burgos Council. Martínez Berasáin
and Arellano were deputed to lead a delegation to Saint-Jean de Luz
where Don Javier would be 'required' to implement the change of
leadership and accept the principle of the single party. In this way
the Navarrese hoped to use the unification issue in order to reverse
the *'coup'* of 1934. On 6 April they faced the Regent with an ultimatum. Carlism, they told him, was torn by crisis. The National
War Junta no longer enjoyed the confidence of the rank and file,
and to make matters worse certain of its members – specifically
Zamanillo, Arauz de Robles and Lamamié – were regarded unfavour-
ably at Franco's Headquarters. They, and better still the entire Junta
must be replaced. Furthermore, unification with the Falange by
government decree was imminent and the Communion had no
choice but to fall in line. Already, it seems, the Navarrese had come
to the conclusion that it was too late to achieve unification 'spontaneously'. Don Javier, who had difficulty in accepting that unification
was anything worse than a distant prospect, responded amiably
but showed signs of wishing to consult Fal Conde. He was given
eight days to decide whether to accept the Navarrese demands;
the alternative was not stated, but there could be no doubt that it
was open rebellion against the Regency.[66]

Don Javier's week of grace still had two days to run when events
took another crucial turn. Martínez Berasáin, as the official head
of Navarrese Carlism, was summoned to meet Franco on 12 April.
Sensing what was coming, Martínez Berasáin telegrammed Rodezno
in Cáceres, and accompanied by Martínez Morentín they went to
Salamanca where, as they expected, Franco informed them of the
main lines of a decree unifying the political forces of Nationalist
Spain. As in the summer of 1936, so now again the military leadership had preferred to deal directly with the flexible, realistic Navarrese rather than with the proud and prickly Fal Conde;[67] and again
the manoeuvre succeeded. News of the meeting quickly leaked out,[68]
and when the Caudillo's Carlist confidants returned to Navarre they
informed the Navarrese War Junta of what they had learned. In turn
the Junta called an assembly of all the province's leading Carlists
to discuss the terms of unification. The assembly, consisting of
around a hundred provincial and local figures, met on 16 April and

straightway learned from Rodezno that the Carlists were merely being informed and not consulted about the details of unification, which were already settled. Without much difficulty Rodezno succeeded in quashing a move to send a delegation to Franco to urge upon him the defence of Traditionalist principles; this, he argued, would be futile and possibly prejudicial to Carlist interests, besides which a purely Navarrese assembly could not claim to speak for Carlism as a whole. What it could and must do, Rodezno insisted, was send representatives to Don Javier demanding that he and Fal Conde accept the decree. This recommendation, together with Navarre's acceptance of the decree, was approved unanimously.[69]

As the meeting broke up, a group led by the Baleztenas left for Saint-Jean de Luz to inform Don Javier of the impending decree, urge his acceptance, and above all dissuade him from publishing a statement hostile to unification which he was believed to be preparing.[70] This statement remains something of a mystery. It was never published, whether thanks to the Navarrese or not, and when the Alfonsist Areilza visited Don Javier on the afternoon of 18 April, hopeful of persuading him to accept the inevitable, the Regent calmly assured him that unification was 'a remote and unlikely possibility'.[71] The decree unifying the political forces of Nationalist Spain was announced over the radio that same evening, and published the next day.

The Decree of Unification referred disingenuously to the need to avoid creating an 'artificial party' and stated that what Spain needed was 'a single national political entity, a link between state and society, guarantee of political continuity and the vital adhesion of the people to the state'. This was to be achieved through the unified organization, uncomfortably denominated the *Falange Española Tradicionalista y de las JONS* (FET), embracing not only the Falange and the Communion but also Acción Española and Renovación. All existing political organizations were declared dissolved and their militias conjoined under the direct authority of the Head of State. Franco would also be head of the single party, assisted by a Secretariat or Political Committee and a National Council. The party's programme would consist of the Falange's 'points', though an attempt was made to silence possible Carlist complaints with the assurance that these would be subject to continuous 'revision and improvement'.[72] The document bore the clear stamp of its drafter,

Serrano Súñer. Like most Falangists, José Antonio included, Serrano
Súñer was careful to pay tribute to Carlism's popular vitality and
the courage of its militants, while at the same time regarding it as too
backward-looking to serve as the basis of the modern totalitarian
state which he and Franco increasingly had in mind. As he later
wrote:

A large part of [Traditionalist] doctrine was also to be found in the
programme of the Falange, but the latter was more in tune with that
proletarian, social, in a word revolutionary concept which could permit
Nationalist Spain ideologically to absorb Red Spain. That, truth to tell,
was our overriding ambition, our essential obligation.[73]

On paper, at least, this was not much for which to surrender the
independent life of the Traditionalist Communion.

Whatever they may have felt inwardly, the Carlists of Spain
greeted the Decree of Unification with similar dutiful celebration
to that displayed by the Falangists. The rank and file in the rearguard, especially in Navarre, manifested its acceptance in street
demonstrations; juntas, *jefes* and commissioners sent letters and
telegrams of loyalty and congratulation to Franco; newspapers
editorialized over the fraternal relations of Carlists and Falangists
and the recognition of Traditionalism enshrined in the decree.[74]
Although part of this response derived from sheer prudence, much
of it was perfectly sincere, if not altogether rational. One who
refused to play his part in it, Jaime del Burgo, later described it as
'a collective psychosis' bearing no relation to the actual terms of
unification or the reasonable expectations of Carlism.[75]
At the highest levels of the Communion a variety of reactions
showed themselves. These ranged from the unqualified acceptance
of most of the leading Navarrese – Burgo was very much the exception in his province – to the almost deafening silence of Fal Conde
and Don Javier. Trapped between these equally predictable reactions
were those many Carlists who lacked the positive enthusiasm of the
Navarrese yet regarded the rigidity of the Regent and his Delegate
as an unrealistic luxury open only to exiles. This position was
epitomized by Valiente, who on the day of Unification wrote to
Don Javier resigning his post as secretary of the National War Junta
and acting head of the Communion within Spain during Fal Conde's
exile. Valiente admitted that the Unification conflicted with his

personal feelings, but argued that as something far more than a 'vulgar electoral alliance' it must be unconditionally accepted. Above all it must not be allowed to provide the occasion for a split between Navarre and the national leadership. Carlists were divided on matters of temperament and procedure, and since there was no simple means of deciding which was the correct Carlist way to behave in a complex political situation, the attitude of Navarre, which was after all the heart of Carlism, had to be respected. If the consequences of the Unification should prove harmful, then 'our Sacred Cause would always be reborn out of its own ashes'.[76] Valiente's personal acceptance of Unification was followed by that of other members of the National War Junta, among them Lamamié and Arauz de Robles. Fal Conde's closest ally, Zamanillo, demonstrated his loyalty by remaining silent and, considering his political responsibilities at an end, took the patriotic way out by enlisting in a combatant unit of the Requeté which he had done so much to create.[77]

The rewards for those Carlists most active in supporting fusion and latterly in co-operating with Franco were not long in coming. The Secretariat of the FET was named within a week of the Unification, and four of its nine members were Carlists — Rodezno, the Conde de Florida, Arellano and José María Mazón, former Commissioner of Logroño.[78] They were balanced by four Falangists; Hedilla, who had recently emerged from a leadership crisis even more acute than Carlism's with his position apparently improved, was appointed to preside over what was evidently to be a largely ceremonial body. However, he proved so firm in his adherence to the agreement made at Villarreal de Álava and consequent refusal to accept office that he was eventually arrested on a charge of military rebellion and, after a death-sentence had been commuted, was consigned to a term of life-imprisonment which actually lasted nine years.[79] Fal Conde, now *Jefe-Delegado* of what strictly speaking was a non-existent movement, was understandably passed over completely.

During the rest of 1937 Franco and Serrano Súñer pressed forward with a determined policy of 'co-ordination' on the basis of the new single party. All anterior juntas and *jefaturas* were suppressed, and Falangist and Carlist activities suspended; the *Obra Nacional Corporativa* was amalgamated with — and soon engulfed by — the Falangist workers' and employers' organizations, and Arauz de Robles removed from his position as its delegate.[80] The separate

party hierarchies were replaced by fourteen new National Delegations, a mere three of which were headed by Carlists – Health by
Benigno Oreja, brother of the murdered deputy; Hospitals and
Front-line Aid by Úrraca Pastor; and Administration by Faustino
Gaiztarro.[81] New provincial party *jefaturas* were also created, of
which Carlists occupied only eight. Valiente sealed his acceptance
of the Unification by assuming the *jefatura* of Burgos, the others
being Cárcer (Valencia), Oriol (Vizcaya), Muñoz Aguilar (Guipúzcoa), Echave Sustaeta (Álava), Herrera Tejada (Logroño) and
Garzón (Granada). Implicitly, Carlism was thus allotted a sphere
of influence based firmly upon Navarre, the Basque country and
Logroño, with only odd additional outposts in Valencia, Andalusia
and Old Castile. Carlist *jefes* were generally 'balanced' by Falangist
deputies, and *vice versa*.[82] A number of Carlists were also scattered
around the various National Councils and Inspectorates created to
run the party's affairs. Among these were Rada, who became one
of two deputy heads of the combined militia; Elizalde, who was
appointed one of the militia's two political advisers; and the veteran
columnist from the *Diario de Navarra*, Eladio Esparza, who was
named as Yzurdiaga's deputy in the propaganda section.[83] Even
allowing for the fact that many of these posts were decorative rather
than influential, the Carlists thus received considerably less than their
due in the early distribution of jobs in the single party of the New
State.

The delirium which had surrounded the Unification soon subsided,
as ordinary Carlists and Falangists came face to face with the often
uncomfortable details of 'co-ordination'. As often as not, in fact, the
process went no further than the telegrams via which it was transmitted. As *jefes* wrestled for local and provincial power with their
deputies, blind eyes were turned on the continued existence of
independent offices and organizations, breaches of the regulations
covering uniforms and insignia, and the use of sectarian termin-
ology.[84] Even among those Carlists who embraced Unification and
threw themselves into FET activities, feelings were frequently sensitive; late in 1937 Arauz de Robles, the up-and coming ex-leader of
the AET, José María Zaldívar, and two more Carlists were harshly
disciplined for inspiring a demonstration of independence by Red
Berets at an FET youth rally in Burgos in October. Zaldívar, as the
Requeté leader, was expelled from the FET and the others suspended

for one or two years. The Secretariat announced that it regarded the demonstration as an attempt to 'step backwards' from Unification, a verdict with which it is hard to disagree.[85] Even the most unqualified Carlist 'unifiers' were dissatisfied at the dominance of Falangists and Alfonsists within the FET. During the summer of 1937 they protested to Franco at the Falangists' lack of give and take, and urged, as a possible way of improving the situation, the formation of the National Council referred to in the Decree of Unification.[86] For once Franco agreed to the Carlist requests, and on 19 October 1937 the membership of the National Council of the FET was announced. It can have brought the Carlists little comfort, for out of fifty members of what in any case was unlikely to be a more powerful body than the Secretariat, only eleven were Carlists.[87] One of these was Fal Conde, whose exile was accordingly lifted. He politely declined the olive branch on the grounds, fully consistent with his past statements, that he could not accept 'the idea of the single party as the medium of national union, a base of the state and an inspiration of the government'.[88] After further entreaties had failed to persuade him to change his mind, Fal Conde was removed from the National Council of the FET in March 1938.[89]

From the Carlists' point of view, the most important aspect of the National Council's establishment was that it brought to a head the ill feeling which had been simmering between Don Javier and the Navarrese since long before the Unification. Nominally, at least, the Navarrese still recognized Don Javier's Regency. During the spring and summer of 1937 Rodezno and Arellano repeatedly tried to persuade him to approve the holding of office by Carlists within the FET, but without success. Instead Don Javier, chivvied by Fal Conde, adopted the most inconsistent and divisive course imaginable – to approve office-holding by 'reliable' figures such as Lamamié and Valiente while banning it in the majority of other cases, especially where the Navarrese were concerned.[90] When the Carlists named to the National Council swore the required oath of allegiance without his permission, Don Javier was furious. If anything, he was becoming even more intractable than Fal Conde, who in refusing to take his seat on the National Council did at least assure Franco of his loyalty. In December Don Javier entered Spain and in San Sebastian was visited by numerous Carlists, among them Rodezno, to whom he extended the chilliest of receptions. Finally he issued a note explicitly forbidding participation in the National Council and expelling from the Traditionalist Communion all those who had taken the oath of loyalty to Franco.[91] Not one of the victims took the slightest notice of their expulsion.

Having flouted Valiente's wise advice and provoked a new schism in the ranks of Carlism, Don Javier went on to offend the influential Serrano Súñer by accusing him of mistakenly erecting a police state modelled on Nazi Germany, and Franco by telling him, correctly but tactlessly, that without the Requeté he would never have risen to his present exalted position. After an ominously successful tour of the battle-fronts and of Andalusia, which suggested that by no means all combatant Carlists were happy with Unification, the Regent was ordered to leave Spain. Before doing so he had one last interview with Franco, who not unreasonably accused him of conducting a monarchist campaign during his stay in Spain. Under pressure, the Head of State admitted that the Germans and Italians were urging him to expel Don Javier. The Regent, having informed Franco that he would continue to labour on behalf of Spain but not for him, left Spain for the last time shortly before the end of the year.[92]

Behind him Don Javier left a Carlist cause whose internal divisions and general disorientation were only hidden by the veneer of the single party and the needs and censorship of wartime. For the present at least, the initiative had reverted to the collaborationists, the dominant influence within the movement to Navarre, and its *de facto* leadership to Rodezno. The most fruitful product of collaboration was Rodezno's appointment, with Arellano as his Under-Secretary, as Minister of Justice in the first full Nationalist cabinet formed in January 1938. Partnered by their old Alfonsist friend Sáinz Rodríguez at the Ministry of Education, they successfully overcame Falangist resistance and revoked all the Republic's laic legislation. With education once more firmly controlled by the Church, and an intimate Church–state relationship guaranteed, the 'Catholic Unity' which formed so central a part of the Carlist programme thus became a reality.[93] When seen in conjunction with the destruction of the left and the liberal system, the restoration of law and order, and the introduction of a New State of broadly corporativist character, this could certainly be considered more than adequate justification for Carlist participation in the war and acceptance of political unification.

Nevertheless, the cost was a high one. The thriving organization largely built up by Fal Conde disappeared, as he had feared it would do; as late as 1968 he was to write: 'Circles, press, administration, funds – we lost the lot.'[94] From the beginning of 1938 onwards, as a Nationalist victory in the Civil War drew nearer, the FET became increasingly dominated by Falangists, old and new. When the Secretariat was reconstituted in March 1938 and the provincial *jefaturas* reshuffled in May, Carlist representation was progressively reduced in favour of the Falangists and even the Alfonsists.[95] Except in the religious sphere and in Navarre, Traditionalist propaganda was swamped by the more fashionable verbiage of National Syndicalism, while Franco himself went out of his way to let monarchists of all kinds know that a restoration or installation of monarchy was at best a remote possibility.[96]

As the Civil War drew towards its successful conclusion in the spring of 1939, the great majority of Carlists lost what interest they had had in the FET's affairs and left it in droves. The one big exception was, of course, Navarre, where as anticipated their control of the party and the province was secure. For many Navarrese Carlists this, alongside the institutionalization of Catholicism and Order, made everything worthwhile. Warm in the knowledge that however the New State might evolve there would always be a Carlist Gibraltar in the north, Carlism yet again withdrew into its traditional stronghold, there to wait upon events.

Epilogue
Carlism in the Spain of Franco

In 1939 the Carlists for the first time in their movement's history ended a civil war on the winning side. Even so, this was not the final, triumphant Carlist War which some had dreamed would straightway usher in the Traditional Monarchy. Victory had to be shared with allies – Falangists, Alfonsists and political generals – who were no less eager than the Carlists to pursue their sectarian goals, while seemingly better placed to succeed. As Fal Conde had always feared would happen, Carlists were already being eased out of positions of power and influence when the war ended, and the chances of their gaining acceptance for their ideas, much less the installation of their monarchy, in the military–fascist climate of post-war Spain, were slender. It would nevertheless be over-hasty to conclude that Fal Conde's view of Carlism and its needs was correct, since some of the present problems were the result of the outlook which he represented. Monarchist fusion behind Don Juan and on a fundamentally Traditionalist platform as advocated by Rodezno could well have presented the officer corps and the Falange with serious competition; similarly, less obduracy than was displayed by Fal Conde in his pre-war and wartime dealings with the army might have encouraged warmer relations between Carlism and the military command and thus enhanced the Carlists' post-war prospects. The rival camps' conceptions of the essence and requirements of Carlism were so different as to make judgment between them a matter of definition rather than fact; suffice it to say that 'falcondian' exclusiveness, while having no chance of short-term success itself, seriously damaged what hopes existed of a fusionist policy's producing the swift installation of a Traditional if not exactly Carlist monarchy. The healthier results of Fal Conde's isolationism were much longer in showing themselves.

Post-war Spain confronted Carlism with a totally new situation: a political regime which shared many of its own attitudes, beliefs, bogeys and myths – not least the powerful myth of the 1936 'Crusade', which Carlists embraced as readily as all Nationalists – but which outside the fields of religion and anti-leftism showed little sign of wanting to apply the main *positive* elements in the Carlist programme. The position was not dissimilar to that of 1923–30, with the important difference that the Carlists' initial commitment to Franco's regime was far greater than that to Primo de Rivera. Whatever the future might hold, the Carlists' relationship with the regime could not be the simple one of complete and permanent acceptance, nor yet the straightforward one of independence and opposition habitual in the past. In the strange political setting of Franco Spain it was, in fact, a highly complex relationship, made up in perpetually shifting degrees of collaboration, self-assertion and outright opposition.

By no stretch of the imagination could the Spain which emerged from the Civil War and took shape during the early 1940s be said to conform closely to the prescriptions of Mella, Pradera and the Carlists. To begin with, of course, there was no king and little likelihood of the monarchy's return in the foreseeable future. It was 1947 before Spain's status was officially defined as that of a kingdom, and another twenty-two years before the person of the future monarch was actually identified. If the regime's form, incarnate more and more in Franco himself, left something to be desired, its content was even further from pure Traditionalism.[1] The New State developed along lines more rigidly centralized than those of any which had preceded it; although Navarre and Álava were rewarded for their contribution to the Nationalist cause with a degree of administrative autonomy, Guipúzcoa, Vizcaya and the rest of Spain were brought firmly under the kind of central control adored by soldiers and Falangists. The *fueros*, supposedly a vital part of the Carlist programme since the 1830s, were thus deader than ever before under the first governmental system of which Carlists more or less approved. Centralization of a different sort was represented by the single party which Fal Conde had honestly resisted as utterly foreign to the spirit of Carlism. Within the FET, Carlism soon became little more than a sleeping partner as Falangists, encouraged by their Secretary-General Serrano Súñer, called the tune and created a fascistic climate which survived the Second World War by several years and which most Carlists found distasteful. Like most single parties the FET of the 1940s – its heyday – was riddled with political and economic corruption, welcome to the *arrivistes* of the Falange but frowned on by the more sober Carlists.

Carlist reactions towards the new regime's shortcomings depended very much upon the individual's reception of his consolation prizes, especially in the spheres of social relations and religion. These were undeniable, but negative in terms of more sophisticated Traditionalist aspirations. Liberalism and leftism had certainly been smashed — for the time being; yet the result was a long way from the social consensus on which a harmonious Traditionalist society was likely to be rebuilt. Open class-conflict may have been largely absent in the war-weary Spain of the 1940s, but with economic hardship worse than at any time in living memory while party hacks enriched themselves, class differences stubbornly refused to go away. Likewise, while the Church was restored to its former place as overseer of education and morals, the upsurge in genuine religious faith necessary to underpin the Carlist utopia was no more in evidence than before the Civil War. For a time, especially when viewed against the horrors of the previous decade, the return of 'order' and 'religious freedom' was enough to ensure active or passive Carlist acceptance of the Franco regime. This, combined with control of Navarre and the Carlist lien on the Ministry of Justice, would always be enough for some Carlists; for others, however, the passage of time and the realization that the regime was a semi-permanent fixture made it vital to review their position, as Carlists, *vis-à-vis* a right-wing but non-Traditionalist system.

The passing of years rendered the Spain of Franco still more out of tune with Traditionalism in a further crucial respect. Perhaps the most paradoxical by-product of Carlism's commitment to the 'Crusade' was that after 1959 the Franco regime presided, not as the marxist would have it over the temporary rescue of Spanish capitalism but over its greatest and most dramatic florescence. Thus Carlism's age-old enemies — industrialism, urbanism, materialism, irreligion — advanced further and faster under the New State than under the Liberal Monarchy or the Second Republic. The architectural symbol of the new Spain was not, as the pre-war Carlists would have wished, the Church, but the bank; the country's crowded and desecrated Mediterranean coastline, the industrial tentacles creeping out from Pamplona into the once-rural districts of Navarre, the orange smog often to be seen obscuring the Catalonian monastery of Montserrat, and the building and speculation scandals of Madrid: these and kindred phenomena stood as proof that capitalism and materialism need not, after all, march in step with liberalism – a fact well known to the left but never previously grasped by Spanish Traditionalists. Thus a regime one of whose acknowledged prophets, José Antonio, had offered 'poetry' as a counterweight to material things, and whose other main civilian component, Carlism, invoked Catholic spirituality in the same cause, abandoned itself to greed and consumption. Had the Carlists of 1936 been able to foresee how difficult it would be for a regime of 'order' to resist the more tawdry aspects of 'modernism', their enthusiasm for the rising might well have been a mite dampened.

The end of the Civil War also brought a semblance of peace to the ranks of Carlism. Amid the celebration of victory, the quarrels and expulsions of 1937–8 were quietly papered over; Don Javier remained Regent, Fal Conde his *Jefe-Delegado*, but with both of them still in exile the *de facto* leadership of Spain's Carlists rested unchallengeably with Rodezno and his mainly Navarrese circle. The Unification, it now transpired, had not, except in name, put an end to Carlism as an independent political movement. The numbers and vigour of Carlism in the 1930s were such as to make loss of identity in the FET out of the question, above all when the single party was dominated by Falangists. Throughout the life of Franco's Spain, therefore, Carlism was to maintain a shadowy but definite life of its own, loyal to the 'Movement' yet grasping at independence. In 1939 no Spaniard, or perhaps only one, could predict the longevity of Franco and the regime which was to become so closely identified with him. On the assumption that the regime would be temporary – even if that might still mean years rather than months – the Carlists found themselves grappling with the old problem of installation in a quite novel setting: one in which, instead of pursuing the overthrow of the incumbent system as was their custom, they were obliged to hope for its evolution in a favourable direction. Here the old divisions within the Communion resurfaced, for while Don Javier and Fal Conde still clung to the Regency as a means whereby not only Carlism but also Franco might solve their succession problems, Rodezno and his supporters resumed their quest for a monarchist *rapprochement*.

During the first half of the Second World War the auguries for Spanish monarchists were not good. With a German victory apparently inevitable and Axis influence in Spain strong, the Falange for three years rode roughshod over its political rivals. Relations between Falangists and Carlists were particularly bad, reaching a climax in August 1942 when a Falangist grenade wounded six Carlists as they left a politically tinged religious celebration in Bilbao attended by their most powerful sympathizer: Varela, now Minister of War. Mutual recriminations and accusations of disloyalty flew around wildly; the Falangist responsible was executed and eventually both Varela and Serrano Súñer lost their posts.[2] The incident was merely the most serious outward expression of a jockeying for position inspired by a variety of hopes and fears of an end to the world war. Reacting against the Falange's pro-Axis stance, the Carlists reversed their position of 1914–18 to join the Alfonsists in siding with the Allies. In doing so the Alfonsists, though hardly the pro-Regency Carlists, could hope that an Allied victory would bring with it the elimination of the Falange, perhaps of the Franco regime itself, and a restoration of the monarchy as the least problematical of alternatives. No monarchist, it is worth pointing out, went further in fighting Nazism, or suffered more in consequence, than Don Javier. After participating in the French Resistance he was captured and spent the remainder of the war in Dachau and other concentration camps. The Spanish government made no attempt to secure his release.[3]

By throwing rival monarchists together, the Falange and its Axis patrons gave encouragement to Rodezno's hopes of a dynastic reconciliation based on a Traditionalist programme. Alfonso XIII, plagued by a failing heart, abdicated in January 1941 and died within weeks. His heir, Don Juan, quickly announced his acceptance of Traditionalist principles and from 1943 onwards was in constant correspondence with Rodezno, whose activities were unquestionably made easier to conduct by Don Javier's unhappy absence. The end of the war, though it cast Spain into diplomatic isolation, failed to bring the positive steps on the part of the victorious Allies which were needed in order to bring down Franco or at least force a restoration of the monarchy upon him. Monarchist hopes nevertheless remained high throughout the late 1940s. Don Juan moved from Switzerland to Estoril in 1946, and in April of that year received Rodezno and several like-minded Carlists with whom he discussed terms for a possible Carlist recognition of his crown.[4]

The great stumbling-block for the Carlist fusionists was, of course, the Regency, especially now that Don Javier was back in harness. The Rodezno party was in an awkward position; given a completely free hand its members would probably have preferred simply to repudiate Don Javier in favour of Don Juan, but loyalty to the memory of the late Alfonso Carlos prevented them from lightly setting aside the Regency which he had instituted. It was nevertheless a most unsatisfactory answer to the succession problem, and grew more so as time passed. Had Alfonso Carlos taken his courage in both hands and named Don Javier his heir, then the great majority of Carlists would have swallowed any misgivings and accepted him – more readily, certainly, than they would have done Don Juan. The Regency, by leaving the identity of the Carlist claimant at least theoretically unspecified, allowed Carlists to go on forming factions around prospective 'kings' – Don Javier himself, Don Juan, or even Karl Pius of Habsburg, whose *cruzadista* backers found their numbers swelling after their favourite, in 1943, at last took up his claim as 'Carlos VIII'.[5] As long as Don Javier stopped short of actually claiming the throne himself, Rodezno and the 'Juanists' were bound to pay his Regency formal deference. In the hope of breaking the deadlock, they repeatedly lobbied him to 'name an heir'. Ideally, of course, this would be Don Juan, but this was patently out of the question; were Don Javier to answer their requests and those of his own entourage by asserting his personal claim, however, then at least the 'Juanists' could feel free to reject him and go their own way.

During the late 1940s and early 1950s, a majority of the surviving Carlist leadership of the pre-war generation inclined towards accepting Don Juan, while Don Javier drew his support from Fal Conde and the predominantly ex-Integrist element who had risen in the movement with him. The underlying differences of outlook remained essentially those of the 1930s, modified by Carlism's position within the new Spain. Acceptance of Don Juan would mean that Carlism would survive as an influence within a broad monarchist movement but no longer as a separate cause; this strengthened monarchism, without offering opposition to Franco, might nevertheless provide Spain with an eventual escape route from the existing regime. As with every fusionist approach, it implied recognition of Carlism's limitations and a willingness to settle for something well short of the full Traditionalist programme. Support of the Regency – or of 'Carlos VIII' – reflected on the other hand a desire for a quite distinct Carlist movement capable of independent action in relation to the regime and, should the need arise, of opposition to it. Where the Carlist rank and file stood on the issue it is difficult to say. The Regency certainly aroused little enthusiasm, as much as anything because it *was* a Regency; at the same time, suspicion of a 'Juanist' arrangement was widespread and perhaps restrained only by the enormous prestige of Rodezno.

Friction between the two main Carlist factions, and the flat refusal of Don Javier and Fal Conde to consider recognition of Don Juan, blocked the fusionists' progress for over five years. From 1952 onwards, matters began to move towards a conclusion. In that year the death of Rodezno left the fusionist party leaderless, while Don Javier finally gave way to his supporters and announced his claim to the throne. With Rodezno out of the way, popular resistance to fusion was once again released, but to the apparent benefit of 'Carlos VIII' rather than Don Javier. In 1953, however, 'Carlos VIII', just as his prospects were beginning to look brighter, died at the early age of forty-four. With him died the Habsburg claim; apart from the handful of eccentrics who pushed the claim of Dom Duarte of Portugal, the increasing number of Carlists who looked askance at Don Juan now had only one way to turn: to Don Javier.

Following his initial claiming of the throne in 1952, Don Javier backpedalled more than somewhat, for reasons which remain a mystery. Then in May 1957 his son Hugues, now styling himself Carlos Hugo, addressed the annual rally of Carlists at Montejurra in the name of his father 'the King'. From this point onwards Don Javier's assumption of the Carlist claim was in no doubt. Its most immediate and important result was to sting the fusionists into long-delayed action. Sixty-eight leading Carlists first protested to Don Javier at his abuse – as they saw it – of the prerogatives of Regency, then left for Estoril where a preliminary agreement was made with Don Juan. Local meetings of sympathetic Carlists took place during the summer and autumn of 1957, and in December Don Juan, in return for an affirmation of Traditionalism, was recognized as sole monarchist claimant by forty-four leading Carlists, among them several prominent pre-war personalities such as Arellano, Arauz de Robles, Comín, Elizalde, Rafael Olazábal and the Conde de Florida. The 'schism' of 1937 had repeated itself after an interval of twenty years.[6]

The 'Act of Estoril' was the posthumous fruit of Rodezno's policies since 1931: that is, of willingness to abandon a separate Carlist identity in return for the assurance that the Carlist ethos would infuse any alliance which was entered into. This attitude had expressed itself in the enthusiasm for an agreement with the army in 1936, the ready acceptance of the Unification in 1937 and, on the whole, amiable collaboration with the Franco regime ever since. Strengthening Spanish monarchism in this way hinted at opposition to the Falange, but not to Franco himself; at most Rodezno and those who after his death carried out his wishes sought a way forward from the existing regime to a new one in which the spirit if not the letter of Carlist Traditionalism would govern social and political conduct. In joining Don Juan's established supporters, the Carlist fusionists moved another step closer to Franco, since their new claimant's accession was, as everyone knew, entirely dependent on the Caudillo's will. Recognition of Don Juan was not only an irrevocable decision but a risky one; many Carlists, it could not be doubted, would remain firm in their refusal to flirt with what they still considered 'liberalism', and might well be vindicated in doing so. Don Juan's 'Traditionalism' was widely believed to lie lightly upon him, while the ideological and political opportunism of his closest followers was nothing short of notorious.

During the 1960s Franco finally began to show signs of being willing to consider a restoration – after his own death. Not, however, of Don Juan who, ironically for a claimant who had been insisting on his attachment to Traditionalism since the early 1930s, was regarded by Franco as too liberal to preside over Spain's fortunes. Instead it was Don Juan's son, Juan Carlos, who in 1969 was designated 'Prince of Spain' and future king. Those Carlists who had struggled for years to persuade their movement to accept Don Juan swallowed their embarrassment and loyally accepted the Caudillo's nominee – proof of the extent of their complaisance towards the regime. Pride in their past, their family traditions and their personal sacrifices ensured that come what may they would always consider themselves Carlists, but there were many who believed that they no longer deserved the name.

The Act of Estoril cured the paralysis from which Carlism had been suffering since the Second World War, and cleared the way for the rise of a new Carlism led by the Bourbon–Parmas and supported by those who regarded acceptance of Don Juan and excessive collaboration with Franco as essentially un-Carlist behaviour. Now at last the merits of Fal Conde's defence of Carlism's independence were revealed, for had he and his faction not asserted the movement's individuality throughout the twenty years following the Unification, Carlism might well have died with the recognition of Alfonso XIII's son. In the event it re-emerged during the 1960s as a lively if minority opposition to the Franco regime.

Much of the credit for this remarkable development must go to the 'new' Carlist royal family. While the now-ageing Don Javier provided symbolic leadership, a more active role was played by Carlos Hugo, his wife, Princess Irene of the Netherlands, and his sisters, all of whom worked unflaggingly for the cause. Between them the Bourbon–Parmas provided the Carlist rank and file with a vital focus for its loyalties which had not existed since the death of Alfonso Carlos, an achievement capped in 1970 by the birth of a son and heir to Carlos Hugo and his wife. In view of Carlism's amazing powers of survival, there seems no reason to suppose that the infant Carlos Javier will not in his turn become Pretender to the Spanish throne.

Under the intelligent and flexible leadership of Carlos Hugo, a figure thought by many Spanish monarchists, not all of them Carlists, to compare favourably with Franco's nominee Juan Carlos, Carlism began to reassert itself as an independent force in Spanish politics. Without ever remotely appearing to repudiate the 'Movement' of 1936, it increasingly came to stand for a deeply felt disillusionment with the long-term results of the rising. Gradually during the late 1960s the Carlists' meetings, especially the annual Montejurra *'via crucis'* and rally, grew more euphoric and even aggressive, until clashes with the police and authorities became the regular thing. The Franco regime overreacted to the first signs of Carlist opposition, and in December 1968 expelled the entire Bourbon–Parma family from Spanish soil. This step, and the elevation of Juan Carlos a few months later, decisively alienated much of the Carlist rank and file from the regime. In the early 1970s anti-government demonstrations by Carlists proliferated; young Carlists seized radio stations and broadcast anti-Franco slogans; in the Cortes the three Carlist 'family' *procuradores* (deputies) were among the most resolute critics of the government; and it became conventional for Carlists to describe themselves as an opposition force.[7]

These developments suggest that significant changes must have been occurring within the bosom of the Carlist movement, and such indeed was the case. Having survived the two post-war decades as a junior partner in the Nationalist alliance, Carlism had by now given birth to yet another generation of loyalists. The members of this new generation, however, while raised like their forebears in staunchly Carlist homes and almost automatically accepting the broad validity of the Carlist tradition, nevertheless inevitably interpreted their inheritance in relation not to a long-dead Republic but to an omnipresent repressive apparatus with which they could in no way identify. Since many of the 1930s generation of leading Carlists had either recognized Don Juan or, like an ailing Fal Conde, finally retired into private life, it was this younger element, personified by Carlos Hugo himself, which gave the new Carlism much of its drive.

The Spain in which the Carlists of the 1960s and 1970s found themselves was another world from that of the 1930s or the immediate post-war period: a Spain in which an apparently immovable authoritarian government presided over headlong economic and social transformation, bringing with it an unprecedented materialism and rampant americanization. Living standards for most Spaniards had risen sharply, but class divisions remained wide and open social conflict was reappearing with the revival of left-wing opposition. The old Falange's influence had declined, and the political reins were now held by 'technocrats', many connected with the Catholic lay organization *Opus Dei*. These and associated developments held little attraction for those raised as Carlists, who were now subject to an unaccustomed emotion – that of total disillusionment with a cause to whose success they or their fathers had contributed. In this situation, so different from the usual one in which Carlism's prime enemies were liberalism and the left, the cause did not necessarily cease to possess relevance or purpose; rather, through grappling with new antagonists, certain aspects of its heritage and programme gained enormously in importance over others – so much so that in a short space of time the movement's whole appearance was revolutionized. In the new Carlism, the monarchy retained its pivotal role, but in the form of 'popular' or 'people's' monarchy, emphasis now being placed upon the direct, intimate bond between king and subjects rather than the detailed apparatus of the Traditional Monarchy as depicted by Mella and Pradera. The position of religion altered too, just as the Spanish Church itself was adopting a more independent attitude towards the regime and displaying conspicuous guilt-feelings regarding its defence of privilege in the 1930s. The Spanish Church of the pre-Civil War era, while giving little active encouragement to Carlism, had been of such a nature as to fit comfortably into the Carlist frame of reference; that of the 1960s and 1970s had changed so much that a Carlism founded on narrowness and intolerance was no longer possible. As a result, social-Catholicism at long last began to be taken very seriously within a movement which had previously used it as a largely empty formula.

In short, the Carlism which developed in the years after 1960 was being spurred by its intensifying antagonism towards an authoritarian, oligarchic regime of the right into doing what in the 1930s and before it had been unable to do: throw off its ideological shackles and, by staking everything on its undeniably vital popular tradition, re-form into the kind of radical–populist movement once vaguely envisaged by the students of *a.e.t.* With the Falange institutionalized and no longer truly 'popular', and the left still hemmed in by restrictions, Carlism's relative freedom of action as a partner in the 'Movement' gave it a unique opportunity to pose as a vehicle for otherwise diffuse protest against the repressiveness, centralism and materialism of the Franco regime. By the mid-1970s Carlism was almost unrecognizable as the reactionary movement of the 1930s. Beneath a capacious populist umbrella, held by Carlos Hugo and in many respects resembling a strange, monarchist cousin of Peronism, there was room for Carlists who held firmly to Traditionalism, Carlists who openly proclaimed their atheism, Carlists who worked hand-in-hand with Communists in the illegal Workers Commissions, Carlists who flirted with the revolutionary Basque Nationalists of ETA, and not least self-styled 'Carlist Marxist-Leninists'. If nothing else these extraordinary developments, whose future it would obviously be foolhardy to attempt to predict, testify to the continued strength of that popular tradition which has perhaps always been Carlism's most outstanding feature, a strand so powerful that it appears able to jettison the ideological trappings of a century and still consider itself Carlist.

Since the chief concern of this book has been the Carlists' conduct under the Second Republic, it is perhaps fitting to end with a graphic illustration of how Carlists born since the Civil War now regard the regime which their fathers fought to destroy – and that by which it was replaced:

The fourteenth of April could have represented the day of the People's liberation, but it was frustrated because there was no Revolution to put an end to bourgeois structures. Only the form changed. It is the People who must democratically decide their constitution and government, through the Revolution which will cast from power the privileged caste which tyrannizes us. This ruling caste is attempting to impose on us a system for ensuring the continuity and survival of capitalism and francoism, using violence and repression against a People fighting for their freedom.

This is why we say: NO to the monarchy of Franco! NO to the monarchy of Juan Carlos! NO to the capitalist–Opus monarchy in the service of the Yanks!

NEITHER MONARCHY NOR REPUBLIC IMPOSED FROM ABOVE! NEITHER MONARCHY NOR REPUBLIC OF A TOTALITARIAN CHARACTER!

THE PEOPLE WITH THEIR REVOLUTION WILL DECIDE.[8]

Under the Franco regime, which owed so much to the Carlism of conservatism, the Carlism of protest has been reborn.

Appendix
The Carlist succession

The assumption of the Carlist claim to the Spanish throne by the childless octogenarian Alfonso Carlos in 1931 created an acute and barely soluble problem regarding the Carlist succession. Involved in the tortuous debates on the subject were varying interpretations of the Salic Law, as well as of the so-called 'principle of dual legitimacy', whereby a Carlist claimant, and *ipso facto* a legitimate king of Spain, must accept the postulates of Traditionalism and behave in conformity with them as well as being legitimate in terms of blood. The following is an attempt briefly to clarify a question about which whole books have been written. Attention is drawn to the accompanying genealogical table.

1   The Alfonsist claim

The Alfonsist claim to 'succeed' Alfonso Carlos as Carlist claimant was paradoxically based upon that same strict interpretation of the Salic Law which the Carlists had originally used in their attempts to exclude Isabella II. Thus viewed, even assuming the Carlist claim to have been valid, the claim reverted upon the extinction of the Carlist male line to the direct descendants of Francisco de Paula, younger brother of Ferdinand VII and Carlos V. Since Francisco de Paula's eldest son, Francisco de Asís, had married Isabella II, these descendants were none other than the Alfonsine branch.

Although this argument was genealogically sound, Carlist critics opposed it on the grounds that both the Isabelline and De Paula branches of the Spanish Bourbons were permanently disqualified from the succession as a punishment for their past liberalism; a further black mark against Alfonso XIII and his sons was the highly doubtful paternity of Alfonso XII, which placed in question their very descent from Francisco de Paula. Advocates of a dynastic reconciliation preferred to slide over this last point, while arguing that 'legitimacy of conduct' might yet be established were Alfonso XIII or Don Juan to swear loyalty to Traditionalist principles.

The exclusion of the descendants of Francisco de Paula by virtue of the family's alleged liberalism also affected the Dukes of Seville, a Bourbon line descended from Francisco de Paula's younger brother; the Carlists also considered this line to be unacceptable because of a number of 'unequal marriages', that is marriages with commoners, the issue of which were regarded as automatically ineligible for the throne.

2   The claim of Karl Pius of Habsburg

The *El Cruzado Español* schismatics, as well as some loyal Carlists such as Lizarza, contended that the Spanish succession was governed not by the Salic Law but by a 'semi-Salic' Law, according to which a claim might be transmitted by, but not reside in, a female. On Alfonso Carlos' death the Carlist claim was thus considered to pass through his niece and Don Jaime's sister, Doña Blanca, to her sons by Archduke Leopold of Habsburg–Tuscany. His elders being excluded through divorce, 'unequal marriage' or sheer lack of inclination, it was Doña Blanca's youngest son, Karl Pius, who was boosted as 'Carlos VIII' by the *cruzadistas*. This solution to the long-anticipated succession problem was apparently first suggested by Mella, with Don Jaime's acquiescence, as early as 1914.

3   The Bourbon–Parma claim

Given certain preconditions, none of which were unreasonable by Carlist standards, the Bourbon–Parma claim was stronger than its many critics allowed. Accepting both the full Salic Law and the disqualification of the 'liberal' Alfonsines and Sevilles, only two of the branches of the House of Bourbon could offer a better *prima facie* claim: the descendants of Don Gabriel, youngest son of Carlos III, and the Bourbons of Naples. The former line, however, had been defiled at several points by 'unequal marriage' and was now on the verge of extinction itself. The Neapolitan Bourbons were suspect on the same grounds as well as on account of their closeness to and double intermarriage with the Alfonsines. This admittedly draconic process of elimination left the Bourbon–Parmas.

Although attention tended to focus on the Bourbon–Parmas' position as nephews-by-marriage of both Alfonso Carlos and, through his marriage to their aunt, the eponymous Margarita, of Carlos VII, this was not their only claim nor their strongest. Nor was that through the marriage of their great-great-grandfather Luigi to María Luisa, youngest sister of Ferdinand VII: even according to the 'semi-Salic' Law, this claim was inferior to that both of Doña Blanca's progeny and of the Portuguese Braganzas, who descended from María Luisa's elder sister. Indeed, a few Carlists, Larramendi for example, actually upheld the claim of Dom Duarte Nuño of Bra-

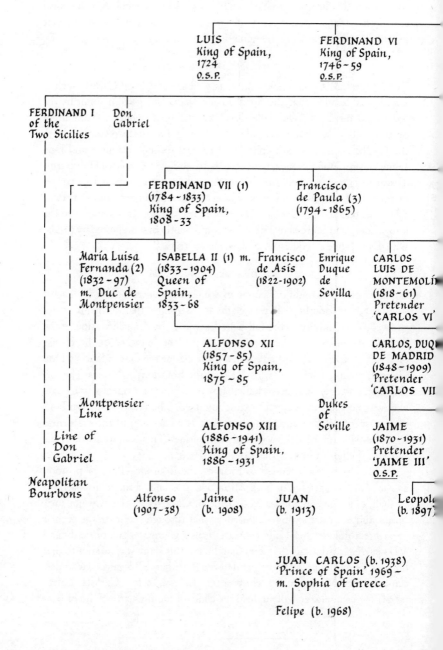

LUIS
King of Spain,
1724
O.S.P.

FERDINAND VI
King of Spain,
1746-59
O.S.P.

FERDINAND I
of the
Two Sicilies

Don
Gabriel

FERDINAND VII (1)
(1784-1833)
King of Spain,
1808-33

Francisco
de Paula (3)
(1794-1865)

María Luisa
Fernanda (2)
(1832-97)
m. Duc de
Montpensier

ISABELLA II (1) m.
(1833-1904)
Queen of
Spain,
1833-68

Francisco
de Asís
(1822-1902)

Enrique
Duque
de
Sevilla

CARLOS
LUIS DE
MONTEMOLÍ
(1818-61)
Pretender
'CARLOS VI'

ALFONSO XII
(1857-85)
King of Spain,
1875-85

CARLOS, DUQ
DE MADRID
(1848-1909)
Pretender
'CARLOS VII'

Montpensier
Line

Line of
Don
Gabriel

ALFONSO XIII
(1886-1941)
King of Spain,
1886-1931

Dukes
of
Seville

JAIME
(1870-1931)
Pretender
'JAIME III'
O.S.P.

Neapolitan
Bourbons

Alfonso
(1907-38)

Jaime
(b. 1908)

JUAN
(b. 1913)

Leopol
(b. 1897)

JUAN CARLOS (b. 1938)
'Prince of Spain' 1969 –
m. Sophia of Greece

Felipe (b. 1968)

Appendix

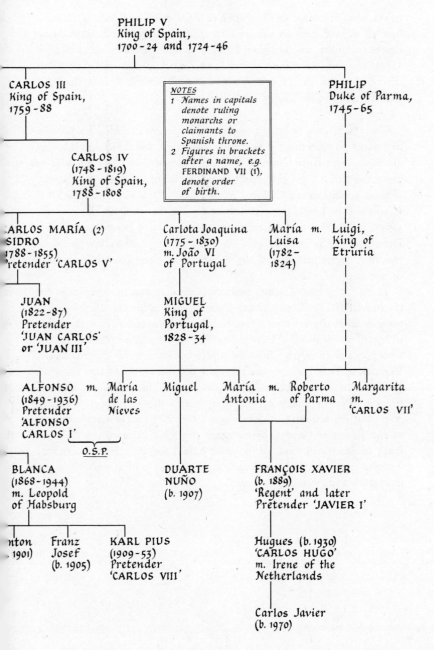

ganza, also Pretender to the throne of Portugal. The Bourbon—Parmas' best claim, and perhaps the least mentioned, derived from their being descended in the male line from Philip, Duke of Parma, brother of Carlos III. It was this line of descent which, after the ruthless process of exclusion described above, gave the Bourbon—Parmas a serious, if far from indisputable, claim to the Carlist succession.

There was thus no easy answer to the succession riddle. By holding to a purist position that the Salic Law was sacred, that the issue of 'unequal marriages' was barred from the succession, and that liberalism was an inexpiable sin, a valid case could be made out for the Bourbon—Parmas. If these conditions were relaxed to the extent of invoking the 'semi-Salic' Law, then the best claim was unquestionably that of Doña Blanca's offspring, followed at a considerable distance by that of Dom Duarte Nuño. Defence of the Salic Law combined with a willingness to allow the expiation of a liberal past opened the succession to a repentant Alfonso XIII or to one of his sons.

In so far as most Carlists probably supported one or other claim for reasons far removed from abstract genealogical argument, all these positions demanded an element of sophistry and compromise. It is reasonable to regard the 'semi-Salic' Law as largely a contrivance employed by those who opposed equally an Alfonsist *rapprochement* and the Integrist-tinged Regency of Don Javier, while the most dubious aspect of the 'fusionist' case was the degree of repentance to be expected from Alfonso XIII and his sons. Perhaps the most surprising feature of the eventual 'solution' arrived at by Alfonso Carlos was that a better defence was never offered of the Bourbon—Parmas' by-no-means negligible combination of legitimacy of descent in terms of the strict Salic Law, disinclination towards 'unequal marriage', and outstanding legitimacy of conduct throughout the nineteenth and twentieth centuries.

Notes

Chapter 1: A classic form of counter-revolution

1 On the fall of the Liberal Monarchy, see Raymond Carr, *Spain 1808–1939* (Oxford, 1966), 591–602.

2 *El Correo Catalán* (Barcelona), 15 April 1931.

3 *El Siglo Futuro* (Madrid), 14 April 1931 (hereafter *SF*).

4 *El Cruzado Español* (Madrid), 24 April 1931 (hereafter *CE*).

5 Richard Herr, *The Eighteenth Century Revolution in Spain* (Princeton, 1958), 201–35; C. C. Noel, 'The Clerical Confrontation with the Enlightenment in Spain', *European Studies Review*, v, 2 (April 1975).

6 On the rising against the French and the War of Independence, see Gabriel Lovett, *Napoleon and the Birth of Modern Spain*, 2 vols. (New York, 1965); *La Guerra de Independencia española y los sitios de Zaragoza*, a symposium (Zaragoza, 1958); and Carr, *Spain*, 106–10.

7 F. Suárez Verdaguer, *La crisis política del Antiguo Régimen en España (1800–1840)* (Madrid, 1950) provides a neo-Traditionalist interpretation of this ideological conflict; see also Carlos Corona Baratech, *Revolución y reacción en el reinado de Carlos IV* (Madrid, 1957). For discussion of early liberalism, see A. Elorza, *La ideología liberal en la Ilustración española* (Madrid, 1970) and M. Artola, *Los orígenes de la España contemporánea* (Madrid, 1959).

8 Suárez Verdaguer, *Crisis política*, 88–100; María del Carmen Pintos Vieites, *La Política de Fernando VII entre 1814 y 1820* (Pamplona, 1958), 94–100.

9 J. L. Comellas, *Los realistas en el trienio constitucional* (Pamplona, 1963) and Rafael Gambra, *La primera guerra civil de España (1821–23)* (Madrid, 1950) deal with this period. The best contemporary accounts are: 'J. M. y R.', *Memorias para la historia de la última guerra civil de España*, 2 vols. (Barcelona, 1826) and F. Galli, *Memorias sobre la guerra de Cataluña en los años 1822 y 1823*, tr. D. E. P. (Barcelona, 1835). The possible links between Don Carlos and the early royalist bands are traced in J. del Moral Ruiz, 'Sociedades secretas "apostólicas" y partidas "realistas" en el trienio constitucional', in M. Tuñón de Lara et al., *Sociedad, política y cultura en la España de los siglos XIX–XX* (Madrid, 1973), 21–32.

10 J. Torras Elías, *La guerra de los Agraviados* (Barcelona, 1967), *passim*.

11 F. Suárez, *Los sucesos de La Granja* (Madrid, 1951) describes this hectic and complicated period in great detail.

12 Román Oyarzun, *Historia del Carlismo* (Bilbao, 1939 and Madrid, 1969) is a single-volume narrative history of Carlism; on a vaster scale but still

narrative, M. Ferrer et al., *Historia del Tradicionalismo español*, 30 vols. (Seville, 1941–58).

13 Sources on the Carlist pretenders include: Conde de Rodezno, *Carlos VII, Duque de Madrid*, 3rd ed. (Madrid, 1944) and *La princesa de Beira y los hijos de Don Carlos* (Santander, 1938); Theo Aronson, *Royal Vendetta* (London, 1966); F. M. de Melgar, *Veinte años con Don Carlos* (Madrid, 1940) and *Don Jaime, el Príncipe caballero* (Madrid, 1932).

14 J. N. Schumacher S.J., 'Integrism', *Catholic Historical Review*, XLVIII (1962), 344–63; Stanley G. Payne 'Spain', in H. Rogger and E. Weber (eds.) *The European Right. A Historical Profile* (London, 1965); R. M. Blinkhorn, 'Ideology and Schism in Spanish Traditionalism, 1874–1931', *Iberian Studies*, I, 1 (Spring 1972); Marcial Solana, *El tradicionalismo político español y la ciencia hispana* (Madrid, 1951), 17–28.

15 On Mella's schism, see Blinkhorn, 'Ideology and Schism'; Melgar, *Príncipe caballero*, 205–8; and F. M. de Melgar, *El noble final de la escisión dinástica* (Madrid, 1964), 62–5.

16 There being no remotely adequate socio-economic analysis of nineteenth-century Carlism, the section which follows draws on a mass of largely peripheral works too numerous to mention, and more specifically on materials in the Archivo Histórico Nacional of Madrid, Sección de Consejos and Sección del Estado. For brief studies of the socio-economic background to Carlism, see Gerald Brenan, *The Spanish Labyrinth*, 3rd ed. (Cambridge, 1962), 87–101, and Carr, *Spain*, 1–37.

17 Recent research is at last proving the importance of artisans to nineteenth-century Carlism. Outstanding in this regard is the work by Julio Aróstegui, *El carlismo alavés y la guerra civil de 1870–1876* (Vitoria, 1970), which reveals the extent to which artisans in Álava left towns to join the guer-rillas. *AHN*, Estado, Leg. 8128 contains numerous lists of Carlist exiles petitioning Spanish consuls in France for permission to return to Spain during the 1850s; the lists contain a remarkably high proportion of artisans – though it must be borne in mind that this class was more liable to be forced into exile than were members of farming families.

18 Brenan, *Spanish Labyrinth*, 97. Like the rest of his book, Brenan's short section (203–14) on Carlism is full of illuminating insights.

19 J. Fontana, *La quiebra de la monarquía absoluta* (Barcelona, 1971) is primarily concerned with the social and economic crises of the years 1814–20.

20 *AHN*, Consejos, Leg. 12206, 12217.

21 On Basque society and culture, see J. Caro Baroja, *Los vascos* (Madrid, 1971) and Rodney Gallop, *A Book of the Basques* (London, 1930); on landholding in the Basque–Navarrese region, Brenan, *Spanish Labyrinth*, 95–7. R. Rodríguez Garraza, *Navarra de Reino a provincia (1828–1841)* (Pamplona, 1968), deals with Navarrese politics during Carlism's early years.

22 C. Seco Serrano, *Tríptico carlista* (Barcelona, 1973), 123–56.

23 For a selection of the writings of Donoso Cortés, see Juan Donoso Cortés, *Textos políticos* (Madrid, 1954).

24 Antonio Aparisi y Guijarro, *En defensa de la libertad* (ed. S. Galindo

Herrero) (Madrid, 1957) is an interesting anthology of his writings and speeches.

25 Oyarzun, *Historia del Carlismo* (1939 ed.), 533; Melgar, *Veinte años con Don Carlos*, 151; A. Pirala, *España y la Regencia. Anales de diez y seis años*, (1885–1902) II (Madrid, 1904–7), 113–14.

26 Juan Vázquez de Mella, *Política tradicionalista*, II (Madrid, 1932), 3.

27 *Ibid.* 83–5.

28 Solana, *El tradicionalismo político español*, 74, 82; Juan Vázquez de Mella, *Ideario*, II (Madrid & Barcelona, 1931), 376–77.

29 Mella, *Ideario*, I, 343–6; II, 377.

30 *Ibid.* I, 9–13, 87; II, 379–80.

31 *Ibid.* II, 380–2.

32 Mella, *Política tradicionalista*, II, 7–9.

33 Mella, *Ideario*, I, 287–8.

34 *Ibid.* III, 178–9.

35 *Ibid.* III, 162–3, 179.

36 M. García Venero, *Historia del nacionalismo vasco (1793–1936)* (Madrid, 1945), 222–3, 244–5, 267; Arturo Campión, *Discursos políticos y literarios* (Pamplona, 1907), *passim*.

37 Campión, *Discursos*, 225–78.

38 García Venero, *Nacionalismo vasco*, 235–9, 261, 269–70.

39 Mella, *Ideario*, III, 296–304.

40 Juan Vázquez de Mella, *Regionalismo y monarquía* (ed. S. Galindo Herrero) Madrid, 1957), 68–74, 107–11, 138–42.

41 Payne, 'Spain', in Rogger and Weber, *European Right*, 181.

42 Mella, *Ideario*, III, 316–21.

43 *Ibid.* III, 328–9.

44 'Acto de Loredán', in Carlos de Borbón y de Austria Este, *Escritos políticos de Carlos VII*, (ed. M. Ferrer) (Madrid, 1957), 224–6.

45 Edgar Holt, *The Carlist Wars in Spain* (London, 1967) gives a lively account of the wars, mainly the First.

46 Stanley G. Payne, *Politics and the Military in Modern Spain* (Stanford and London, 1967), 5–43, and E. Christiansen, *The Origins of Military Power in Spain, 1800–1854* (Oxford, 1967), *passim*, deal with the army's development into a 'liberal' body.

47 I. Romero Raizábal, *El Carlismo en el Vaticano* (Santander, 1968), 84–5, describes the role of the Papal Nuncio, Cardinal Rampolla, in preparing the Spanish Church for Alfonso XII's restoration and reducing Carlist influence within it.

48 'Manifiesto de Pau', in Ferrer (ed.), *Escritos políticos de Carlos VII*, 224–6.

49 M. Fernández Almagro, *Historia política de la España contemporánea*, II, (Madrid, 1959), 39; Pirala, *Anales*, II, 170; E. Ortiz de Zárate, *Políticos... en cuadrilla y el partido carlista* (Madrid, 1898), 60; Tirso de Olazábal, *Don Jaime en España* (Bilbao, 1895), 191. For details of the Carlist organization immediately before Cerralbo's reforms, see 'D. F. de P. O.' (Francisco de Paula Oller), *Álbum de personajes carlistas con sus biografías* (Barcelona, 1887–90), I, 144–53.

50 M. Martínez Cuadrado, *Elecciones y partidos políticos de España (1868–*

1931), II (Madrid, 1969), 882–921. Martínez Cuadrado's estimates appear to err on the low side; Ortiz de Zárate (*Políticos . . . en cuadrilla*, 56) wrote of 11 Carlist deputies in, presumably, 1894, while a figure of 12 appears in *Biblioteca Popular Carlista* (Barcelona), May 1896. Any discrepancies can probably be explained in terms of differing attribution of independent 'Catholic' deputies. On Carlism's involvement in *Solidaridad Catalana*, see S. Canals, *La Solidaridad Catalana* (Madrid, 1907), 26–7, and Martínez Cuadrado, *Elecciones*, II, 946–7.

51 Martínez Cuadrado, *Elecciones*, II, 946–73, 982–96. The rough geographical strength of Carlism in the 1899–1914 period is revealed in the *Boletín de Orientación Tradicionalista* (Madrid) (hereafter *BOT*), 11 November 1934, which shows that during these years all Carlist deputies were returned from Navarre, the Basque provinces, Catalonia, the Levant, Mallorca and the Leonese province of Palencia. Occasional Integrists were elected in other areas such as Salamanca and western Andalusia.

52 Stanley G. Payne, 'Catalan and Basque Nationalism', *Journal of Contemporary History* VI, 1 (January 1971), 20, appears to agree with this view; for a general study of Catalanism, see M. García Venero, *Historia del nacionalismo catalán (1793–1936)* (Madrid, 1944).

53 Campión, *Discursos*, 35–47; García Venero, *Nacionalismo vasco*, 227–8; Fernández Almagro, *España contemporánea*, I, 374–5.

54 In the national election of 1918, the PNV for the first time returned more deputies than the Carlists in the Basque–Navarrese region. This was, however, mainly the result of overwhelming strength in Vizcaya (Martínez Cuadrado, *Elecciones*, II, 972–3).

55 Carr, *Spain*, 186.

56 O. Alzaga Villaamil, *La primera democracia cristiana en España* (Barcelona, 1973), 129–131, 149–152 and *passim*.

57 M. Fernández Almagro, *Historia del reinado de Alfonso XIII* (Barcelona, 1934), 155–6; Carr, *Spain*, 487–9. For a biography of Maura, see D. Sevilla Andrés, *Antonio Maura: la revolución desde arriba* (Barcelona, 1954).

58 M. García Venero, *Víctor Pradera. Guerrillero de la unidad* (Madrid, 1943), 93.

59 C. F. Henningsen, *A Twelve Months' Campaign with Zumalacárregui* (London, 1836) remains not only the most revealing study of Zumalacárregui but also one of the best on the First Carlist War as a whole. On Cabrera, see Román Oyarzun, *Vida de Ramón Cabrera y las guerras carlistas* (Barcelona, 1961).

60 'Cataluña autónoma. Los carlistas en acción', *El Correo Catalán* (Barcelona), 26 & 29 April 1931.

61 Mella, *Política tradicionalista*, II, 10.

62 *Ibid.* II, 67–8.

63 Ferrer (ed.), *Escritos políticos de Carlos VII*, 221.

64 Melgar, *Veinte años con Don Carlos*, 216.

65 Mella, *Ideario*, I, 335–9.

66 J. E. Casariego, *La verdad del tradicionalismo* (Madrid, 1940), 235–6; L. Redondo and J. de Zavala, *El Requeté (la Tradición no muere)*, 2nd ed. (Barcelona, 1957), 211–12.

67 Gabriel Maura Gamazo, *Bosquejo histórico de la dictadura* (Madrid, 1930), 33.
68 García Venero, *Víctor Pradera*, 67–8, 145–6.
69 Mella, *Ideario*, I, 279.

Chapter 2: The Vaticanist Gibraltar

1 *CE*, 1 May 1931.
2 *SF*, 14, 16 & 17 April 1931.
3 *El Pensamiento Navarro* (Pamplona), 16 April 1931 (hereafter *PN*).
4 *CE*, 17 April 1931.
5 Although until October 1931 Carlism was more properly Jaimism, the former term has been preferred in this chapter save where it is crucial to perceive the distinction between Jaimism and Integrism or Mellism.
6 *El Correo Catalán*, 16 April 1931; J. Arrarás Iribarren (ed.), *Historia de la segunda República española* (Madrid, 1956–68), I, 64 (hereafter *HSRE*).
7 *CE*, 1 May 1931.
8 The relevant results appeared in *PN*, 13 April 1931; *SF*, 14 April 1931; *El Debate* (Madrid), 14 April 1931. The figures given by S. Galindo Herrero, *Los partidos monárquicos bajo la segunda República*, 2nd ed. (Madrid, 1956), 70–2, are incomplete. Exact details of local elections during the 1930s are virtually impossible to arrive at owing to the imprecise nature of party and coalition labels, especially on the right.
9 In Pamplona there were ten Jaimists out of 17 'anti-revolutionaries'; the Republicans won 12 and the PNV, going it alone, 3. In Vitoria 13 assorted Traditionalists dominated the victorious coalition of 19 councillors. Large numbers of Carlists were also returned in the villages and small towns of the region. Of the Basque provinces only Vizcaya, thanks to its capital Bilbao, saw both a Republican victory and a decisive success for the PNV.
10 *PN*, 22 April 1931.
11 *CE*, 1 May 1931.
12 *SF*, 6 May 1931.
13 Anthony Rhodes, *The Vatican in the Age of the Dictators, 1922–1945* (London, 1973), 117; José M. Sánchez, *Reform and Reaction. The Politico-Religious Background of the Spanish Civil War* (Chapel Hill, 1962), 80–8.
14 *SF*, 12, 13 & 14 May 1931; *PN*, 12 & 19 May 1931.
15 *SF*, 9, 22 & 23 May, 17 June 1931.
16 *PN*, 25 May 1931; *SF* 25 & 28 May 1931.
17 *PN*, 28 April 1931.
18 *SF*, 4 May 1931. The definition was admittedly a broad one which could include CNT-inspired unrest most unlikely to be connected in any way with the Soviet Union.
19 *SF*, 8 & 10 June 1931.
20 R. Sierra Bustamante, *Euzkadi* (Madrid, 1941), 123.
21 *PN*, 21 & 25 April, 1 May 1931; *Diario de Navarra* (Pamplona), 24 & 25 April 1931; D. de Arrese, *El País Vasco y las Constituyentes de la segunda República* (Madrid, 1932), 12–13.
22 *PN*, 25 & 26 April 1931.

23 J. A. de Agiŕe Lekube (= Aguirre Lecube), *Entre la libertad y la revolución 1930–1935: la verdad de un lustro en el País Vasco* (Bilbao, 1935), 35, 45–6.
24 *PN*, 7 June 1931, published the text of the proposals.
25 *PN*, 9 & 10 June 1931.
26 Aguirre, *Entre la libertad*, 59; *Diario de Navarra*, 13 June 1931.
27 *CE*, 19 June 1931; *PN*, 11 June 1931.
28 Aguirre, *Entre la libertad*, 56–8.
29 *La Voz de Navarra* (Pamplona), 8 June 1931.
30 *PN*, 9 & 18 April, 2 June 1931.
31 *SF*, 10 June 1931; Aguirre, *Entre la libertad*, 60–1.
32 Aguirre, *Entre la libertad*, 61–3.
33 *SF*, 15 June 1931; *PN*, 16 June 1931.
34 *PN*, 16 June 1931.
35 *SF*, 16 June 1931.
36 *El Socialista* (Madrid), 16 June 1931.
37 *CE*, 1 May 1931.
38 *SF*, 22 & 29 April, 6 June 1931.
39 *PN*, 19 June 1931.
40 *SF*, 27 & 29 April 1931; Arrarás, *HSRE*, I, 68–9.
41 Galindo Herrero, *Los partidos*, 52; M. Fernández Almagro, *Historia de la República española (1931–1936)* (Madrid, 1940), 81.
42 *La Unión* (Seville), 5 & 19 May 1931.
43 *La Unión*, 6 May 1931.
44 *SF*, 9 May, 3 & 6 June 1931.
45 *SF*, 3 June 1931.
46 *SF*, 15 & 22 June 1931.
47 *PN*, 19 June 1931.
48 *SF*, 3 & 18 June 1931.
49 *La Voz de Navarra*, 30 & 31 May 1931; *PN*, 2 June 1931.
50 *PN*, 23 June 1931.
51 *El Correo Catalán*, 20 June 1931.
52 *El Correo Catalán*, 25 & 27 June 1931.
53 *La Unión*, 17 June 1931.
54 Complaints were frequent (e.g. in *SF*, 23 & 27 June 1931) not so much that censorship was making electioneering difficult as that Republican crowds were breaking up meetings. This certainly happened to members of other right-of-centre parties, and there is no reason to suppose that Carlist complaints were groundless.
55 *PN*, 26 June 1931; *SF*, 27 June 1931.
56 *PN*, 21 June 1931.
57 *SF*, 18 June 1931.
58 *PN*, 24 June 1931; *El Correo Catalán*, 28 June 1931.
59 *Manifiesto de Hernando Larramendi* (Madrid), June 1931.
60 Throughout the Second Republic, seats in the Cortes were distributed within each provincial constituency according to a 'majority and minority' system. This reserved the greater number (usually between two-thirds and four-fifths) of the seats at stake for the party or alliance of parties heading

the poll, and the remainder for the leading runner-up. In each case a minimum proportion of the votes cast was necessary, failure to achieve this meaning the repeat of the election two weeks after the main round. It was this provision which encouraged parties to group together in order to avoid splitting the vote.

61 The right won 5 out of 7 seats in Navarre; 4 out of 6 in Guipúzcoa; and all 3 in Vizcaya-Province (Bilbao was a separate constituency). In Álava, which sent only 2 deputies to the Cortes, Oriol came a close second to the Republican candidate and took the 'minority' seat. Only in Bilbao was there a clear Republican win, and even there 2 Basque Nationalists took the 'minority' seats (*PN*, 30 June 1931; *El Debate*, 30 June 1931).

62 *El Debate*, 30 June, 1, 2 & 3 July 1931; *SF*, 30 June 1931; *PN*, 30 June 1931; *El Correo Catalán*, 30 June 1931; *La Unión*, 30 June 1931; *El Sol* (Madrid), 30 June, 1, 2 & 3 July 1931.

63 *CE*, 3 July 1931.

64 Arrese, *El País Vasco y las constituyentes*, 53–65. Arrese was secretary to the Basque–Navarrese group in the Constituent Cortes, and the editor of Oriol's newspaper *Heraldo Alavés* (Vitoria).

65 *SF*, 11 & 17 July, 1 August 1931.

66 *SF*, 14 July 1931; Aguirre, *Entre la libertad*, 99–106.

67 *SF*, 15 July 1931. The choice of Beunza represented an attempt to hold the Carlists and Basque Nationalists together. The Carlists probably would not have willingly followed a Basque Nationalist, nor the Basque Nationalists Rodezno, given his ambivalence towards autonomy. Beunza, a member of the Society for Basque Studies, was sufficiently keen on the Statute to be acceptable to the Basque Nationalists; as he himself put it, he represented 'the point of convergence between the heterogeneous elements' in the group (*Diario de sesiones de las Cortes Costituyentes*, 29 July 1931 [hereafter *DSCC*]).

68 *SF*, 15 July 1931.

69 A. Ossorio y Gallardo, *Mis memorias* (Buenos Aires, 1946), 189–99.

70 *SF*, 6, 9 & 13 July 1931.

71 *SF*, 27 July 1931. On the composition of the committee, see L. Jiménez de Asúa, *Proceso histórico de la constitución de la República española* (Madrid, 1932), 166.

72 Gabriel Jackson, *The Spanish Republic and the Civil War* (1931–1939) (Princeton, 1965), 43–4.

73 *SF*, 25 July 1931.

74 *DSCC*, 28 July 1931 (Beunza), 29 July 1931 (Estévanez).

75 *DSCC*, 29 July 1931.

76 *DSCC*, 10 September 1931 (Estévanez).

77 *DSCC*, 30 July 1931 (Beunza).

78 Sánchez, *Reform and Reaction*, 117–19.

79 Arrarás, *HSRE*, I, 132–3; Jackson, *Spanish Republic*, 73.

80 *Reacción* (Barcelona), 25 July 1931; *El Correo Catalán*, 15 & 26 July 1931.

81 *El Correo Catalán*, 4 August 1931. Also *Reacción*, 8 August 1931 and *Joventut* (Valls), 4 August 1931.

82   *El Correo Catalán*, 4 August, 5, 15 & 16 September 1931.
83   Aguirre, *Entre la libertad*, 183.
84   *PN*, 26 July, 11 August 1931. The figures for Navarre were:

    For a Basque–Navarrese Statute   304,351
    For a Navarrese Statute   2,808
    For regional autonomy   2,561
    Against any Statute   30,290

The *pueblos* hostile to any Statute, mostly left-wing-dominated towns and villages in the Navarrese *ribera* (the Ebro valley), were Armañanzas, Cabanillas, Caparroso, Fitero, Isaba, Jaurrieta, Larraga, Lodosa, Mélida, Mendavia, Mendaya, Peralta, Sartaguda, Torres del Río and Urdiáin. The subsequent vote on the Statute of Estella was 172,026 to 147,977 – a majority of 24,049 and not, as claimed by Aguirre (*Entre la libertad*, 112) 30,000.

85   *DSCC*, 30 July 1931 (Ansó); *SF*, 25 August 1931.
86   *SF*, 22 & 24 August 1931.
87   *SF*, 25 & 26 August 1931. *El Siglo Futuro* continued to appear throughout this period, but suffered a six-week suspension beginning on 10 September.
88   *SF*, 22 August 1931.
89   A. Lizarza Iribarren, *Memorias de la conspiración. Como se preparó en Navarra la Cruzada, 1931–1936* (Pamplona, 1953), 16–17; Jaime del Burgo Torres, *Requetés en Navarra antes del Alzamiento* (San Sebastian, 1939), 14, and interview with the author, Pamplona, 1966.
90   Lizarza, *Conspiración*, 16; Redondo and Zavala, *El Requeté*, 235.
91   J. Arrarás Iribarren (ed.), *Historia de la Cruzada española*, I–4 (Madrid, 1939–40), 486 (hereafter *HCE*).
92   Aguirre, *Entre la libertad*, 150–60; Arrarás, *HSRE*, I, 181–3; Sierra Bustamente, *Euzkadi*, 120, 124–30.
93   Payne, *Politics and the Military*, 280.
94   *PN*, 19 September 1931; Aguirre, *Entre la libertad*, 133. The Temporary Committees, particularly that of Navarre, were just as discouraging. The Navarrese Committee said that the time for presentation would not be ripe until the Statute had been approved by a plebiscite like that of Catalonia.
95   *DSCC*, 25 & 26 September 1931.
96   Aguirre, *Entre la libertad*, 179–80.
97   *Voto particular* of Leizaola and Gil Robles to Article 42, *DSCC*, 20 August 1931, Appendix.
98   *DSCC*, 6 October 1931.
99   *DSCC*, 10 October 1931 (Beunza).
100   *DSCC*, 13 October 1931.
101   *SF*, 27 October 1931. The attribution of the withdrawal to Lamamié's initiative appears in *SF*, 21 November 1931 and *El Debate*, 1 November 1931.
102   *PN*, 21 October 1931.
103   Arrarás, *HSRE*, I, 197.
104   *SF*, 1 December 1931.
105   *PN*, 20 November 1931.
106   *SF*, 23 December 1931.

Chapter 3: The national arena

1 *PN*, 22 December 1931. According to Aguirre (*Entre la libertad*, 189) there was 'nothing else to do' or, as *La Voz de Navarra* put it (23 December 1931), since the Temporary Committees were going to do the job whether the PNV liked it or not, and since the Basques would have to accept the result or nothing, it was better to collaborate in order to make the new Statute as palatable as possible.

2 *SF*, 4 November 1931.

3 *Reacción*, 14 November 1931.

4 *SF*, 9 December 1931.

5 Galindo Herrero, *Los partidos*, 115–16; Arrarás, *HCE*, I–4, 486.

6 L. M. Ansón Oliart, *Acción Española* (Madrid, 1960), 48–9.

7 For a more detailed examination of this process, see Chapter 6.

8 From, for example, the president of the Juventud Monárquica of Valladolid (*Tradición Vasca* (San Sebastian), 23 August 1931) and a member of that of Valencia (*Reacción*, 29 August 1931).

9 J. A. Ansaldo, *¿ Para qué . . . ? (De Alfonso XIII a Juan III)* (Buenos Aires, 1951), 22.

10 A fuller discussion of the succession problem can be found in the appendix.

11 F. Melgar, *El noble final de la escisión dinástica*, 105–6.

12 *Ibid.* 108; J. Danvila Rivera, 'Datos para la historia', *ABC* (Madrid), 20 July 1954 (hereafter 'Datos').

13 This, it should be stated, is Melgar's view, though no authority is given for it (Melgar, *El noble final de la escisión dinástica*, 109).

14 Galindo Herrero, *Los partidos*, 117–18.

15 J. M. Lamamié de Clairac, 'Notas para la historia de la segunda República. Negociaciones e intentos de pactos entre las dos ramas dinásticas', *Informaciones* (Madrid), 7–8 July 1954 (hereafter 'Negociaciones'); Danvila, 'Datos'; Melgar, *El noble final de la escisión dinástica*, 110, 114–15.

16 Melgar, *El noble final de la escisión dinástica*, 116–17.

17 No firm explanation can be given for the apparent abandonment of an agreement signed only two weeks before. Danvila states that Alfonso very soon realized that the Carlists were as yet unlikely to accept any member of his family as Don Jaime's heir. Melgar, the Pretender's secretary, argues that the pact 'could never have been effective' and it seems probable that he and other prominent Jaimists not previously consulted advised Don Jaime, after his arrival in Paris, against pursuing the points of the 12 September agreement any further. See Danvila, 'Datos' and Melgar, *El noble final de la escisión dinástica*, 110.

18 Melgar, *El noble final de la escisión dinástica*, 118. The Bourbon–Parma princes were related in four distinct ways to the Carlist branch of the Spanish royal house, a fact of some importance in the succession question. See appendix.

19 Alfonso Carlos to F. de P. Oller, 1 December 1931, Alfonso Carlos de Borbón y de Austria Este, *Documentos*, ed. Melchor Ferrer, 170 (hereafter *DAC*). The title 'Alfonso XII' would have implied that both Alfonso XII

and Alfonso XIII were illegitimate monarchs; that of 'Alfonso XIV' would, of course, have amounted to recognizing that legitimacy. The addition of the name 'Carlos' had the additional attraction of allowing his followers to resume the term 'Carlist'.

20 · Both Lamamié and Galindo Herrero (*Los partidos*, 122–3) assume that Alfonso Carlos was referring in this message to the details of the Territet pact. However, there is no evidence that he was as yet aware of the pact's contents, as distinct from its existence. In his letter to Oller, cited above, Alfonso Carlos mentioned the pact of 12 September with approval, but clearly assumed its provisions to be identical with the vague pieties of the press statements of 25–26 September. For example he referred to its signatories' determination to 'save Spain from Communism', an intention explicitly included in the press statements but not in the Territet pact. That Alfonso Carlos would not have welcomed the pact had he not been thus confused is shown by Lamamié's description of his reaction when informed of its details.

21 Alfonso Carlos to Oller, 1 December 1931, *DAC*, 171–2.

22 *SF*, 30 October, 17 November 1931.

23 *SF*, 10, 12 & 18 November, 15 & 18 December 1931; *PN*, 8, 9 & 10 December 1931.

24 *PN*, 8 & 12 January 1932.

25 *PN*, 2 February 1932. Olazábal was rewarded by being appointed to the position of second-in-command of the important Provincial Junta of Guipúzcoa (*PN*, 3 January 1932).

26 *Reacción*, 27 February 1932; *SF*, 20 February 1932.

27 *SF*, 8 April 1932.

28 *SF*, 2 November 1931.

29 *SF*, 29 April 1932.

30 *SF*, 18 November 1931; 7 January, 15, 18 & 24 March, 4, 5 & 6 April 1932. A similar degree of expansion occurred in the third Levantine province of Alicante.

31 *SF*, 21 November, 1 & 12 December 1931, 19 January 1932.

32 In Godojos (Zaragoza), four of the eight junta members, including the president and vice-president, came from the Castejón family (*SF*, 14 April 1932); the case of Málaga was even more noteworthy, for here the local junta was headed by Carlos Huelín while his three sons ran the provincial organization. In the words of a surviving member of the Huelín family, Carlism in Málaga was 'a family concern' (interview with Srta María Teresa Huelín, Málaga, 1966). Newly formed local juntas normally had from six to eight members, or rather more in the cities.

33 Fernando Contreras was named regional *jefe* of Jaén in January 1932 (*SF*, 22 February 1932), and the amount of activity in Jaén during the Traditionalist Week of March testifies to his energy. When a provincial *jefe* was appointed to assist him in June, *El Siglo Futuro* (14 June 1932) claimed that 'most villages' in Jaén now had circles. Although this was a gross exaggeration many local juntas had been formed, and a number of circles, e.g. at Villacarrillo. Contreras' brother Ramón in Granada and Alvear in Córdoba had less success as yet in expanding beyond their respective pro-

vincial capitals, but greater achievement was registered in Seville and Cádiz.

34 This conclusion is drawn from a mass of particular cases published in the Carlist press during 1931–3; in particular from descriptions of local organizations and their activities and preoccupations, lists of juntas and the occupations of their members, statements by Carlist speakers etc. As sociological analysis this is admittedly impressionistic, unquantified and unsatisfactory, but in the absence of harder information it must serve.

35 *Reacción*, 11 June 1932.

36 Sometimes referred to also as *Agrupación Estudiantil Tradicionalista*, the AET was founded early in 1930 upon the recognition of the moribundity of the old *Agrupación Estudiantil Católica*. Until the coming of the Republic it included not only Traditionalists but 'all who could call themselves anti-Republicans' (D. Jato, *La rebelión de los estudiantes (Apuntes para la historia del alegre SEU)* (Madrid, 1953), 41).

37 Except in Navarre, Red Berets had little to do at this stage save act as guards of honour at meetings. See *SF*, 17 November 1931 for one of many such instances, in this case at Orihuela (Alicante).

38 *SF*, 4 January, 18 February, 12 April, 5 June, 28 July 1932.

39 *SF*, 26 March–5 April, 4–7 May 1932.

40 See below, pp. 87–8.

41 *PN*, 19, 20, 21 & 22 January 1932.

42 *PN*, 20, 21 & 23 April 1932.

43 *SF*, 5, 6 & 7 April 1932.

44 *PN*, 16 & 22 March, 28 June 1932; *SF*, 8 January, 21 & 28 March, 4 April, 20 June 1932; *Reacción*, 25 June 1932.

45 *SF*, 21 January, 5 April 1932; *PN*, 20 April 1932.

46 *SF*, 20 April 1932.

47 E.g. in Valencia (*SF*, 19 February), Granada (*SF*, 3 March), Jerez (*La Unión*, 30 March), Cádiz (*SF*, 28 April), Madrid and Salamanca (*SF*, 8 July).

48 *SF*, 13 January 1932; *PN*, 3 March 1932.

49 *SF*, 12 March, 17 June 1932.

50 *PN*, 19 & 26 January 1932.

51 *PN*, 20 April, 29 May 1932; *SF*, 14 & 16 June 1932. Similar cases of detention were reported from Barcelona (*Reacción*, 16 September 1932) and Haro (*SF*, 13 June 1932).

52 *DSCC*, 29 January 1932 (Lamamié).

53 *DSCC*, 2 February 1932 (Beunza).

54 *PN*, 12 February 1932; *SF*, 6 & 10 February 1932.

55 During the early months of the Republic, Civil Guard incursions into Casas del Pueblo and violence against left-wing meetings was widespread throughout large areas of Andalusia and Extremadura, leading on occasions to loss of life. I owe the confirmation of what had previously been only a suspicion to my research student Raymond Steele, who is currently studying this and related questions.

56 *Criterio* (Madrid), 10 January 1932. (*Criterio* was a review edited by the veteran Hernando Larramendi.) Also *Reacción*, 9 January 1932; *PN*, 2 & 3 January 1932.

57 *SF*, 2 January 1932.
58 *DSCC*, 5 January 1932 (Beunza).
59 E.g. in San Sebastian (*SF*, 8 January 1932) and Valencia (*SF*, 12 January 1932).
60 For a detailed discussion of the bill's terms, the Cortes debate, and the final Act see Edward E. Malefakis, *Agrarian Reform and Peasant Revolution in Spain* (New Haven, 1970), 196–235.
61 *SF*, 10 & 18 May 1932.
62 *PN*, 15 July 1932.
63 *DSCC*, 7 June 1932 (Estévanez), 23 July 1932 (Lamamié and Rodezno).
64 *PN*, 22 March 1932.
65 *Reacción*, 30 January 1932.
66 *Reacción*, 21 May 1932.
67 *SF*, 18 May 1932.
68 *PN*, 19 July 1932.
69 *PN*, 2 February 1932. Most outright opposition continued to come from left-dominated *pueblos* in the Ebro valley.
70 Aguirre, *Entre la libertad*, 194–5; *PN*, 27 & 28 February, 9 March 1932.
71 *PN*, 26 April 1932.
72 *La Constancia* (San Sebastian), 7 January 1932.
73 *PN*, 29 May 1932.
74 *PN*, 17 June 1932. Rodezno now believed that Navarre had erred in opting for the 'Single Statute', and not its own Statute, in January.
75 *La Constancia*, 13 May 1932; *SF*, 17 June 1932; Aguirre, *Entre la libertad*, 234–5.
76 Aguirre, *Entre la libertad*, 235–6.
77 *PN* & *SF*, 18 June 1932.
78 Aguirre, *Entre la libertad*, 267–8.
79 *PN*, 21 June 1932. See also Aguirre's account (Aguirre, *Entre la libertad*, 269–87).
80 *La Voz de Navarra*, 21, 22 & 23 June 1932.
81 Aguirre, *Entre la libertad*, 289–95.
82 The discussion which follows is pursued in greater detail in my article '"The Basque Ulster"; Navarre and the Basque Autonomy question under the Spanish Second Republic', *Historical Journal* XVII, 3, (September 1974).
83 Aguirre, *Entre la libertad*, 297–8.
84 *SF*, 28 June 1932.
85 *PN*, 28 June 1932.
86 *PN*, 24 June 1932.
87 *SF*, 2 August 1932; *PN*, 2 August 1932; Aguirre, *Entre la libertad*, 302–3.
88 *PN*, 27 & 28 July 1932.
89 *PN*, 10 July 1932.
90 *PN*, 29 July 1932; Aguirre, *Entre la libertad*, 308–15. The Bishop of Vitoria cleared the PNV of any such complicity, but it was over a year before his statement was made public.
91 *PN*, 6 July 1932.
92 Discrepancies exist between the account given of these talks by Galindo

Herrero in the first edition of *Los partidos* ((Madrid, 1954), 66) and that of Lamamié, as regards both their personnel and their significance. Galindo claims that there existed an official committee of negotiation, created by the two claimants and consisting of Esteban Bilbao, Rafael Olazábal, Luis Zuazola, Gómez Pujadas and Senante for the Communion, and Vallellano, the Marqueses de Albayda and Cartagena, Quiñones de León and Julio Danvila for the Alfonsists. Lamamié's version in 'Negociaciones' is based primarily upon the evidence of Senante and appears the more convincing. He asserts that the committee had no formal existence, that the personnel changed from one day to the next and were different from Galindo's, and that 'no pact was either prepared or signed' though Alfonso Carlos was present for part of the time. Yet it seems unlikely, given the propensity of those involved to draft agreements at the slightest opportunity, that the 'pact' did not exist in some form. Probably it was drafted but not signed – and it was certainly never circulated. In his second edition (Madrid, 1956, 135–6) Galindo adds Lamamié's account without commenting or attempting to reconcile the differences.

93 Melgar, *El noble final de la escisión dinástica*, 122–3; Arrarás, *HCE*, 1–4, 460–1 gives the full text of Alfonso Carlos' manifesto, which was drafted by Rodezno. Also Galindo Herrero (*Los partidos*, 2nd ed.) 143–5. Alfonso XIII's manifesto was drawn up by Vallellano.

94 Melgar, *El noble final de la escisión dinástica*, 123–6. Melgar, keen as he is to stress the common ground between Alfonso Carlos and Alfonso XIII, points out that the latter's refusal to cease regarding himself as king was the main barrier preventing an accommodation. He was, Melgar states, ignorant of 'the state of monarchist opinion' within Spain.

95 Lamamié, 'Negociaciones', and Melgar, *El noble final de la escisión dinástica*, 127–8. Both are Carlist accounts but intrinsically plausible, especially given Melgar's subsequent acceptance of Don Juan's leadership.

96 According to D. Luis Arellano, at this time a young *protégé* of Rodezno, 'absolutely everyone knew' (interview with the author, Pamplona, 1966); see also J. del Burgo, *Conspiración y guerra civil* (Madrid & Barcelona, 1970), 329.

97 Sáenz's reason for resigning was initially given as 'ill health'; the true reason was not made public until April (*PN*, 25 February 1932; *CE*, 5 April 1932).

98 Burgo, *Conspiración*, 339.

99 *SF*, 26 February 1932.

100 J. Cora y Lira, *Estudios jurídicos, históricos y políticos. El futuro caudillo de la Tradición española* (Madrid, 1932).

101 Burgo, *Conspiración*, 388.

102 *SF*, 2 May 1932. The expulsion was dated 11 April – an example of the delays usual between the issuing and publication of the National Junta's official declarations.

103 *CE*, 26 April 1932.

104 *SF*, 7 April 1932; *CE*, 17 May 1932.

105 Burgo, *Conspiración*, 350.

106 *CE*, 15 & 26 April 1932; *SF*, 8 April 1932. The three concerned were the *jefe señorial* of Álava and the provincial *jefes* of Granada and Málaga. The last two were replaced by Ramón Contreras and Ricardo Huelín respectively.

107 *CE*, 21 June 1932; *SF*, 8 April 1932. The centre in Madrid was actually described as 'Radical Carlist'.

108 Burgo, *Conspiración*, 351–4.

109 One more attempt at dynastic reconciliation was in fact made in autumn 1932, but it was a modest and somewhat desperate affair, and came even less close to success than the earlier attempts.

110 *El Debate*, 15 February 1932; *SF*, 22 February, 28 April 1932; *La Unión*, 11, 26, 29 & 31 March 1932.

111 Arrarás, *HCE*, I–4, 486–90; Arrarás, *HSRE*, I, 435–8.

112 Arrarás, *HCE*, I–4, 489. As the discussion which follows will show, the authors' use of the word 'collaboration' to apply to the attitude of Rodezno and other prominent Carlists is acceptable if held to imply discussion, exchange of information and general sympathy, but not if implying combined pursuit of a common end.

113 Arrarás, *HCE*, I–4, 489–90. During 1932 police in Navarre carried out repeated searches of Carlist meeting places and private houses, often unsuccessfully but on other occasions unearthing large quantities of weapons, ammunition and explosives (*SF*, 13 January, 19 April, 16 June 1932).

114 Arrarás, *HCE*, I–4, 489. This official account is again vague. The Catalonian Carlists are described as having been 'in complete agreement' with the conspirators. So, in principle, they no doubt were, but hardly to the extent of joining, for the reasons stated above.

115 *Reacción*, 16 & 23 July 1932.

116 E. Esteban-Infantes, *General Sanjurjo* (Barcelona, 1957), 191; J. Romano, *Sanjurjo, el caballero del valor* (Madrid, 1940), 128.

117 Ansaldo, *¿Para qué...?*, 36–7.

118 This is the figure given in Arrarás, *HCE* (1–4, 493). After the rising Sanjurjo was actually asked why he had not called on the Navarrese Carlists and replied that he was informed that they were insufficiently armed to be a dependable force. This was, of course, true, and neither question nor answer seems compatible with the alleged promise of Navarrese aid (Romano, *Sanjurjo*, 194–5).

119 *PN*, 1 & 8 June 1932. The two reports apparently appeared in *La Prensa* of San Sebastian, but I have been unable to verify this.

120 For further discussion of Ledesma, Redondo and Spanish fascism see Chapters 4 and 7.

121 E. Esteban-Infantes, *La sublevación del general Sanjurjo, relatada por su ayudante*, 2nd ed. (Madrid, 1933), 31–2; Arrarás, *HCE*, I–4, 493.

122 J. I. Luca de Tena, *Mis amigos muertos* (Barcelona, 1971), 80.

123 Arrarás, *HSRE*, I, 475.

124 Ansaldo, *¿Para qué...?*, 41.

125 Burgo, in interview with the author, Pamplona, 1966.

126 *La Unión*'s evening edition was the only newspaper in Seville to publish a detailed and uncensored account of the day's events – under the headline 'Spain has need of all her sons and issues this day a call to provide the nation

with healthier institutions' (L. de Taxonera, *10 agosto 1932. Madrid: Sevilla: perfiles de un episodio histórico* (Madrid, 1933), 145, 154). (The relevant issue of *La Unión* is missing from the run consulted in the Hemeroteca Municipal of Madrid.)

127 The figure is that of Redondo and Zavala (*El Requeté*, 242). At this time it was usual in Seville and the other Andalusian cities to import Red Berets from the Madrid AET for major meetings, a practice which ceased as the Andalusian Requeté expanded after 1933.

128 Arrarás, *HSRE*, I, 452.

129 Arrarás, *HCE*, 1–4, 525.

130 *PN*, 17 September, 18 October 1932; *SF*, I, 3, 8 & 17 October 1932; *Reacción*, 12 November 1932.

131 Circles were closed in, for example, Molina de Segura, Villacarrillo, Valencia and Olot (*SF*, 20 & 27 September, 1 & 28 October 1932); Carlist property and circles were attacked by crowds in Seville and Granada (*SF*, 22 September 1932; Arrarás, *HCE*, 1–4, 589).

132 'Anonymous' (Luis Bolín, F. R. de Bertodano y Wilson, M. del Moral and Douglas Jerrold), *The Spanish Republic* (London, 1933), 44.

133 *PN*, 12 October 1932; *DSCC*, 17 & 18 August 1932.

134 *PN*, 18 September 1932; Arrarás, *HSRE*, I, 510n1.

135 *SF*, 24 September 1932.

136 *SF*, 7 October 1932.

Chapter 4: Rivals on the right

1 *PN*, 10 September 1932.

2 *El Observador* (Seville), 20 November 1932; *SF*, 12 October 1932.

3 Galindo Herrero, *Los partidos*, 158–9.

4 *PN*, 7 December 1932, 27 July 1933; *SF*, 10 December 1932.

5 *La Unión*, 3, 6, 8 & 26 December 1932; *El Observador*, 29 January 1933.

6 *DSCC*, 15 February 1933 (Rodezno).

7 *La Unión*, 3 April 1933.

8 The Communion's press and deputies protested vigorously but in vain against the use of a decrepit and insanitary vessel, the *España No. 5*, to transport the prisoners, as well as against the unconstitutionality of deporting anyone more than 250 km from his place of residence (*SF*, 20, 24 & 27 September, 8 & 14 October 1932; *DSCC*, 28 December 1932 (Lamamié)). *El Siglo Futuro* carried a regular diary reporting in minute and stultifying detail on life in the penal colony; the series was later published as a book: see Antonio Cano Sánchez-Pastor, *Cautivos en las arenas* (Madrid, 1933).

9 *DAC*, 199; F. García de Vinuesa, *De Madrid a Lisboa por Villa Cisneros* (Madrid, 1933), 253–4.

10 A. Coll, *Memorias de un deportado* (Madrid, 1933), 180, 218; *El Observador*, 24 December 1932, 29 January 1933; *La Unión*, 19 January 1933.

11 *DAC*, 207.

12 J. M. Pemán y Pemartín, *Un soldado en la historia. Vida del capitán general Varela* (Cádiz, 1954), 121–31.

13 *Ibid.* 242–4.
14 Ansaldo, *¿Para qué . . .?*, 47–8.
15 J. M. Gil Robles, *Spain in Chains* (New York, 1937), 1.
16 For a summary of the assembly's discussions see R. A. H. Robinson, *The Origins of Franco's Spain* (Newton Abbot, 1970), 107–9.
17 On Casas Viejas, see Jackson, *Spanish Republic,* 101–2. An interesting recent analysis of the situation in Casas Viejas itself is given by Gérard Brey and Jacques Maurice, 'Casas-Viejas: réformisme et anarchisme en Andalousie (1870–1933), *Le Mouvement Social*, 83, (April–June 1973).
18 *Reacción,* 14 January 1933; *SF*, 12 & 13 January 1933; *La Unión,* 12 January 1933.
19 *El Observador*, 2 April 1933.
20 *La Unión*, 25 February 1933.
21 *SF*, 10, 11 & 16 February 1933.
22 Luis Lucía Lucía, *En estas horas de transición hacia una política de principios cristianos, de afirmación de soberanías sociales y de preocupación por las realidades regionales* (Valencia, 1930).
23 Arrarás, *HSRE*, II, 145.
24 Paul Preston, 'The "Moderate" Right and the Undermining of the Second Republic in Spain, 1931–1933', *European Studies Review* III, 4 (October 1973), 369–94; also Robinson, *Origins of Franco's Spain,* 113–17. Detailed consideration of the relationship between CEDA ideology and policies and that of Carlism will be found in Chapter 6.
25 *SF*, 27 December 1932. Unfortunately *El Siglo Futuro* failed to report what the other nine allegedly were.
26 Information concerning the sociological composition of the CEDA's support is as scanty as for most Spanish political parties in this period. Robinson (*Origins of Franco's Spain*) has little to say on the subject, but see p. 116; rather more information appears in the article by Paul Preston referred to above.
27 *SF*, 15 November 1932.
28 *SF*, 29 December 1932, 11 January 1933.
29 E.g. reports of speeches by Rodezno (*SF*, 18 January; *PN*, 16 March), Lamamié (*SF*, 30 January, 27 March), Bilbao (*SF*, 30 January, 22 February), Oreja (*PN*, 22 April) and Fal Conde (*La Unión*, 7 February; *PN*, 4 July).
30 *Reacción,* 7 January 1933.
31 *PN*, 16 March 1933.
32 *PN*, 22 March 1933.
33 *SF*, 6 February 1933.
34 *El Observador*, 14 May 1933.
35 *SF*, 25 February 1933.
36 *El Observador*, 14 May 1933; *La Unión*, 15 May, 27 June, 19 July 1933.
37 *PN*, 16 August 1933.
38 *PN*, 16 March 1933.
39 *El Observador*, 9 July 1933.
40 Arrarás, *HSRE*, II, 117; Jackson, *Spanish Republic,* 104. Interpretations of these results, as of all elections during the Republic, differ widely. Jackson,

for example, stresses the Republican majority, Arrarás that of the anti-governmental parties.

41 *PN*, 26 April 1933.

42 *SF*, 3 June 1933.

43 *SF*, 6 June 1933.

44 *El Observador*, 16 July 1933.

45 On the Rural Leases Bill see Malefakis, *Agrarian Reform and Peasant Revolution*, 269–73.

46 *SF*, 27 June, 17 & 30 August 1933.

47 In a pamphlet, *La Confederación Española de Derechas Autónomas*, which he published in Valencia in 1933, Lucía declared his belief that these two parties, which in many respects resembled the DRV, were in fundamental agreement with the CEDA though not attached to it.

48 *SF*, 28 October 1932; *Reacción*, 12 November 1932.

49 *Reacción*, 19 November 1933; *SF*, 15 & 16 November 1933; *PN*, 20 November 1933.

50 See *SF*, 22 November 1933 for the most complete results.

51 *Reacción*, 26 November 1933.

52 *PN*, 26 October 1932.

53 *PN*, 27 October 1932. Ironically, the original promoters of the idea of a Navarrese Statute, Aizpún and Gortari, were now abandoning it in favour of special status for Navarre within a single Basque–Navarrese Statute (*PN*, 4 October 1932).

54 *PN*, 23 September 1932.

55 *PN*, 19 & 29 October, 8 December 1932; Arrarás, *HSRE*, II, 18. The committee was to consist of four Republicans, three Basque Nationalists, two members of the minute Acción Nacionalista Vasca, and two Carlists. The Carlists' complaint that this underestimated their strength while grotesquely flattering that of the Republican parties and ANV was amply vindicated by the local and national election results of 1933 (see below, pp. 115, 122–3).

56 *SF*, 6 November 1933. Oriol later claimed that the true figure was actually between 23% and 25% but that the results were falsified (*SF*, 8 June 1934).

57 *PN*, 26 July, 26 October 1933.

58 J. M. Gil Robles, *No fue posible la paz* (Barcelona, 1968), 84–5.

59 *PN*, 20 December 1932.

60 *SF*, 19 December 1932.

61 Gil Robles, *No fue posible la paz*, 86.

62 *PN*, 11 & 12 January 1933.

63 Arrarás, *HSRE*, II, 135.

64 No precise date has been published for the formal creation of Renovación Española, but references to its existence appeared in the press early in February.

65 See below, Chapter 6.

66 Gil Robles, *No fue posible la paz*, 85–6; *SF*, 5 January 1933.

67 Ansaldo, *¿Para qué . . . ?* 54; Paul Preston, 'Alfonsist Monarchism and the Coming of the Spanish Civil War', *Journal of Contemporary History* VII, 3–4 (July–October 1972), 89–114.

68   *SF*, 23 January 1933.
69   *SF*, 18 & 30 January 1933.
70   Gil Robles, *No fue posible la paz*, 79.
71   *Ibid.* 87.
72   *SF*, 13 & 20 February, 18 March 1933.
73   Goicoechea told *El Siglo Futuro* (20 March 1933) that Renovación was linked to the Communion by 'a community of ideals growing closer all the time'. Goicoechea, who besides being leader of Renovación Española was also its most frequent public speaker, continued to do everything possible to identify the party with Traditionalism and to stress that only the dynastic question stood between the two movements.
74   See below, Chapter 5.
75   Burgo, *Conspiración*, 367–81 provides a lengthy description of the conversations.
76   *DAC*, 125.
77   Burgo, *Conspiración*, 389.
78   *PN*, 6 March 1932.
79   Stanley G. Payne, *Falange. A History of Spanish Fascism* (London, 1962), 10; Galindo Herrero, *Los partidos*, 50. Albiñana received favourable coverage in the veteran Larramendi's review *Criterio*, to which he also contributed (*Criterio*, 24 January, 3 April 1932).
80   *SF*, 13 February 1933. The Carlists and Renovación held a joint meeting in Madrid on behalf of the release of Albiñana and the Alfonsist Miralles brothers.
81   Payne, *Falange*, 11–20. A detailed account of the early years of the JONS is given in the most recent Spanish biography of Ledesma: Tomás Borrás, *Ramiro Ledesma Ramos* (Madrid, 1971), 145–356.
82   Arrarás, *HSRE*, II, 150–1.
83   *Reacción*, 4, 11 & 25 March 1933.
84   *La Unión*, 11 March 1933.
85   *La Unión*, 14 March 1933.
86   *SF*, 16 & 17 March 1933.
87   See below, p. 154.
88   *SF*, 24 & 25 July 1933; *La Unión*, 25, 27 & 29 July 1933; *PN* 27 & 30 July 1933.
89   *PN*, 3 August 1933.
90   *SF*, 31 August 1933.
91   Jato, *La rebelión de los estudiantes*, 59.
92   *PN*, 29 September 1933.
93   *La Unión*, 14 October 1933.
94   *El Observador*, 19 February 1933; *SF*, 7 & 8 March, 2 May 1933.
95   *PN*, 25, 26, 27 & 28 April 1933; *SF*, 28 April 1933. Enormous discrepancies exist among the various authorities regarding the party allegiances of those elected. Galindo Herrero (*Los partidos*, 184–5) gives a total of 419 Traditionalists and Jaimists (*sic*) elected, while *El Siglo Futuro* claimed 1,324. Much depends upon the allegiance ascribed to those elected as Independent Catholics and Agrarians; since *El Pensamiento Navarro*'s detailed results give a minimum of 900 Carlists in Navarre and the Basque provinces, and bearing in mind the National Junta's tribute to numerous

Carlists standing under other labels elsewhere, *El Siglo Futuro*'s claim does not seem unreasonable. It claimed 77 out of 1,086 councillors elected in Burgos, 57 out of 1,111 in Salamanca, 37 out of 264 in Castellón and 32 out of 443 in Logroño. Only in Madrid, Murcia, Oviedo, Soria and Santa Cruz de Tenerife were no Carlist successes claimed.

96   *SF*, 7 April 1933.

97   *El Observador*, 12 March 1933.

98   *SF*, 26, 29 & 30 June, 1 July 1933.

99   For details of this aspect of the 1932 Act see Malefakis, *Agrarian Reform and Peasant Revolution*, 206–7, 212–14, 217–19. Malefakis' book makes it possible to deduce what remains unclear from purely Carlist sources, i.e. the reasons why a number of middling proprietors aligned themselves with Carlism – or with other right-wing elements – during 1933–4. The Andalusian Carlist press, though given to general lamentations about 'the condition of the countryside', seldom indulged in specific analysis of the problems.

100 In March 1933, for example, Youth Sections were inaugurated in Pilas, Sanlúcar la Mayor, Huelva, Écija and Castro del Río (*El Observador*, 9 & 10 March, 2 & 9 April 1933).

101 *El Observador*, 9 April 1933.

102 See Jackson, *Spanish Republic*, 112 for a description of interunion rivalry in Seville.

103 *El Observador*, 9 April 1933. The Workers Section was the outcome of the same meeting of the Regional Junta as the Youth Federation. On the CEDA Workers Section see J. Monge Bernal, *Acción Popular* (Madrid, 1936), 1077–94.

104 *El Observador*, 4 July, 6 & 13 August, 8 October 1933.

105 *SF*, 27 May 1933.

106 *El Observador*, 13 August 1933. Joaquín Valdís, Fal Conde's biographer, is unfortunately less restrained than his subject, and claims that by the end of 1933 the Workers Section numbered 8,000. This utterly incredible figure at least makes that of *El Observador* appear reasonable ('Villarín y Willy' [pseudonym of Joaquín Valdís], *El Secretario de S. M. Biografía de Fal Conde* (Seville, 1954), 84).

107 *SF*, 28 March 1933.

108 *SF*, 27 May 1933. Fal Conde stated that the Seville organization contained 1,000 workers, with 924 in the Youth and 1,000 in its main circle. The overlap between the three figures must have been considerable; nevertheless, assuming their rough accuracy the total number of Carlists in Seville by the spring of 1933 may be estimated at the not unimpressive figure of around 1,500.

109 *DAC*, 220–1; 'Villarín y Willy', *Fal Conde*, 88–9; *La Unión*, 23 June 1933.

Chapter 5: A young man to lead the young

1   The Carlists, Basque Nationalists and Agrarians, as well as Maura's Conservatives and Alcalá Zamora's Progressives, opposed the Act which created the Court, mainly on the grounds that it would not be em-

powered to judge Republican legislation prior to its own establishment (*DSCC*, 7 June 1933).

2   *SF*, 1 September 1933.

3   *PN*, 5 September 1933; *SF*, 4, 5 & 7 September 1933. The percentages for each province were:

	Carlists	PNV	Government	Radicals
Álava	52	37	11	–
Guipúzcoa	30·5	57	12·5	–
Vizcaya	21	57	22	–
All Basque provinces	32·3	51·3	16·3	–
Navarre	77·5	–	15·5	7

4   *PN*, 13 September 1933.
5   *Reacción*, 16 September 1933.
6   *PN*, 23 February 1933.
7   *La Unión*, 24 April 1933.
8   *SF*, 12 September 1933.
9   *SF*, 9 October 1933.
10 *SF*, 10 October 1933.
11 *SF*, 12 & 13 October 1933; *La Unión*, 18 October 1933; *PN*, 17 October 1933.
12 Gil Robles, *No fue posible la paz*, 95–6; *SF*, 13 October 1933. The original idea that the Agrarian Bloc should carry out this task came from the *cedista* Calderón; the committee's other members were Gil Robles, Casanueva and Calderón (CEDA), Royo Villanova (liberal Agrarian) and Sáinz Rodríguez (Alfonsist).
13 *PN*, 15 & 22 October, 7 & 15 November 1933. Four of the seven candidates in Navarre were Carlists: Rodezno, Bilbao, Arellano and Martínez Morentín; Oriol was the lone right-wing candidate in Álava; Oreja was one of two candidates in Vizcaya-Province; and the Communion provided two of the four rightists in Bilbao – Lezama Leguizamón and Hermógenes Rojo.
14 *El Observador*, 22 October, 12 November 1933; *SF*, 30 October, 1 November 1933. The speedy agreement between the Carlists and the CEDA in Seville was no doubt facilitated by their shared detestation of Martínez Barrio.
15 *SF*, November 1933 *passim*.
16 *El Observador*, 5 November 1933; *SF*, 2 & 13 November 1933.
17 *SF*, 19, 25 & 31 October 1933.
18 *SF*, 28 October, 2 & 11 November 1933.
19 *Reacción*, 21 October 1933.
20 They were (names in italics are those of candidates elected): Álava: *J. L. Oriol*; Alicante: Manuel Senante; Burgos: *F. Estévanez*, Gómez Rojí; Barcelona-Province: J. Soler Janer, J. Clavería Puvé; Cádiz: *Juan José Palomino*, M. *Martínez Pinillos*; Castellón: *Juan Granell*, Jaime Chicharro; Corunna: Rafael Díaz-Aguado Salaverría; Gerona: María Rosa Úrraca Pastor, P. Llosas, J. M. Arauz de Robles; Guipúzcoa: Úrraca Pastor, A.

Pagoaga, A. Tellería; Lérida: *Casimiro Sangenís*; Logroño: *Miguel de Miranda*; Madrid-City: *Romualdo Toledo*; Málaga: J. M. Hinojosa; Navarre: *Rodezno, Bilbao, Arellano, Martínez Morentín*; Salamanca: *Lamamié de Clairac*; Santander: *José Luis Zamanillo*; Seville-City: *Ginés Martínez*; Seville-Province: *Domingo Tejera*, J. Díaz Custodio; Tarragona: *Joaquín Bau*; Valencia-City: *Barón de Cárcer*; Valencia-Province: Carlos Llinares; Vizcaya-City (Bilbao): L. Lezama Leguizamón, Hermógenes Rojo; Vizcaya-Province: *Marcelino Oreja*; Zaragoza-Province: *Jesús Comín*, J. *Ramírez Sinués*. *El Siglo Futuro* claimed five more candidates, four of whom were actually *cedistas* and the fifth of whom withdrew before polling day.

21 *SF*, 14 October 1933.

22 E.g. *La Unión* 10, 15, 17 & 18 November 1933; *SF*, 31 October, 1, 9, 14 & 15 November 1933; *PN*, 14, 15 & 17 November 1933; *Reacción*, 21 October 1933. The tone of the campaign is admirably conveyed in a pamphlet distributed by TYRE:

'MARXISM – Negation of God. Class War. Negation of patriotism. Free Love. Power of the State over children. Negation of Private Property. Exaltation of Force. Utopias.

'ANTI-MARXISM – True Religion. Social Peace. Exaltation of Spain. Sanctification of Matrimony. Parental Rights over Children. Respect for the Property of Others. Rule of Law. Realism. VOTE FOR THE RIGHT!'

23 *SF*, 3, 13 & 16 November 1933.

24 *PN*, 10 November 1933. *El Pensamiento Navarro*, like other Carlist newspapers, actually went so far as to suggest that Catholic women were less corruptible and more sensible than their menfolk.

25 *SF*, 11 & 12 October 1933.

26 This and other election results are taken from *El Debate*, 21 November 1933. *El Debate*, together with *El Sol*, published the most complete and reliable election figures during the Republic. Results given in Carlist newspapers tended to be neither accurate nor final.

27 *Boletín de Información Bibliográfica y Parlamentaria de España y del Extranjero*, Año I, Tomo I, No. 6 (Madrid, November–December 1933). The figure of 21 given by this official publication is correct. Galindo Herrero (*Los partidos*, 210) names 24, but errs in including three members of the CEDA – Meras (Asturias), García Bedoya (Burgos) and Zaforteza (Baleares) – and one Carlist who was actually defeated – Chicharro (Castellón) – while omitting Ramírez Sinués (Zaragoza) and attaching Oreja to Valencia instead of Vizcaya. This confusion is in part understandable since *El Siglo Futuro* and the Traditionalist Secretariat itself wrongly or at least overoptimistically claimed Meras and Zaforteza until after the new Cortes assembled.

28 Estévanez (Burgos), Sangenís (Lérida), Miranda (Logroño), Lamamié (Salamanca), Zamanillo (Santander), Ginés Martínez (Seville-City) and Tejera (Seville-Province) all trailed behind most of their CEDA or Lliga allies. Similarly Chicharro (Castellón), Salaverría (Corunna), Díaz Custodio (Seville-Province), Senante (Alicante) and Hinojosa (Málaga) all failed to

gain election despite right-wing successes in their constituencies. In Madrid-City Larramendi came next to last. (*El Debate* & *SF* 23 & 30 November, 1 December 1933, *El Día* [Alicante], 24 November 1933).

29 The following information concerning the Carlist deputies elected in 1933 derives almost entirely from the press as follows: *SF*, 14 & 24 November, 1 December 1933; *El Observador*, 19 February, 22 October 1933; *La Unión*, 1 November 1933 (all concerning Ginés Martínez); *SF*, 2 December 1933 (Martínez Pinillos); *SF*, 4 December 1933 (Palomino); *La Unión*, 7 November 1933; *El Observador*, 22 October 1933; *SF*, 5 December 1933 (all dealing with Tejera); *SF*, 13 February, 16 March 1934 (Arellano); *SF*, 8 March 1934 (Toledo). *SF*, 19 March 1934 (Martínez Morentín); *SF*, 27 March 1934 (Cárcer); *SF*, 21 March 1934 (Comín); *SF*, 18 April 1934 (Ramírez Sinués); *SF*, 20 April, 3 September 1934 (Bau); *SF*, 7 May 1934 (Sangenís); *SF*, 21 May 1934 (Zamanillo).

30 *SF*, 23 November 1933.

31 *El Día*, 30 November, 1 December 1933; *SF*, 4 December 1933. In Alicante the excluded Carlist, Senante, and his Alfonsist partner presented an independent candidature but were overwhelmingly defeated with barely 20,000 votes compared with almost 75,000 in the first round.

32 Arrarás, *HSRE*, II, 242–3.

33 Gil Robles, *No fue posible la paz*, 107; Arrarás, *HSRE*, II, 243.

34 *El Debate*, 15 & 17 December 1933; *SF*, 15 December 1933.

35 *Diario de las sesiones de las Cortes* (hereafter *DSC*), 19 December 1933.

36 *PN*, 19 December 1933.

37 *SF*, 19 December 1933.

38 *El Observador*, 17 & 24 December 1933.

39 *PN*, 9 January 1934.

40 *SF*, 25 & 31 January 1934.

41 This was a group of some seventeen deputies of social-Catholic leanings, which aimed at publicizing social-Catholicism both inside and outside the Cortes and ultimately at sponsoring a Catholic rival to the UGT and CNT. The Carlists were represented in it by Ginés Martínez and Arellano. In effect it appears to have limited itself to discussion, thereby epitomizing the preference of Spanish social-Catholics for words over action in the political sphere (*El Observador*, 14 January 1934; *PN*, 14 January 1934; Arellano, interview).

42 *SF*, 22 & 31 December 1933.

43 *PN*, 28 February 1934; *DSC*, 28 February, 5 April 1934; *SF*, 1 March 1934.

44 *PN*, 28 & 31 January 1934; *SF*, 29 January 1934.

45 *SF*, 6 April 1934.

46 *SF*, 27 & 29 December 1933.

47 *La Unión*, 28 January 1934; *SF*, 29 January 1934.

48 Gil Robles, *No fue posible la paz*, 113–14; *SF*, 17 January 1934. Gil Robles says that the press statement censured his conduct, whereas in fact it merely reiterated the monarchists' demands.

49 See Rodezno in *SF*, 24 March 1934 and Comín in *SF*, 31 March, 4 April 1934.

50 *DSC*, 20 April 1934; *SF*, 20 April 1934. According to *El Siglo Futuro* the glass, one of many being thrown around, was aimed at Rodezno's head but hit his hand, 'which bled copiously'. The Carlists then threw themselves upon the far more numerous Socialists and blows were exchanged. The uproar lasted half an hour, and the next day the Carlists formally protested against the 'shameful events' which had taken place.

51 *SF*, 5 April 1934; *DSC*, 4 April 1934. The Alfonsist Honorio Maura, brother of Miguel, described the day's session as 'the most monarchist session since 1909'.

52 In June Lamamié emphasized how many of the 'laicizing measures of the unhappy biennium' remained untouched; in July Bilbao stated that the Cortes had achieved some negative good, but not enough (*PN*, 4 July 1934), and *La Unión* claimed that 'scarcely any' of the November programme had been fulfilled (*La Unión*, 9 July 1934). New Carlist deputies repeatedly declared their dissatisfaction with the Cortes: for example Arellano (*SF*, 13 February 1934), Toledo (*SF*, 8 March 1934), Cárcer (*SF*, 27 March 1934), Ramírez Sinués (*SF*, 18 April 1934), Ginés Martínez (*PN*, 14 February 1934), Comín (*SF*, 16 April 1934) and Zamanillo (*SF*, 21 May 1934).

53 E.g. Lamamié (*PN*, 2 February 1934; *SF*, 19 February, 15 & 17 May 1934), Arellano (*SF*, 13 February, 15 March 1934), Cárcer (*SF*, 27 March, 21 May 1934), Ginés Martínez (*El Observador*, 14 January 1934; *La Unión*, 16 May 1934), plus a host of editorials in all the main Carlist newspapers.

54 *a.e.t.* (Pamplona), 2 & 9 February 1934.

55 *SF* (8 February 1934) declared that Gil Robles, far from 'controlling the government' was now controlled by it; Rodezno concluded that 'it is beyond question that there is no room for the right within the regime'.

56 *SF*, 19 February 1934.

57 *El Observador*, 22 April 1934.

58 *SF*, 2 July 1934.

59 *El Observador*, 22 April 1934.

60 *SF*, 7 June 1934.

61 *La Unión*, 12 May 1934; *SF*, 4 June 1934.

62 *PN*, 10 April 1934.

63 J. Cortés Cavanillas, *Confesiones y muerte de Alfonso XIII*, 2nd ed. (Madrid, 1951), 79–82; Arrarás, *HCE*, II–1, 81. Gil Robles later denied responsibility for Valiente's visit, a move followed by the latter's resignation from the presidency of the JAP and later by his departure from the CEDA to join the Carlists (see below, p. 199). Valiente's resignation was announced in *La Unión* on 10 June 1934.

64 Ansaldo, ¿*Para qué . . . ?*, 79–82; Payne, *Falange*, 60–3. What Ansaldo calls this 'curious document' apparently stated that the Falange would refrain from anti-monarchist acts and propaganda in return for a cash payment. The money did not materialize and the agreement never took effect.

65 Payne, *Falange*, 68.

66 F. Bravo Martínez, *Historia de la Falange Española de las JONS* (Madrid,

1940), 76–7; F. Ximénez de Sandoval, *José Antonio*, 2nd ed. (Madrid, 1949), 361–2; Jato, *Rebelión de los estudiantes*, 123. On 16 February 1935 Eliseda published in *El Pensamiento Navarro* an article entitled 'Towards the New State', outlining a typically neo-Traditionalist version of the corporate state.

67 Ximénez de Sandoval, *José Antonio*, 372–6.
68 *SF*, 21 May 1934.
69 *SF*, 14 June 1934.
70 *SF*, 3 March 1934. This report concerned the re-formation of Acción Española's committee, falsely stated by Ansón (*Acción Española*, 141) to have taken place in the subsequent June.
71 These figures are quoted in J. E. Casariego, *La verdad del Tradicionalismo* (Madrid, 1940), 16–17, and in Redondo and Zavala, *El Requeté*, 254. Their authenticity is thrown into question by the fact that they never appeared in the Carlist press and that they are at variance with the more realistic figures published in 1935 (see below, 210).
72 *SF*, 11 March 1933.
73 *El Observador*, 7 May 1933. Although the *Sociedad Editorial Tradicionalista* took over *El Siglo Futuro* from its owner Juan Olazábal in the hope of lessening its identification with Integrism, the inescapable importance of former Integrists within the Communion was only highlighted since the Society's committee was dominated by Lamamié and Senante. In December 1933, however, it was reconstituted under Rodezno's chairmanship and with a wider, more representative membership (*SF*, 12 December 1933).
74 The only member who might be considered an 'organizer' was Oriol, who was naturally enough too preoccupied with Álava and the Statute to be able to devote much attention to the national organization.
75 As the Secretariat's figures, however exaggerated, clearly show.
76 *BOT*, 30 December 1934, 13 January 1935.
77 Arellano, interview. The actual phrase used was 'hacer tonterías'.
78 Burgo, in an interview with the author, admitted that the strident tone of *a.e.t.* was adopted deliberately in order to counteract the quietism of the older Navarrese Carlists.
79 *a.e.t.*, 9 March 1934.
80 *a.e.t.*, 2 February 1934.
81 *a.e.t.*, 16 February 1934.
82 *a.e.t.*, 2 March 1934.
83 *SF*, 19 February 1934.
84 *PN*, 27 February 1934. The term was coined by *a.e.t.* (2 March 1934).
85 *SF*, 7 April 1934.
86 *SF*, 4 January 1934.
87 *La Unión*, 27 February 1934.
88 Pemán, *Varela*, 135. The meeting, according to Pemán's source, Santiago Arauz de Robles, resembled something out of the early nineteenth century and was noteworthy less in terms of real achievement than for the mere fact that it happened at all. Varela was forced to flee in haste when an alarm was given.
89 *DAC*, 235.

90 *SF*, 11 April 1934.
91 Lizarza, *Conspiración*, 22–4.
92 The following account derives mainly from W. C. Askew, 'Italian Intervention in Spain. The Agreements of March 31, 1934 with the Spanish Monarchist Parties', *Journal of Modern History*, XXIV, 2 (June 1952); and from Lizarza, *Conspiración*, 24–8.
93 The chief sources for the meeting of regional *jefes* and the events leading up to it are *DAC*, 241; *SF*, 12 May 1934; and Burgo, *Conspiración*, 392–7.
94 *La Unión*, 17 April 1934; *SF*, 16 April 1934; 'Villarín y Willy', *Fal Conde*, 124–50.
95 *SF*, 17 April 1934.
96 *DAC*, 240–1.
97 *DAC*, 243. TYRE's activity was officially suspended, but the office continued in existence – evidence, perhaps, that the traditional Spanish formula 'Obedezco pero no cumplo' was able to operate within the Communion.
98 *La Unión*, 3 July 1934. On his first visit to Seville after Fal Conde's appointment, Rodezno paid public tribute to the new Secretary-General's energy, describing him as 'this modest, good and constructive man' – which by normal Carlist standards of effusiveness amounted almost to damning him with faint praise.
99 Arrarás, *HSRE*, II, 354; confirmed in interviews by both Burgo and Arellano.
100 *SF*, 14 May 1934.
101 *La Unión*, 15 May 1934.
102 *a.e.t.*, 18 May 1934.

Chapter 6: Traditionalism and the contemporary crisis

1   *SF*, 21 July, 13 August 1931.
2   *SF*, 29 October 1931.
3   *PN*, 28 & 31 October 1931; see also *SF*, 29 & 31 October 1931.
4   *Reacción*, 9 April 1932; *SF*, 20 July 1932.
5   *SF*, 9 November 1934.
6   *PN*, 5 March 1933.
7   *SF*, 7 February 1934.
8   *SF*, 24 May, 6 July 1934.
9   *PN*, 19 August 1933.
10 *SF*, 30 April 1936.
11 *PN*, 29 April 1932.
12 *SF*, 24 November 1933.
13 For further discussion of the relationship between Traditionalism and fascism, see Chapter 7.
14 *PN*, 6 July 1932, 26 July 1934, 28 February 1935; *SF*, 24 March, 6 October 1933, 27 June, 2 August 1934.
15 *PN*, 22 August 1935.
16 *SF*, 11 October 1935.

17 For example by Estévanez in the Cortes (*DSCC*, 10 September 1931). For an example of Carlist approval of Salazar, see *La Unión*, 11 October 1933.

18 *SF*, 23 & 25 September 1933.

19 A succinct examination of Dollfuss' ideas and of the 1934 Austrian constitution is that by R. J. Rath, 'Authoritarian Austria', in Peter F. Sugar (ed.), *Native Fascism in the Successor States* (Santa Barbara, California, 1971), 24–35.

20 *SF*, 26 & 27 July 1934.

21 On Degrelle and Rexism see Jean Steyers, 'Belgium', in H. Rogger and E. Weber (eds.), *The European Right*, 156–64; Eugen Weber, *Varieties of Fascism* (New York, 1964), 122–9; and the sympathetic account by Robert Brasillach, *Léon Degrelle et l'avenir de 'Rex'* (Paris, 1936).

22 *SF*, 4 & 8 June 1936.

23 Víctor Pradera, *El Estado Nuevo* (Madrid, 1935). In the discussion which follows, reference is made to the excellent English translation published at the end of the Civil War: Víctor Pradera, *The New State*, tr. B. Malley (London, 1939) (hereafter *TNS*).

24 *TNS*, 28.

25 *TNS*, 38.

26 *TNS*, 54–6.

27 *TNS*, 77.

28 *TNS*, 49.

29 *TNS*, 81–4.

30 *TNS*, 86–7, 95–7.

31 *TNS*, 108, 113.

32 *TNS*, 98.

33 *TNS*, 120–1.

34 *TNS*, 110.

35 *TNS*, 114–17.

36 *TNS*, 119.

37 *TNS*, 151, 173.

38 *TNS*, 179–83.

39 *TNS*, 184–8.

40 *TNS*, 139.

41 *TNS*, 140, 153, 207–8, 212.

42 *TNS*, 167–8.

43 *TNS*, 124.

44 *TNS*, 129–30.

45 *TNS*, 253–9.

46 *TNS*, 244–7.

47 *TNS*, 228–30, 255.

48 *TNS*, 271–2.

49 *TNS*, 80.

50 *TNS*, 297–305.

51 *TNS*, 88–92.

52 *TNS*, 320.

53 E.g. Arellano (*SF*, 16 March 1934): 'Fascist organization is from the top downwards, whereas ours is from the bottom upwards.'

54 This being the view propagated by Lizarza (*Conspiración*, 31) and accepted by Payne (*Politics and the Military*, 336).
55 Arellano, interview.
56 Alfonso XIII told his intimates that his personal experience had convinced him that 'new routes' were now being revealed (J. Cortés Cavanillas, *Alfonso XIII en el destierro* (Madrid, 1933), 79–80).
57 Preston, 'Alfonsist Monarchism', 89–95.
58 J. M. Pemán, *Cartas a un escéptico en materia de formas de gobierno*, 2nd ed. (Madrid, 1935). References given here are actually from the later renamed reissue: *Cartas a un escéptico ante la monarquía*, 4th ed. (Madrid, 1956).
59 *La Época* (Madrid), 21 June 1934.
60 *La Época*, 28 March, 15 August 1934.
61 José Calvo Sotelo, *El estado que queremos* (Madrid, 1958), 74.
62 Ramiro de Maeztu, *Defensa de la Hispanidad* (Madrid, 1934), 298.
63 E. Aunós Pérez, *La reforma corporativa del Estado* (Madrid, 1935), xvii.
64 *La Época*, 16 June 1934.
65 *La Época*, 8 June 1934.
66 Pemán, *Cartas*, 118, 123, 128–30, 147.
67 Calvo Sotelo, *El estado que queremos*, 77–8, 93–6.
68 Pemán, *Cartas*, 181, 191.
69 Calvo Sotelo, *El estado que queremos*, 97–8.
70 Aunós, *Reforma corporativa*, 230–1, 257 ff.
71 Gil Robles, quoted in Robinson, *Origins of Franco's Spain*, 211.
72 *DSC*, 6 November 1934.
73 A position first labelled by the Marqués de Quintanar as 'national traditionalism' (Preston, 'Alfonsist Monarchism', 95).
74 Ramiro de Maeztu, *Frente a la República* (ed. G. Fernández de la Mora) (Madrid, 1956), 125–6.
75 Aunós, *Reforma corporativa*, xv, xvi.
76 Pemán, *Cartas*, 100.
77 For example Villores in *El Siglo Futuro*, 1 December 1931. The political leader of the Communion planned the creation of a Technical Council of Jurists to revise the fundamental statutes of the realm prior to the effective 'installation' of the monarchy. This unusual practical suggestion for coping with the 'transition' problem still avoided the central questions of coercion and security; it soon sank without trace and later leaders showed even less inclination to face the issue.
78 *DSC*, 6 June 1935.
79 *La Época*, 29 March, 21 June 1934.
80 Aunós, *Reforma corporativa*, 120–1.
81 Calvo Sotelo, *El estado que queremos*, 80–1; *SF*, 4 February 1935.
82 Preston, 'Alfonsist Monarchism', 103–14.
83 The discussion which follows derives mainly from the most useful examination of Gil Robles' ideas in Robinson, *Origins of Franco's Spain*, 207–11, and from Gil Robles, *No fue posible la paz*, passim.
84 Gil Robles, quoted in Robinson, *Origins of Franco's Spain*, 211.
85 *SF*, 12 November 1934.

Chapter 7: Carlism and fascism

1 *La Unión*, 14 March 1933.
2 *SF*, 11 September 1935.
3 *SF*, 4 & 5 October 1935.
4 *SF*, 3 October 1935.
5 *SF*, 19, 28 & 30 September, 17 October 1935.
6 *DSC*, 17 May 1935 (Rodezno).
7 *SF*, 1 February, 10 April 1933.
8 *Reacción*, 1 April 1933.
9 *PN*, 2 & 6 January 1935.
10 *SF*, 9 March 1936.
11 *SF*, 27 July 1934.
12 *SF*, 20 February 1935.
13 *PN*, 6 January 1935.
14 *SF*, 2 August 1935.
15 *SF*, 15 & 19 June 1934.
16 *SF*, 24 March, 5 April 1933.
17 *PN*, 21 March 1933.
18 *Reacción*, 8 April 1933.
19 *El Observador*, 26 March 1933.
20 *PN*, 22 April 1933; *SF*, 2 September, 10 October 1933.
21. *El Observador*, 26 March 1933; *SF*, 4 April 1933. A Canadian article, 'The Glorious Work of Hitler', was reprinted in *El Siglo Futuro* with the accompanying comment: 'Spanish Traditionalism has no need to copy any of Hitler's programme, but his courage, patriotism and constancy *are* worthy of imitation.'
22 Víctor Pradera, in *Acción Española*, 16 December 1933.
23 *La Unión*, 4 February 1935.
24 See Ledesma's *Manifiesto político* (1931), reprinted in Borrás, *Ramiro Ledesma Ramos*, 158–64.
25 Payne, *Falange*, 70, 78. Payne suggests that the last time José Antonio accepted the term was in April 1934 – a mere six months after the Falange's foundation.
26 José Antonio Primo de Rivera, *Obras completas* (ed. A. del Río Cisneros and E. Conde Gargollo) (Madrid, 1942), 569, 571.
27 Payne, *Falange*, 80.
28 Primo de Rivera, *Obras*, 553–64. The twenty-fifth of the Falange's twenty-seven points stated that the Falange was faithfully Catholic and reverent towards the Church, but that the latter's activities must nonetheless be strictly circumscribed. In particular the Falange went along with the Republic in stressing the educative role of the state as against that of the Church – though needless to say the state education prescribed by Falangists would have been very different from that encouraged by Republicans.
29 Borrás, *Ramiro Ledesma Ramos*, 256–68.
30 Primo de Rivera, *Obras*, 483–508, 558; Payne, *Falange*, 79; Frederick B. Pike, *Hispanismo, 1898–1936. Spanish Conservatives and Liberals and their Relations with Spanish America* (Notre Dame & London, 1971), comments interestingly on this theme.

31 *La Unión*, 3 August 1934.
32 *SF*, 8 March 1934 (Romualdo Toledo); *El Observador*, 8 March 1934.
33 *La Unión*, 20 March 1934; *SF*, 16 March 1934 (Arellano).
34 *Tradición* (Santander), 1 January, 1 February 1934; *La Unión*, 9 November 1933, 9 January, 9 April, 16 May 1934; *SF*, 24 November 1933, 14 February, 1 June 1934.
35 *a.e.t.*, 23 February 1934.
36 *a.e.t.*, 9, 16 & 23 February 1934.
37 *a.e.t.*, 13 April 1934.
38 *a.e.t.*, 9 February 1934.
39 *a.e.t.*, 25 May 1934.
40 *PN*, 14 February 1934.
41 *La Unión*, 5 & 29 July 1933, 24 August 1934.
42 *El Observador*, 27 August 1933; *SF*, 14 November 1933, 14 February 1934.
43 *PN*, 14 February 1934; *El Observador*, 10 June 1934.
44 *a.e.t.*, 27 April 1934.
45 Ginés Martínez, in *El Observador*, 27 August 1933.
46 *a.e.t.*, 16 March 1934.
47 See Payne, *Falange*, 75.
48 Primo de Rivera, *Obras*, 571. This is essentially the argument put forward by a later Secretary-General of the Falange, J. L. de Arrese, in *El Estado totalitario en el pensamiento de José Antonio* (Madrid, 1945), as well as in V. Marrero, *La guerra española y el trust de cérebros*, 2nd ed. (Madrid, 1962), 293–5. The neo-Traditionalist Marrero connects José Antonio's repudiation of modern totalitarianism with his ideological debt to Traditionalism.
49 I am conscious that to introduce this concept carries as many dangers as too cavalier a use of the term 'fascism'. For a general and particularized discussion of populism, see Ghita Ionescu and Ernest Gellner (eds.), *Populism. Its Meanings and National Characteristics* (London, 1969), and in particular the chapter 'Latin America' by Alistair Hennessy (28–61).
50 On fascism and 'modernization from above' see Barrington Moore, jun., *Social Origins of Dictatorship and Democracy. Lord and Peasant in the Making of the Modern World* (London, 1969), 433–53.
51 *SF*, 17 November 1934.
52 Preston, 'Alfonsist Monarchism', 100. CEDA anti-semitism has been little documented, despite being a far from elusive phenomenon. It was almost as commonplace in *El Debate* as social-Catholicism, notwithstanding which Robinson largely ignores it in *The Origins of Franco's Spain*.
53 Ramiro Ledesma Ramos, 'Discurso a las juventudes de España' in *¿Fascismo en España? Discurso a las juventudes de España* (Barcelona, 1968), 302.
54 See above, Chapter 2.
55 *SF*, 29, 30 & 31 December 1931 *et seq.*
56 *La Unión*, 14, 15, 16 & 19 March 1932 *et seq.*
57 *SF*, 9 February 1933.
58 *La Unión*, 7 January 1934; *PN*, 6 April 1934.
59 *SF*, 4 April 1934.
60 *SF*, 13 February 1935.
61 *SF*, 26 March 1935.

62 *SF*, 23 August 1933. There was, of course, no implied connection with the Green International of European Agrarian parties during the interwar period.
63 *BOT*, 15 December 1935.
64 *PN*, 26 January 1935.
65 *SF*, 17 October 1935.
66 *La Unión*, 21 March 1935.
67 *La Unión*, 21 & 27 July, 21 September 1935.
68 *SF*, 30 January, 11 April 1936.
69 *SF*, 24 August 1933.
70 *SF*, 9 March, 27 April 1935.
71 *SF*, 31 March, 9 June 1936.
72 M. García Venero, *Falange en la guerra de España: la Unificación y Hedilla* (Paris, 1967), 23, 86.
73 Burgo, interview.
74 See below, p. 317.

Chapter 8: The politics of counter-revolution

1 E.g. Lamamié (*PN*, 2 February 1934; *SF*, 19 February, 15 May 1934); Rodezno (*SF*, 16 February, 5 March 1934); Arellano (*SF*, 16 March, 9 April 1934); Cárcer (*SF*, 27 March 1934); Toledo (*SF*, 29 May 1934).
2 For a variety of views on the Socialists' move leftwards see Edward Malefakis, 'The Parties of the Left and the Second Republic' in Raymond Carr (ed.), *The Republic and the Civil War in Spain* (London, 1971), 35–7; Arrarás, *HSRE*, II, 295–9; R. de la Cierva, *Historia de la guerra civil española* (Madrid, 1969) (hereafter *HGCE*) I, 343–52; Robinson, *Origins of Franco's Spain*, 181–5.
3 Jackson, *Spanish Republic*, 134–7, 142–3.
4 *SF*, 5 March 1934.
5 *SF*, 9 April 1934.
6 *a.e.t.*, 16 March 1934.
7 *PN*, 11 & 12 August 1934; *SF*, 11 & 29 August 1934. The Regional Junta of Navarre now declared its intention to concentrate its efforts on obtaining the restoration of a genuinely elected Diputación for Navarre – and thus tacitly abandoned the Statute campaign (*PN*, 23 August 1934).
8 On the Basque troubles of 1934 see Arrarás *HCE*, II–1, 88–92, 97–101; García Venero, *Nacionalismo Vasco*, 450–7.
9 *PN*, 2 & 5 September 1934; *SF*, 2, 10 & 11 September 1934. 'Gernikako Arbola' = 'The Tree of Guernica'.
10 On Catalonia during 1934 see La Cierva, *HGCE*, I, 288–93; Arrarás, *HSRE*, II, 365–6; García Venero, *Historia del nacionalismo catalán*, 537.
11 *BOT*, 16 September 1934; *SF*, 16 July, 10 September 1934.
12 Arrarás, *HSRE*, II, 437.
13 *PN*, 20, 21 & 22 September 1934; *SF*, 14 & 21 September 1934; *La Unión*, 28 September 1934; Gil Robles, *No fue posible la paz*, 131.
14 *SF*, 25 September 1934.

15 The CEDA ministers were Anguera de Sojo (Labour), Giménez Fernández (Agriculture) and Aizpún (Justice). *El Pensamiento Navarro* (5 October 1934) extended the coldest of congratulations to the Navarrese Aizpún, but pointed out that this was not what the voters had in mind when they elected him.

16 *SF*, 6 October 1934.

17 *La Unión*, 5 October 1934.

18 Paul Preston, 'Spain's October Revolution and the Rightist Grasp for Power', to appear in *Journal of Contemporary History*, 1975.

19 *BOT*, 7 October 1934; *SF*, 8 October 1934.

20 *BOT*, 21 October 1934; *SF*, 11 October 1934.

21 *El Siglo Futuro* (13 June 1934) reported the closure of Carlist circles in and around Barcelona, together with the suspension of *Reacción* and *El Correo Catalán*. See also Arrarás, *HSRE*, II, 368–9.

22 *SF*, 11–22 September 1934.

23 *BOT*, 14 & 21 October, 4, 11 & 25 November 1934; *PN*, 6 October 1934; *SF*, 6 & 18 October 1934. A further death, that of the local *jefe* of Galdácano, was reported in Bilbao as late as 31 October.

24 *BOT*, 18 November 1934.

25 E.g. *PN*, 24, 25 & 26 October 1934; *SF*, 20, 23, 24 & 25 October 1934.

26 *PN*, 30 October 1934. Another party – Tejera, Granell, Comín and Ramírez Sinués – paid a similar visit to Barcelona (*SF*, 31 October 1934).

27 *PN*, 13 October 1934. Olazábal's *La Constancia* published several articles charging the PNV with complicity in the revolutions, later collected together in a pamphlet: *El nacionalismo vasco con la revolución de octubre 1934* (San Sebastian, 1936).

28 *BOT*, 14 October 1934.

29 *SF*, 30 October, 5 November 1934; *PN*, 23 & 24 October 1934.

30 *SF*, 16 October (Salaverría), 17 October (statement by the Special Delegation of Youth), 15 November 1934 (Lamamié).

31 *PN*, 15 & 24 November 1934; *SF*, 12 November 1934 (Arauz de Robles); *BOT*, 11 November 1934 (Bilbao).

32 *La Unión*, 25 November 1934.

33 *SF*, 24 November 1934.

34 The full text and list of signatories of the National Bloc's manifesto appears in R. A. H. Robinson, 'Calvo Sotelo's *Bloque Nacional* and its Manifesto', *University of Birmingham Historical Journal* x, 2 (1966).

35 *SF*, 8 December 1934. La Cierva (*HGCE*, 499) appears to imply that the Carlists, on Fal Conde's orders, played no part whatsoever in the National Bloc. This, obviously, is incorrect.

36 Lamamié, 'Negociaciones'. Note that even in the 1950s Carlists were still bemoaning the exaggeration of Calvo Sotelo's role.

37 Cf. reports of Bloc activities in *SF*, 11, 18 & 25 March, 27 May, 12, 14 & 25 November 1935.

38 *BOT*, 24 March 1935.

39 Arellano, interview.

40 *BOT*, 14 April 1935.
41 The full debate appeared in *El Siglo Futuro*, 26, 27 & 29 December 1934.
42 *SF*, 4 & 8 January 1935.
43 *SF*, 14 January 1935.
44 *SF*, 15 & 18 January 1935.
45 Arrarás, *HSRE*, III, 11–17, 47–8.
46 Gil Robles, *No fue posible la paz*, 142–3; Jackson, *Spanish Republic*, 162–5.
47 *DSC*, 5 December 1934 (Bau), 6 December 1934 (Sangenís). The Statute's rescindment was proposed on 11 December by the Alfonsist Honorio Maura and was supported by the Carlists, Renovación, José Antonio and one ultra-centralist CEDA deputy (*DSC*, 11 December 1934, 25 January 1935).
48 *DSC*, 20 & 21 March 1935.
49 *PN*, 23 March 1935.
50 *La Unión*, 29 & 31 May 1935.
51 The *yunteros* were sub-tenants, so called because of their ownership of a team (*yunta*) of mules, used in ploughing (see Malefakis, *Agrarian Reform and Peasant Revolution*, 127–8). For discussion of Giménez Fernández's tenure of the Ministry of Agriculture, see Malefakis, *op. cit.* 347–55 and Robinson, *Origins of Franco's Spain*, 200–2.
52 *SF*, 28 November 1934.
53 *DSC*, 7 December 1934.
54 *El Sol*, 13 December 1934. In his memoirs Gil Robles appears to accept that these words were actually uttered, even though they do not appear in the official record of the Cortes. He describes Lamamié's attitude, with which many *cedistas* sympathized, as 'incomprehensible' (*No fue posible la paz*, 179).
55 *DSC*, 1 February 1935 (Lamamié); 5 February 1935 (Lamamié and Estévanez); 7 February 1935 (Lamamié and Rodezno).
56 *DSC*, 20 February 1935 (Lamamié and Estévanez).
57 Malefakis, *Agrarian Reform and Peasant Revolution*, 351; Gil Robles, *No fue posible la paz*, 177–82.
58 *SF*, 12 June, 13 July 1935.
59 Ansaldo, *¿Para qué...?*, 103–4; Arrarás, *HSRE*, III, 119.
60 *DSC*, 8 May 1935 (Rodezno).
61 *PN*, 7 May 1935.
62 *SF*, 8 & 20 May 1935.
63 *SF*, 20 May 1935.
64 *SF*, 26 June 1935. Earlier in the year (3 May) *El Siglo Futuro* had suggested that the Socialists would play Sagasta and Gil Robles share the role of Cánovas with Lerroux.
65 *DSC*, 25 June 1935.
66 *SF*, 8 & 12 July 1935.
67 *DSC*, 20 July 1935. See also Arrarás, *HSRE*, III, 167–8. Arrarás, no pro-Republican, admits that there was no serious evidence against Azaña.
68 *SF*, 23 July 1935.
69 Arrarás, *HSRE*, III, 163–5.

70 *SF*, 17 & 19 June, 16 August 1935.
71 *La Unión*, 5 June 1935 (Pradera); *PN*, 22 September 1935; *SF*, 9 & 16 September 1935.
72 In the Cortes, for example, Lamamié urged, 'Let us establish a regime . . .' (*DSC*, 3 October 1935).
73 *SF*, 12 June, 11 & 13 July 1935.
74 Malefakis, *Agrarian Reform and Peasant Revolution*, 356–61.
75 *DSC*, 26 July 1935.
76 *BOT*, 3 March, 14 April 1935.
77 *La Unión*, 6 July 1935; *SF*, 16 July, 12 August 1935.
78 *BOT*, 3 & 10 February 1935. Attention was also paid to rumoured provincial unrest within the CEDA and a supposed grass-roots desire to ditch the Radicals in favour of a reforged alliance with the monarchist parties (*SF*, 31 July, 1 August 1935).
79 E.g. *SF*, 12 March 1935 (Toledo).
80 *PN*, 5 September 1935.
81 *SF*, 24 & 28 May 1935.
82 *PN*, 12 June, 20 August 1935. Gil Robles' version of this dispute is given in *No fue posible la paz*, 189–210.
83 Arrarás, *HSRE*, III, 133.
84 *PN*, 10 August 1935; *La Unión*, 18 August 1935; *SF*, 13 August, 14 November 1935.
85 Arrarás, *HSRE*, III, 89, claims that the CEDA held ten meetings for every one held by the monarchists.
86 Ansaldo, *¿Para qué . . . ?*, 103–4.
87 *PN*, 11 September 1935.
88 *BOT*, 4 August 1935.
89 *SF*, 26 September, 10 October 1935.
90 *PN*, 22 October 1935; *SF*, 21 October 1935.
91 E.g. *SF*, 8 March, 9 & 14 May, 30 July 1935; *PN*, 2 July 1935; *La Unión*, 15 May 1935.
92 *SF*, 24, 26, 29 & 30 October 1935.
93 *DSC*, 28 October, 7 December 1935; *PN*, 31 October 1935.
94 *SF*, 9 December 1935.
95 The cabinet was made up of independents – Chapaprieta and Portela – and representatives of the Radical, Progressive, Agrarian, Lliga and Liberal Democratic parties. See Arrarás, *HSRE*, III, 267–74.
96 *SF*, 14 December 1935.
97 *PN*, 15 & 17 December 1935.
98 *SF*, 16 & 17 December 1935.
99 Throughout 1935 the Carlist authorities had been warning the Communion's members to prepare for an election at the slightest notice (e.g. *PN*, 5 April 1935; *BOT*, 4 August 1935).
100 *SF*, 4 May, 4 October 1935.
101 *BOT*, 22 December 1935; *SF*, 18 & 21 December 1935.
102 Gabriel Jackson, 'The Spanish Popular Front, 1934–37', *Journal of Contemporary History* v, 3 (July 1970), 27–8. To be precise, the contracting parties were: The Republican Left, a fusion of Azaña's Republican

Action, the Radical Socialists and the Galician ORGA; Martínez Barrio's Republican Union, a minority of Radicals who had broken with Lerroux in 1934 over the Amnesty; the Esquerrà; the Socialist Party; the Communist Party; the anti-Stalinist marxists led by Andrés Nin and Joaquín Maurín; and the tiny Syndicalist Party of the maverick Anarcho-Syndicalist Ángel Pestaña.

103 *El Día*, 22 January 1936; Arrarás, *HSRE*, IV, 41.
104 Gil Robles, *No fue posible la paz*, 409–10.
105 *BOT*, 29 December 1935; *SF*, 18, 27 & 28 January 1936.
106 *SF*, 4 January 1936.
107 *SF*, 8 February 1936.
108 *El Día*, 8 February 1936; *SF*, 3, 7 & 12 February 1936; García Venero, *Hedilla*, 86. It would appear that in each case the exclusion was the initiative of the local CEDA organization, anxious once again for ties with the moderate Republican parties. Despite the exclusions the Carlists still had the agreed 30 candidates.
109 *La Unión*, 30 January, 8 February 1936.
110 *SF*, 27 & 29 January 1936; *La Unión*, 6 February 1936.
111 For Rada's activities in the Communion, see Chapters 9 and 10.
112 *SF*, 10 February 1936.
113 *PN*, 21 January 1936.
114 *PN*, 24 January 1936; *SF*, 22, 23 & 30 January 1936; *La Unión*, 5 February 1936; *DAC*, 298.
115 Arrarás, *HSRE*, IV, 39–42.
116 *SF*, 4 & 16 January 1936.
117 *PN*, 14, 15 & 29 January 1936; *SF*, 3 & 12 January 1936.
118 *PN*, 2, 11, 12 & 13 February 1936; *SF*, 22 January, 10, 12 & 15 February 1936.
119 *PN*, 17 January 1936; *SF*, 20 January 1936.
120 *La Unión*, 1 January 1936. The Carlist candidate-to-be in Vizcaya-Province, Gaytán de Ayala, hoped that the PNV would be 'wiped out' in the election (*SF*, 13 January 1936).
121 *La Voz de Navarra*, 7 & 13 February 1936.
122 *SF*, 21 December 1935 (Pradera), 7 January 1936 (Lamamié); *La Unión*, 1 January 1936 (Rodezno); *PN*, 2 January 1936 (Pradera).
123 Gil Robles, *No fue posible la paz*, 423.
124 *SF*, 4 January, 23 February 1936.
125 *PN*, 14 & 16 February 1936; *La Unión*, 11 February 1936; *SF*, 5 February 1936.
126 Interpretations of the result differ widely. Compare, for example, those of Jackson and Galindo Herrero:

Jackson (*Spanish Republic*, 193):

Left	4,700,000
Right	3,997,000
Centre & PNV	579,000

Galindo Herrero (*Los partidos*, 305):

Left	3,912,000
Right	4,187,571

See Arrarás (*HSRE*, IV, 75) for a detailed and not unfair examination of the results.

127 *SF*, 26 February, 2 March 1936. They were: Rodezno, Arellano, Martínez Morentín, Elizalde (Navarre); Oriol (Álava); Comín (Zaragoza); Bau (Tarragona); Valiente, Estévanez (Burgos); Lamamié (Salamanca); Requejo (Toledo); Arauz de Robles (Granada); and Ginés Martínez (Seville).
128 *SF*, 17 February 1936.
129 *SF*, 20 February 1936.

Chapter 9: Preparation for rebellion

1 A fact admitted even by Fal Conde's political enemy Melgar (*El noble final de la escisión dinástica*, 129).
2 *DAC*, 244–8; *BOT*, 9 & 16 December 1934.
3 *SF*, 2 June 1934; *DAC*, 261.
4 *DAC*, 253.
5 *BOT*, 16 & 23 September 1934.
6 *BOT*, 2 December 1934. The Grand Council consisted of some 46 representatives of the Delegations and the general organization, several other prominent figures having been consulted previously. It was to have met in October 1934 but the meeting was postponed on account of the revolution.
7 *BOT*, 18 November 1934.
8 *DAC*, 248, 253.
9 *BOT*, 22 July, 23 September 1934.
10 *BOT*, 9 & 12 December 1934; see below pp. 214–15.
11 *SF*, 18 June 1934.
12 Arellano, interview.
13 *BOT*, 18 November 1934.
14 *SF*, 23 January 1935.
15 *BOT*, 13 January 1935.
16 *SF*, 24 April 1935. During 1934 and 1935 the *Boletín* published several detailed accounts of provincial organizations, listing all local bodies together with their *jefes* etc. These details tend to confirm the Secretariat's statements, but not the more dubious ones of Casariego and Redondo/Zavala.
17 *BOT*, 9 December 1934.
18 *BOT*, 10 & 24 March, 5 May, 7 July, 6 & 13 October 1935; *SF*, 15 January, 2, 16 & 23 March, 6 May, 13 July, 8 & 29 October 1935.
19 *BOT*, 31 March, 20 October 1935; see also *SF*, 3 December 1935. The provincial *jefe* of the Canaries, *in absentia*, was the Sevillian Tejera.
20 *DSC*, 27 June 1935 (Toledo).
21 *SF*, 14 May 1935.
22 *SF*, 8 November 1933. In autumn 1935 the Communion joined other Spanish Catholics in demanding and obtaining the international withdrawal of Josef von Sternberg's Paramount film *The Devil Is a Woman*, which they alleged was 'a travesty of Spanish life' and 'insulted the Spanish armed forces'. In *La Unión* (28 April 1935) Molina Nieto, a priest influenced by Integrism, described 75% of all movies as 'pagan'.
23 *La Unión*, 15 May 1935.

24 *SF*, 28 May, 20 June, 2 & 6 July 1935; *La Unión*, 3 March 1935. The Youth of Seville rejoiced in the membership of the Spanish national goalkeeper, described by the *Boletín* as 'the pride of our race'. (*BOT*, 7 July, 20 October 1935).

25 *BOT*, 22 July 1934.

26 *BOT*, 17 February, 17 November 1935.

27 These included Córdoba and Montilla (*BOT*, 13 January 1935), Tarragona (*SF*, 20 June 1935) and Málaga (*SF*, 1 July 1935). By the end of 1935 the development was general.

28 *BOT*, 20 January 1935.

29 For example the Workers Section of Montilla, founded in the summer of 1934, made special reference to stonemasons, carpenters, shoemakers, printers, barbers, blacksmiths – and rural labourers (*SF*, 20 July 1934).

30 S. Dávila and J. Pemartín, *Hacia la historia de la Falange. Primera contribución de Sevilla* (Jerez de la Frontera, 1938), 91.

31 *La Unión*, 14 April 1935.

32 *La Unión*, 11 December 1935.

33 The leadership of the Gerona organization was fairly typical: the provincial *jefe* was the Conde de Valdellano; the Youth Delegate a doctor of medicine; the Requeté *jefe* a retired army officer; the propaganda delegate a lawyer; and the financial delegate a professional economist. The least characteristic feature here was leadership by an aristocrat, an increasing rarity by 1935 (*BOT*, 27 October 1935).

34 Burgo, *Requetés en Navarra*, 149–51. The description of the Seville circle appears in Redondo and Zavala, *El Requeté*, 280; on the training mission to Italy, see Lizarza, *Conspiración*, 35, and Payne, *Politics and the Military*, 295.

35 E.g. *BOT*, 17 March 1935.

36 *BOT*, 9 & 16 December 1934; 17 March 1935.

37 *BOT*, 19 & 26 May 1935.

38 See below, pp. 222–4.

39 *BOT*, 10 February 1935.

40 *DAC*, 293.

41 Arellano, interview. As an intimate of Rodezno, Arellano expressed the views of Fal Conde's critics, but freely acknowledged his exceptional powers of organization and the admiration which many Carlists felt for him.

42 *CE*, 30 November, 11 December 1934, 25 January, 26 April 1935.

43 *CE*, 25 January 1935. See appendix.

44 *BOT*, 14 April 1935.

45 *CE*, 24 May 1935.

46 *SF*, 17 & 25 May 1935; *BOT* 26 May, 2 June 1935.

47 *CE*, 28 June 1935.

48 *DAC*, 285.

49 *BOT*, 4 August 1935.

50 *PN*, 31 July 1935; Cortés Cavanillas, *Confesiones y muerte de Alfonso XIII*, 121–2.

51 *DAC*, 287; *BOT*, 8 September 1935.

52 *SF*, 21, 28 & 30 May 1934.

53 E.g. *SF*, 24 February 1934.

54 This was particularly true of Fal Conde's *El Observador*, which intermittently serialized the book, beginning on 28 January 1934 and continuing into the spring. Alfonso Carlos' manifesto of July was followed in *La Unión* (13 July 1934) by a recommendation to read Castro Albarrán's book as 'a healthy injection of patriotic optimism' setting out the right path for Spain to follow.

55 *La Unión*, 3 August 1934.

56 *BOT*, 21 July 1935; see also 10 & 24 February, 28 April, 16 June 1935.

57 *SF*, 12 March 1935.

58 *SF*, 27 April 1935 *et seq.*

59 *SF*, 23 June 1935.

60 *PN*, 4 June 1935.

61 *PN*, 15 October 1935.

62 *PN*, 22 May 1935.

63 *SF*, 23 December 1935.

64 *SF*, 4 June 1935.

65 *SF*, 27 November 1935.

66 Pemán, *Varela*, 135; Redondo and Zavala, *El Requeté*, 244, 267.

67 Lizarza, *Conspiración*, 58–9.

68 *Ibid.* 68 *et seq.*

69 *SF*, 26 June 1935.

70 Esteban-Infantes, *General Sanjurjo*, 244–5; Romano, *Sanjurjo*, 182, 194.

71 'El Requeté a punto', *Informaciones* (Madrid), 18 July 1956 (hereafter cited as 'El Requeté a punto').

72 La Cierva, *HGCE*, I, 745.

73 Redondo and Zavala, *El Requeté*, 327–9.

74 'El Requeté a punto'.

75 Lizarza, *Conspiración*, 50–1.

76 Redondo and Zavala, *El Requeté*, 328–9; Lizarza, *Conspiración*, 49.

77 'El Requeté a punto'.

78 B. Félix Maíz, *Alzamiento en España. De un diario de la conspiración* (Pamplona, 1952), 164; Lizarza, *Conspiración*, 83.

79 Lizarza to Zamanillo, 21 March 1935, quoted in Lizarza, *Conspiración*, appendix. The actual figure was 5,964.

80 Redondo and Zavala (*El Requeté*, 326) suggest that there were 8,400 Red Berets ready for combat in Navarre by 1936 – a perfectly credible figure given the continued increase over the previous year, and knowing what we do of the Navarrese role in the actual fighting (see Chapter 11). Redondo and Zavala also claim, more dubiously, that '15 *tercios*' of combat troops and 16 of auxiliary troops existed in Catalonia. The rough total for Catalonia of over 23,000 would appear grossly inflated, although the course of the war in Catalonia makes any serious check impossible. Their figure of 1,500–2,000 for Álava seems more reasonable, if not indeed on the conservative side. Other regions are even harder to assess. The 600 Andalusian Red Berets of 1934 had increased appreciably by the start of 1936, as had numbers in the south-east and the Levant. For Madrid, Casariego (*La*

verdad del Tradicionalismo, 246) gives a figure of 1,716 Red Berets, credible in view of the strength of the Madrid AET.

A more recent and cautious estimate is that offered by Maximiano García Venero, *Historia de la Unificación (Falange y Requeté en 1937)* (Madrid, 1970), 149. García Venero suggests that the basic strength of the Requeté in February 1936 was around 6,000. If other estimates exaggerate the Requeté's size, this surely errs in the opposite direction. Presumably, although he does not say so, García Venero is referring only to fully trained, armed Red Berets; if so his underestimate may not be very great. If partially trained and reserve Red Berets are included – and the war was to prove their effectiveness – then the true figure must be very much higher.

81 *SF*, 18 January 1935.
82 *SF*, 13 & 15 April, 11 November 1935; *BOT*, 21 October, 4 November 1934.
83 *DSC*, 15 February 1935.
84 *DSC*, 21 & 24 June 1935. Tarduchy (*SF*, 22 June 1935) complained that in the Cortes only Cárcer had treated the question with the seriousness that it deserved.
85 *PN*, 4 June 1935.
86 J. W. D. Trythall, *El Caudillo. The Political Biography of Franco* (New York, 1970), 76–7; Payne, *Politics and the Military*, 298, 300, 302–7.
87 Pemán, *Varela*, 136–7, 139.
88 A. Cacho Zabalza, *La Unión Militar Española* (Alicante, 1940), 13–14; Payne, *Politics and the Military*, 293–4.
89 Cacho Zabalza, *La Unión Militar Española*, 26–7.
90 Arrarás, *HCE*, III–13, 442–3; Cacho Zabalza, *La Unión Militar Española*, 19.
91 Payne, *Politics and the Military*, 300–1.
92 'El Requeté a punto'.
93 *SF*, 8 & 9 August 1935.

Chapter 10: *Adveniat Regnum Tuum*

1 Trythall, *El Caudillo*, 80–2.
2 *SF*, 7 March 1936.
3 *PN*, 8 March 1936; *SF*, 18 March 1936.
4 *La Unión*, 11 March 1936.
5 *SF*, 25 February, 26, 27 & 28 March, 11 April 1936; *La Unión*, 15 April 1936.
6 *SF*, 3, 4 & 6 March 1936; Gil Robles, *No fue posible la paz*, 575; Arrarás, *HSRE*, IV, 91.
7 *SF*, 26 & 27 February 1936.
8 *SF*, 28 February 1936.
9 *La Unión*, 29 March 1936. This problem is freely admitted by Gil Robles (*No fue posible la paz*, 573–4). He states that the CEDA was suffering serious losses both of extremists and of those undergoing frustrated *empleomanía*, and that by 16 June 15,000 JAP members had joined the Falange.
10 Payne, *Politics and the Military*, 318.

11 Robinson, *Origins of Franco's Spain*, 264.
12 See below, pp. 245–6, 248, for Gil Robles' interventions in the conspiracy.
13 *SF*, 18 February 1936.
14 *PN*, 17 March 1936.
15 *BOT*, 6 April 1936. The announcement was actually dated 21 January.
16 *DAC*, 299.
17 Melgar, *El noble final de la escisión dinástica*, 132–3; Oyarzun, *Historia del Carlismo*, 575–80; Arellano, interview; Arrarás, *HSRE*, IV, 11–12. See appendix.
18 See below, 320 *et seq.*
19 *SF*, 16 April 1936.
20 *La Unión*, 3 March 1936; *SF*, 1 January 1936. Oyarzun, in his history of Carlism, asserts that enthusiasm for the National Bloc was greatest among the deputies and in the provinces where Carlism was weak. It has already been shown, however, that only six or seven of the deputies were active in it, while opposition was, if anything, more intense in the 'weaker', organizationally minded south than in Navarre and the north generally, where Carlists were more numerous (Oyarzun, *Historia del Carlismo*, 573–4).
21 *SF*, 20, 25 & 28 March, 1, 2 & 3, April 1936.
22 Jackson, *Spanish Republic*, 196, 211–15; La Cierva, *HGCE*, I, 652–60.
23 *DSC*, 30 March, 4 June 1936; *SF*, 5 June 1936.
24 *PN*, 11 April 1936.
25 *SF*, 11 & 12 May 1936.
26 *SF*, 23 & 26 May, 2 June 1936.
27 *La Unión*, 25 May 1936.
28 Jackson, *Spanish Republic*, 215–16; Claude G. Bowers, *My Mission to Spain* (London, 1954), 200–9.
29 E.g. *La Unión*, 5 & 23 May 1936.
30 *SF*, 9 March 1936.
31 *SF*, 17 April 1936.
32 Payne (*Falange*, 103–5) estimates that 'some forty Falangists, several conservatives and well over fifty liberals or leftists were killed' in this period. The Falange, more than ever before, was now receiving financial support from Spanish conservatives.
33 Payne, *Falange*, 98, 104; Gil Robles, *No fue posible la paz*, 573–4. Serrano Súñer was never, as Payne and many others have suggested, the leader of the JAP.
34 García Venero, *Hedilla*, 87.
35 Jato, *La rebelión de los estudiantes*, 209–11. Serious collaboration among students seems to have begun in December 1935, when a 'general strike' of right-wing students was held in protest against the lifting of restrictions on the Generalitat (*ibid.*, 199–204).
36 Gil Robles, *No fue posible la paz*, 637.
37 *SF*, 20 February, 18 April, 22 May 1936.
38 *PN*, 29 March 1936; Burgo, *Requetés en Navarra*, 171–3.
39 E.g. Tejera, in *La Unión*, 27 March 1936.
40 *SF*, 1 June 1936.

41 Stanley G. Payne, *The Spanish Revolution* (London, 1970), 211.
42 Hugh Thomas, *The Spanish Civil War*, 2nd ed. (Harmondsworth, 1965), 150n; for an extended examination of the Communist conspiracy myth, see Herbert R. Southworth, *El Mito de la Cruzada de Franco* (Paris, 1963).
43 *PN*, 25 & 29 January 1935.
44 Arrarás, *HSRE*, IV, 295–6.
45 *El Socialista*, 19 February 1936.
46 García Venero, *Hedilla*, 112.
47 Redondo and Zavala, *El Requeté*, 345.
48 Lizarza, *Conspiración*, 76–7.
49 Félix Maíz, *Alzamiento*, 162.
50 García Venero, *Hedilla*, 113.
51 Pemán, *Varela*, 140–1.
52 Joaquín Bau, 'Calvo Sotelo y la Cruzada', *ABC* (Madrid) 13 July 1954; Ansaldo, *¿Para qué...?* 123.
53 Redondo and Zavala, *El Requeté*, 356.
54 Payne, *Falange*, 108–9.
55 Payne, *Politics and the Military*, 314–15.
56 Pemán, *Varela*, 140–1.
57 Félix Maíz, *Alzamiento*, 56.
58 J. Vigón, *General Mola (El Conspirador)*, (Barcelona, 1957), 88–9. Nevertheless it seems no coincidence that on the day of Mola's arrival in Pamplona, *El Pensamiento Navarro* published an article all but urging military rule.
59 'El Requeté a punto'; Redondo and Zavala, *El Requeté*, 349–50.
60 B. Copado, S. J., *Con la columna de Redondo* (Seville, 1937), 87; *La Unión*, 18 July 1937; Redondo and Zavala, *El Requeté*, 350.
61 'El Requeté a punto'; Romano, *Sanjurjo*, 202; Redondo and Zavala, *El Requeté*, 350. Galindo Herrero (*Los partidos*, 321) writes that Sanjurjo was intended to lead the Cáceres rising. This point is unclear; Cáceres would have been geographically convenient given Sanjurjo's presence in Portugal, but the 'northern' role would have been politically far more dramatic and logical.
62 *SF*, 29 June 1936.
63 Pemán, *Varela*, 144, 147; Arrarás, *HSRE*, IV, 302–3.
64 Bravo Martínez, *Historia de la Falange*, 97.
65 J. M. Iribarren, *El general Mola*, 2nd ed. (Madrid, 1945), 45–7; Félix Maíz, *Alzamiento*, 69–70.
66 Arrarás, *HSRE*, IV, 314; Payne, *Politics and the Military*, 322, 325.
67 Raimundo García was widely known by his journalistic pen-name of 'Garcilaso'.
68 Esteban-Infantes, *General Sanjurjo*, 254–5; Romano, *Sanjurjo*, 203; Iribarren, *Mola*, 51.
69 Lizarza, *Conspiración*, 99–100.
70 Gil Robles (*No fue posible la paz*, 731) is the only authority to mention Arraiza's intervention.
71 Iribarren, *Mola*, 53–5; Arrarás (*HSRE*, IV, 313) gives 27 June as the date of the raid, but there seems no reason to doubt the accuracy of the very different date quoted by all other sources.

72 Iribarren, *Mola*, 55; Vigón, *General Mola*, 94–5; Félix Maíz, *Alzamiento*, 206; Arrarás, *HCE*, III–13, 449.

73 Lizarza, *Conspiración*, 92–3.

74 *Ibid.* 94.

75 Félix Maíz, *Alzamiento*, 149–50; Arrarás, *HCE*, III–13, 449; Lizarza, *Conspiración*, 94–5.

76 The point was acknowledged in an article published in the Carlist *La Unión* on 15 July 1937, as well as by Redondo and Zavala (*El Requeté*, 356–7), who imply that Mola had little objection to the principles themselves.

77 García Venero (*Hedilla*, 129) quotes Zamanillo's own account of the meeting; also Lizarza, *Conspiración*, 97–100.

78 Fal Conde, quoted in *ABC*, 3 May 1968; García Venero, *Hedilla*, 135–6; Payne, *Politics and the Military*, 335.

79 Fal Conde, *loc. cit.*; Payne, *Politics and the Military*, 335–6.

80 Vigón, *General Mola*, 98–9; Esteban-Infantes, *General Sanjurjo*, 255.

81 Iribarren, *Mola*, 76.

82 Lizarza, *Conspiración*, 100.

83 *Ibid.* 101–2; Arrarás, *HCE*; III–13, 457–8; Arrarás, *HSRE*, IV, 319.

84 Bau, 'Calvo Sotelo y la Cruzada'; Vigón, *General Mola*, 102; Robinson, *Origins of Franco's Spain*, 287.

85 Lizarza, *Conspiración*, 103–4.

86 *Ibid.* 105–6. From Félix Maíz's account (*Alzamiento*, 252) it would appear that he too was now operating as a go-between and went to Saint-Jean de Luz with a similar letter. Félix Maíz claims that his letter bore Mola's agreement, but this can hardly have been the case.

87 Cacho Zabalza, *La Unión Militar Española*, 39; M. Silva Ferreiro, *Galicia y el Movimiento Nacional* (Santiago de Compostela, 1938), 112, 272–3; F. Lacruz, *El alzamiento, la revolución y el terror en Barcelona* (Barcelona, 1943), 8; A. Pérez de Olaguer, *El terror rojo en la Montaña* (Barcelona, n.d.), 67–8; A. Gollonet Megías and J. Morales López, *Rojo y azul en Granada* (Granada, 1937), 109.

88 Gil Robles, *No fue posible la paz*, 733.

89 This account is distilled from: Lizarza, *Conspiración*, 107–8; Iribarren, *Mola*, 71–8; Vigón, *General Mola*, 103; Arrarás, *HCE*, III–13, 458; and Arrarás, *HSRE*, IV, 393. The accounts differ somewhat; Iribarren suggests that Don Javier was in basic agreement with the Navarrese, Arrarás that he was hostile but forced to give way.

90 Lizarza, *Conspiración*, 106.

91 Iribarren, *Mola*, 78–80; Arrarás, *HCE*, III–13, 458–9.

92 Robinson, *Origins of Franco's Spain*, 274–5; Payne, *Politics and the Military*, 337–8. The only source which actually mentions Rodezno as one of the assassins' targets is A. Lerroux, *La pequeña historia*, 2nd ed., (Madrid, 1964), 480.

93 Félix Maíz, *Alzamiento*, 255.

94 Arrarás, *HCE*, III–13, 459.

95 Lizarza, *Conspiración*, 109–11.

96 Félix Maíz, *Alzamiento*, 282–3; Lizarza, *Conspiración*, 112; Arrarás, *HCE*, III–13, 459.

97 Lizarza, *Conspiración*, 108.

98 Arellano, interview.
99 Bau, 'Calvo Sotelo y la Cruzada'. Bau was an eye-witness of the crash.

Chapter 11: The Fourth Carlist War

1 J. Pérez Madrigal, *Memorias de un converso* (Madrid, 1943–52), VI, 128–30. The term 'wild-boar' (*jabalí*) was commonly used by the right to describe the rabid anti-clericals of the Radical left wing and the Radical-Socialist Party; 'cave-dwellers' and 'troglodytes' were terms applied to the Carlists by the left.
2 Iribarren, *Mola*, 81.
3 Redondo and Zavala, *El Requeté*, 462.
4 Copado, *Con la columna de Redondo*, 29–30.
5 E. Julio Téllez, *Historia del Movimiento Libertador de España en la provincia gaditana* (Cádiz, 1944), 93, 101–2, 106, 109; Copado, *Con la columna de Redondo*, 10–11.
6 Gollonet Megías and Morales López, *Rojo y azul en Granada*, 107–9; A. Gollonet Megías and J. Morales López, *Sangre y fuego, Málaga* (Granada, 1937), 26–44; G. Gómez Bajuelo, *Málaga bajo el dominio rojo* (Cádiz, 1937), 93–7; Thomas, *Spanish Civil War*, 188–9.
7 F. Bertrán Güell, *Preparación y desarrollo del Alzamiento Nacional* (Valladolid, 1939), 312–13; J. Díaz de Villegas, *Guerra de Liberación* (Barcelona, 1957), 57; J. García Mercadal, *Frente y retaguardia* (Zaragoza, 1937), 124–5.
8 *Boletín de Campaña de los Requetés* (Burgos), 5 December 1936 (hereafter *BCR*); Ansaldo, *¿Para qué...?*, 129.
9 Redondo and Zavala, *El Requeté*, 431–2.
10 J. M. Zugazaga, *Cruz de Requetés* (Madrid, 1942), 18–21, 27.
11 J. M. Resa, *Memorias de un Requeté* (Barcelona, 1968), 40–1; Thomas, *Spanish Civil War*, 202.
12 Gollonet Megías and Morales López, *Rojo y azul en Granada*, 109, 165.
13 The escape of two leading Red Berets from Santander is described in A. Pérez de Olaguer, *El terror rojo en la Montaña*, 67–71; such attempts continued as long as Santander remained in Republican hands. Lamamié's son, a priest, lived for four months in Santander under an assumed name before crossing into Nationalist territory in November 1936 (A. Pérez de Olaguer, 'Piedras vivas'. *Biografía del Capellán Requeté José María Lamamié de Clairac y Alonso* (San Sebastian, 1939), 109–77 *passim*).
14 Lacruz, *Barcelona*, 63–7, 97. Lacruz's figures are substantially those published in *BCR*, 28 August 1936.
15 See below, p. 260.
16 The best first-hand account of this phase in Madrid is probably that of Arturo Barea, in the third and final volume of his autobiography *La forja de un rebelde*. See the most recent edition of the English translation: Arturo Barea, *The Forging of a Rebel* (London, 1972), 514–32.
17 R. de la Cierva y de Hoces, 'The Nationalist Army in the Spanish Civil War', in Carr (ed.), *The Republic and the Civil War in Spain*, 188–9.
18 *PN*, 23 July 1936.

19 García Mercadal, *Frente y retaguardia*, 128–30; *PN*, 23 July 1936.
20 For a more detailed discussion of Mola's problems, see M. Aznar, *Historia militar de la Guerra de España*, 3rd ed., (Madrid, 1958), I, 183.
21 *PN*, 25 July 1936; *BCR*, 25 August 1936; Thomas, *Spanish Civil War*, 266. Resa, *Memorias de un Requeté*, 43–4, gives the figure as 1,600.
22 *PN*, 19 July 1936; Redondo and Zavala, *El Requeté*, 422–3; Aznar, *Historia militar*, 189–90; Díaz de Villegas, *Guerra de Liberación*, 102–3.
23 *PN*, 23 & 25 July 1936; Aznar, *Historia militar*, 213–14.
24 For accounts of this campaign see P. Cía Navascués, *Memorias del Tercio de Montejurra* (Pamplona, 1941); R. Sáinz de los Terreros, *Horas críticas. Como se desarrolló el movimiento revolucionario en la frontera de Bidasoa* (Burgos, 1937); and G. L. Steer, *The Tree of Gernika* (London, 1938).
25 C. G. Ortiz de Villajos, *De Sevilla a Madrid. Ruta libertadora de la columna Castejón* (Granada, 1937), 36–52; A. Olmedo Delgado and J. Cuesta Monereo, *General Queipo de Llano* (Barcelona, 1958), 145; *La Unión*, 25 July 1936.
26 *La Unión*, 27 July, 1 August 1936; *BCR*, 25 August 1936; Copado, *Con la columna de Redondo*, 33–4.
27 Ortiz de Villajos, *De Sevilla a Madrid*, 167 *et seq.*
28 *BCR*, 23 August 1936; *La Unión*, 17 August 1936.
29 *La Unión*, 4 September 1936; *BCR*, 3 October, 7 November 1936 (the latter being a statement by Fal Conde).
30 A figure suggested by Iribarren (*Mola*, 132) and accepted by Thomas (*Spanish Civil War*, 450, n. 1). In the Requeté's bulletin on 3 October, Fal Conde quoted a figure of 35,000 Navarrese out of a total enlistment of 70,000.
31 *BCR*, 17 & 28 August, 26 September 1936; Silva Ferreiro, *Galicia y el Movimiento Nacional*, 294.
32 *PN*, 18 August 1936; Redondo and Zavala, *El Requeté*, 401.
33 *BCR*, 5 September 1936. Towards the end of the year, Fal Conde also created a Special Committee for Catalonian affairs.
34 For examples of the opening of new local organizations, see *PN*, 26 February 1937; *BCR*, 3 October 1936; *La Unión*, 25 September 1936.
35 *La Unión*, 14 October 1936. For independent corroboration of the drift, see R. Serrano Súñer, *Entre Hendaya y Gibraltar* (Madrid, 1947), 25; Aznar, *Historia militar*, I, 82.
36 *BCR*, 20 February 1937; *PN*, 24 January 1937.
37 *PN*, 8 & 9 January 1937.
38 Burgo, *Conspiración*, 63, 66–9.
39 Interview with Antonio Márquez, a former member of the JAP and the Falange in Arriate.
40 These details are drawn from the valuable work by S. Nonell Bru, *Así eran nuestros muertos* (Barcelona, 1965), *passim*.
41 *BCR*, 14 November 1936; *La Unión*, 10 April 1937; Redondo and Zavala, *El Requeté*, 405; F. M. Noriega (ed.), *Fal Conde y el Requeté*, (Burgos, 1937), 29–30; Thomas, *Spanish Civil War*, 794.
42 Burgo, *Conspiración*, 55.
43 Peter Kemp, *Mine Were of Trouble* (London, 1957); an interesting

fictionalized version of Kemp's experiences appears in the novel by Peter Elstob, *The Armed Rehearsal* (London, 1964).

44 Bernard Bergonzi, 'Roy Campbell: Outsider on the Right', *Journal of Contemporary History* II, 2 (April 1967), refutes the account in the anonymously edited collection, *Hommage à Roy Campbell* (Montpellier, 1958).

45 See Harold Cardozo, *March of a Nation* (London, 1937), 32 (this being the account by the *Daily Mail* correspondent), and F. McCullagh, *In Franco's Spain* (London, 1937), 126–7.

46 *BCR*, 7 November 1936.

47 Nonell Bru, *Así eran nuestros muertos, passim.*

48 J. de Ramón-Laca, *Bajo la férula de Queipo. Como fue gobernada Andalucía* (Seville, 1939), 32.

49 Burgo, *Conspiración*, 834–5.

50 *PN*, 25 December 1936, 23 January 1937; *BCR*, 21 August 1936; Iribarren, *Mola*, 132; Ignacio Romero Raizábal, *Boinas rojas en Austria* (San Sebastian, 1939), 52.

51 Zugazaga, *Cruz de Requetés*, 36.

52 Burgo, *Conspiración*, 687; Redondo and Zavala, *El Requeté*, 407–11.

53 *PN*, 23, 25 & 29 July 1936; *BCR*, 13 August, 1 September 1936.

54 *La Unión*, 5 August 1936.

55 *BCR*, 24 October 1936; Marqués de San Juan de Piedras Albas, *Héroes y mártires de la aristocracia española* (Madrid, 1945), 281.

56 José Echeandía, *La persecución roja en el País Vasco* (Barcelona, 1945), *passim*; A. de Castro Albarrán, *Este es el cortejo. Héroes y mártires de la Cruzada española* (Salamanca, 1938), 168–73; F. Carasa Torre, *Presos de los rojo-separatistas* (San Sebastian, 1938), 29–30, 170–1; *PN*, 8 & 17 September 1936; *BCR*, 30 January 1937.

57 *PN*, 25 September 1936, 5 February 1937; E. Puig Mora, *La tragedia roja. Memorias de un evadido* (Zaragoza, 1937), 39–40, 57; T. Caballé y Clos, *Barcelona roja. Dietario de la revolución* (Barcelona, 1939), 32, 62; Lacruz, *Barcelona*, 121 *et seq.*

58 J. Gutiérrez-Ravé, *Las Cortes errantes del Frente Popular* (Madrid, 1953), 202.

59 Gómez Bajuelo, *Málaga*, 152; Gollonet Megías and Morales López, *Málaga*, 332; Redondo and Zavala, *El Requeté*, 471; Srta María Teresa Huelín, interview.

60 Payne, *Falange*, 138–41; Borrás, *Ramiro Ledesma Ramos*, 777–82; Redondo and Zavala, *El Requeté*, 394.

61 In Ernest Hemingway's *For Whom the Bell Tolls* (London, 1941) for example, the Requeté appears as the incarnation of Nationalist fanaticism; see also Elstob, *The Armed Rehearsal* and William Herrick, *Hermanos!* (Harmondsworth, 1973), 284.

62 On the repression in Navarre, see Thomas, *Spanish Civil War*, 220–4, and Thomas' chief sources: Juan de Iturralde, *El catolicismo y la Cruzada de Franco*, II (Bayonne, 1960) and Fr. Iñaki de Aberrigoyen, *Sept mois et sept jours dans l'Espagne de Franco* (Paris, 1938). For the best pro-Nationalist account: Burgo, *Conspiración*, 87–107.

63 Burgo, *Conspiración*, 91. The actual figure accepted by Burgo is 678 judicial and summary executions.

64 Burgo, *Conspiración*, 96–101.
65 F. Díaz-Plaja (ed.), *La historia de España en sus documentos. El siglo XX. La Guerra (1936–39)* (Madrid, 1963), 167–8.
66 Félix Maíz, *Alzamiento*, 307–10.
67 *Boletín Oficial de la Junta de Defensa Nacional de España* (Burgos), 25 July, 4 August 1936 (hereafter *BOJD*).
68 Burgo, *Conspiración*, 31–2.
69 Díaz-Plaja, *Documentos*, 174–6.
70 *BOJD*, 30 July 1936.
71 *PN*, 30 July 1936.
72 *PN*, 31 July, 1 August 1936.
73 *PN*, 23 July, 2 August 1936.
74 *PN*, 25 & 26 July 1936.
75 *PN*, 2, 8, 14 & 18 August 1936.
76 *PN*, 21, 22 & 25 August 1936. After the capture of Irún in September, non-PNV representatives of Irún and Fuenterrabía apparently besought their Navarrese 'liberators' to admit their towns into Navarre (*PN*, 23 September 1936; Burgo, *Conspiración*, 165–71).
77 *BCR*, 8 August 1936.
78 *La Unión*, 19 August 1936.
79 *BCR*, 19 September 1936.
80 *PN*, 18 August 1936.
81 *PN*, 21 October 1936.
82 Burgo (*Conspiración*, 682) says that *El Pensamiento Navarro* was fervently pro-Regency. If this was indeed the case with its editorial board, then no evidence of its feelings was permitted to appear in the newspaper itself.
83 *BCR*, 12 December 1936.
84 *PN*, 31 December 1936.
85 *PN*, 22 October 1936.
86 Lizarza, *Conspiración*, 108.
87 *PN*, 5, 9 & 18 August, 8 September, 13 October 1936.
88 *Diario de Navarra*, 2 September 1936; *PN*, 15 & 19 August 1936; G. Orizana and J. M. Martín Liébana, *El Movimiento Nacional* (Valladolid, 1937), 70–2; Burgo, *Conspiración*, 43.
89 Burgo, *Conspiración*, 49–51.
90 *Ibid.* 41–2.
91 *BCR*, 1 September 1936.
92 *BCR*, 26 September 1936.
93 *La Unión*, 20 August 1936; *BCR*, 17 August, 19 September 1936.
94 Payne, *Falange*, 121–2.
95 Some Carlists, however, were worried without saying so publicly. See Burgo, *Conspiración*, 576–8.
96 *La Unión*, 14, 21 & 26 September 1936; *El Pensamiento Alavés* (Vitoria), 31 August 1936.
97 E.g. Fal Conde (*BCR*, 17 August 1936) and Arellano (*PN*, 28 August 1936).
98 *BCR*, 3 August 1936. García Venero (*Hedilla*, 291) speaks of Falangist respect for Fal Conde.

Chapter 12: The New State

1   *Documents on German Foreign Policy 1918–1945. Series D, vol. 3: Germany and the Spanish Civil War 1936–1939* (London, 1951), no. 43, 42–3; also no. 16, 16 (hereafter *DGFP*).

2   This account derives mainly from A. Kindelán, *Mis cuadernos de guerra* (Madrid, 1945), 49–56; Vigón, *General Mola*, 252–4; and Payne, *Politics and the Military*, 369–73.

3   *BOJD*, 30 September 1936.

4   Romero Raizábal, *Boinas rojas en Austria*, 17–20, 35–6, 50–2.

5   *PN*, 30 September, 7 October 1936.

6   *Boletín Oficial del Estado* (Burgos), 2 October 1936 (hereafter BOE).

7   *PN*, 11 October 1936.

8   The Italian ambassador, Roberto Cantalupo, formed the definite impression that the Carlists 'openly protected the Franco government' whereas the Falange represented an adversary. However, Cantalupo's contacts with the Communion appear to have centred on Rodezno, and hence he perhaps tended to generalize from his knowledge of the most flexible of Carlists. See Roberto Cantalupo, *Embajada en España* (Barcelona, 1951), 104–5.

9   Preston, 'Alfonsist Monarchism', 114.

10   *PN*, 15 October 1936.

11   *BCR*, 3 October 1936.

12   *DAC*, 319.

13   *La Unión*, 21 October 1936.

14   M. García Venero, *Historia de la Unificación*, 169; Romero Raizábal, *Boinas rojas en Austria*, 192–3, claims that Fal Conde was now desirous of giving up his leadership, but there is no evidence to support this statement.

15   *BCR*, 7 November 1936 *et seq*. See below, p. 279.

16   An argument forcefully expressed by Román Oyarzun in *El Pensamiento Navarro*, 31 December 1936 and 10 January 1937, and leading to a lively correspondence.

17   *BCR*, 12 September 1936.

18   *BCR*, 19 September 1936.

19   For lengthy exposition of the theory underlying the *Obra Nacional Corporativa*, see *La Unión*, 30 December 1936; *BCR*, 16 January, 5 February 1937; *PN*, 16 & 21 January 1937.

20   *BCR*, 13, 20 & 27 February, 13 March 1937.

21   On 5 February 1937, the Bulletin bore a banner headline which stated unambiguously: 'The *Obra Nacional Corporativa* and the *Movimiento Nacional-Agrario*, bases of our State when it reaches completion'.

22   *La Unión*, 30 December 1936, 2 February 1937; *Hoja Oficial del Lunes de Guipúzcoa* (San Sebastian), 25 January 1937.

23   *Diario de Burgos*, 9 March 1937. The incorporation of the CESO into the *Obra Nacional Corporativa* was actually sealed in March, having been expected since November (*La Unión*, 12 November 1936). This confederation of Catholic unions was founded in 1935 with 276,000 members; presumably this membership increased after the start of the Civil War. See

J. N. García-Nieto Paris, *El sindicalismo cristiano en España. Notas sobre su origen y evolución hasta 1936* (Bilbao, 1960), 190.

24 García Venero, *Hedilla*, 291–3 (testimonies of Fal Conde and Zamanillo); Burgo, *Conspiración*, 687–8.

25 *PN*, 16, 17 & 18 December 1936 (serialized text of decree).

26 Payne, *Falange*, 143.

27 The above account is distilled from: García Venero, *Hedilla*, 291–4 and *Historia de la Unificación*, 157–8; Burgo, *Conspiración*, 692–3; Payne, *Politics and the Military*, 376; and Thomas, *Spanish Civil War*, 449–50.

28 *DGFP*, 268.

29 Burgo, *Conspiración*, 702–3.

30 *BOE*, 19 December 1936.

31 *BOE*, 30 December 1936.

32 *BOE*, 22 December 1936.

33 *BOE*, 28 January, 1 February 1937.

34 *PN*, 5 & 7 February 1937.

35 E.g. in *El Pensamiento Navarro*, 1 November 1936, Elizalde expressed complete confidence in the generals 'who achieve what they promise'. Later the same month an editorial in *El Pensamiento Navarro* praised Franco's Catholicism.

36 *BCR*, 2 January, 5 & 20 February 1937; *La Unión*, 3 January 1937.

37 *BCR*, 27 February 1937.

38 E.g. *La Rioja* (Logroño), 29 August 1937; *Arriba España* (Pamplona), 20 January 1937.

39 Payne, *Falange*, 128–9.

40 Payne, *Falange*, 149–54; R. de la Cierva y de Hoces, 'Un aspecto de la evolución política de la zona nacional en la guerra: la trayectoria de la Falange hasta la unificación de 1937', in V. Palacio Atard, R. de la Cierva y de Hoces and R. Salas Larrazábal, *Aproximación histórica a la Guerra española (1936–1939)* (Madrid, 1970), 209–14.

41 Antonio Bahamonde, *Memoirs of a Spanish Nationalist* (London, 1939), 23–4.

42 García Venero, *Hedilla*, 171–3.

43 All Carlist sources agree on this. See, for example, M. R. Úrraca Pastor, *Así empezamos. Memorias de una enfermera* (Bilbao, n.d.), 123; independent corroboration is provided by Héctor Colmegna, *Diario de un médico argentino en la guerra de España* (Madrid, 1941), 53.

44 Burgo, *Conspiración*, 576.

45 *Arriba España*, 16 & 20 January, 7 February 1937.

46 *DGFP*, 107.

47 *Diario de Navarra*, 31 October 1936.

48 García Venero, *Hedilla*, 324.

49 *PN*, 19 December 1936.

50 *Arriba España*, 3 January 1937.

51 *Arriba España*, 6 January 1937.

52 *Diario de Burgos* (Burgos), 24 May 1937 (testimony of Sancho Dávila).

53 García Venero, *Hedilla*, 323–4 (testimonies of Gamero and Escario).

54 Sancho Dávila, *José Antonio, Salamanca y otras cosas* ... (Madrid, 1967), 106–7.

55 *Ibid.* 107.

56 Fal Conde (*PN*, 17 November 1968) has suggested that they did not have Hedilla's permission to make the trip; García Venero says (*Hedilla*, 324) that Gamero and Escario did have Hedilla's blessing but that he knew nothing of Dávila's involvement.

57 Burgo, *Conspiración*, 754.

58 The following account draws principally from: García Venero, *Hedilla*, 324–7; Payne, *Falange*, 154–7; and Burgo, *Conspiración*, 754–60.

59 Sancho Dávila, *José Antonio*, 114.

60 Burgo, *Conspiración*, 763; Sancho Dávila, *José Antonio*, 114–15; García Venero, *Historia de la Unificación*, 169–72.

61 Serrano Súñer, *Entre Hendaya y Gibraltar*, 26–30. At this time Franco was under pressure from the German Ambassador to hand over power to the Falange, which von Faupel was doing his best to Nazify (see Cantalupo, *Embajada en España*, 101–6). Cantalupo also suggests that the leaders of the 'militias' – i.e. of the Communion and the Falange – knew nothing of the impending unification, but this is incredible. On Serrano Súñer, see García Venero, *Historia de la Unificación*, 173–81.

62 Burgo, *Conspiración*, 764–6.

63 *Ibid.* 767.

64 García Venero, *Hedilla*, 354–5; *Historia de la Unificación*, 181, 188.

65 García Venero, *Historia de la Unificación*, 188–9; *Hedilla*, 351; Payne, *Falange*, 156.

66 Burgo, *Conspiración*, 767–8.

67 *Ibid.* 773. It is also possible (see García Venero, *Historia de la Unificación*, 189) that two more Carlists were present, namely the Conde de Florida and Marcelino Ulibarri, but this detail is uncertain.

68 García Venero, *Historia de la Unificación*, 209.

69 Burgo (*Conspiración*, 773–84) provides a detailed description of the assembly's proceedings; García Venero, *Historia de la Unificación*, 190–1, gives a briefer account.

70 Burgo, *Conspiración*, 783.

71 García Venero, *Hedilla*, 355.

72 *BOE*, 20 April 1937.

73 Serrano Súñer, *Entre Hendaya y Gibraltar*, 34.

74 E.g. *La Unión*, 20 & 21 April 1937; *PN*, 20–7 April 1937.

75 Burgo, *Conspiración*, 814.

76 *Ibid.* 790–4.

77 García Venero, *Historia de la Unificación*, 216.

78 *BOE*, 25 April 1937.

79 Thomas, *Spanish Civil War*, 533–4.

80 *Boletín del Movimiento de FET y de las JONS* (Salamanca), 15 August 1937 (hereafter *BMFET*). The orders were transmitted in a series of telegrams from the FET Secretariat during April, May and June and summarized in this, the second issue of the FET bulletin.

81 *BMFET*, 15 August 1937.

82 *BMFET*, 1 September 1937.
83 *BMFET*, 15 August 1937.
84 Bahamonde, *Memoirs of a Spanish Nationalist*, 24–5; Ansaldo, *¿Para qué ...?*, 78; Sir Robert Hodgson, *Spain Resurgent* (London, 1953), 95–6. See also the complaints in *BMFET*, 15 September 1937 *et seq.*
85 *BMFET*, 1 November 1937.
86 Burgo, *Conspiración*, 843–5.
87 *BMFET*, 1 November 1937. They were: Rodezno, Bilbao, Muñoz Aguilar, Joaquín Baleztena, Úrraca Pastor, Valiente, Fal Conde, Oriol, Dolz Espejo (Conde de Florida), Arellano, Romualdo Toledo.
88 Payne, *Falange*, 192; Burgo, *Conspiración*, 847–8.
89 *BMFET*, 15 March 1938.
90 Burgo, *Conspiración*, 837–9.
91 *Ibid.* 845–6.
92 Thomas, *Spanish Civil War*, 613–14.
93 Payne, *Falange*, 192–3.
94 *PN*, 17 September 1968.
95 *BMFET*, 1938 *passim*, especially the issues of 15 March and 1 June.
96 F. Franco y Bahamonde, *Palabras del Caudillo* (Madrid, 1939), 168–9.

Epilogue: Carlism in the Spain of Franco

1 On the political and administrative structure of Franco Spain, see Kenneth M. Medhurst, *Government in Spain* (Oxford, 1973), *passim*; and Stanley G. Payne, *Franco's Spain* (London, 1968), 16–47.
2 Payne, *Falange*, 234–6.
3 I. Romero Raizábal, *El prisionero de Dachau 156.270* (Zaragoza, 1972).
4 Burgo, *Conspiración*, 450–62.
5 *Ibid.* 444–5; Melgar, *El noble final de la escisión dinástica*, 139.
6 Melgar, *El noble final de la escisión dinástica*, 146–57, 203–8; Burgo, *Conspiración*, 464–88.
7 On the expulsion and related matters, see E. Alvarez Puga, 'El Carlismo en la encrucijada', *Mundo* (Madrid), 29 May 1971; also *Montejurra* (Pamplona), March 1971 for the subsequent expulsion of Doña Cecilia of Bourbon–Parma, sister of Carlos Hugo.
8 Flysheet circulated by the A.E.C. (Carlist Students' Association), Madrid, 1972.

Bibliography

Note. The bibliography contains all those primary and secondary sources which are either cited in the text or which, while not directly cited, nevertheless contributed something to the author's general appreciation of the problems examined in the book. Those acquainted with Carlist and Spanish Civil War bibliography will note the absence of any reference to the so-called 'Carlist Archive' in Seville. The archive, actually a private collection compiled by the Carlist historian Melchor Ferrer, was closed after Ferrer's death in 1965, shortly after access had been granted to the author but before research could actually begin. Thanks to the prior efforts of other historians such as Jaime del Burgo and Professors Thomas and Payne, however, it seems unlikely that the loss has been more than marginal.

1. UNPUBLISHED SOURCES

Archivo Histórico Nacional, Madrid (AHN)
  Sección del Estado: Legajos 8110, 8111, 8114, 8115, 8122, 8124, 8125, 8126, 8128, 8129, 8130, 8143.
  Sección de Consejos: Legajos 12206, 12215, 12217.

2. PUBLISHED DOCUMENTARY SOURCES

(i) *Parliamentary debates*

Diario de sesiones de las Cortes Constituyentes de la República española, comenzaron el 14 de julio de 1931. 25 vols. (Cited as *DSCC.*)
Diario de las sesiones de Cortes, Congreso de los Diputados, comenzaron el 8 de diciembre de 1933. 17 vols. (Cited as *DSC.*)
Diario de las sesiones de Cortes, Congreso de los Diputados, comenzaron el 16 de marzo de 1936. 3 vols. (Cited as *DSC.*)

(ii) *Printed documents*

Borbón y de Austria Este, Alfonso Carlos de (Duque de San Jaime). *Documentos* (ed. Melchor Ferrer). Madrid, 1950. (Cited as *DAC.*)
Borbón y de Austria Este, Carlos de (Carlos VII). *Autógrafos de D. Carlos. Manifiestos, proclamas, alocuciones, cartas y otros documentos del augusto Sr. Duque de Madrid* (ed. M. Polo de Peyrolón). Valencia, 1900.

Testamento político. Reprinted edition. Pamplona, 1934.

Cartas inéditas (Prologue, notes and appendices by J. de Carlos Gómez-Rodolfo). Madrid, 1959.

Borbón-Parma, Francisco Javier de (Príncipe Regente de la Comunión Tradicionalista y los Carlistas). *Manifiestos y objetivos de la Regencia*. n.pl., 1941.

Cierva y de Hoces, Ricardo de la. *Los documentos de la primavera trágica. Análisis documental de los antecedentes inmediatos del 18 de julio de 1936*. Madrid, 1969.

Cortés Cavanillas, Julián. *Acta de acusación: epístolas, documentos, frases y diálogos para la historia de la segunda República*. Madrid, 1933.

Crónica de la Asamblea General Jaimista celebrada en Zaragoza los días 13, 14, 15 y 16 de octubre de 1921. Zaragoza, 1923.

Declaración colectiva del Episcopado español sobre el espíritu y actuación de los católicos en las presentes circunstancias. Madrid, 1932.

Díaz-Plaja, Fernando (ed.). *La historia de España en sus documentos. El siglo XX. Dictadura ... República (1923–1936)*. Madrid, 1964.

La historia de España en sus documentos. El siglo XX. La guerra (1936–1939). Madrid, 1963.

Documents on German Foreign Policy 1918–1945. Series D, vol. 3: Germany and the Spanish Civil War 1936–1939. London, 1951. (Cited as *DGFP*.)

Ferrer, Melchor (ed.). *Antología de los documentos reales de la dinastía carlista*. Madrid, 1951.

La Iglesia y la guerra civil española (documentos eclesiásticos). Buenos Aires, 1947.

Manifiesto de D. Hernando Larramendi. Madrid, 1933.

Ministerio de Justicia. *Causa General. La dominación roja en España. Avance de la información instruida por el ministerio público*. Madrid, 1944.

(iii)   *Government and official bulletins*

Boletín de Información Bibliográfica y Parlamentaria de España y del Extranjero (Madrid). November 1933–August 1934.

Boletín Oficial de la Junta de Defensa Nacional de España (Burgos), July–September 1936. (Cited as *BOJD*.)

Boletín Oficial del Estado (Burgos), October 1936–May 1937. (Cited as *BOE*.)

Boletín del Movimiento de Falange Española Tradicionalista y de las JONS (Salamanca), May 1937–April 1939. (Cited as *BMFET*.)

3.   NEWSPAPERS AND PERIODICALS

Acción Española (Monarchist monthly review, Madrid), 1932–1936.

a.e.t. (Carlist Youth weekly, Pamplona), February–July 1934. (Cited as *a.e.t.*)

Arriba España (Falangist daily, Pamplona), November 1936–May 1937.

Boletín de Campaña de los Requetés (Carlist weekly, Burgos), August 1936–April 1937. (Cited as *BCR*.)

Boletín de Orientación Tradicionalista (Carlist weekly, Madrid), July 1934–April 1936. (Cited as *BOT*.)

La Constancia (Integrist, then Carlist daily, San Sebastian), April 1931–July 1936.

El Correo Catalán (Carlist daily, Barcelona), March 1931–December 1932.

Criterio (Carlist weekly, Madrid), January–June 1932.

El Cruzado Español (Carlist weekly, then twice weekly, Madrid), April 1931–December 1935. (Cited as *CE*.)

El Debate (Independent Catholic, then CEDA daily, Madrid), April 1931–July 1936.

El Día (Independent Catholic, pro-Carlist daily, Alicante), October–December 1933 and January–April 1936.

Diario de Burgos (Nationalist daily, Burgos), July 1936–December 1937.

Diario de Navarra (Independent Catholic, pro-Carlist daily, Pamplona), January 1931–December 1937.

La Época (Monarchist daily, Madrid), November 1931–December 1935.

España (Carlist weekly, then monthly, Las Palmas), March 1935–April 1936.

F.E. (Falangist weekly, Madrid and Seville), December 1933–July 1934.

Montejurra (Carlist monthly, Pamplona), 1970–1.

El Observador (Carlist weekly, Seville), November 1932–July 1934.

El Pensamiento Navarro (Carlist daily, Pamplona), December 1930–March 1939. (Cited as *PN*.)

Reacción (Carlist weekly, Barcelona), July 1931–December 1933.

El Siglo Futuro (Integrist, then Carlist daily, Madrid), January 1930–July 1936. (Cited as *SF*.)

El Socialista (Socialist daily, Madrid), April 1931–July 1936.

El Sol (Independent Republican daily, Madrid), April–July 1931, October–December 1933, December 1934, January–March 1936.

Tradición (Carlist fortnightly, Santander), December 1933–March 1934.

La Unión (Independent, then Carlist daily, Seville), January 1931–July 1938.

La Voz de España (Carlist daily, San Sebastian), December 1936–July 1937.

La Voz de Navarra (Basque Nationalist daily, Pamplona), January 1931–July 1936.

In addition to the above continuous runs of newspapers and periodicals, numerous short runs and odd copies were also consulted. These included:

ABC (Madrid), 1931–6, 1954, 1968.

La Actualidad Española (Madrid), 1968, 1971.

Ayer (Jerez de la Frontera), 1937.

Biblioteca Popular Carlista (Barcelona), 1896–7.

Boina Roja (Ávila), 1937.

El Castellano (Burgos), 1936.

El Católico (Madrid), 1840–8.

El Correo de Andalucía (Seville), 1936.

Diario de Ávila (Ávila), 1936.

Diario de Jerez (Jerez de la Frontera), 1936–7.

F.E. (Seville), 1936–7.

Heraldo Alavés (Vitoria), 1931–2.

Hoja Oficial del Lunes de Guipúzcoa (San Sebastian), 1937.

Hoy (Badajoz), 1936–7.

Ideal (Granada), 1936–7.

El Ideal Gallego (Corunna), 1936.

Informaciones (Madrid), 1954, 1956.

Joventut (Valls), 1931.

El Lunes (Zaragoza), 1936–7.

El Norte de Castilla (Valladolid), 1936–7.

El Pensamiento Alavés (Vitoria), 1933–7.

La Provincia Nueva (Castellón), 1933.

Rádica (Pamplona), 1931.

Reconquista (Palma de Mallorca), 1934.

La Restauración (Valencia), 1843–4.

Ribereño Navarro (Tudela), 1936–7.

La Rioja (Logroño), 1936–7.

Tradición Navarra (Pamplona), 1931.

Tradición Vasca (San Sebastian), 1931.

Unidad (San Sebastian), 1936–7.

4. ANTHOLOGIES, COLLECTED WRITINGS, THEORETICAL WORKS
   AND SPEECHES

Aparisi y Guijarro, Antonio. *La cuestión dinástica*. Madrid, 1869.

   En defensa de la libertad (ed. S. Galindo Herrero). Madrid, 1957.

Aunós Pérez, Eduardo. *La reforma corporativa del Estado.* Madrid, 1935.

Balmes, Jaime. *Obras completas.* 6 vols. Madrid, 1948–50.

Borbón y de Austria Este, Carlos de (Carlos VII, Duque de Madrid).
   Escritos políticos (ed. Melchor Ferrer). Madrid, 1957.

   Antología (ed. Jaime del Burgo). Pamplona, 1947.

Campión y Jaime-Bon, Arturo. *Discursos políticos y literarios*. Pamplona, 1907.

Castro Albarrán, Aniceto de. *El derecho a la rebeldía*. Madrid, 1934.

Donoso Cortés, Juan. *Textos políticos.* Madrid, 1954.

Escobar, José Ignacio (Marqués de Valdeiglesias); Vigón, Jorge, & Vegas Latapié, Eugenio. *Escritos sobre la instauración monárquica.* Madrid, 1955.

Franco y Bahamonde, Francisco. *Palabras del Caudillo.* Madrid, 1939.

Gil Robles, José María. *Discursos políticos.* Madrid, 1971.

Giménez Caballero, Ernesto. *La nueva catolicidad. Teoría general sobre el fascismo — en Europa; en España.* Madrid, 1933.

Gutiérrez-Ravé, José (ed.). *Habla el Rey: discursos de don Alfonso XIII.* Madrid, 1955.

Herrera Oria, Ángel. *Obras selectas* (ed. J. M. Sánchez de Muniáin & J. L. Gutiérrez García). Madrid, 1963.

Lamamié de Clairac, José María. *Documentos parlamentarios. En defensa de la Compañía de Jesús.* Madrid, 1932.

Ledesma Ramos, Ramiro. *Antología* (ed. A. Macipe López). Barcelona, 1940.

¿Fascismo en España? Discurso a las juventudes de España. Barcelona, 1968.

Maeztu, Ramiro de. *Defensa de la Hispanidad.* Madrid, 1934.

Frente a la República (ed. G. Fernández de la Mora). Madrid, 1956.

El nuevo tradicionalismo y la revolución social (ed. Vicente Marrero). Madrid, 1959.

Antología (ed. F. González Navarro). Madrid, 1960.

Marrero, Vicente (ed.). *El tradicionalismo español del siglo XIX.* Madrid, 1955.

Menéndez Pelayo, Marcelino. *Textos sobre España* (ed. F. Pérez Embid). Madrid, 1962.

Mola y Vidal, Emilio. *Obras completas.* Valladolid, 1940.

Nocedal y Rodríguez de la Flor, Cándido. *Discursos.* Madrid, 1860.

Pemán, José María. *Cartas a un escéptico ante la monarquía.* 4th edn., Madrid, 1956.

Pradera, Víctor. *El Estado Nuevo.* Madrid, 1935.

The New State (tr. B. Malley). London, 1939. (Cited as *TNS.*)

Obra completa. 2 vols. Madrid, 1945.

Primo de Rivera, José Antonio. *Obras completas* (ed. A. del Río Cisneros & E. Conde Gargollo). Madrid, 1942.

Textos inéditos y epistolario (ed. A. del Río Cisneros & E. Pavón Pereyra). Madrid, 1956.

Redondo, Onésimo. *Obras completas (edición cronológica).* 2 vols. Madrid, 1954–5.

Río Cisneros, Agustín del (ed.). *El pensamiento de José Antonio.* Madrid, 1962.

Sáinz Rodríguez, Pedro. *La Tradición nacional y el Estado futuro.* Madrid, 1935.

Sardà y Salvany, Félix. *Propaganda católica.* 9 vols. Barcelona, 1883–94.

Thomas, Hugh (ed.). *José Antonio Primo de Rivera. Selected Writings.* London, 1972.

Torras Bages, José; Maragall, Juan, & Cambó, Francisco. *La actitud tradicional en Cataluña* (ed. J. B. Solervicens). Madrid, 1961.

Vázquez de Mella y Fanjul, Juan. *Ideario*. 3 vols. Madrid & Barcelona, 1931.

Política general. 2 vols. Madrid & Barcelona, 1932.

Política tradicionalista. 2 vols. Madrid & Barcelona, 1932.

Regionalismo. 2 vols. Madrid & Barcelona, 1935.

Regionalismo y monarquía (ed. S. Galindo Herrero). Madrid, 1957.

Vegas Latapié, Eugenio. *Escritos políticos*. Madrid, 1940.

Vidal i Barraquer, Arxiu. *Esglesia i Estat durant la segona Republica Espanyola 1931–1936*. I, Montserrat, 1971.

5. MEMOIRS, EYE-WITNESS ACCOUNTS AND BIOGRAPHIES

(i) *Memoirs and eye-witness accounts*

Aberrigoyen, Iñaki de. *Sept mois et sept jours dans l'Espagne de Franco*. Paris, 1938.

Agire Lekube, de (= Aguirre Lecube), José Antonio. *Entre la libertad y la revolución 1930–1935: la verdad de un lustro en el País Vasco*. Bilbao, 1935.

Freedom was Flesh and Blood. London, 1945.

Albiñana, José María. *Confinado en Las Hurdes*. Madrid, 1933.

Alcalá Zamora, Niceto. *Los defectos de la Constitución de 1931*. Madrid, 1936.

Ansaldo, Juan Antonio. *¿Para qué . . .? (De Alfonso XIII a Juan III)*. Buenos Aires, 1951.

Armiñán Odriozola, L. de. *Por los caminos de guerra (De Navalcarnero a Gijón)*. Madrid, 1939.

Avilés, G. *Tribunales rojos vistos por un abogado defensor*. Barcelona, 1939.

Ayerra Redín, Marino. *No me avergoncé del Evangelio*. Buenos Aires, 1959.

Azaña, Manuel. *Obras completas*. vol. IV. Mexico City, 1968.

(Azaña, Manuel). *Memorias íntimas de Azaña* (ed. J. Arrarás). 5th ed. Madrid, 1950.

Bahamonde, Antonio. *Memoirs of a Spanish Nationalist*. London, 1939.

Barea, Arturo. *The Forging of a Rebel*. London, 1972.

Bauer, Eddy. *Rouge et Or (Chroniques de la 'Reconquête' espagnole 1937–1938)*. Neuchâtel, 1939.

Berenguer, Damaso (Conde de Xauen). *De la Dictadura a la República. Crisis del reinado de Alfonso XIII*. Madrid, 1946.

Bernanos, Georges. *A Diary of My Times* (tr. Pamela Morris). London, 1938.

Bolín, Luis A. *Spain: the Vital Years*. London, 1967.

Borbón y de Austria Este, Alfonso (Carlos) de. *Mis memorias*. Madrid, 1934.

Borbón y de Austria Este, Carlos de (Carlos VII). *Memorias y diario de Carlos VII* (ed. B. Ramos Martínez). Madrid, 1957.

Borkenau, Franz. *The Spanish Cockpit. An Eye-Witness Account of the Political and Social Conflicts of the Spanish Civil War*. Ann Arbor, 1963.

Bowers, Claude G. *My Mission to Spain: Watching the Rehearsal for World War II.* London, 1954.

Braganza y de Borbón, María de las Nieves de. *Mis memorias ... de 1872, '3, '4.* Madrid, 1934.

Buckley, Henry. *Life and Death of the Spanish Republic.* London, 1940.

Burgo Torres, Jaime del. *Requetés en Navarra antes del Alzamiento.* San Sebastian, 1939.

Caballé y Clos, T. *Barcelona roja. Dietario de la revolución.* Barcelona, 1939.

Cadena y Brualla, R. de la. *Entre rojos y azules.* Zaragoza, 1939.

Calvo Sotelo, José. *Mis servicios al Estado. Seis años de gestión. Apuntes para la Historia.* Madrid, 1931.

Cano Sánchez-Pastor, Antonio. *Cautivos en las arenas. Crónicas de un confinado.* Madrid, 1933.

Cantalupo, Roberto. *Embajada en España* (tr. A. V. de Avilés). Barcelona, 1951.

Cardozo, Harold. *March of a Nation. My Year of Spain's Civil War.* London, 1937.

Cavero y Cavero, F. *Con la segunda bandera en el frente de Aragón.* Zaragoza, 1938.

Cía Navascués, Policarpo. *Memorias del Tercio de Montejurra (por su capellán).* Pamplona, 1941.

Cierva Peñafiel, Juan de la. *Notas de mi vida.* Madrid, 1955.

Coll, Andrés. *Memorias de un deportado.* Madrid, 1933.

Colmegna, Héctor. *Diario de un médico argentino en la guerra de España.* Madrid, 1941.

Conill y Mataró, Antonio. *Codo: de mi diario de campaña.* Barcelona, 1954.

Copado, Bernabé, S.J. *Con la columna de Redondo. Combates y conquistas. Crónica de guerra.* Seville, 1937.

'Córdoba, Juan de'. *Estampas y reportajes de retaguardia.* Seville, 1939.

Cortés Cavanillas, Julián. *Confesiones y muerte de Alfonso XIII.* 2nd ed. Madrid, 1951.

Cossió, Francisco de. *Hacia una nueva España. De la revolución de octubre a la revolución de julio: 1934–1936.* Valladolid, 1937.

Cuesta, Teodoro. *De la muerte a la vida. Veinte meses de una vida insignificante en el infierno rojo.* Burgos, 1939.

Dávila, Sancho. *José Antonio, Salamanca y otras cosas....* Madrid, 1967.

Dávila, Sancho & Pemartín, Julián. *Hacia la historia de la Falange. Primera contribución de Sevilla.* Jerez de la Frontera, 1938.

Domenech Puig, R. *Diario de campaña de un Requeté.* Barcelona, 1959.

Esteban-Infantes, Emilio. *La sublevación del general Sanjurjo, relatada por su ayudante. Apuntes para la historia.* 2nd ed. Madrid, 1933.

Félix Maíz, B. *Alzamiento en España. De un diario de la conspiración.* Pamplona, 1952.

García Mercadal, J. *Frente y retaguardia (impresiones de guerra).* Zaragoza, 1937.

García de Vinuesa, Fernando. *De Madrid a Lisboa, por Villa Cisneros.* Madrid, 1933.

Gil Robles, José María. *No fue posible la paz.* Barcelona, 1968.

Gómez Acebo, J. *La vida en las cárceles de Euzkadi.* Zarauz, 1938.

Gutiérrez, Ricardo. *Memoria de un azul.* Salamanca, 1937.

Gutiérrez-Ravé, José. *Yo fui un joven maurista (historia de un movimiento de ciudadanía).* Madrid, 1945.

Hayes, Carlton. *Wartime Mission in Spain, 1942–1945.* New York, 1945.

Henningsen, C. F. *A Twelve Months' Campaign with Zumalacárregui.* London, 1836.

Hidalgo, Diego. *¿Por qué fui lanzado del Ministerio de la Guerra? Diez meses de actuación ministerial.* Madrid, 1934.

Hoare, Samuel (Viscount Templewood). *Ambassador on Special Mission.* London, 1946.

Hodgson, Sir Robert M. *Spain Resurgent.* London, 1953.

Hoyos Vinent, José María de (Marqués de Hoyos). *Mi testimonio.* Madrid, 1962.

Iribarren, José María. *Con el general Mola. Escenas y aspectos inéditos de la guerra civil.* Zaragoza, 1937.

Jerrold, Douglas. *Georgian Adventure.* London, 1937.

Jiménez de Asúa, Luis. *Proceso histórico de la constitución de la República española.* Madrid, 1932.

Kemp, Peter. *Mine Were of Trouble.* London, 1957.

Kindelán, Alfredo. *Mis cuadernos de guerra.* Madrid, 1945.

Lerroux, Alejandro. *La pequeña historia. Apuntes para la Historia grande vividos y redactados por el autor.* 2nd ed. Madrid, 1964.

Lizarza Iribarren, Antonio. *Memorias de la conspiración. Como se preparó en Navarra la Cruzada, 1931–1936.* Pamplona, 1953, 4th ed. Pamplona, 1957.

López de Medrano, L. *986 días en el infierno.* Madrid, 1939.

López Ochoa, Eduardo. *Campaña militar de Asturias en octubre de 1934 (narración táctico-episódica).* Madrid, 1936.

Luca de Tena, J. I. *Mis amigos muertos.* Barcelona, 1971.

McCullagh, Francis. *In Franco's Spain.* London, 1937.

Maisky, Ivan. *Spanish Notebooks.* London, 1966.

Manning, Leah. *What I Saw in Spain.* London, 1935.

Maura, Miguel. *Así cayó Alfonso XIII . . . .* Mexico City, 1962.

Melgar, Francisco Martín de. *Veinte años con Don Carlos. Memorias de su secretario.* Madrid, 1940.

Mola Vidal, Emilio. *Memorias de mi paso por la Dirección General de Seguridad.* Madrid, 1932.

Morales, Mauricio Emiliano. *La guerra civil en Guipúzcoa, julio–agosto 1936 (con la columna del Comandante Galbís).* Valladolid, 1937.

Nadal, Joaquín María. *Seis años con don Francisco Cambó (1930–36). Memorias de un secretario político.* Barcelona, 1957.

Noriega, Fernando Miguel (ed.). *Fal Conde y el Requeté (juzgados por el extranjero).* Burgos, 1937.

Olazábal, Tirso de. *Don Jaime en España. Crónica del viaje de S.A.R.* Bilbao, 1895.

Ortiz de Villajos, Cándido García. *De Sevilla a Madrid. Ruta libertadora de la columna Castejón.* Granada, 1937.

Ossorio Gallardo, Ángel. *Mis memorias.* Buenos Aires, 1946.

Oudard, Georges. *Chemises noires, brunes, vertes en Espagne.* Paris, 1938.

Paul, Elliott. *The Life and Death of a Spanish Town.* London, 1937.

Pérez Madrigal, Joaquín. *Augurios, estallado y episodios de la guerra civil. Cincuenta días con el ejército del norte.* Ávila, 1936.

Memorias de un converso. 9 vols. Madrid, 1943–52.

Pérez (vida y trabajos de uno). Madrid, 1955.

Puig Mora, E. *La tragedia roja en Barcelona. Memorias de un evadido.* Zaragoza, 1937.

Resa, José María. *Memorias de un Requeté.* Barcelona, 1968.

Romero Raizábal, Ignacio. *Boinas rojas en Austria. Impresiones de un viaje a Viena, cuando la muerte de D. Alfonso Carlos.* San Sebastian, 1939.

Ruiz Vilaplana, Antonio. *Burgos Justice. A Year's Experience of Nationalist Spain* (tr. W. H. Carter). London, 1938.

Salazar Alonso, Rafael. *Bajo el signo de la Revolución.* Madrid, 1935.

Serrano Súñer, Ramón. *Entre Hendaya y Gibraltar (noticia y reflexión, frente a una leyenda, sobre nuestra política en dos guerras).* Madrid, 1947.

Steer, G. L. *The Tree of Gernika.* London, 1938.

Úrraca Pastor, María Rosa. *Así empezamos. Memorias de una enfermera.* Bilbao, n.d.

Young, Sir George. *The New Spain.* London, 1933.

(ii) *Biographies and biographical studies*

Acedo Colunga, Felipe. *José Calvo Sotelo (la verdad de un muerte).* Barcelona, 1957.

Aguado, Emiliano. *Ramiro Ledesma en la crisis de España.* Madrid, 1942.

Aguirre Prado, Luis. *Ruiz de Alda.* Madrid, 1955.

Ramiro de Maeztu. 2nd ed. Madrid, 1959.

Vázquez de Mella. 2nd ed. Madrid, 1959.

Alcázar de Velasco, Ángel. *Serrano Súñer en la Falange.* Barcelona, 1941.

Aracil, Antonio. *Dolor y triunfo. Héroes y mártires en pueblos de Andalucía durante el movimiento nacional.* Barcelona, 1944.

Arjona, Emilio de. *Páginas de la historia del partido carlista: Carlos VII y Don Ramón Cabrera.* Paris, 1875.

Arrábal, Juan. *José María Gil Robles: su vida, su actuación, sus ideas.* Madrid, 1933.

Arrarás Iribarren, Joaquín. *Francisco Franco* (tr. J. M. Espinosa). London, 1938.

Aunós Pérez, Eduardo. *Calvo Sotelo y la política de su tiempo.* Madrid, 1941.

Bernard, Ino. *Mola, mártir de España.* Granada, 1938.

Bertrán Güell, Felipe. *Caudillo, profetas y soldados.* Madrid, 1939.

Boissel, Antony. *Un chef: Gil Robles.* Paris, 1934.

Bordoy Oliver, Miguel. *Don Carlos considerado como patriota, militar y político.* Palma de Mallorca, 1900.

Borrás, Tomás. *Ramiro Ledesma Ramos.* Madrid, 1971.

Botella y Serra, C. *Don Cándido Nocedal.* Barcelona, 1913.

Bourgade, William. *Don Carlos. Histoire d'un prince et d'un peuple, 1848—1909.* Paris, 1909.

Bravo Martínez, Francisco. *José Antonio: el hombre, el jefe, el camarada.* 2nd ed. Madrid, 1940.

Calleja López, Juan José. *Yagüe, un corazón al rojo.* Barcelona, 1963.

Camba, Francisco. *Lerroux: el caballero de la libertad.* Madrid, 1935.

Castro Albarrán, Aniceto de. *Este es el cortejo. Héroes y mártires de la Cruzada española.* Salamanca, 1938.

Coles, S. F. A. *Franco of Spain: a full-length biography.* London, 1955.

Corma, Enrique. *El general Mola.* 2nd ed. Madrid, 1956.

Corral, Enrique del. *Calvo Sotelo.* 2nd ed. Madrid, 1956.

Cortés Cavanillas, Julián. *Alfonso XIII en el destierro.* Madrid, 1933.

Alfonso XIII, el Rey romántico. Madrid, 1943.

Crozier, Brian. *Franco. A Biographical History.* London, 1967.

Esteban-Infantes, Emilio. *General Sanjurjo (un laureado en el penal de Dueso).* Barcelona, 1957.

Fernández Arias, A. *Gil Robles ¡La esperanza de España!* Madrid, 1935.

Fernández de Castro Pedrera, Rafael. *Franco, Mola, Varela. Vidas de soldados ilustres de la nueva España.* 2nd ed. Melilla, 1938.

Galinsoga, Luis de, & Franco Salgado, F. *Centinela de occidente (semblanza biográfica de Francisco Franco).* Barcelona, 1956.

García de la Escalera, Inés. *General Varela.* 2nd ed. Madrid, 1959.

El general Yagüe. 2nd ed. Madrid, 1959.

García y García de Castro, R. *Vázquez de Mella.* Madrid, 1940.

García Sánchez, Narciso. *Onésimo Redondo.* 2nd ed. Madrid, 1956.

García Venero, Maximiano. *Víctor Pradera. Guerrillero de la unidad.* Madrid, 1943.

Vida de Cambó. Barcelona, 1952.

Falange en la guerra de España: la Unificación y Hedilla. Paris, 1967.

General Fanjul. Madrid, 1967.

Goded, Manuel. *Un 'faccioso' cien por cien.* Zaragoza, 1938.

González Piedra, Juan. *Vida y obra de Menéndez Pelayo.* Madrid, 1952.

González Ruano, César. *General Sanjurjo.* 2nd ed. Madrid, 1959.

Guinea Suárez, Carlos. *Víctor Pradera.* 2nd ed. Madrid, 1953.

Gutiérrez-Ravé, José. *El Conde de Barcelona.* Madrid, 1962.

Gil Robles, caudillo frustrado. Madrid, 1967.

Antonio Goicoechea. Madrid, 1965.

Hills, George. *Franco. The Man and his Nation.* London, 1967.

Iribarren, José María. *Mola; datos para una biografía y para la historia del Alzamiento Nacional.* Zaragoza, 1938.

El general Mola. 2nd ed. Madrid, 1945.

Joaniquet, Aurelio. *Calvo Sotelo.* Santander, 1939.

Lapuente Benavente, Pablo A. *El Príncipe Don Javier de Borbón Parma.* Madrid, 1955.

Mariñas, Francisco Javier. *General Varela (de soldado a general).* Barcelona, 1956.

Marrero, Vicente. *Maeztu.* Madrid, 1955.

Martin, Claude. *Franco, soldat et chef d'état.* Paris, 1959.

Melgar, Francisco Martín de. *Don Jaime, el Príncipe caballero.* Madrid, 1932.

Millán Astray, J. *Franco el caudillo.* Salamanca, 1939.

Mugieta, J. *Los valores de la Raza: Víctor Pradera, Ramiro de Maeztu, José Calvo Sotelo, José Antonio Primo de Rivera.* San Sebastian, 1938.

Nonell Bru, Salvador. *Así eran nuestros muertos.* Barcelona, 1965.

Olmedo Delgado, Antonio, & Cuesta Monereo, José. *General Queipo de Llano (aventura y audacia).* Barcelona, 1958.

Ortega, Teófilo. *Presidente: Martínez de Velasco.* Barcelona, 1935.

Ortiz Estrada, Luis. *Alfonso XIII, artífice de la II República española.* Madrid, 1947.

Ossorio Gallardo, Ángel. *Vida y sacrificio de Companys.* Buenos Aires, 1943.

Oyarzun, Román. *Vida de Ramón Cabrera y las guerras carlistas.* Barcelona, 1961.

Pabón Suárez, Jesús. *Cambó.* 3 vols. Barcelona, 1952–69.

Paula Oller, Francisco de ('D.F. de P.O.'). *Álbum de personajes carlistas con sus biografías.* Barcelona, 1887–90.

Pemán y Pemartín, José María. *Un soldado en la historia. Vida del capitán general Varela.* Cádiz, 1954.

Pérez Madrigal, Joaquín. *Tipos y sombras de la tragedia. Mártires y héroes, bestias y farsantes.* Ávila, 1937.

El general Sanjurjo a presidio. Madrid, 1955.

Pérez de Olaguer, Antonio. *'Piedras vivas'. Biografía del Capellán Requeté José María Lamamié de Clairac y Alonso.* San Sebastian, 1939.

Pérez Olivares, R. *Excmo. Sr. General D. Emilio Mola Vidal, jefe de los ejércitos del Norte.* Ávila, 1937.

Petrie, Sir Charles. *Alfonso XIII and His Age.* London, 1963.

Pi Navarro, Manuel. *Los primeros veinticinco años de la vida de José Calvo Sotelo (apuntes para una biografía).* Zaragoza, 1961.

Polo y Peyrolón, Manuel. *Don Carlos. Su pasado, su presente y su porvenir.* Valencia, 1900.

Don Carlos de Borbón y de Austria-Este. Su vida, su carácter y su muerte. Valencia, 1909.

Ramírez, Luis. *Francisco Franco. Historia de un mesianismo.* Paris, 1964.

Requejo San Román, Jesús. *El cardenal Segura.* Toledo, 1932.

Rodezno, Conde de (Domínguez Arévalo, Tomás). *La princesa de Beira y los hijos de Don Carlos.* Santander, 1938.

Carlos VII, Duque de Madrid. 3rd ed. Madrid, 1944.

Romano, Julio. *Sanjurjo, el caballero del valor.* Madrid, 1940.

Weyler, el hombre de hierro. Madrid, 1944.

Romero Raizábal, Ignacio. *El príncipe requeté.* Santander, 1965.

El prisionero de Dachau 156.270. Zaragoza, 1972.

Sallent, Valentín. *Carlos VII, el Rey caballero.* Barcelona, 1946.

Salmador, Víctor G. *Juan Antonio Ansaldo, caballero de la lealtad.* Montevideo, 1962.

Salvá Miguel, Francisco, & Vicente, Juan. *Francisco Franco (historia de un español).* Barcelona, 1959.

San Juan de Piedras Albas, Marqués de (Melgar y Abreu, Bernadino). *Héroes y mártires de la aristocracia española.* Madrid, 1945.

Sánchez del Arco, Manuel. *Horas y figuras de la guerra de España.* Madrid, 1939.

Sanz Díaz, José. *Escritores asesinados por los rojos.* Madrid, 1953.

Sedwick, Frank. *The Tragedy of Manuel Azaña and the Fate of the Spanish Republic.* Columbus, 1963.

Sencourt, Robert. *King Alfonso. A Biography.* London, 1942.

Sevilla Andrés, D. *Antonio Maura: la revolución desde arriba.* Barcelona, 1954.

Suárez, Federico. *Introducción a Donoso Cortés.* Madrid, 1964.

Tomás, Mariano. *Ramón Cabrera. Historia de un hombre.* Barcelona, 1939.

Trythall, J. W. D. *El Caudillo. The Political Biography of Franco.* New York, 1970.

Valdesoto, Fernando de. *Francisco Franco.* Madrid, 1943.

Vallotton, Henry. *Alphonse XIII.* Lausanne, 1943.

Vigón, Jorge. *General Mola (El Conspirador).* Barcelona, 1957.

'Villarín y Willy' (Valdís, Joaquín). *El Secretario de S. M. Biografía de Fal Conde.* Seville, 1954.

Ximénez de Sandoval, Felipe. *José Antonio.* 2nd ed. Madrid, 1949.

6. OTHER BOOKS

(i) *Works published before and during 1939*

Albiñana, José María. *España bajo la dictadura republicana (crónica de un período putrefacto).* 2nd ed. Madrid, 1933.

Alcalá Galiano, Alvaro. *The Fall of a Throne* (tr. S. Erskine). London, 1933.

Altabella Gracia, Pedro. *El catolicismo de los nacionalistas vascos.* Vitoria, 1939.

'Anonymous' (Bolín, Luis; Bertodano y Wilson, F. R.; Marqués del Moral & Jerrold, Douglas). *The Spanish Republic. A survey of Two Years of Progress.* London, 1933.

Antequera, José María. *La desamortización eclesiástica.* Madrid, 1885.

Arauz de Robles, José María. *Plan (Obra Nacional Corporativa).* Burgos, 1937.

Arrese, Domingo de. *El País Vasco y las Constituyentes de la segunda República.* Madrid, 1932.

Bajo la Ley de Defensa de la República. Madrid, 1933.

Barrail, Henri. *L'autonomie régionale en Espagne.* Lyons, 1933.

Bertrán Güell, Felipe. *Preparación y desarrollo del Alzamiento Nacional.* Valladolid, 1939.

Rutas de la victoria. Barcelona, 1939.

Brandt, Joseph A. *Toward the New Spain.* Chicago, 1933.

Brasillach, Robert. *Léon Degrelle et l'avenir de "Rex".* Paris, 1936.

Brasillach, Robert & Bardèche, Maurice. *Histoire de la guerre d'Espagne.* Paris, 1939.

Calvo Sotelo, José. *En defensa propia.* Madrid, 1932.

La voz de un perseguido. Madrid, 1933.

Campión y Jaime-Bon, Arturo. *Carlismo, integrismo y regionalismo.* Barcelona, 1912.

Canals y Vilaró, Salvador. *La Solidaridad Catalana (apuntes para un estudio).* Madrid, 1907.

Apuntes para la Historia. La caída de la Monarquía. Problemas de la República. Instalación de un régimen. Madrid, 1932.

De como van las cosas de España. Estudios políticos y económicos. Madrid, 1933.

Carasa Torre, F. *Presos de los rojo-separatistas.* San Sebastian, 1938.

Casares, Francisco. *La CEDA va a gobernar (notas y glosas de un año de vida pública nacional).* Madrid, 1934.

Casariego, Jesús Evaristo. *Flor de hidalgos (ideas, hombres y escenas de la guerra).* Pamplona, 1938.

Castillejo, José. *War of Ideas in Spain: Philosophy, Politics and Education.* London, 1937.

Clarke, H. Butler. *Modern Spain.* Cambridge, 1906.

(La Constancia). *El nacionalismo vasco con la revolución de octubre 1934.* San Sebastian, 1936.

'Constancio'. *El tradicionalismo español.* San Sebastian, 1934.

Conze, Edward. *Spain Today: Revolution and Counter-Revolution.* London, 1936.

Cora y Lira, Jesús. *Estudios jurídicos, históricos y políticos. El futuro Caudillo de la Tradición española.* Madrid, 1932.

Cortés Cavanillas, Julián. *Gil Robles ¿monárquico?* Madrid, 1935.

Dean Berro, Emilio. *Descoriendo el velo. La conjuración Juanista y la fidelidad de los modernos cruzados de la causa.* Madrid, 1933.

Espinosa y del Río, José María. *La agonía de la dictadura rojo-separatista en Vizcaya.* San Sebastian, 1938.

Ezquiaga, Simón. *Gran álbum tradicionalista 1833–1933. Centenario de la gloriosa Comunión.* Beasáin, 1933.

Farmborough, Florence. *Life and People of Nationalist Spain.* London, 1938.

Fernández Almagro, Melchor. *Catalanismo y República española.* Madrid, 1932.

Historia del reinado de Alfonso XIII. Barcelona, 1934.

Foss, William, & Gerahty, Cecil. *The Spanish Arena.* London, 1938.

Fuembriena, Eduardo. *Guerra en Aragón.* Zaragoza, 1938.

Galli, F. *Memorias sobre la guerra de Cataluña en los años 1822 y 1823* (tr. D. E. P.). Barcelona, 1835.

Gallop, Rodney. *A Book of the Basques.* London, 1930.

Garcerán, Rafael. *La Falange espagnole de février 1936 jusqu'au Gouvernement National.* San Sebastian, 1938.

García Palacios, L. *El segundo bienio· (España en escombros) 1933–35.* n.pl. 1936.

García Sanchiz, Federico. *Del Robledal al Olivar. Navarra y el Carlismo.* San Sebastian, 1939.

Gerahty, Cecil. *The Road to Madrid.* London, 1937.

Gil Robles, José María. *Spain in Chains* (tr. C. de Arango). New York, 1937.

Gollonet Megías, Ángel & Morales López, José. *Rojo y azul en Granada.* Granada, 1937.

Sangre y fuego, Málaga. Granada, 1937.

Gomá Tomás, Isidro. *Antilaicismo.* 2 vols. Barcelona, 1935.

Gómez Bajuelo, Gil. *Málaga bajo el dominio rojo*. Cádiz, 1937.

González Oliveros, W. *Falange y Requeté*. Valladolid, 1937.

Gracia, V. *Aragón, baluarte de España*. Zaragoza, 1938.

Grossi, Manuel. *La insurrección de Asturias*. Barcelona, 1935.

Gutiérrez-Ravé, José. *España en 1931*. Madrid, 1932.

Guzmán de Alfarache, J. *¡18 de julio! Historia del Alzamiento glorioso de Sevilla*. Seville, 1937.

'Hispanicus'. *How Mussolini Provoked the Spanish War*. London, 1938.

(ed.). *Foreign Intervention in Spain*. vol. I. London, 1937.

Hume, Martin A. S. *Modern Spain*. London, 1899.

'J. M. y R.' *Memorias para la historia de la última guerra civil de España*, 2 vols. Barcelona, 1826.

Jellinek, F. *The Civil War in Spain*. London, 1938.

Knickerbocker, C. R. *The Siege of the Alcázar*. Philadelphia, 1936.

Larramendi, Hernando de. *Crisis del tradicionalismo. Omisiones y desvarios de Mella*. Madrid, 1919.

Lassala, M. *Historia política del partido carlista*. Madrid, 1841.

Llado y Figueres, José María. *El 19 de julio en Barcelona*. Barcelona, 1938.

Loveday, Arthur F. *World War in Spain*. London, 1939.

Lucía Lucía, Luis. *En estas horas de transición hacia una política de principios cristianos, de afirmación de soberanías sociales y de preocupación por las realidades regionales*. Valencia, 1930.

La Confederación Española de Derechas Autónomas. Valencia, 1933.

McNeill-Moss, Geoffrey. *The Epic of the Alcázar*. London, 1937.

Manuel, Frank E. *The Politics of Modern Spain*. New York, 1938.

Maura Gamazo, Gabriel. *Bosquejo histórico de la dictadura*. Madrid, 1930.

Dolor de España. Madrid, 1932.

Medina Togores, José de. *Un año de Cortes Constituyentes (impresiones parlamentarias)*. Madrid, 1932.

Melgar, Francisco Martín de. *Germany and Spain. The Views of a Spanish Catholic* (tr. Thomas Okey). London, 1916.

Mendizábal, Alfredo. *The Martyrdom of Spain (Origins of a Civil War)*. (tr. C. H. Lumley). London, 1938.

Monge Bernal, José. *Acción Popular (estudios de biología política)*. Madrid, 1936.

Montalbán, V. & Domi, Carlos. *Realidades presentes. Aspectos de la guerra civil española*. Zaragoza, 1937.

Moral, Joaquín del. *Lo del '10 de agosto' y la Justicia*. Madrid, 1933.

Nazi Conspiracy in Spain, The (tr. E. Burns). London, 1937.

Orizana, G. & Liébana, J. M. Martín. *El Movimiento Nacional*. Valladolid, 1937

Ortega y Gasset, José. *España invertebrada*. 12th ed. Madrid, 1962.

Ortiz de Zárate, Enrique. *Políticos . . . en cuadrilla y el partido carlista.* Madrid, 1898.

Oyarzun, Román. *Historia del Carlismo.* Bilbao, 1939; Madrid, 1969.

Peers, Edgar Allison. *The Spanish Tragedy, 1930–1936. Dictatorship, Republic, Chaos.* 3rd ed. London, 1936.

Catalonia Infelix. London, 1937.

Spain, the Church and the Orders. London, 1939.

Pérez de Olaguer, Antonio. *El terror rojo en Cataluña.* Burgos, 1937.

El terror rojo en Andalucía. Burgos, 1938.

El terror rojo en la Montaña. Barcelona, n.d.

Pérez Solis, Oscar. *Sitio y defensa de Oviedo.* Valladolid, 1938.

Pirala, Antonio. *Historia contemporánea. Segunda parte de la guerra civil. Anales desde 1843 hasta la conclusión de la actual guerra civil.* Madrid, 1875–9.

Historia de la guerra civil y de los partidos liberal y carlista. 3 vols. Madrid, 1889–91.

España y la Regencia. Anales de diez y seis años (1885–1902). 3 vols. Madrid, 1904–7.

Ramón-Laca, Julio de. *Bajo la férula de Queipo. Como fue gobernada Andalucía.* Seville, 1939.

Rodríguez, Teodoro. *El problema social y las derechas: nuevas orientaciones.* El Escorial, 1935.

Royo Villanova, Antonio. *La Constitución española de 9 de diciembre de 1931, con glosas jurídicas y apostillas políticas.* Valladolid, 1934.

Sáinz de los Terreros, Ramón. *Horas críticas. Como se desarrolló el movimiento revolucionario en la frontera de Bidasoa.* Burgos, 1937.

Sanabría, F. *Madrid bajo las hordas.* Ávila, 1938.

Sánchez del Arco, Manuel. *El sur de España en la Reconquista de Madrid.* Seville, 1937.

Sencourt, Robert. *Spain's Ordeal. A Documented Survey of Recent Events.* London, 1938.

Silva Ferreiro, M. *Galicia y el Movimiento Nacional.* Santiago de Compostela, 1938.

Smith, Rhea M. *The Day of the Liberals in Spain.* London, 1938.

Taxonera, Luciano de. *10 agosto 1932. Madrid: Sevilla: perfiles de un episodio histórico.* Madrid, 1933.

Toni Ruiz, Teodoro. *La lección de Navarra.* Burgos, 1938.

Torres, Manuel. *L'oeuvre social du nouvel état espagnole.* Paris, 1938.

Toynbee, Arnold J. & Boulter, V. M. *Survey of International Affairs, 1937.* Vol. II. *The International Repercussions of the War in Spain (1936–7).* London, 1938.

Tusquets, Juan. *Orígenes de la revolución española.* Barcelona, 1932.

Villarín, Jorge. *Guerra en España contra el judaïsmo bolchevique. Crónicas del frente.* Cádiz, 1937.

Wall, Bernard. *Spain of the Spaniards.* London, 1938.

(ii) *Works published since 1939*

Aguado Bleye, Pedro & Alcázar Molina, Cayetano. *Manual de historia de España, Tomo III.* 6th ed. Madrid, 1956.

Aguirre Prado, Luis. *The Church and the Spanish War.* Madrid, 1965.

Alba, Victor. *Historia de la segunda República española.* Mexico City, 1961.

Albert Despujol, Carlos de. *La gran tragedia de España, 1931–9.* Madrid, 1940.

Almagro San Martín, Melchor de. *Ocaso y fin de un reinado (Alfonso XIII. Los Reyes en el destierro).* Madrid, 1947.

Altamira, Rafael. *A History of Spain from the Beginnings to the Present Day* (tr. M. Lee). New York, 1952.

Alzaga Villaamil, Oscar. *La primera democracia cristiana en España.* Barcelona, 1973.

Ansón Oliart, Luis María. *Acción Española.* Zaragoza, 1960.

Aronson, Theo. *Royal Vendetta. The Crown of Spain, 1829–1965.* London, 1966.

Aróstegui, Julio. *El carlismo alavés y la guerra civil de 1870–1876.* Vitoria, 1970.

Arrarás Iribarren, Joaquín (ed.). *Historia de la Cruzada española.* 8 vols. Madrid, 1939–40. (Cited as *HCE.*)

    Historia de la segunda República española. 4 vols. Madrid, 1956–68. (Cited as *HSRE.*)

Arrese, José Luis de. *El Estado Totalitario en el pensamiento de José Antonio.* Madrid, 1945.

Artola, Miguel. *Los orígenes de la España contemporánea.* Madrid, 1959.

Aunós, Eduardo. *España en crisis (1874–1936).* Buenos Aires, 1942.

Aznar, Manuel. *Historia militar de la Guerra de España, Tomo I.* 3rd ed. Madrid, 1958.

Balcells, A. *Crisis económica y agitación social en Cataluña (1930–1936).* Barcelona, 1971.

Barrington Moore, Jr. *Social Origins of Dictatorship and Democracy. Lord and Peasant in the Making of the Modern World.* London, 1969.

Bécarud, Jean. *La deuxieme république espagnole, 1931–1936. Essai d'interprétation.* Paris, 1962.

Beneyto, Juan. *Historia social de España y de Hispanoamérica.* Madrid, 1961.

Bolloten, Burnett. *The Grand Camouflage. The Communist Conspiracy in the Spanish Civil War.* London, 1961.

Bonafulla, Leopold. *La revolución de julio en Barcelona.* Barcelona, 1943.

Bravo Martínez, Francisco. *Historia de la Falange Española de las JONS.* Madrid, 1940.

Brenan, Gerald. *The Spanish Labyrinth.* Cambridge, 1943, 3rd ed, 1962.

Broué, Pierre & Témime, Émile. *The Revolution and the Civil War in Spain* (tr. Tony White). London, 1972.

Bruguera, F. G. *Histoire contemporaine d'Espagne, 1789–1950.* Paris, 1954.

Burgo, Jaime del. *Cien anos después. Recuerdos del Alzamiento Nacional.* Pamplona, 1951.

Conspiración y guerra civil. Madrid & Barcelona, 1970.

Cacho Zabalza, Antonio. *La Unión Militar Española.* Alicante, 1940.

Calvo Serer, Rafael. *Franco frente al Rey. El proceso del régimen.* Paris, 1972.

Caro Baroja, Julio. *Los pueblos del Norte de la península ibérica.* Madrid, 1943.

Los vascos. Madrid, 1971.

Carr, Raymond. *Spain 1808–1939.* Oxford, 1966.

(ed.). *The Republic and the Civil War in Spain.* London, 1971.

Carrasco Verde, Manuel et al. *Cien años en la vida del Ejército español.* Madrid, 1956.

Casariego, Jesús Evaristo. *La verdad del Tradicionalismo.* Madrid, 1940.

Castro Albarrán, Aniceto de. *La gran víctima: la Iglesia española mártir de la revolución roja.* Salamanca, 1940.

Cattell, David T. *Communism and the Spanish Civil War.* Berkeley, 1955.

Christiansen, Eric. *The Origins of Military Power in Spain, 1800–1854.* Oxford, 1967.

Cierva y de Hoces, Ricardo de la. *Historia de la guerra civil española. Tomo I: Perspectivas y antecedentes 1898–1936.* Madrid, 1969. (Cited as *HGCE*).

Colodny, Robert. *The Struggle for Madrid: the Central Epic of the Spanish Conflict (1936–7).* New York, 1958.

Comellas, J. L. *Los realistas en el trienio constitucional.* Pamplona, 1963.

Comín Colomer, Eduardo. *Historia secreta de la segunda República.* 2 vols. Madrid, 1954–55.

De Castilblanco a Casas Viejas. 2nd ed. Madrid, 1959.

Corona Baratech, Carlos. *Revolución y reacción en el reinado de Carlos IV.* Madrid, 1957.

Crow, John A. *Spain, the Root and the Flower. A History of the Civilization of Spain and of the Spanish people.* New York, 1963.

Díaz, Guillermo. *Como llegó Falange al poder. Análisis de un proceso contrarrevolucionario.* Buenos Aires, 1940.

Díaz-Plaja, Fernando. *España, los años decisivos: 1931.* Barcelona, 1970.

Díaz de Villegas, José. *Guerra de Liberación (la fuerza de razón).* Barcelona, 1957.

Eby, Cecil. *The Siege of the Alcazar. Toledo: July to September 1936.* London, 1965.

Echeandía, José. *La persecución roja en el País Vasco.* Barcelona, 1945.

Elorza, Antonio. *La ideología liberal en la Ilustración española.* Madrid, 1970.

Epton, Nina. *Navarre: The Flea Between Two Monkeys.* London, 1957.

Esparza, Eladio. *Pequeña historia del reino de Navarra. El Rey, el Fuero, la Cruzada.* Madrid, 1940.

Estado Mayor Central del Ejército (Servicio Histórico Militar). *Historia de la guerra de liberación (1936–1939). Tomo I: Antecedentes de la guerra.* Madrid, 1945.

Fernández, Jaime. *Cartas a un tradicionalista.* Pamplona, 1951.

Fernández Almagro, Melchor. *Historia de la República española (1931–1936).* Madrid, 1940.

Historia política de la España contemporánea. 2 vols. Madrid, 1956–59.

Fernsworth, Lawrence. *Spain's Struggle for Freedom.* Boston, 1957.

Ferrer, Melchor. *Breve historia del legitimismo español.* Madrid, 1958.

'Veinticinco años atrás . . .' el Requeté vela las armas. En el XXV aniversario del Quintillo. Seville, 1959.

Ferrer, Melchor, Tejera, Domingo, & Acedo, José F. *Historia del Tradicionalismo español,* 30 vols. Seville, 1941–58.

Fogarty, M. P. *Christian Democracy in Western Europe.* London, 1957.

Foltz, Charles Jr. *The Masquerade in Spain.* Boston, 1948.

Fontana, J. *La quiebra de la monarquía absoluta.* Barcelona, 1971.

Fontana, José María. *Los Catalanes y la guerra de España.* Madrid, 1951.

Galindo Herrero, Santiago. *Breve historia del tradicionalismo español.* Madrid, 1956.

Los partidos monárquicos bajo la segunda República. 1st ed. Madrid, 1954, and 2nd ed. Madrid, 1956.

Gallo, Max. *Spain Under Franco: a History* (tr. Jean Stewart). London, 1973.

Gambra, Rafael. *La primera guerra civil de España (1821–23).* Madrid, 1950.

La monarquía social y representativa en el pensamiento tradicional. Madrid, 1954.

García Escudero, José María. *De Cánovas a la República.* 2nd ed. Madrid, 1953.

García-Nieto Paris, Juan N. *El sindicalismo cristiana en España. Notas sobre su origen y evolución hasta 1936.* Bilbao, 1960.

García Venero, Maximiano. *Historia del nacionalismo catalán (1793–1936).* Madrid, 1944.

Historia del nacionalismo vasco, 1793–1936. Madrid, 1945.

Historia de los Internacionales en España. Tomo II (Desde la primera guerra mundial al 18 de julio de 1936). Madrid, 1957.

Historia de los movimientos sindicalistas españoles (1840–1933). Madrid, 1961.

Historia de la Unificación (Falange y Requeté en 1937). Madrid, 1970.

Georges-Roux. *La guerre civile d'Espagne.* Paris, 1964.

González Bueno, Jesús. *Paz en guerra.* Cádiz, 1944.

Guerra de Independencia española y los sitios de Zaragoza, La, a symposium. Zaragoza, 1958.

Gutiérrez-Ravé, José. *Las Cortes errantes del Frente Popular.* Madrid, 1953.

Hamilton, Thomas J. *Appeasement's Child. The Franco Regime in Spain.* London, 1943.

Hennessy, C. A. M. *The Federal Republic in Spain.* Oxford, 1962.

Modern Spain. London, 1965.

Herr, Richard. *The Eighteenth Century Revolution in Spain.* Princeton, 1958.

Holt, Edgar. *The Carlist Wars in Spain.* London, 1967.

Hommage à Roy Campbell. Montpellier, 1958.

Horizonte Español 1972. 3 vols. Paris, 1972.

Howard, Michael (ed.). *Soldiers and Governments. Nine Studies in Civil–Military Relations.* London, 1957.

Ionescu, Ghita and Gellner, Ernest (eds.). *Populism. Its Meanings and National Characteristics.* London, 1969.

Iturralde, Juan de (pseud). *El catolicismo y la Cruzada de Franco.* vol. I, Bayonne, 1956; vol. II, Bayonne, 1960; vol. III, Toulouse, 1965.

Jackson, Gabriel. *The Spanish Republic and the Civil War, 1931–1939.* Princeton, 1965.

Jato, David. *La rebelión de los estudiantes (Apuntes para la historia del alegre SEU).* Madrid, 1953.

Julio Téllez, Eduardo. *Historia del Movimiento Libertador de España en la provincia gaditana.* Cádiz, 1944.

Lacruz, Francisco. *El alzamiento, la revolución y el terror en Barcelona.* Barcelona, 1943.

Lizarra, A de. *Los Vascos y la República española. Contribución a la historia de la guerra civil 1936–1939.* Buenos Aires, 1944.

López Sanz, Francisco. *Navarra en la Cruzada.* Pamplona, 1949.

De la historia Carlista. Abnegación, renunciamiento, heroísmo, sacrificio. Pamplona, 1951.

Loveday, Arthur F. *Spain 1923–48: Civil War and World War.* Ashcott, 1948.

Lovett, Gabriel. *Napoleon and the Birth of Modern Spain.* 2 vols. New York, 1965.

Lyle, Rob, & Lizarza, Francisco Xavier. *The Destiny of Spain.* Glasgow, 1952.

Madariaga, Salvador de. *Spain. A Modern History.* 3rd ed. London, 1961.

Malefakis, Edward C. *Agrarian Reform and Peasant Revolution in Spain.* New Haven, 1970.

Marcotte, V. A. *L'Espagne nationale-syndicaliste.* 2nd ed. Brussels, 1943.

Marrero, Vicente. *La guerra española y el trust de cérebros.* 2nd ed. Madrid, 1962.

Martínez Barrio, Diego. *Orígenes del Frente Popular español.* Buenos Aires, 1943.

Martínez de Campos y Serrano, Carlos. *España bélica, el siglo XIX.* Madrid, 1961.

Martínez Cuadrado, Miguel. *Elecciones y partidos políticos de España (1868–1931).* 2 vols. Madrid, 1969.

Matthews, Herbert. *The Yoke and the Arrows.* New York, 1957.

Maura, Duque de & Fernández Almagro, Melchor. *Por que cayó Alfonso XIII. Evolución y disolución de los partidos históricos durante su reinado.* Madrid, 1948.

Maurras, Charles. *Vers l'Espagne de Franco.* Paris, 1943.

Mayer, Arno J. *Dynamics of Counterrevolution in Europe, 1870–1956: An Analytic Framework.* New York, 1971.

Medhurst, Kenneth. M. *Government in Spain.* Oxford, 1973.

Melgar, Francisco de (Conde de Melgar). *Pequeña historia de las guerras carlistas.* Pamplona, 1958.

El noble final de la escisión dinástica. Madrid, 1964.

Montero Moreno, Antonio. *Historia de la persecución religiosa en España, 1936–1939.* Madrid, 1961.

Morrow, Felix. *Revolution and Counter-Revolution in Spain.* London, 1963.

Narbona, F. *Frentes del sur.* Madrid, 1959.

La quema de conventos. Madrid, 1959.

Nonell Bru, Salvador. *Los Requetés catalanes del Tercio de Nuestra Señora de Montserrat.* Barcelona, 1956.

Nuevo Estado Español, El. Madrid, 1963.

Ossorio y Gallardo, Ángel. *La guerra de España y los católicos.* Buenos Aires, 1942.

Oyarzun, Román. *Pretendientes al trono de España.* Barcelona, 1965.

Pabón Suárez, Jesús. *La otra legitimidad.* Madrid, 1965.

Palacio Atard, V; Cierva y de Hoces, Ricardo de la, & Salas Larrazábal, R. *Aproximación histórica a la Guerra española (1936–1939).* Madrid, 1970.

Payne, Stanley G. *Falange. A History of Spanish Fascism.* London, 1962.

Politics and the Military in Modern Spain. London, 1967.

Franco's Spain. London, 1968.

The Spanish Revolution. London, 1970.

A History of Spain and Portugal II, Madison, 1973.

Peers, Edgar Allison. *Spain in Eclipse.* London, 1943.

Peirats, José. *La CNT en la revolución española.* 3 vols. Toulouse, 1951–52.

Los anarquistas en la crisis política española. Buenos Aires, 1964.

Peña y Ibáñez, Juan José. *Las guerras carlistas. Antecedentes del Alzamiento Nacional de 1936.* San Sebastian, 1940.

Pérez de Olaguer, Antonio. *Estampas carlistas.* Madrid, 1950.

Petrie, Sir Charles. *The Spanish Royal House.* London, 1958.

Pike, Frederick B. *Hispanismo, 1898–1936. Spanish Conservatives and Liberals and their Relations with Spanish America.* Notre Dame & London, 1971.

Pintos Vieites, María del Carmen. *La política de Fernando VII entre 1814 y 1820.* Pamplona, 1958.

Plá, José. *Historia de la segunda República española.* 4 vols. Barcelona, 1940–41.

Polo, Fernando. *¿Quién es el Rey? La actual sucesión dinástica en la Monarquía española.* Madrid, 1949.

Puzzo, Dante A. *Spain and the Great Powers, 1936–1941.* New York, 1962.

Rama, Carlos M. *Ideología, regiones y clases sociales en la España contemporánea.* Montevideo, 1958.

La crisis española del siglo XX. Mexico City, 1960.

Ramos Oliveira, A. *Politics, Economics and Men of Modern Spain, 1808–1946.* London, 1946.

Redondo, Luis & Zavala, Juan de. *El Requeté (la Tradición no muere).* 2nd ed. Barcelona, 1957.

Reguengo, Vicente. *Guerra sin frentes.* 3rd ed. Barcelona, 1955.

Rhodes, Anthony. *The Vatican in the Age of the Dictators, 1922–1945.* London, 1973.

Risco, A. *La epopeya del Alcázar de Toledo.* San Sebastian, 1941.

Robinson, R. A. H. *The Origins of Franco's Spain. The Right, the Republic and Revolution, 1931–1936.* Newton Abbot, 1970.

Rodríguez Garraza, R. *Navarra de Reino a provincia (1828–1841).* Pamplona, 1968.

Rogger, H. & Weber, E. (eds.). *The European Right. A Historical Profile.* London, 1965.

Romero Raizábal, Ignacio. *Altar y trono. Los Papas y los Reyes Carlistas.* n.pl. 1960.

Héroes de romance. Cosas del Requeté. Santander, 1952.

El Carlismo en el Vaticano. Santander, 1968.

Royo Villanova, Antonio. *Treinta años de política antiespañola.* Valladolid, 1940.

Sánchez, José Mariano. *Reform and Reaction. The Politico-Religious Background of the Spanish Civil War.* Chapel Hill, 1962.

Schulte, H. F. *The Spanish Press, 1470–1966: Print, Power and Politics.* Urbana, 1968.

Seco Serrano, Carlos. *Historia de España, Tomo VI: Época contemporánea.* Barcelona, 1962.

Alfonso XIII y la crisis de la Restauración. Barcelona, 1969.

Tríptico carlista. Barcelona, 1973.

Segura, Francisco. *La Iglesia y el Alzamiento Nacional.* Madrid, 1961.

Sierra Bustamente, Ramón. *Euzkadi (de Sabino Arana a José Antonio Aguirre. Notas para la historia del nacionalismo vasco).* Madrid, 1941.

Smith, Rhea Marsh. *Spain. A Modern History.* Ann Arbor, 1965.

Solana y González Camino, Marcial. *El tradicionalismo político español y la ciencia hispana.* Madrid, 1951.

Southworth, Herbert Rutledge. *El mito de la Cruzada de Franco.* Paris, 1963. *Antifalange. Estudio crítico de 'Falange en la guerra de España: la Unificación y Hedilla' de Maximiano García Venero* (tr. J. Martínez). Paris, 1967.

Spain and Franco: Quest for International Acceptance 1949–59. New York, 1973.

Suárez Verdaguer, Federico. *Los sucesos de La Granja.* Madrid, 1951. *La crisis política del Antiguo Régimen en España (1800–1840).* Madrid, 1950.

Sugar, P. F. (ed.). *Native Fascism in the Successor States.* Santa Barbara, 1971.

Thomas, Hugh. *The Spanish Civil War.* 2nd ed. Harmondsworth, 1965.

Torras Elías, J. *La guerra de los Agraviados.* Barcelona, 1967.

Trend, J. B. *The Civilization of Spain.* London, 1944.

Tuñón de Lara, M., *et al. Sociedad, política y cultura en la España de los siglos XIX–XX.* Madrid, 1973.

Valynseele, Joseph. *Les prétendants aux trônes d'Europe.* Paris, 1967.

Vegas Latapié, Eugenio. *El pensamiento político de Calvo Sotelo.* Madrid, 1941.

Vicens Vives, Jaime. *Historia social y económica de España y América. Tomo IV, vol. 2: Burguesía, industrialización, obrerismo.* Barcelona, 1959. *Aproximación a la Historia de España.* 2nd ed. Barcelona, 1959. *Cataluña en el siglo XIX* (tr. from the Catalan by E. Borras Cubells). Madrid, 1961. *Coyuntura económica y reformismo burgués y otros estudios de historia de España.* Barcelona, 1969.

Vilar, Pierre. *Histoire de l'Espagne.* Paris, 1958.

Weber, Eugen. *Varieties of Fascism.* New York, 1964.

Wilson, Francis G. *Political Thought in National Spain.* Champaign, Illinois, 1967.

Zugazaga, José María. *Cruz de Requetés. Apuntes del Alzamiento en Burgos.* Madrid, 1942.

Zugazagoitia, J. *Guerra y vicisitudes de los Españoles.* 2 vols. Paris, 1968–69.

7. NOVELS

Elstob, Peter. *The Armed Rehearsal.* London, 1964.

Hemingway, Ernest. *For Whom the Bell Tolls.* London, 1941.

Herrick, William. *Hermanos!* Harmondsworth, 1973.

Malraux, André. *Days of Hope (L'Espoir)* (tr. Stuart Gilbert and Alistair Macdonald). London, 1938.

8. ARTICLES AND ESSAYS

Alvarez Puga, Eduardo. 'El Carlismo en la encrucijada', *Mundo* (Madrid), 29 May 1971.

Askew, William C. 'Italian Intervention in Spain. The Agreements of March 31, 1934 with the Spanish Monarchist parties', *Journal of Modern History*, XXIV, 2, June 1952.

Bau, Joaquín. 'Calvo Sotelo y la Cruzada', *ABC* (Madrid), 13 July 1954.

Bergonzi, Bernard. 'Roy Campbell: Outsider on the Right', *Journal of Contemporary History*, II, 2, April 1967.

Blinkhorn, R. Martin. 'Ideology and Schism in Spanish Traditionalism, 1874–1931', *Iberian Studies*, I, 1, Spring 1972.

'Carlism and the Spanish Crisis of the 1930s', *Journal of Contemporary History*, VII, 3–4, July–October 1972.

'"The Basque Ulster": Navarre and the Basque Autonomy Question under the Spanish Second Republic'. *Historical Journal*, XVII, 3, September 1974.

Brey, Gérard, & Maurice, Jacques. 'Casas-Viejas: réformisme et anarchisme en Andalousie (1870–1933)', *Le Mouvement Social*, No. 83, April–June 1973.

Danvila Rivera, Julio. 'Datos para la historia', *ABC*, 20 July 1954.

Gutiérrez-Ravé, José. 'Algunas entrevistas históricas de don Alfonso XIII', *ABC*, 28 February 1964.

Hubbard, John R. 'How Franco financed his war', *Journal of Modern History*, XXV, 4, December 1953.

Jackson, Gabriel. 'The Azaña regime in perspective (Spain, 1931–1933)', *American Historical Review*, LXIV, 2, January 1959.

'The Spanish Popular Front, 1934–37', *Journal of Contemporary History*, V, 3, July 1970.

Lamamié de Clairac, José María. 'Notas para la historia de la segunda República. Negociaciones e intentos de pactos entre las dos ramas dinásticas', *Informaciones* (Madrid), 7–8 July 1954.

Noel, C. C. 'The Clerical Confrontation with the Enlightenment in Spain', *European Studies Review*, V, 2, April 1975.

Payne, Stanley G. 'Catalan and Basque Nationalism', *Journal of Contemporary History*, VI, 1, January 1971.

'Spanish Fascism in comparative perspective', *Iberian Studies*, II, 1 Spring 1973.

Preston, Paul. 'Alfonsist Monarchism and the Coming of the Spanish Civil War', *Journal of Contemporary History*, VII, 3–4, July–October 1972.

'The "Moderate" Right and the Undermining of the Second Republic in Spain, 1931–1933', *European Studies Review*, III, 4, October 1973.

'Spain's October revolution and the Rightist Grasp for Power', to appear in *Journal of Contemporary History*, 1975.

Robinson, Richard A. H. 'Calvo Sotelo's *Bloque Nacional* and its Manifesto', *University of Birmingham Historical Journal*, X, 2, 1966.

'Genealogy and function of the monarchist myth of the Franco regime', *Iberian Studies*, II, 1, Spring 1973.

Sánchez, José M. 'The Spanish Church and the revolutionary Republican movement, 1930–1931', *Church History*, XXXI, 4, December 1962.

'The Second Spanish Republic and the Holy See, 1931–1936', *Catholic Historical Review*, XLIX, 1, April 1963.

Schumacher, John N., S. J. 'Integrism. A Study in nineteenth-century Spanish political thought', *Catholic Historical Review*, XLVIII, 3, October 1962.

Suárez Verdaguer, Federico. 'El manifiesto realista de 1826', *Príncipe de Viana* (Pamplona), IX, XXX, 77–100.

'La formación de la doctrina política del carlismo', *Revista de Estudios Políticos*, XIV, 25–6, 1946.

Thomas, Hugh, 'The Hero in the Empty Room – José Antonio and Spanish Fascism', *Journal of Contemporary History*, I, 1, January 1966.

Vegas Latapié, Eugenio. 'Maeztu y "Acción Española"', *ABC*, 2 November 1952.

N.B. Unsigned press articles appear in footnotes where cited in the text.

9. BIBLIOGRAPHIES AND WORKS OF REFERENCE

British Admiralty, The (Naval Intelligence Division). *Spain and Portugal*. vol. III. *Spain*. London, 1944.

Burgo, Jaime del. *Bibliografía de las Guerras Carlistas y de las luchas políticas del siglo XIX, antecedentes desde 1814 y apéndice hasta 1936; fuentes para la historia de España*. 4 vols. and Supplement. Pamplona, 1953–66.

Cierva y de Hoces, R. de la. *Bibliografía general sobre la Guerra de España (1936–1939) y sus antecedentes históricos: fuentes para la historia contemporánea de España*. Madrid, 1968.

Diccionario de Historia de España desde sus orígenes hasta el fin del reinado de Alfonso XIII. 2 vols. Madrid, 1952.

García Moreno, Melchor. *Ensayo de bibliografía e iconografía del Carlismo español*. Madrid, 1950.

Gutiérrez-Ravé, José. *Diccionario histórico de la guerra de liberación (1936–1939)*. 2 *folletos* only. Madrid, n.d.

Informaciones estadísticas de la vida local. Madrid, 1935.

Index

4/4/76 **DATE DUE**